Taiwan's Social Movements under Ma Ying-jeou

In the spring of 2014, the Sunflower Movement's three-week occupation of the Legislative Yuan brought Taiwan back to international media attention. It was the culmination of a series of social movements that had been growing in strength since 2008 and have become even more salient since the spring of 2014. Social movements in Taiwan have emerged as a powerful new actor that needs to be understood alongside those players that have dominated the literature such as political parties, local factions, Taishang, China and the United States.

This book offers readers an introduction to the development of these social movements in Taiwan by examining a number of important movement case studies that focus on the post-2008 period. The return of the Kuomintang (KMT) to power radically changed the political environment for Taiwan's civil society and so the book considers how social activists responded to this new political opportunity structure. The case chapters are based on extensive fieldwork and are written by authors from a variety of disciplinary backgrounds and methodological approaches; in some cases, authors combine being both academics and activists themselves. Together, the chapters focus on a number of core issues, providing the book with four key aims. First, it investigates the roots of the movements and considers how to best explain their emergence. Second, it examines the development trajectories of these movements. Third, it looks at the best way to explain their impact and development patterns, and finally it assesses their overall impact, questioning whether they can be regarded as successes or failures.

Covering a unique range of social movement cases, the book will be of interest to students and researchers interested in Taiwanese society and politics, as well as social movements and civil society.

Dafydd Fell is the reader in comparative politics with special reference to Taiwan at the Department of Political and International Studies, School of Oriental and African Studies (SOAS), University of London. He is also the director of the SOAS Centre of Taiwan Studies.

Routledge Research on Taiwan
Series editor: Dafydd Fell
SOAS, UK

The Routledge Research on Taiwan series seeks to publish quality research on all aspects of Taiwan studies. Taking an interdisciplinary approach, the books will cover topics such as politics, economic development, culture, society, anthropology and history.

This new book series will include the best possible scholarship from the social sciences and the humanities and welcomes submissions from established authors in the field as well as from younger authors. In addition to research monographs and edited volumes, general works or textbooks with a broader appeal will be considered.

The series is advised by an international editorial board and edited by *Dafydd Fell* of the Centre of Taiwan Studies at the School of Oriental and African Studies.

12 **Political Changes in Taiwan under Ma Ying-jeou**
Partisan Conflict, Policy Choices, External Constraints and Security Challenges
Edited by Jean-Pierre Cabestan and Jacques deLisle

13 **Border Crossing in Greater China**
Production, Community and Identity
Edited by Jenn-hwan Wang

14 **Language, Politics and Identity in Taiwan**
Naming China
Hui-Ching Chang and Richard Holt

15 **Place, Identity, and National Imagination in Post-war Taiwan**
Bi-yu Chang

16 **Environmental Governance in Taiwan**
A New Generation of Activists and Stakeholders
Simona A. Grano

17 **Taiwan and the 'China Impact'**
Challenges and Opportunities
Edited by Gunter Schubert

18 **Convergence or Conflict in the Taiwan Strait**
The Illusion of Peace?
J. Michael Cole

19 **Taiwan's Social Movements under Ma Ying-jeou**
From the Wild Strawberries to the Sunflowers
Edited by Dafydd Fell

Taiwan's Social Movements under Ma Ying-jeou
From the Wild Strawberries to the Sunflowers

Edited by Dafydd Fell

LONDON AND NEW YORK

First published 2017
by Routledge
2 Park Square, Milton Park, Abingdon, Oxon OX14 4RN

and by Routledge
711 Third Avenue, New York, NY 10017

Routledge is an imprint of the Taylor & Francis Group, an informa business

© 2017 selection and editorial matter, Dafydd Fell; individual chapters, the contributors

The right of Dafydd Fell to be identified as the author of the editorial matter, and of the authors for their individual chapters, has been asserted in accordance with sections 77 and 78 of the Copyright, Designs and Patents Act 1988.

All rights reserved. No part of this book may be reprinted or reproduced or utilized in any form or by any electronic, mechanical, or other means, now known or hereafter invented, including photocopying and recording, or in any information storage or retrieval system, without permission in writing from the publishers.

Trademark notice: Product or corporate names may be trademarks or registered trademarks, and are used only for identification and explanation without intent to infringe.

British Library Cataloguing in Publication Data
A catalogue record for this book is available from the British Library

Library of Congress Cataloging in Publication Data
A catalog record for this book has been requested

ISBN: 978-1-138-67567-4 (hbk)
ISBN: 978-1-315-56053-3 (ebk)

Typeset in Times New Roman
by Wearset Ltd, Boldon, Tyne and Wear

Contents

List of figures	vii
List of tables	viii
Notes on contributors	ix
Acknowledgements	xiv

1 Social movements in Taiwan after 2008: from the strawberries to the sunflowers and beyond 1
DAFYDD FELL

2 Civic activism and protests in Taiwan: why size doesn't (always) matter 18
J. MICHAEL COLE

3 Virtual ecologies, mobilization and democratic groups without leaders: impacts of Internet media on the Wild Strawberry Movement 34
HSIAO YUAN

4 A tale of two offshore islands: anti-casino movements in Penghu and Mazu 54
TSAI I-LUN AND HO MING-SHO

5 Not wanting Want: the Anti-Media Monopoly Movement in Taiwan 71
ROWENA EBSWORTH

6 This land is your land? This land is *MY* land: land expropriation during the Ma Ying-jeou administration and implications on social movements 92
KETTY W. CHEN

Contents

7 **The Sunflower Movement: origins, structures and strategies of Taiwan's response against the Black Box**   113
ANDRÉ BECKERSHOFF

8 **The China factor and Taiwan's civil society organizations in the Sunflower Movement: the case of the Democratic Front against the Cross-Strait Service Trade Agreement**   134
HSU SZU-CHIEN

9 **The evolution of the anti-nuclear movement in Taiwan since 2008**   154
SIMONA GRANO

10 **The revival of Taiwan's Green Party after 2008**   177
DAFYDD FELL AND PENG YEN-WEN

11 **Rising from the ashes? The trade union movement under Ma Ying-jeou's regime**   199
CHIU YU-BIN

12 **A team player pursuing its own dreams: rights-claim campaign of Chinese migrant spouses in the migrant movement before and after 2008**   219
LARA MOMESSO AND ISAEELLE CHENG

13 **All our relations: indigenous rights movements in contemporary Taiwan**   236
SCOTT SIMON

14 **Uneasy alliance: state feminism and the conservative government in Taiwan**   258
HUANG CHANG-LING

Index   273

Figures

3.1	The interface of the BBS where users can choose boards	41
3.2	The interface of the BBS where users can choose posts	41
9.1	Anti-nuclear rock concert in Gongguan, Taipei, 5 November 2011	159
9.2	National 'No-Nuke Action Campaign', Taipei, 30 April 2011	162
11.1	Union membership in Taiwan, 1989–2015	203
11.2	Number of unions in Taiwan, 1989–2015	204
11.3	The amendment of Trade Union Law in 2011	209
11.4	Employees by size of workplace, 2014	210

Tables

3.1	Description of the Wild Strawberry Movement	39
3.2	Categories of posts on the official Wild Strawberry Movement BBS site	40
8.1	Important events of the Cross-Strait Agreement Watch (CSAW) 2010–12	141
8.2	China factor and the three contexts of the Sunflower Movement	149
A8.1	Membership of DFACSSTA	150
A8.2	Interview list	151
10.1	Green Taiwan Party performance in national-level elections (National Assembly: NA and Legislative Yuan: LY)	179
10.2	Green Taiwan Party performance in local-level elections	180
14.1	Cabinet Commission on the Promotion of Women's Rights (CPWR) member composition	264

Contributors

André Beckershoff is research fellow at the European Research Center on Contemporary Taiwan (ERCCT) at the University of Tübingen, Germany. In 2011 and 2012 he was visiting research fellow at the Department of Political Science at the National Chengchi University (NCCU), Taipei, Taiwan. His research interests include critical theory, international political economy and social movements. His recent publications analyse the cross-strait rapprochement from a critical perspective.

Ketty W. Chen is the vice president of the Taiwan Foundation for Democracy. Prior to assuming her current position, Dr Chen was the director of research at the Association of Public Issues and Studies in Taipei, Taiwan. She also taught US–China relations as visiting professor at Austin College in Sherman, Texas, and American government in Collin College in Plano, Texas. Her research fields include: comparative politics, international security, democratization, and civil societies and social movements in Taiwan. Dr Chen has been referenced regularly by media outlets such as the *Wall Street Journal*, the *Associated Press*, *Al Jazeera*, the *LA Times*, the *New York Times*, the *Financial Times*, *Voice of America* and *BBC World*.

Isabelle Cheng (程念慈) is the senior lecturer in East Asian and international development studies at the School of Languages and Area Studies (SLAS) at the University of Portsmouth. She received her doctoral degree from the School of Oriental and African Studies (SOAS) of the University of London. She is a board member of the European Association of Taiwan Studies (EATS) and a research associate of the Centre of Taiwan Studies at SOAS. Her research concentrates on marriage migration, citizenship, multiculturalism, immigrants' political participation, and overseas Chinese studies. Her research is published by *Asian Ethnicity* under the titles of *Making Foreign Women the Mother of Our Nation: The Exclusion and Assimilation of Immigrant Women in Taiwan* and *Bridging Across or Sandwiched Between? Political Re-socialisation of Chinese Immigrant Women in Taiwan* and by the *Journal of Current Chinese Affairs* under the title of *Taiwan's Claim to Multiculturalism before and after 2008: The Impact of Changing Ruling Parties on Immigration Policies* (co-authored with Dafydd Fell). Her research on marriage among immigrant women from Indonesia and China is included in *Migration to and from Taiwan* under the titles of *Home-Going or Home-Making? The Citizenship Legislation and Chinese Identity of Indonesian-Chinese Immigrant Women in Taiwan* and *The politics of the mainland spouses' rights movement in Taiwan* (co-authored with Tseng Yu-chin and Dafydd Fell).

Chiu Yu-bin (邱毓斌) is an assistant professor at the Department of Social Development at National Pingtung University in Taiwan and has a PhD in sociology from Essex University. Prior to his academic career, he was a union organizer and served as the first general secretary of the Taiwan Confederation of Trade Unions (2000–01). He was the founding member of the Taiwan Tertiary Education Union in 2012 and has served as a union representative since. His research interests focus on comparative labour movements, social movements and NGOs in new democracies.

J. Michael Cole (寇謐將) is a Taipei-based senior non-resident fellow with the China Policy Institute (CPI) at the University of Nottingham and an associate researcher at the Centre d'Études Français sur la Chine contemporaine (CEFC). He was a journalist and deputy news chief at the *Taipei Times* (2006–13) and editor at the Thinking Taiwan Foundation (2014–16); he is currently chief editor of The News Lens International. He is a frequent contributor to CNN, *The Diplomat*, *The National Interest*, CPI blog and *Jane's Defence Weekly*. Prior to moving to Taiwan in 2005, he was an analyst at the Canadian Security Intelligence Service (CSIS). He has a master's degree in war studies from the Royal Military College of Canada (RMC).

Rowena Ebsworth is a PhD candidate at the Australian Centre on China in the World (CIW), Australian National University. Her dissertation is focused on student activism in contemporary Taiwan. She completed her BA with first class honours from the University of Tasmania in 2013. Her thesis was on *The Anti-Media Monopoly Movement in Taiwan*.

Dafydd Fell (羅達菲) is the reader in comparative politics with special reference to Taiwan at the Department of Political and International Studies, School of Oriental and African Studies (SOAS), University of London. He is also the director of the SOAS Centre of Taiwan Studies. In 2004 he helped establish the European Association of Taiwan Studies. He has published numerous articles on political parties and electioneering in Taiwan. His first book was *Party Politics in Taiwan* (Routledge, 2005), which analysed party change in the first 15 years of multiparty competition. His latest book is *Government and Politics in Taiwan* (Rouledge, 2011). He recently co-edited *Migration to and from Taiwan* (Routledge, 2013) and is also the book series editor for the new Routledge Research on Taiwan Series.

Simona A. Grano is the senior lecturer at the Department of Sinology, Institute for Asian and Oriental Studies, University of Zürich. She received her doctoral degree from Ca' Foscari University of Venice, Department of Chinese Studies in 2008. She is a board member of the European Association of Taiwan Studies (EATS) and an associate fellow of the European Research Center on Contemporary Taiwan (ERCCT), at Tübingen. Her research interests focus on environmental management and politics, state-society relations, and judicial sector reforms. She has published various articles on environmental politics and social movements in Taiwan and China.

In 2005 she published *Environmental Governance in Taiwan: A New Generation of Activists and Stakeholders* with Routledge, which deals with environmental governance mechanisms and actors in Taiwan through a multidisciplinary research approach.

Ho Ming-sho (何明修) is a professor at the Department of Sociology, National Taiwan University. He studies social movement, labour and environmental issues. He recently published *Working Class Formation in Taiwan: Fractured Solidarity in State-owned Enterprises, 1945–2012* (New York: Palgrave Macmillan).

Hsiao Yuan (蕭遠) is a graduate student in the Department of Sociology at the University of Washington. Yuan is interested in collective action, Internet and social media, social psychology and quantitative methods. His 2011 research on the Wild Strawberry Movement in Taiwan was published in *Taiwan Democracy Quarterly* and has been listed as required reading in several courses at several universities in Taiwan. He received his BA in Sociology from National Taiwan University.

Hsu Szu-chien (徐斯儉) is associate research fellow of the Institute of Political Science at Academia Sinica in Taipei and the director of the Center for Contemporary China at the National of Tsinghua University in Hsinchu, Taiwan. His recent publications include an edited volume, *The Big Chessboard of Xi Jinping: The Limits of the Transformation of a Post-totalitarian Authoritarianism* (in Chinese), in 2016; a co-edited book (with Yushan Wu), *Transformation of the Party-State: Elite and Policies in the Chinese Communist Regime* (in Chinese), in 2007; and book chapters such as 'A tale of two party states: Comparing authoritarianism across the Taiwan Strait', in Guoguang Wu and Helen Landsdowne (eds) (2015) *New Perspectives on China's Transition from Communism*, and 'Whither the local autonomy under the "China Model"? The political economy of China's 2008 stimulus' (co-authored with Hans Tung), in TK Leng and Yushan Wu (eds) (2014) *The Chinese Models of Development*.

Huang Chang-Ling is associate professor of political science at the National Taiwan University. She received her PhD from the University of Chicago and her research interests are gender politics and minority politics. She has published in various academic journals such as the *American Journal of Public Health*, *Developing Economies*, *Issues & Studies*, and *Politics & Gender*. She was also a contributor to several edited volumes. Her current research interests focus on comparative studies of gender quotas and state feminism. Professor Huang is a recipient of the Outstanding Teaching Award and the Outstanding Social Service Award from the National Taiwan University. Besides teaching and research, she has been actively involved in Taiwan's social movements. Since 2000, she has been a board member of the Awakening Foundation, the earliest established feminist organization of postwar Taiwan, and between 2004 and 2007 she was the president of the foundation. Over the past decade she has also served on various government gender commissions. Since 2013, she has been the president of the Taiwan Association for Truth and Reconciliation, a social movement organization that works on transitional justice in Taiwan.

Lara Momesso is a postdoctoral researcher at the Centre for European and International Studies Research (CEISR), University of Portsmouth, with a project on contemporary marriage migration and family formation in the context of China–Taiwan relations. She received her doctoral degree from the School of Oriental and African Studies (SOAS), University of London. Currently she is a board member of the European Association of Taiwan Studies (EATS), a research associate of the Taiwan Studies Centre (SOAS) and an associate fellow at the European Centre of Contemporary Taiwan (ERCCT), University of Tüebingen. She lives between Portsmouth, Taipei and Xiamen to carry out her current research project.

Peng Yen-wen (彭渰雯) is an associate professor at the Institute of Public Affairs Management, National Sun Yat-sen University, Taiwan. She received her PhD from the School of Planning and Public Policy, Rutgers University, USA (2004). She has published widely in peer-reviewed journals on gender politics, social movements and democratic governance. She has also been actively involved in Taiwan's women's activism and is a former Green Party chair and election candidate.

Scott Simon is a professor in the School of Sociological and Anthropological Studies at the University of Ottawa, where he holds a research chair in Taiwan studies. With a PhD in anthropology from McGill University, Simon began his career working in the anthropology of development. Two separate research projects led to his books *Tanners of Taiwan: Life Strategies and National Cultures* (2005) and *Sweet and Sour: Life-Worlds of Taipei Women Entrepreneurs* (2003). Taking an interest in indigenous peoples of Taiwan, from 2004 to 2008 he did ethnographic research with Truku and Sediq groups in Hualien and Nantou on various issues related to development and politics. The results of this research have been published as chapters in edited volumes and journals such as *Human Organization, Oceania, American Ethnologist* and *Anthropologie et Sociétés*. His book *Sadyaq Balae! L'autochtonie formosane dans tous ses états* (2012) is an ethnographic exploration of state–indigenous relations, including the social movements that often contest state projects on indigenous territory. In more recent annual trips to Taiwan, he has been working closely with Truku-speaking trappers and hunters, who have been teaching him about ethno-biology and human–animal relations, in addition to sharing their discontent about Taiwan's legal regime, which criminalizes most hunting activities.

Tsai I-lun (蔡依倫) is an associate professor at the General Education Center, Penghu University of Science and Technology. She received her PhD from the College of Management at National Sun Yat-sen University. Her current research interests include new institutionalism, social movements and organization theory.

Acknowledgements

As a scholar who has mainly written on Taiwan's political parties and electoral politics, the idea of editing a book on social movements requires some explanation. Naturally I had covered social movements when teaching courses on Taiwan's politics. The readings we discussed in class tended to be focused on movements involved in Taiwan's democratic transition and the period immediately after transition in the Lee Teng-hui era. Our reading lists suggested that the literature on the period after the first change of ruling parties in 2000 seemed sparser. Back in 2006 I had co-authored a book chapter on Taiwan's women's movement, but I was the second author and not involved in the primary fieldwork. Thus, despite the fact that I covered social movements in my teaching, as late as mid-2012 this was not yet one of my core research topics.

The importance of social movements became increasingly clear in the period after the second change of ruling parties in 2008. This was highlighted by numerous speakers who came to SOAS, as well as in films we screened, such as Chiang Wei-hua's (江偉華) documentary about the Wild Strawberry Movement, *The Right Thing* (廣場). Reading the writings of Michael Cole and Ho Ming-sho (何明修) and speaking to scholars such as Chiu Kuei-fen (邱貴芬) and Fan Yun (范雲) made it clear me that something transformative was developing in Taiwanese civil society. In late 2012 I attempted to build on my earlier work on Taiwan's small parties by starting a research project on Taiwan's Green Party (GPT) with Peng Yen-wen (彭渰雯) (my co-author in this volume). I am so grateful to my former student Yu Wan-ru (余婉如) for inviting me to bid for a research grant focused on the GPT. Those initial interviews and focus groups with environmental activists linked to the GPT opened a new world for me in my understanding of Taiwanese politics and society.

Thus, almost as soon as I had completed the previous co-edited volume *Migration to and from Taiwan* in late 2013 I began the preparations for the June 2014 conference on Taiwan's social movements after 2008. The Sunflower occupation in March–April 2014 reinforced the timeliness of the conference theme. The conference included a mix of academics working on Taiwan's social movements, social movement activists and scholar activists. We were not able to include the papers of all participants in the current volume but here I would like to thank the following scholars for their paper presentations and contributions to

Acknowledgements xv

the conference discussions: Fan Yun, Malte Kaeding, Lorna Kung (龔尤倩), Chang Jung-che (張榮哲), Jeng Hsiao-ta (鄭小塔), Mark Harrison and Chiu Hua-mei (邱花妹). In addition, the papers and discussion benefitted from the contribution of the following discussants: Niki Alsford, Chang Bi-yu, Antony Fielding, Nora Fee Kroeger, Liu Lili, Tim Pringle, Stuart Thompson, Tseng Yu-chin and Heidi Wang. I would also like to thank my wonderful colleagues Chang Bi-yu and Jewel Lo (羅寶珠) for their organizational support for this memorable event.

I also need to thank the main funder of this conference and the SOAS Taiwan studies programme, the Taipei Representative Office (TRO) to the United Kingdom. I particularly need to thank Ms Chen Ya-hui for logistical support and to the deputy representative, Ms Hsu Fen-chuan (許芬娟), for hosting the memorable conference dinner. The debates over social movements were as lively over dinner as in the conference.

The process of turning the set of conference papers into an edited volume was quite a challenge. I have to say this was the most challenging volume I have edited so far. A first challenge was the fact that, unlike earlier volumes or special editions, I was the sole editor. None of the participants at the conference volunteered to join my editorial team. A second challenge was the fact that many of the participants were either activists or scholars who were also activists. Therefore, when we held the June conference we had a mix of academic papers and rich activist PowerPoint presentations. Many of the presenters had become so involved in social movements that they did not have time to write their conference papers. In the aftermath of the conference, many also became heavily involved in party politics in the run-up to the 2014 and 2016 elections.

This meant that I had a group of very reliable chapter authors but also some authors who found it very difficult to deliver rounded academic papers due to the pressure of their activist, academic, family and party political lives. In some cases, authors had to withdraw from the project and so I had to try to find alternative chapter authors to ensure that critically important social movements were not neglected. I am so grateful for the way that Rowena Ebsworth, Hsiao Yuan and André Beckershoff joined the project in time so that they were part of the manuscript that went to the external reviewers. I really do not remember how many nagging emails I sent out in my bid to get the first draft of the manuscript ready but I do apologize to those chapter authors who had to put up with my constant nagging. It was a great relief to submit that first manuscript 15 months after the June 2014 conference.

At this point I also need to express my gratitude for the support of my colleagues at Routledge. I first raised the book proposal idea with the Asian studies editorial assistant, Hannah Mack, who joined a number of the June 2014 conference panels. Subsequently after Hannah left Routledge, I worked closely with her replacement, Rebecca Lawrence, through the rest of the project.

In addition to the original chapters, I was delighted to include a chapter by Huang Chang-ling on the feminist movement. Once it was clear that Fan Yun would not be able to contribute a chapter, I had felt that this was a topic sadly missing in the original manuscript. Huang's chapter is the only piece that had been previously published and I would thus like to express my appreciation to the *Journal of Gender Studies* at Ochanomizu University, Japan, for agreeing to allow us to republish the piece.

I naturally would like to thank the anonymous external reviewers for their constructive and encouraging suggestions for revisions. The revisions process was not straight forward. One major challenge was the fact that so much had happened in the social movement and political scene since our first drafts. In particular, we (largely) made our final revisions and updates during the transition period between the DPP's January 2016 election victories and Tsai's inauguration in May. Last, I would like to thank all my wonderful chapter authors. It has been a pleasure to work with you and you have taught me so much! However, I think I will leave the task of a book on social movements in the Tsai Ing-wen era to others.

Dafydd Fell
Upper Caldecote, Bedfordshire
July 2016

1 Social movements in Taiwan after 2008

From the strawberries to the sunflowers and beyond

Dafydd Fell

From 18 March to 10 April 2014, the Sunflower Movement's occupation of Taiwan's parliament, the Legislative Yuan, brought the country global media attention. The occupation only ended after the Legislative Yuan speaker pledged that parliamentary ratification of the proposed Cross-Strait Service Trade Agreement (CSSTA) would be put aside until legislation was brought in for reviewing future agreements with China. After a series of economic agreements between Taiwan and China in the aftermath of the Kuomintang (KMT) returning to power in 2008, this was the first time that the process had been stalled. Thus this alliance of student activists and a diverse range of social movements had achieved something that had eluded the main opposition party, the Democratic Progressive Party (DPP), and its allies. After years of cross-strait stalemate from 1995–2008, the post-2008 China–Taiwan détente had led some observers to believe that Taiwan was no longer a potential flashpoint to rival the Korean peninsula. However, the Sunflower Movement revealed that many of the fundamental issues in China–Taiwan relations remained unresolved.

The lasting impact of the new era of Taiwanese social movement was made apparent in the 2015 Golden Melody music awards ceremony. Fire Ex's (滅火器) *Island's Sunrise* (島嶼天光), which had been an anthem for the Sunflower Movement, won the award for best song. As the group arrived at the ceremony they unfurled a banner in support of Dapu village, which had been at the centre of a land rights social movement (discussed in this volume by Ketty Chen). The banner read: 'Today Demolish Dapu, Tomorrow Demolish the Government' (今天拆大埔, 明天拆政府).[1] The sensitivity of this award was revealed when coverage of Fire Ex was cut from broadcasts of the ceremony in both China and Singapore. In those two countries' broadcasts no award was given for best song. The importance of social movements was again highlighted in the inaugural ceremony for the new DPP president, Tsai Ing-wen, on 20 May 2016. In addition to Fire Ex performing *Island's Sunrise*, the ceremony included performances by musicians associated with environmental protests movements such as Lin Sheng-hsiang (林生祥) and Panai Kusui (巴奈·庫穗).[2]

The key focal points of academic studies of Taiwan have shifted over time. In the post-war era, when fieldwork in the People's Republic of China (PRC) was impossible for Western scholars, Taiwan represented a surrogate for China.

Taiwan began to be studied in its own right as a result of its economic growth in the 1980s and early 1990s. The next big topic was Taiwan's democratization and democratic consolidation, which featured heavily in the 1990s and into the DPP era (2000–08). From the mid-1990s, cross-strait economic integration and China–Taiwan political tensions became another popular topic for research. As Taiwan's democracy matured, its electoral and party politics have also captured the attention of scholars abroad. Although there have been a number of scholars working on Taiwan's social movements since the lifting of martial law, these movements have been much less studied than the themes mentioned above. The wave of social movements that emerged in the post-2008 period, however, has contributed to a blossoming of interest and research into Taiwanese civil society. At my own university, as soon as the Sunflower occupation ended we found a huge interest among students to write their dissertations on Taiwanese social movements. As I write, in mid-2016, a considerable body of Chinese-language book publications, documentaries and academic journal articles have been released that examine this increasingly important actor in Taiwan. Our volume attempts to give readers a sense of this resurgence in Taiwan's civil society.

The Sunflower Movement was viewed as a shock and a worrying development for Taiwan's democracy by many observers. For some, the fact that the KMT government had won strong majorities in the 2008 and 2012 national elections gave it a mandate to govern as it saw fit. Detractors of the movement condemned it as violent and anti-democratic. Another common theme was that the movement damaged Taiwan's international reputation and prospects for regional economic integration.[3] In contrast, the Sunflower Movement's key source of legitimacy was that it was protecting Taiwan's democracy. In fact, one of the slogans most frequently used during the Sunflower Movement was 'Protect Democracy, Return the CSSTA' (捍衛民主, 退回服貿). From this perspective, Taiwan's party politics were not working and needed to be saved.

The Sunflower Movement did not come from nowhere. As many of the chapters here show, it represented the culmination of social tensions that had been building up since the autumn of 2008, just a few months after the KMT returned to power. Although there was much continuity before and after 2008, we feel that the development trajectory of social movements after the KMT returned to power makes this a useful starting point for our analysis. In the initial stage of post-martial law development, social movements tended to ally with the opposition party, the DPP. They largely welcomed the DPP's rise to national power in 2000. With the DPP holding executive power after 2000, some social movement activists experienced their first taste of government. Some were appointed as government ministers, for instance two figures from the anti-nuclear movement served as environmental ministers under the DPP. Social movement leaders were invited to join a wide array of government advisory committees where they had previously been excluded. Rather than being oppositional to the state, many activists became part of the state or at least financially dependent on the state. However, the relationship between the DPP and social movement activists became increasingly strained as the DPP was seen as giving in to big business.

Increasingly, social movements attempted to regain their autonomy from political parties. In fact, during the DPP era Taiwan's largest social movement protests, the Red Shirt anti-corruption movement in 2006 was starkly different from those of the Lee Teng-hui era. It was closely allied to the KMT and its allied parties and called for the DPP president to resign over corruption allegations. By the end of the DPP era, many of those in social movements had become quite disillusioned with their former ally.

The landslide KMT victories in parliamentary elections in January 2008 and the presidential election in March radically changed the environment for social movements. Activists were no longer welcome in government bodies and they now faced a KMT that took policy positions at odds with most social movements. As we see in the chapters in this volume, it took a highly developmentalist approach to land disputes, pushed ahead with the controversial Fourth Nuclear Power Station and ended the moratorium on death sentences. Although Taiwan had been increasingly economically integrated with China under the DPP, the process was accelerated under the KMT and the closer political relations meant that the China factor became increasingly influential on Taiwanese politics and society. Many of the case studies in our book reveal that fear of China undermining Taiwan's democracy and way of life played a key role in social movement activism. The KMT's election victories between 2005 and 2008 gave it control of most local authorities and all branches of national government, giving it the confidence to ignore protests. Relations between social movements and their former ally, the DPP, were now distant, partly as a result of the experience of DPP rule and the DPP's wish to project an image of a moderate party ready for returning to government. Although the KMT has often tried to argue that the social movements after 2008 were controlled by the DPP, our studies have found that activists harboured deep distrust towards the DPP. In short, the KMT's return to power in 2008 created a radically different environment for Taiwan's civil society.

In this book we attempt to offer a picture of the development and diversity of Taiwanese civil society. We do this by examining a series of social movement case studies in the post-2008 period. The authors contributing to the volume come from a wide range of disciplinary backgrounds and use a range of methodological approaches. Most of the chapters are based on extensive fieldwork and in some cases authors are trying to navigate the delicate balance of being both academics and also activists themselves. Despite the diversity in our approaches and disciplines, we examine the development of Taiwan's social movements by addressing four core themes. First, we consider the root causes leading to the emergence of our social movement cases. Second, we consider the patterns of movement development seen in our cases. Third, we are interested in how to best assess or measure the success of our social movement cases? Last, we consider how we can best explain the pattern of development seen in our cases. Through the detailed case studies of social movements we hope to give the reader a vivid picture of the state of Taiwan's civil society and to dispel some of the common misconceptions about Taiwan's social movements.

Overview of the book

The book is divided into three sections. We start with seven chapters that consider movement cases that are specific to the Ma Ying-jeou era (2008–16). This we call this section from the Wild Strawberries to the Sunflowers. We start with Michael Cole's chapter, which sets the scene in the field of social activism after the KMT returned to power in 2008. He focuses on how best to explain the variation in social movement impact by comparing the cases of Citizen 1985 and the Black Island Nation Youth Alliance. Cole argues that mobilization size is not necessarily the most important variable in explaining the impact of movements, instead a key source of movement strength was the way it 'challenged the government in the realm of ideas'. The next chapter, by Hsiao Yuan, considers the social movement that is viewed as the pioneer of the era, the Wild Strawberry student movement, which emerged in late 2008 in response to police violence against protests over China–Taiwan talks. It particularly focuses on the impact of new Internet technologies on social movement organization and mobilization. Although the Wild Strawberry Movement failed to achieve its core demands, it would have a long-term impact on the social movement scene through the use of technology and many of its activists moved on to play prominent roles in a range of other social movements discussed in this volume. This is then followed by a chapter by one of the most prolific writers on Taiwan's social movements, Ho Ming-sho, together with Tsai I-lun. This chapter considers two cases of anti-casino movements on offshore islands. The first is from Penghu during the first Ma term and the second is from Mazu during his second term. Ho and Tsai highlight the importance of local political conditions, particularly the strength of local civil society in explaining why the Penghu campaign was more successful. The next two chapters consider two of the key movements in the run-up to the Sunflower Movement. First, Rowena Ebsworth looks at the Anti-Media Monopoly Movement, which challenged the attempt by Want Want's Tsai Eng-meng (蔡衍明) to dominate the Taiwanese media market. This is followed by Ketty Chen's examination of two important land dispute movements, the Huaguang Community in Taipei and Dapu in Miaoli. Both the Chen and Ebsworth chapters feature activists who had their first taste of activism in the Wild Strawberry Movement and would go on to play an even more prominent role in the Sunflower Movement. This section ends with two chapters on the Sunflower Movement itself. First, André Beckershoff discusses the origins, organizational structures and strategies of the Sunflower Movement. This is followed by Hsu Szu-chien's examination of the role of the China factor on creating the anti-CSSTA alliance of civil society organizations.

The next section examines cases from the social movement that has been the most heavily studied in Taiwan, the environmental movement. We start with Simona Grano's examination of the anti-nuclear movement. After briefly sketching the historical evolution of the movement, Grano examines why it was able to grow in momentum and make its critical breakthrough in the second KMT era. The section ends with my chapter with Peng Yen-wen on the development of the

Green Party Taiwan (GPT) after 2008. In many western European cases the Green Party has played a leading role in environmental movements. By contrast, the Green Party has been a late developer in Taiwan.

The third and final section of the book looks at four long-term social movements that emerged prior to the DPP's time in power and have featured quite different development trajectories even after 2008. First, Chiu Yu-bin looks at the challenges faced by the labour union movement, which first emerged in the late martial law era. In this case the movement faced similar challenges before and after the KMT returned to power. While the majority of movements have been oppositional to the KMT, Chinese migrant spouse NGOs, examined in the chapter by Momesso and Cheng, have tended to work more closely with the KMT. Unlike the other movements, it could be argued the Chinese spouse support movement actually benefitted from the KMT's return to power in 2008. In contrast, Scott Simon's chapter on indigenous rights groups argues that this movement is also quite unlike other cases and has its own internal dynamics, which are relatively unaffected by the shifting balance of party politics in Taipei. The final chapter, by Huang Chang-ling, examines a social movement that is often regarded as the most successful, the women's movement. Key ingredients in its successful formula have been its attempt to stay above party politics and its direct engagement with the state to promote its agenda of gender equality. However, Huang shows how this state feminism approach became increasingly challenged under the conservative government after 2008.

Movement roots

The social movements examined in this book feature cases that emerged in the post-2008 period as well as those originating in the late martial era. For instance, labour, indigenous rights and anti-nuclear movements all emerged in the mid- to late 1980s, while the GPT and migrant spouse rights movements first appeared in the mid- and late 1990s, respectively. However, even for the older movements, the KMT's return to power did have a significant effect on their development. One of the most common causes of the social movement emergence or growing activism among existing movements was the combination of the KMT's return to power with the new post-2008 China–Taiwan relationship, or the China factor. For example, for Ebsworth, 'the roots of the Anti-Media Monopoly Movement lie in the convergence of debates over freedom of the press, cross-Strait relations and distrust of Taiwan's political institutions'.

We see this in the chapter on the Wild Strawberries, a movement emerging soon after the KMT's return to power. Although the movement should not be viewed as an anti-China movement, its emergence was closely connected to the resumption of China–Taiwan negotiations in 2008. It emerged as a result of excessive police violence in dealing with protests against the Chinese envoy, Chen Yunlin (陳雲林), and the reluctance of the KMT government to reform the Assembly and Parade Act. Two documentaries that also give a vivid sense of the interplay between the China factor and the new political environment surrounding the Wild Strawberry Movement are *The Right Thing* (廣場) by Chiang Wei-hua (江偉華) and *Civil Disobedience* (公民不服從) by Chen Yu-ching (陳育青). We see a similar pattern in the anti-casino movement chapter by Ho and Tsai. In this case the China factor is less explicit. Local political support for casinos had been building up in the 2000s but it was not until the KMT returned to power that legislation to allow casinos to be established on the offshore islands was passed. However, the vision of developers is that the offshore island gambling industry will develop on a model similar to Macau and thus their main prospective customers were to be from China. This became a potential target market after Chinese package tours and independent Chinese tourist markets were liberalized after 2008.

The causal link between social movement activism and the China factor under KMT rule became even more powerful in the second Ma term. Cole suggests that both Ma and the Chinese administration led by Xi Jinping (習近平) were attempting to accelerate the process of integration after 2012. As we see in the Ebsworth chapter, the Want Want media empire emerged soon after the KMT returned to power and its openly pro-PRC/CCP editorial line played a key role in motivating the Anti-Media Monopoly Movement activism. Similarly, as we see in the Hsu chapter, the China factor was critical in bringing together the very diverse collection of groups of the alliance of NGOs that formed the Democratic Front against the Cross-Strait Service Trade Agreement (DFACSSTA). However, he also shows how these civil society organizations, with diverse issue concerns and ideological backgrounds, had very different perceptions of the China factor. Hsu distinguishes between the cross-strait, anti-globalization and democracy/human rights contexts that embodied the China factor for these groups and which played a key motivating role in their participation in the build-up to and actual Sunflower Movement. A related movement not covered in our volume concerns revisions to high school curricula. This movement emerged in protest against the attempt by the Ma administration to bring back what it perceived as a new China-centric curriculum. At the height of the movement, protesters were forcibly ejected from a brief occupation of the Ministry of Education.[4] A thread common to these cases is a concern that closer economic and political integration with China threatens to undermine Taiwan's freedom and democracy.

We can also see the China factor in the emergence of a strong migrant spouse rights movement with the high levels of marriage migration from China. However, in this case it was the attempt to impose discriminatory regulations against the Chinese spouses in the DPP era that was critical in the movement's emergence (Tseng *et al.* 2013). In contrast with the other cases, the KMT's return to power created a much more favourable political opportunity structure for this movement. It will be interesting to see how this movement fares now that the DPP has returned to power in 2016.

In some of our cases, though, it was the KMT's economic and development policies that lay at the heart of the movement's renewed activism. For instance, the KMT's much more explicit support for nuclear power and, in particular, the

Fourth Nuclear Power Station benefitted the GPT and anti-nuclear movement. However, these environmental movements were also affected by the shift in public opinion following the Fukushima Dai-ichi nuclear disaster in 2011. The KMT's electoral dominance and control of local and national government gave it the confidence to press ahead with controversial development projects regardless of local opposition and at times also regardless of losing court cases. We see this pattern in the Dapu case, discussed in Ketty Chen's chapter, and also the Miramar resort case in Taitung County.

In a number of our chapter cases, a perception of a return to authoritarian government practices played an important shaping role on activism. Grano, for instance, makes this argument in her chapter on the anti-nuclear movement. The widespread use of excessive police violence and even gangsters against protesters are a feature of this authoritarianism that we see in the land dispute, Wild Strawberry and Sunflower case studies chapters.

A number of contributors attribute the rise of social movement activism to the failures of the main opposition party. Cole, for instance, notes how large DPP protests, even in Ma's second term, such as in January 2013, failed to derail Ma's agenda. We see similar patterns in the environmental movement chapters, whereby disillusionment with the DPP contributed to growing activism. The words of a GPT supporter in the Fell and Peng chapter illustrates this well: 'In fact you can't say the GPT particularly attracts me, but that the other parties hold no attraction at all to me.' Similarly, an interviewee in Hsu's chapter explained how 'After approaching the DPP, they came to understand that the DPP had too many pragmatic considerations and constraints in political operation and was not likely to take prompt and decisive action [in the Legislative Yuan against CSSTA].'

When it comes to the causal variables, the chapters by Scott Simon on indigenous rights groups, Chiu in the labour movement, Huang on the feminist movement and Momesso and Cheng on migrant spouse rights groups reveal some different patterns. While these cases see movements reacting to contemporary issues, long-term causal factors (prior to 2008) have been especially influential. In the latter case, the movement came to prominence as a result of both the sociological impact of large-scale marriage migration from China and South East Asia and, more importantly, the discriminatory policy proposals towards spouses from China by the DPP administration. Huang shows how the feminist movement attempted to maintain its state feminist mode of operation even after the change in ruling parties in 2008. For Chiu, 'the trade union movement after 2008 was deeply conditioned by the mindset of organizing and the strength of national union federations which have been significantly shaped by the legacy of the KMT decades long authoritarian rule'. Simon argues that the indigenous movement simply has much deeper historical roots going back to the Japanese colonial era.

Patterns of development

With such a diversity of social movement case studies, it is not surprising that our chapters display quite distinct patterns of development. The authors also adopt a variety of methods of portraying the ebb and flow of movements. For instance, in the Chiu Yu-bin chapter we can get a sense of development through the decline in union numbers and union members, while in the Fell and Peng chapter development is measured though changing numbers of votes and vote shares for the GPT in elections.

The size of protests is another method commonly used for tracking movement development. For instance, Cole notes how after the first protests against Chen Yunlin's visit in late 2008 the size of protests dropped during the remainder of the first Ma term. Cole contrasts this with a pattern of growing momentum in the second Ma term, not only in the scale of protests but more importantly in the improved strategies and broadened alliances in these movements. Cole and Ketty Chen both talk of a process of cross-pollination and strategic consolidation (of social movements). The idea of a progressively widening alliance is also well illustrated in the two chapters on the Sunflower Movement. For example, Hsu shows how groups that had previously not worked together and were originally wary of each other gradually built up an alliance that culminated in the DFAC-SSTA. Nevertheless, Cole's comparative cases reveal that the importance of the size of mobilization alone should not be focused on in isolation.

The Ho and Tsai chapter on the Penghu anti-casino movement case also gives readers a picture of movement momentum. In this case the anti-casino movement was quite weak compared to the pro-casino local lobby and this was clear in the early non-binding referendums in the DPP era, with clear pro-casino majorities. However, we see how the opposition movement grew rapidly in the build-up to the successful defeat of the referendum proposal. In contrast, the Mazu movement struggled to get off the ground and held its first rally only two months prior to the referendum.

We also have a sense of movement momentum in Grano's chapter. The anti-nuclear movement had hit a low point early in the DPP era after the resumption of construction of the Fourth Nuclear Power Station in 2001. Moreover, the movement had been divided as some activists had joined the government. However, we see a quantitative and qualitative increase in the movement after 2008. Grano shows this in the size of protests, but also in the style of anti-nuclear events such as concerts. This process culminated in the growing pressure on the government, which eventually led to the mothballing of the Fourth Nuclear Power Station in April 2014. Similarly, Fell and Peng present a picture of the GPT progressively getting closer to its goal of an electoral breakthrough.

In the case of the Simon, Huang and Momesso and Cheng chapters on the indigenous rights, feminist and migrant spouse rights movements, we see evidence of continued movement momentum from earlier pre-2008 periods. Simon, however, prefers not to talk of movement development but instead focuses on what he calls four movement unfoldings after 2008. These are the shift in focus from name rectification to livelihood issues, in the rise in the role of non-church movement actors, the greater use of alternative or new media and the attempt to establish autonomy from the mainstream parties by creating a new political party. In the case of the migrant spouse rights movement, we see a continued effort to improve relevant legislation and to remove discrimination.

Naturally movement strength will ebb and flow over time rather than being a linear process. This pattern is well captured in the Beckershoff chapter on the Sunflower Movement and Ebsworth's piece on the Anti-Media Monopoly Movement. Even though the occupation lasted less than a month, Beckershoff reveals how the Sunflower Movement swung between high points (such as the 30 March rally) and low points of crisis as the KMT tried to wait for the movement to collapse from exhaustion and for public opinion to swing away.

The movement that perhaps represents the best example of one that eventually runs out of steam is the Wild Strawberry Movement, discussed in the chapter by Hsiao Yuan. Another way that readers can get a sense of this gradual loss of momentum is the wonderful documentary film by Chiang Wei-hua *The Right Thing*. We can see this not only in the gradual decline in the numbers involved in the Liberty Square occupation but also in the mood of participants. However, even in this case many of these activists went on to join a wide range of subsequent social movements, having learned lessons from the setback. It is quite likely that viewers will see a renewed energy among ex-Wild Strawberry activists in Chiang's forthcoming film *The Mob*, which will look at what happened to them afterwards in the build-up to the Sunflower Movement.

Assessing the impact

During our conference on Taiwanese social movements in the summer of 2014, a question that we constantly came back to was how to best assess the impact of our case studies. Have the movements been successes or failures? All our chapters attempt to answer this question in their own styles. Carter (2007: 164–5) suggests a framework for assessing the types of impact of environmental pressure groups that I will use to summarize some of the key trends in our book. He first distinguishes between internal and external impacts. The key internal impact for Carter refers to the levels of politicization of movement supporters. He then suggests four types of external impacts: (1) Sensitizing impacts, such as changing the public agenda or public opinion; (2) Procedural impacts, such as movement access to decision-making bodies; (3) Structural impacts, such as changes in institutions or alliance structures; and (4) Substantive impacts, such as closing a polluting plant or new legislation. In addition, I will also add a fifth, external impact category of political effect, such as the impact on election results and establishment and strength of movement political parties.

First, we can see a significant effect on the politicization of movement members and supporters in a number of our chapters. The experience of involvement in the series of protests movements is likely to have a lasting effect on the political consciousness and career trajectory of activists in this period. The closest historical parallel to such an impact on the identity of movement activists is that of the immediate post-martial law era, in particular the Wild Lily Movement of 1990. In our volume we see how the numbers joining social movement activities have progressively increased over the Ma Ying-jeou era and this experience will leave a long-term imprint. As we saw with the Wild Lily Movement, many of the activists of this current period will go on to be opinion leaders in academia, party politics and the cultural realm, as well in a wide range of social movements. Hsu's chapter gives a vivid sense of the politicization of movement supporters. In one case we see how members of the Taiwan Alliance for Advancement of Youth Rights and Welfare, which originally did not have a clear anti-China identity, ended up joining the movement due to concerns about how CSSTA could affect the rights of young Taiwanese in the hair and beauty salon sectors.

External impacts

The chapters in this book reveal that the social movements in the post-2008 period have had a remarkable sensitizing impact by not only placing neglected issues on the public agenda but also influencing public opinion. Moreover, they also managed to make a number of highly technical issues understandable to broader audiences. To use Carmines and Stimson's (1990) terminology, they made a number of hard issues into easy issues. For these writers, easy issues are those that are often symbolic and do not require extensive knowledge to understand, while hard issues tend to be highly technical and require a degree of sophistication to understand.

There are numerous examples where we can see this effect. For instance, the Tapu case, discussed in Ketty Chen's chapter, has effectively placed the topic of land justice firmly on the political agenda. The use of the simple but effective slogan of 'Today Demolish Dapu, Tomorrow Demolish the Government' helped make this local developmental issue into an easily understandable national issue. The issue of nuclear power had become quite marginal after the DPP government's unsuccessful attempt to halt the construction of the Fourth Nuclear Power Station in 2000. Moreover, at that point most public opinion supported completing construction of the controversial power station. In the Ma Ying-jeou era the anti-nuclear movement was not only able to bring the issue back on to the public agenda but also contributed to the radical swing in public opinion away from nuclear energy. We see a similar pattern in a number of chapters that look at movements concerned with the risks of economic integration with China. During the first Ma term, public opinion was generally quite supportive of Ma's economic agreements with China and polls suggested that this contributed to his re-election in 2012. In contrast, in cases such as the Anti-Media Monopoly and Sunflower Movement chapters we see how movements were able to raise awareness of the risks of economic integration and contributed to a shift to a much more conservative position on economic ties. One way that we can measure this effect is that, if there had been a referendum in June 2010 on ECFA, it probably would have won; in contrast, a referendum on CSSTA in mid-2014 would undoubtedly have been defeated. This shift in public opinion on both the anti-nuclear and economic ties with China cases was achieved despite the relatively lukewarm role of the main opposition party, the DPP, as well a limited interest in social movement concerns in the mainstream media. Instead, it was civil society actors who changed what the government had framed as highly technical hard issues into easy issues.

In the two anti-casino cases we also see how public opinion changed. In both cases the local political establishment was firmly behind the casinos and, at least in the Penghu case, we have the earlier non-binding unofficial referendums to show broad support. However, public opinion clearly did swing in both cases, enough to block the casino motion in Penghu and almost enough in Mazu. The fact that the Mazu vote was as close as it was is a genuine achievement for the movement as this county had long been a barren area for the DPP and its allied social movements.

We can see the sensitizing effect of social movements in issue areas on which we were not able to include chapters in this volume. For instance, there has been growing awareness and support for the idea of gay marriage as a result of movement activism. This did feature in the GPT chapter by Fell and Peng, as the party has nominated openly gay candidates and used LGBT appeals in election campaigns. We also see in Huang's chapter how the issue of LGBT rights moved on to the political agenda as draft bills on legalizing same-sex marriage were debated in parliament from 2013. Another important case has been the issue of constitutional revisions, something that had largely fallen off the agenda in the second DPP era but was brought back to life as a consequence of the Sunflower Movement. For instance, key reforms that were placed firmly on the political agenda and that generated significant public support included lowering the threshold for smaller parties to be elected to parliament and also lowering the voting age to 18.

One of the biggest differences between the DPP era and the KMT's return to power has been the reduction in social movement activists' access to decision-making bodies after 2008. This difference is seen in the Grano chapter on the anti-nuclear movement. Under the DPP, activists were selected as environmental ministers and featured heavily on the Nuclear-Free Homeland Committee and Environmental Impact Assessment Review Committee. Such access was lost as soon as the KMT returned to power. As Grano notes, the Nuclear-Free Homeland Committee was closed down. Social movements were largely not viewed as a negotiating partner by the KMT. In fact, neither side trusted each other sufficiently. We see this in the Beckershoff chapter's description of the public dialogue between the Sunflower leaders and Premier Jiang on 22 March 2014 and the fact that there was no meeting with Ma. Even when the DPP tried to act as a go-between such as during Lin I-hsiung's hunger strike over the Fourth Nuclear Power Station, the DPP and KMT chairmen, though in the same room, just talked past each other. However, not all of Taiwan's social movements have stood in opposition to the KMT after 2008. For instance, the feminist NGOs have attempted to maintain their non-partisan style of operation regardless of which party is in power (Fell and Weng 2006). Even here, as we see in Huang's chapter, Ma attempted to undermine state feminism by bringing in more conservative figures into bodies such as the Commission on Gender Equality Education. In Simon's chapter there is a similar sense that indigenous rights NGOs have tried to stay above party politics. The case in our volume that stands out as most exceptional is of course the migrant spouse movement groups, who have tended to develop closer links with the KMT and actually gained much greater government access after 2008.

Unlike in the DPP era, under the KMT movement activists have had almost no ability to promote the establishment of new government institutions. In contrast, a key feature of the period has been the creation of a starkly different alliance structure. The KMT has tried to paint the rise of social movements as a product of DPP manipulation. It is true that some movements and activists have an ambiguous relationship with the DPP and most are very anti-KMT. However, in many of our cases, such as the GPT and the indigenous rights movement, there is a clear distrust of the DPP and a desire to retain movement autonomy. In a number of our cases there was a clear attempt to keep a distance from the DPP, even where they held similar policy aims. At times NGOs were prepared to cooperate with the DPP but only on an issue-by-issue basis.

The area where we see the greatest alliance effect, though, is between other social movements. In the first Ma term, movements often worked in isolation. However, over time much broader networks of alliances were built up. We get a sense of this growing alliance in the Cole chapter and in even more detail in Hsu's chapter. One way we can see this is by comparing the extensive NGO support networks, which were critical for the Sunflower occupation to be sustained for over three weeks, with the much more limited support for the Wild Strawberries in 2008. These alliances were gradually built up through the accumulated experience of numerous protest movements. For instance, the Dapu and Anti-Media Monopoly Movement cases appear to have been particularly influential in this process of alliance building in the run-up to the Sunflower occupation. As Cole put it,

> the Sunflower Movement's greatest success, and that of the many movements that came before it, may be that it has reanimated civic activism and empowered youth in a way that makes it impossible for political institutions to ignore them, as they often did prior to 2012.

Generally, social movements are not successful in achieving substantive impacts, especially when faced with a highly hostile ruling party that enjoyed such strong control over the executive and legislative branches of government. What is especially surprising in the cases examined in this book is the number of substantive successes, though it should be noted that in many cases the successes are partial ones or cases where the final outcome has been postponed.

When it comes to blocking controversial projects, our studies show a mixed picture. In Grano's chapter we see how the Fourth Nuclear Power Station has been mothballed rather than scrapped. Clearly the KMT would like to resurrect the project and bring the power station into operation. However, it looks unlikely that this will happen in the near future. The idea of a ruling party proposing a fifth nuclear power station is unimaginable and it looks likely that we will see a gradual but accelerated decommissioning of the three existing nuclear power stations. When I have shown the film *Gongliao How are you?* (貢寮你好嗎?) to British anti-nuclear activists they have been impressed with the Taiwanese movement, especially when considering how little resistance there has been in Britain to building a new generation of nuclear power stations. We see a similar mixed picture on the casino projects, where one of the two referendums, in Penghu, was defeated and the other, in Mazu, passed. The outcome is not fully complete in either case. In Mazu, for instance, little progress has been made in actually following through after the referendum passed. In fact, Chinese officials have indicated that they do not approve of the Mazu plan and even indicted that they might cut transport links if the casinos are opened. In Penghu, there is also local renewed political pressure to restart a new casino referendum campaign in 2016.

The Anti-Media Monopoly and Sunflower Movements also show a mixed picture when it comes to substantive effects. In the former case, though the Want Want Group's attempt to take over Next Media and CNS were successfully blocked, draft legislation that would prevent media monopolies has not been successfully passed. Similarly, despite the halting of the CSSTA and the emergence of a number of drafts for cross-strait agreement supervision legislation, nothing has yet made progress in the Legislative Yuan. It will be interesting to see whether the new post-2016 DPP administration is able to pass this legislation. Even after the Sunflower occupation ended, the Ma government still hoped that the CSSTA could be approved and rejected the idea of renegotiation of CSSTA. We see a similar pattern on the key issues being pushed for by groups such as the GPT and other NGO groups, including gay marriage, reducing the voting age, lowering the referendum threshold, lowering the PR threshold for parliamentary seats and revising the Assembly and Parade Act. Although there was greater political support for such legislation and draft bills do now exist, these were unable to make parliamentary progress in the final two years of the second Ma term. Interestingly, the case chapter where we can see the clearest substantive impact in terms of legislation has been the migrant spouse case, where we do see significant improvement in work rights and equalization of time required for receiving citizenship. Now that the DPP holds the presidency and a parliamentary majority after 2016, there are expectations that many of the key reforms demanded by civil society will be addressed. If the Tsai administration fails to deliver, it is likely that large-scale social protests will soon reappear.

We can measure the political effect in a number of ways. A basic starting point is whether the social movement's main opponent performs badly and loses support. Here we can at least see a correlation with the post-2012 rise in activism and the decline in KMT support. Although the first draft of most of the chapters here were written prior to the November 2014 local elections, we can see the rise in social movements as playing a role in this KMT defeat. One variable has been greater interest in politics from younger voters and as we saw in the second DPP term young voters appear to have again turned against the ruling party in Ma's second term. In addition, though, as social movements attempted to preserve autonomy one method has been the creation or strengthening of parties trying to keep clear of the blue–green divide. We can get a sense of the limits to space for the challenger parties in the Fell and Peng chapter on the GPT. It experienced its best elections to date, coming fifth in the party list vote in 2012 and finally making a breakthrough in winning two local council seats in the November 2014 elections. Another interesting development was that the Labour Party's sole local councillor also won re-election in Hsinchu County in 2014. In the 2016 national elections, most social movements actively engaged in the campaign and contributed to the KMT's worst ever election defeats.

Nevertheless, Taiwan's party and electoral systems offer limited space for smaller challenger parties. For instance, the GPT failed to win national seats in 2012 despite coming fifth in vote share, and the vast majority of social activist candidates in 2014 were unsuccessful. A major challenge is whether to maintain autonomy or work with the DPP. Since 2014 the DPP has actively recruited social movement activists and this was especially visible in the DPP's 2016 parliamentary candidate nomination. The alternative has been to establish new parties. In the aftermath of the Sunflower Movement, the Tree Party, the Social Democratic Party (SDP) and the New Power Party (NPP) were established to try to capture the votes of those dissatisfied with the mainstream parties. Like the GPT, all these parties can be viewed as being offshoots of civil society. In 2016, although the SDP and GPT have been able to establish an electoral alliance, there was not a grand coalition of civil society groups and this served to dilute the impact of alternative parties. In the aftermath of the GPT's failure to make a breakthrough in 2016, there is a sense of pessimism over its prospects. Although the NPP has entered parliament, it did so in an alliance with the DPP and thus appears to be more like a splinter party than a genuine alternative party. It remains to be seen whether the NPP can avoid the fate of earlier splinter parties and maintain its social movement advocacy now it has entered parliament.

Explaining patterns of development

Given that our chapter authors look at the social movement issue from such distinct disciplinary perspectives, it is not surprising that there is some diversity in terms of how we explain the impact of our cases. A number of our chapters show how movements took advantage of the changing political environment or political opportunity structure to explain their impacts.

One of the most common themes that explain social movement impact in our book has been technological change, in particular the use of the Internet and social media. Hsiao shows the mobilization benefits but also the organizational challenges of the Internet in the Wild Strawberry case. In contrast, as social media use has become more widespread we see a much more positive effect in the GPT chapter as well as both the Anti-Media Monopoly and Sunflower Movements.

Another important change in the political environment has been the shift towards more supportive public opinion. In other words, this can be regarded as both an impact and an explanatory variable. The shifting attitudes towards nuclear energy, for instance, have benefitted the anti-nuclear movement and GPT. Similarly, we can see how the GPT has tried to benefit from more tolerant views towards homosexuality by its nomination of openly gay activist candidates. Of course, some contextual changes have posed challenges to social movements. For instance, in Huang's chapter we see the rise of a well-organized counter movement against legalizing same-sex marriage.

The shift in public opinion that has been most influential has been that on relations with China. Thus, those movements we examined that are rooted in concern over growing Chinese political influence benefitted from this swing. For instance, we can contrast the limited public support for the Wild Strawberries with much stronger support for the Sunflower Movement. Without such a swing in public opinion it is unlikely that movements such as the Sunflower Movement, which adopted methods as radical as occupying parliament or the Executive Yuan, would have received such strong public support. Thus, what Hsu calls the China factor has played a critical role in bringing together many of the social movements that in the past might not have worked together. Hsu notes that many of these groups have quite different understandings of what constitutes a China factor or China threat, but it clearly has played a dynamic role in bringing them together.

Another variable that features in a number of chapters could be termed a failure of mainstream party politics or a sense of disillusionment with mainstream party politics. This meant that social movements were forced to step in and play the role that could or even should have been played by more responsive political parties. For instance, a number of chapters talk about the KMT's authoritarian governing styles as being a key motivating factor. Generally, the KMT failed to engage in dialogue with civil society. If the party had been more responsive, it is possible that the build-up in tensions could have been – if not avoided – at least reduced. However, a number of the chapters also reveal that dissatisfaction, distrust of the DPP, along with its seeming inability to constrain the KMT, also provided further motivation to social activists.

Agency also matters in our chapter cases, as success or failure is down to more than changes on the political environment. A number of chapters stress the role of improved movement strategies as playing a key role in their impact. For instance, we see the way that activists tried to extend their message abroad in both the Anti-Media Monopoly and Sunflower Movements. Cole, for instance, argued that the unpredictability of the 'guerrilla-style protests' adopted by certain initially smaller groupings such as the Black Island Nation Youth Alliance contributed to their impact. Another strategy effectively used in our cases has been linking campaigns to elections. Grano argues that it was the fear of losing votes in the run-up to 2016 that finally pushed the KMT to reluctantly freeze the Fourth Nuclear Power Station project in 2014. There was an earlier but similar environmental success in the halting of the planned Kuokuang Petrochemical Plant in 2011. On this occasion, as the movement gained momentum in the run-up to the 2012 national elections, the KMT decided to stop the project that could have affected its electoral projects in the swing region of central Taiwan (Grano 2015).

The use of projects or discourses again was critical in explaining movement impact. Tsai and Ho argue that the use of local identities was important in mobilizing opposition to casinos in Penghu and Mazu. In the migrant spouse movement, employing human rights discourses has also been prevalent. For the GPT it was attempting to project an international Green Party set of values with slight revision for the Taiwanese case. This meant its discourse centred on a range of broad and niche appeals such as climate change, nuclear energy, gay rights, grass-roots democracy and animal rights. Some of these international appeals carried risks due to adverse public opinion, such as on the death penalty. Nevertheless, the fact that other parties were either ambiguous or ignored these appeals gave the GPT scope to win support. When it comes to the indigenous rights movement, Simon suggests that a factor in recent momentum has been a shift in appeals towards more down to earth livelihood issues. Last, we see in the Sunflower and Anti-Media Monopoly chapters that appeals on protecting Taiwan's freedom of the media and democracy were highly effective for mobilization.

Conclusion

So our book offers a picture of Taiwan's vibrant civil society by looking at a number of important movement cases studies after 2008. In our case studies we discuss movement roots, movement development, the impact and how we can best explain the movements' impact and development. We hope that through this analysis we can dispel some of the common myths about Taiwan's civil society. The majority of influential movements in this period have not been controlled by the DPP. Although the China factor did play a role in motivating protests in many cases, most movements they should not be seen as anti-Chinese. Instead, what does motivate action has been a fear of PRC-style authoritarian rule undermining Taiwan's freedom and democracy.

One of the major reasons for Taiwan's relatively consolidated democracy has been its strong and stable party system. However, over time its parties have become insufficiently responsive to societal demands. Democracy theorists argue that a strong civil society is important for democratic transition, but even more so in the consolidation period (Grugel 2002). Taiwan is fortunate to have such a strong and diverse civil society. Our case studies suggest that Taiwan's social movements are playing a critical role in the Taiwanese political process by both supervising political parties and attempting to fill the gap in issue advocacy left by parties. We have seen in this book how civil society has attempted to protect and strengthen Taiwan's democracy. In short, a key lesson of the Ma Ying-jeou era is that, if we want to understand Taiwan, alongside political parties and international relations Taiwan's social movements include a variety of other political actors that require equal attention and research.

Notes

1 Michael Cole. 'What the Authoritarians Don't Want you to See'. Available online at http://thinking-taiwan.com/what-the-authoritarians-dont-want-you-to-see.
2 Loa Iok-sin. 2016. 'Democracy focus of celebrations'. *Taipei Times*, 21 May, 1.
3 Charles Chen. 2014. 'Sorry, The Protests have undermined Taiwan's International Reputation'. *The Diplomat*, 15 April.
4 Michael Cole. 2015. 'Taiwanese Students Occupy Education Ministry Over Textbook Controversy'. Available online at http://thediplomat.com/2015/07/taiwanese-students-occupy-education-ministry-over-textbook-controversy.

Bibliography

Carmines, Edwards and James Stimson. 1990. *Issue Evolution: Race and the Transformation of American Politics*. Princeton, NJ: Princeton University Press.
Carter, Neil. 2007. *The Politics of the Environment*. Cambridge: Cambridge University Press.
Fell, Dafydd and Hui-chen Weng. 2006. 'The rootless movement: Taiwan's women's movement'. In Dafydd Fell, Chang, Bi-Yu and Henning Klöter (eds), *What has Changed? Taiwan's KMT and DPP Eras in Comparative Perspective*. Wiesbaden: Harrassowitz.
Grano, Simona. 2015. *Environmental Governance in Taiwan*. London: Routledge.
Grugel, Jean. 2002. *Democratization: A Critical Introduction*. London: SAGE.
Tseng, Yu-chin, Isabelle Cheng and Dafydd Fell. 2013. 'The politics of the mainland spouses' rights movement in Taiwan'. In Dafydd Fell, Chiu Kuei-fen and Lin Ping (eds), *Migration to and From Taiwan*. London: Routledge, pp. 205–26.

2 Civic activism and protests in Taiwan
Why size doesn't (always) matter

J. Michael Cole

Introduction

Taiwan is blessed with a long tradition of street protests, whose origins can perhaps be traced back to its inhabitants' resistance to the many external challenges it faced throughout its history. 'Every three years an uprising, every five years a rebellion' was a phrase used to describe the contentious relationship between its people and whoever sought to govern the island. Though this description was used to characterize the state of things during periods of 'Chinese rule' between the late seventeenth century and 1895, it is also an appropriate representation of the Formosans' reaction to other exogenous groups, from European settlers to Japanese colonial forces (1895–1945) and finally the Chinese Nationalist Party (KMT) administration following World War II and its defeat in the Chinese Civil War in 1949. Throughout Taiwan's modern history, insurrection and protests have played an instrumental role in shaping the political scene. Among those were the agitations organized by Dr Chiang Wei-shui (蔣渭水), the Japanese-trained physician and founder of the Taiwan Cultural Society (臺灣文化協會) in 1921, which were alimented by indigenous nationalism and resistance to the imposition of Japanese culture and language on the population, and which ultimately succeeded in securing a few concessions from the Japanese colonial administration (Fong 2006). Other, and perhaps better known, instances of popular resistance include the February 1947 uprising, which sparked the 228 Massacre and subsequent White Terror (Kerr 1966), the Kaohsiung Incident of 1979 and the Wild Lily (野百合學運) demonstrations at Memorial Square in Taipei in 1990 (Jacobs 2012). With the exception of the Wild Lily sit-in, the other protests took place in the absence of an institutionalized political opposition that could channel public grievances against the government.

With the advent of democracy and the resulting greater responsiveness of government institutions, protests took on a more local, though by no means unimportant, role, especially after the creation in 1986 of the Democratic Progressive Party (DPP), whose founding members had themselves been part of the *dangwai* ('outside the party') movement, which had called for political reform. After years of silence, civil society, which had been almost entirely penetrated by the KMT under martial law, became a factor in Taiwanese politics and 'contributed to Taiwan's democratic transition by not only calling for political and social reforms, but also by eroding the KMT's dominant position in the country's associational life' (Fell 2012). As Fell observes, the end of authoritarian rule resulted in an explosion in social activism. While there were 143 social protests in 1983, the number rose to 676 in 1987. Over time, Taiwan developed one of the most vibrant civil societies in Asia.

Besides the Wild Lilies and other '*dangwai*-turned-DPP' activism, which was, as Chuang (2013) writes, 'entrapped and paralyzed in institutional politics', many protests from the mid-1980s until the late 1990s tended to fall into what came to be known as the *zili jiuji* (自力救濟), or 'self-relief', category, meaning that they tended to focus more on local issues, such as pollution, conflicts of interest in the workplace and the rights of disenfranchised groups, than on questions of identity and democracy (see Chapter 11). In many cases, social movements worked closely with legislators to enact change. Though essential for the democratic consolidation of the island and, as we shall see, to the vibrant web of sub-state actors that would challenge the authorities from 2012 onwards, those issues, which were predominantly local, barely affected the nation as a whole or did so in a much more incremental and indirect manner. In other words, the *political* nature of their activism could be interpreted as being less overt than *dangwai*-inspired protesting, which directly touched issues of identity, democratization and opposition to authoritarian rule.[1]

Although there were some large protests during the two Chen Shui-bian (陳水扁) presidencies (2000–08), among them the KMT-led rallies following Chen's re-election in 2004, the Red Shirts 'anti-corruption' movement of 2006 calling for Chen to step down, and activism over the planned demolition of the Losheng Sanatorium (樂生療養院) outside Taipei (a problem that was passed on to the subsequent administration and which to this day remains a source of contention and a driver for activism), the main forum where the politics of contention were played out decisively was within the Legislative Yuan, where the KMT enjoyed a majority. In other words, during the period between 2000 and 2008, the KMT opposition was the principal actor in countering the ruling party, especially on matters pertaining to state policy. Consequently, though they succeeded in generating some media interest, large protest movements during those eight years only played a peripheral role and for the most part did not succeed in changing Chen's policies.[2]

The 2008 election of President Ma Ying-jeou (馬英九), whose crushing victory over his opponent, the DPP's Frank Hsieh (謝長廷), gave the KMT near-total control over the executive and legislative branches of the government. With the election, the DPP had nearly ceased to exist as a credible counterweight to the government. It would be a few years before it was resurrected as a political entity of any consequence.

It did not take long before Ma's policies, which were regarded as 'pro-China', engendered large protests. Tens of thousands of people took to the streets during the visit to Taiwan by Chen Yunlin (陳雲林), then the chairman of China's

Association for Relations Across the Taiwan Strait (ARATS), in November 2008. The large police force activated for the visit – as many as 10,000 police officers were deployed around Taipei – created controversy among Taiwanese, as did reports of arrests and various restrictions on the display of national flags. During the five-day visit, 149 police officers and between 200 and 300 individuals were reported injured, with 18 arrests (Amnesty International 2008). Despite the protests, which regrouped various pro-localization organizations, the DPP, and the Wild Strawberries Movement (野草莓運動), the Chen visit was never derailed and set the stage for the signing of the Economic Cooperation Framework Agreement (ECFA) between Taiwan and China, a pact that laid the foundations for several future agreements between the two sides. The protests subsided with Chen's return to China, and the Wild Strawberries (see Chapter 3), a group of about 400 students that, among other things, had advocated for amendments to the Assembly and Parade Act (集會遊行法) – a hangover from the authoritarian era – soon disbanded.³ For the duration of President Ma's first four-year term, Chen and other Chinese officials made repeated visits to Taiwan, but with each visit the size of the protests dropped and the popular outcry, such as it was, failed altogether to impact government policy. The initial wave of protests during Chen's 2008 visit was regarded as a one-off affair sparked by deep suspicions about China and the precedent set by the high-level exchanges. For many, the quick disbanding of social movements was evidence of a lack of political awareness and revolutionary spirit.

The DPP and smaller political parties in the pan-green camp organized a handful of large protests during the remainder of Ma's first term, but those were highly symbolic affairs. The gatherings made the front pages of local newspapers but were largely ignored by the international community. More importantly, they had practically no effect on an administration that could afford to ignore them. One exception to this would be the Anti-Kuokuang Petrochemical Industry Movement (反國光石化運動), which succeeded, after a sustained campaign, in killing plans by the 'pro-business' Ma administration to construct a petrochemical plant in Changhua over predominantly environmental fears (Ho 2014).

Ma's second term: a new phase in the politics of contention

By the time that President Ma was elected to a second and final term in 2012, the DPP had rebuilt itself and narrowed the gap in the legislature. Nevertheless, it still held only a minority of seats in the Legislative Yuan and its ability to counter Ma and the KMT was further undermined by factionalism and internal battles. Ma, who had encountered little credible resistance during his first term, was keen to continue the process of liberalization across the Taiwan Strait. His second term also coincided with the rise of Xi Jinping (習近平) in Beijing, whose leadership style was, by many assessments, much less patient than that of his predecessor. As a result, from 2012 onwards the pace of exchanges in the Taiwan Strait showed a marked acceleration, with China pushing for integration in the cultural, educational and media sectors, all areas that had implications for

Taiwan's democracy (unlike the emphasis on purely *economic* exchanges seen under the first Ma administration). Furthermore, with the KMT by some accounts failing to take the lead on cross-strait negotiations, Beijing had the ability to dictate the areas targeted as well as the pace of liberalization, thus putting the Ma administration in a reactive position. With President Ma keen on securing his legacy and purportedly desiring to hold an eventual summit with President Xi before he steps down in 2016, Taipei appeared to have adopted Beijing's accelerated schedule. With a DPP that continued to show signs of weakness and enjoying the support of an international community that welcomed détente in the Taiwan Strait, the road ahead seemed clear for Ma to do as he wished. Consequently, the government became even less responsive to dissent and increasingly authoritarian whenever it encountered opposition, such as when KMT legislators voted against the party line on major policy proposals.

A mass rally organized by the DPP on 13 January 2013, to protest against government policies highlighted the opposition's inability to derail Ma's agenda. Although it succeeded in attracting an estimated 100,000 protesters (the DPP claimed 200,000), the 'Fury' rally hardly made a dent in the government's policies. More than ever, the protest showed that the ability to bus large number of people into Taipei to wave flags and shout slogans was no longer a sign of one's effectiveness in influencing government policy, especially when institutional checks and balances were weakened by a split opposition and the near-total control by the president, who was also KMT party chairman, over both the executive and legislative branches of government.

Unfortunately for the Ma administration, social forces emerged around that period that would directly challenge the government. Aware of the existential threat facing the nation and disillusioned with the DPP's ability to effectively counter the administration, civic movements with memberships in the hundreds or low thousands burst onto the scene and filled the oppositional vacuum. And they succeeded where much larger gatherings had failed, forcing the government to change its policies or keeping controversial issues alive long enough to attract much greater attention from the public and political actors. Large crowds, long a yardstick by which to evaluate 'success', no longer mattered. Instead, size gave way to unpredictability and the ability of social movements to spread the word, usually via social platforms and the Internet. Slightly more radical but eschewing violence, the groups adopted 'guerrilla' tactics to keep the authorities on their toes. Charismatic leaders, some of whom had cut their teeth as members of the Wild Strawberries, also emerged during that period. Just as important was the cross-pollination of various movements that had mobilized over a number of disparate issues, from the monopolization of the media to forced evictions, which fostered an environment in which activists could learn from each other.

The road to the Sunflower Movement: size didn't matter

One of the key phenomena during the second Ma presidency was the coming together of social movements and the connection that occurred between groups that advocated for local issues and those that agitated over matters of the state. In other words, the spirit of the *dangwai*, which in many ways had dissipated following the institutionalization of the DPP, was slowly merging with the now decades-old tradition of *zili jiuji* activism. Such a development would likely not have occurred had the DPP been able to function as a strong counterweight to the KMT in the legislature, or if cabinet agencies had not been cowed into submission by the Ma administration. The DPP's failings were twofold: first, it had not succeeded in securing enough seats in the 2012 legislative elections to break the pan-blue majority in the Legislative Yuan; and, second, the party appeared to have lost sight of its ideals and for the most part ignored the demands of civil society, causing severe disenchantment among social activists, who came to regard it as part of the problem.

Accompanying this loss of faith in the DPP's ability to act as a bridge between civil society and the government were signs of a widening chasm between the Ma administration and the public.[4] Throughout 2012 and 2013, the government and KMT legislators outwitted a divided DPP in the legislature and, with a few exceptions, ignored the demands of civil society. In some instances, officials in the Ma government broke earlier promises and proceeded with policies that sparked great anger among the public. One salient example was the decision in July 2013 to proceed with the demolition of four homes in Dapu, Miaoli County, despite an earlier promise by the then-premier (and now vice president), Wu Den-yih (吳敦義), to spare them. A high-profile eviction case in Shilin District (士林),[5] Taipei, as well as the razing of the Huaguang Community (華光社區), also exacerbated tensions between civil society and the authorities and often resulted in sizeable police deployments. Besides the increasingly frequent land and eviction issues (see Chapter 6), other controversies in 2012–13 included the continued battle for the preservation of the Losheng Sanatorium, the deaths of military conscripts, veiled corporate interests, the wind turbine controversy in Yuanli, the Taoyuan Aerotropolis project, the A7 Airport MRT project, a 16-year-old government court case against laid-off factory workers, the theft of Aboriginal ancestral lands, 'unsafe' nuclear energy, the aforementioned Assembly and Parade Act and many others. Increasingly, government mechanisms meant to ensure transparency and accountability were seen to be failing, and, with an opposition DPP that seemed unable or unwilling to take action,[6] civil society felt compelled to take matters into its own hands. In most instances, activism was met with government indifference, and when they realized that the activists would not give up, with increasing use of police shields, arrests, fines and court summons.

The China factor was also a critical component in the coming together of social movements. Having lost trust in government accountability over domestic issues, social movements became especially wary of the Ma administration's reliability when it came to negotiations with authoritarian China, talks that furthermore often occurred behind closed doors and which tended, so the belief went, to favour the business interests of a small coterie of wealthy entrepreneurs on both sides of the Taiwan Strait. The Youth Alliance Against Media Monsters

(反媒體巨獸青年聯盟), created in 2012 to block the acquisition of Next Media's (壹傳媒) operations in Taiwan by Tsai Eng-meng (蔡衍明), chairman of the Want Want China Times Group (旺旺中時集團), was just as keen to prevent the monopolization of Taiwan's media environment as it was to ward off the 'black hand' of China within Taiwan (see Chapter 5). One of the key reasons why the group came into being was the lack of trust in the ability of the National Communications Commission (NCC), the Fair Trade Commission (FTC) and legislators' ability to properly review the controversial deal. Ultimately, Tsai, a billionaire who made his fortune in China and who had a long history of editorial meddling, would retract his bid for the group, in part because of the negative impact the drawn-out case was having on his empire's image. This decision, a rare victory for civic groups in 2012, was a direct result of the sustained campaign organized by the Alliance, which augmented its series of street protests outside the NCC, the FTC and the Legislative Yuan with a highly creative use of imagery, an Internet campaign and efforts to internationalize the matter by involving prominent foreign academics such as Noam Chomsky. The many protests organized by the Alliance from the summer of 2012 until Tsai announced he was dropping out never consisted of more than a few hundred individuals.

The Alliance yielded the emergence of two highly charismatic leaders, Lin Fei-fan (林飛帆) and Chen Wei-ting (陳為廷), both of them graduate students who would spearhead other efforts in subsequent months. Just as importantly, the dozens of tier-two leaders and foot soldiers who participated in the protests began supporting other issues, engendering a process of cross-pollination that strengthened the otherwise unconnected causes. Amid this constellation of movements, two standouts were the Youth Alliance for Miaoli (捍衛苗栗青年聯盟), a group opposing forced evictions in the county, and the Black Island Nation Youth Alliance (黑色島國青年聯盟), which came into being in July 2013 to oppose the just-signed Cross-Strait Service Trade Agreement (CSSTA), a follow-on pact to the ECFA, between Taiwan and China. As with other causes, the groups received the support of many academics and civic organizations, among them the Taiwan Rural Front (台灣農村陣線).

As with the Alliance Against Media Monster, the two movements had very humble beginnings. The first protest against the CSSTA, held outside the Executive Yuan on 24 June 2013, attracted about a dozen participants. Initially, most protests by the Youth Alliance for Miaoli also involved no more than a few dozen activists, many of them veterans of other campaigns. Over the months, the level of participation grew, in large part because of a sustained Internet campaign, nationwide outreach efforts and 'guerrilla-style' and highly symbolic acts that succeeded in attracting media attention and that fed into a growing sense of disillusionment with the government.[7] The groups also relied heavily on paraphernalia, including T-shirts, stickers and ribbons, to spread their propaganda. Three slogans in particular, 'F**k the Government', 'Civil Revolt' and 'Today Dapu, Tomorrow the Government', became highly successful and known nationwide. Furthermore, they broke with post-Confucian traditions, prevalent in

Taiwanese society, of politeness, a linguistic radicalization that, reflecting a sense of urgency, may have played a role in generating foreign interest in their cause.

During the period between June 2013 and the Sunflower Occupation of the Legislative Yuan in March 2014, the two groups held several dozen protests each, most of them small, spontaneous and resulting in the mobilization of large police forces. With the exception of the 18 August 2013 rally on Ketagalan Boulevard against nationwide forced evictions, which attracted several thousands of people and was followed by a 24-hour occupation of the Ministry of the Interior (MOI),[8] most protests over urban renewal involved at most a few hundred people. The same applied to the Black Island, which on repeated occasions held protests outside the legislature as it tried to gain entry to public hearings, only to be pushed out by several hundred police officers.

The key to the movements' success was their resilience. Despite the absence of initial results, government intransigence, lack of media interest and a distracted DPP, the groups persisted and never lost sight of their objectives. Unlike the Wild Strawberries (of which Lin Fei-fan was a veteran), they were here to stay.[9] The Black Island and Miaoli alliances travelled around the country and held public meetings, forums and concerts to educate the population and recruit new members, efforts that clearly paid dividends. Judging from the large police deployments at every one of their activities outside the Presidential Office, the Legislative Yuan, the MOI, the Executive Yuan and other venues, as well as efforts by the administration to discredit the protesters by portraying them as 'violent' and 'irrational', the government was taking notice, a stark departure from its apparent indifference to the DPP-organized 'Fury' protest, held earlier that year.

These groups' relatively small number of participants and inability to attract the sustained attention of domestic media (foreign media ignored them altogether) was in stark contrast with the three large protests organized by Citizen 1985 (公民 1985) during the second half of 2013 over the death of army conscript Hung Chung-chiu (洪仲丘) and the subsequent cover-up by the military. Arising out of nowhere (the original members were netizens), Citizen 1985 held its first protest outside the Ministry of National Defense (MND) on 20 July, attracting as many as 30,000 people – among them the families of other victims of abuse in the military. The rally was held 17 days after the 24-year-old Hung died of complications resulting from hyperthermia-induced disseminated intravascular coagulation, or DIC. Citizen 1985, whose leaders, unlike the student alliances, were not well known and in fact secretive to 'avoid detracting attention from the issues', organized a second rally on 3 August, this time on Ketagalan Boulevard. The slick affair, with a large stage, giant screens, music bands and strictly enforced seating rules, drew approximately 250,000 white-clad protesters. Citizen 1985 demanded both the truth behind Corporal Hung's death and reforms to the court martial system, which had been implemented 57 years ago. The group held a final rally on 10 October, National Day, which also attracted several thousands of citizens.

Since its inception, Citizen 1985 had sought to distance itself from other social movements such as the Black Island Nation Youth Alliance, often distinguishing itself as a 'high class' movement that shunned the 'violent' behaviour of the other organizations. The organizers' efforts to portray the movement as peaceful and rational were hard to miss. As already mentioned, Citizen 1985 events adhered to rigid seating rules, so much so that that journalists and photographers (including the author) often complained about their inability to conduct their work. Freedom of movement was limited and protest areas were literally cordoned off. Foot soldiers, furthermore, were deployed to watch out for potential troublemakers. Sources close to the movement's leadership explained that the strict enforcement was meant to reassure Taiwanese 'who were not ready to engage in more hardline forms of protest' and encourage them to come out.[10] In their view, only by offering a safe environment for young people and families could tens of thousands, if not hundreds of thousands of people be mobilized. The tactic worked, but the high predictability of the Citizen 1985 events also meant that the authorities did not feel threatened. The contrast between police deployments at Citizen 1985 rallies and the much smaller ones organized by the Black Island and Miaoli alliances, along with several others (e.g. the Yuanli Self-Help Organization against wind turbines, Losheng activists and members of the Huaguang Community and their supporters), was astonishing. While the police-to-protester ratio on 10 October to counter the Black Island's early-morning protest on Ketagalan Boulevard was about $3:1$,[11] the police were nowhere to be found when Citizen 1985 gathered on Jinnan Road outside the Legislative Yuan, or when it 'occupied' the steps outside Chiang Kai-shek Memorial Hall.[12] Similar ratios had been observed in earlier months, where police officers vastly outnumbered protesters who often were forcefully removed and taken away on buses. In many cases, the protests had been held in defiance of the Assembly and Parade Act and protest leaders were fined or prosecuted for doing so. The highest police-to-protester ratios were observed at protests organized by the Miaoli and Black Island alliances, an indication of the groups' unpredictability and ability to escalate when necessary (e.g. throwing eggs, climbing fences around the Executive and Legislative Yuans, briefly 'occupying' government agency compounds and so on). There is also evidence that the National Security Bureau (NSB) became involved in monitoring protest sites and removing protest leaders. A campaign in mid-2013 to throw shoes at government officials, organized by the National Alliance for Workers of Closed Factories (NAWCF), also resulted in large police mobilizations, as would later efforts to counter protests by laid-off tollbooth workers (the 'e-Tag' protests).

In terms of generating photogenic events and attracting the attention of the media, Citizen 1985 was far more successful than its smaller counterparts. The size of the crowds alone was sufficient to ensure such results. However, it soon became apparent that Citizen 1985 was having little, if any, impact on government policy. This was largely because its one-off events, however large, were predictable, controlled and non-threatening to the authorities. The rallies succeeded in mobilizing large numbers of people but they never *involved* or *responsibilized* them. Tens of thousands of white-clad citizens gathered on the streets, chanted slogans and waved 'Big Citizen is Watching You' flags and banners, but unlike their counterparts in the smaller organizations they never took ownership of the issue; furthermore, there was nothing *between* events to keep the issue alive. Consequently, as with the large DPP rallies held since 2008, the Ma administration for the most part ignored them. In many ways, the response was similar to that of the government to the large rallies held against the continued use of nuclear energy following the incident at the Fukushima Dai-ichi in Japan. Large groups thronged the streets and made the front pages of all the major dailies, but, once people went home, life returned to normal and the administration stuck to its initial policy. Tellingly, the anti-nuclear movement (see Chapter 9) would enjoy greater success following the Sunflower occupation of the Legislative Yuan in March/April 2014, in part due to the involvement of the Sunflower leadership in the occupation of Zhongxian West Road.

Citizen 1985's shortcomings were also in part due to their failure to follow through. Government officials and legislators never faced any consequences if they failed to listen to public grievances or went back on their word. It is hardly surprising, then, that the Ma administration broke its promises on reform in the military justice system or that the punishment meted out on the officers responsible for Hong's death were so minor as to be meaningless. Wrong-footed, the best that Citizen 1985 could do when Taipei broke its word was to encourage its followers to call legislators.

By the end of 2013, Citizen 1985 showed every sign that it was a spent force. At best, it had succeeded in raising awareness about the issue of deaths in the military, but it had little to show in terms of results. Moreover, by October 2013 it had lost its focus and sought to grab other issues (school textbooks, the CSSTA, the Referendum Act, the Election and Recall Act for Public Servants, subsidies for political parties), to little success. Several of its founders had left the group and joined other organizations, including the Black Island Nation Youth Alliance, a group that, months before, it had sought to discredit. Above all, Citizen 1985 lacked the identifiable charismatic leadership that had turned the student movements into powerful agents for change. In fact, unlike the groups headed by Lin Fei-fan and Chen Wei-ting, the top cadres of Citizen 1985 shunned the limelight, arguing that high-profile leadership would be counterproductive. Given the outcome, this was a strategy of questionable validity.[13]

That is not to say that the 50-odd groups that in March 2014 coalesced into what came to be known as the Sunflower Movement had clearly identified or permanent leaders. In fact, while leaders like Lin and Chen were recurrent figures (as leaders or simply lending their support, such as at Huaguang), the key organizers were constantly changing. For example, Lin, who had headed the Alliance Against Media Monster, eventually handed over powers to another student before assuming a leadership position within Black Island. As they increased their interactions, the constellation of organizations developed new leaders and became progressively skilful at organizing beyond the scrutiny of law enforcement agencies, which were becoming increasingly wary of their activities. Cells were formed and decision-making was rarely the sole remit of a senior leadership; it was primarily in the hands of a *horizontal* rather than *vertical* leaders, though at the height of the occupation the Sunflower Movement would eventually develop a more traditional leadership structure. Splinter organizations and ever-changing alliances, which often but not always worked as a single unit, only added to the complexity of the challenge that the state apparatus was facing in keeping tabs on their activities, a situation that was reflected in the increasing presence of police barricades, gates and barbed wire around government buildings and outside KMT headquarters. Although efforts in that domain would dramatically increase in the wake of the Sunflower Movement, law enforcement authorities were also starting to pay greater attention to social media, Internet chat rooms and Facebook, which the various groups had been using to organize their activities and to share information.[14] In some instances, police monitoring forced the groups deeper underground and the leadership was compelled to hold meetings at secret physical locations.

It all came together on 18 March 2014, when about 200 protesters climbed the gate around the Legislative Yuan and launched an unprecedented (and in many ways unplanned) 24-day occupation. Unlike what critics would say at the time, there was nothing spontaneous about the event, which stemmed from tensions that had accumulated during the previous two years, caused largely by perceptions of government unresponsiveness. Just as importantly, the occupation was sparked by a convergence of two principal grievances: the perceived failure of government organs and the 'China threat'.[15] As noted above, this was a marriage between the *dangwai* spirit and traditional social activism. The Sunflower Movement (see Chapters 7–8), named after the delivery of a large quantity of sunflowers to the legislature, became an umbrella organization for as many as 54 civic groups, whose aims and ideology did not always perfectly coincide. Pro-localization groups – some of them 'deep green'[16] and others animated by notions of 'civic nationalism' – joined forces with labour organizations. Though there was an 'anti-China' sentiment, by no means did all participants support that view, which tended more towards scepticism and a desire to prevent the influence of Chinese authoritarianism on Taiwan's democratic institutions. The same applied to anti-globalization ideology, which was espoused by a small number of activists within the Black Island Nation Youth Alliance and other leftist groups. Other issues, such as stagnant wages, lack of opportunities for youth, government corruption and unresponsive legislators, also fed the general anger, both inside and outside parliament.

As several thousands of people (most of them of student age) gathered outside the Legislative Yuan, the composition of the leadership inside the chambers of the legislature was very familiar to those who had followed civic groups since 2012. Almost every one of them was a veteran of one or (in most cases) many previous campaigns. Over the past 24 months they had learned lessons, understood what worked and what did not and had a more refined understanding of how to reach out to the public to make their case effectively.[17] That formidable stock of institutional memory was furthermore compounded by the assistance of various academics, many of them veterans of the Wild Lily Movement in the 1980s, who reminded them of the need to educate themselves about the issues, to become subject matter experts. Tellingly, some leaders of the Citizen 1985 movements also played a role, albeit a secondary one, inside the legislature.[18]

Ironically, despite the Sunflowers' success in bringing the government to a halt and sustaining interest with an international audience over a period of more than three weeks (helped in part by the brief but escalatory occupation of the Executive Yuan on 23 March), the yardstick most often used to evaluate the movement's success was the 30 March mass rally held outside the legislature, which attracted a crowd estimated at 350,000 to 500,000 people, possibly the largest in the nation's history. Just as with the Citizen 1985 rallies, the event was high in emotion and yielded reams of eye-catching footage.[19] However, size notwithstanding, there is every reason to believe that the rally had only marginal influence on government policy. Or, put differently, it would have gone the way of large DPP rallies or the three protests organized by Citizen 1985 were it not for the fact that it was held in the context of the unprecedented occupation of the legislature. Much more effective than the rally were the small things: the emotional speeches held inside the chambers, the interviews given to international media by the movement's leaders, the hundreds of small Sunflower protests held around the globe, the support by activists such as Tiananmen Square veterans Wang Dan (王丹) and Wu'er Kaixi (吾爾開希), or independence fighter Su Beng (史明), the songs and videos recorded in support of the movement[20] and the extraordinary scene outside the parliament, where over the 24-day occupation tens of thousands of participants helped turn the scene into a gigantic classroom, art gallery and concert hall.[21] Lingering images from the occupation are much more likely to be scenes of students clashing with police, or the festooned chambers of the legislative chamber, than the hundreds of thousands of people who gathered on Zhongshan South Road and Ketagalan Boulevard. The police crackdowns, the contradictory and often inept government responses and the involvement of gangsters on the side of the administration added drama to the situation and were all caused not by the large assembly of people but by the firm stance of the movement's unpredictable and creative leadership, its understanding of the issues and its proven track record of defiance, which convinced their followers that they would not be abandoned at the first sign of trouble. It is unlikely that Lin, Chen and the hundreds of others who brought the nation to a standstill and defied Taipei and Beijing would have succeeded in captivating the world – and perhaps change the face of Taiwanese politics – had they not graduated over the years from the hard school of small protests.

In the end, tactical victories notwithstanding (e.g. as of 2016 the CSSTA has yet to be implemented, and negotiations on follow-on pacts, such as the trade-in-goods agreement, have stalled) the Sunflower Movement's greatest success, and that of the many movements that came before it, was that it reanimated civic activism and empowered youth in a way that made it impossible for political institutions to ignore them, as they often did prior to 2012. Activism, though it did not enjoy universal support, had become 'cool' and served as a platform to educate the population on pressing issues, often by connecting the local (issue), the national (party governance) and the external (China). The July 2015 occupation of the Ministry of Education building in Taipei over controversial (and Sino-centric) changes to high school textbook curriculum guidelines highlighted the trickle-down effect of years of activism; new faces emerged, with recognizable ones from the Sunflower Movement providing only moral support to a new generation of protesters, some of whom were as young as 16. Indicatively, the occupation of the MoE followed a very similar trajectory as that of the Sunflower Movement, with months of small yet persistent protesting that eventually gathered momentum and succeeded in attracting larger numbers to their cause – in this case including a number of former KMT members. The new activism, which has shaken Taiwanese politics since 2012, also had the effect of politicizing many young people who eventually decided to enter politics and run for office.

Conclusion

In an era of large protests, such as those seen across the Maghreb and the Muslim world during the Arab Spring, the experience of Taiwan shows that size and violence are not indispensable components for the ability of non-state actors to influence government policy (Danahar 2013). More than anywhere else, Taiwan's youth movements have demonstrated that wit and charisma, along with perseverance, can be just as powerful as bullets. Several factors have contributed to this. Chief among them is the fact that Taiwan is a democracy, which cannot be said of the other countries that have experienced civil unrest in recent years. Taiwan's activists have not sought to overthrow the system but rather were seeking remedial measures to improve the quality of their country's flawed democracy, which furthermore was subject to external, and possibly intensifying, influence by an authoritarian regime. Given the self-imposed restrictions on their objectives, Taiwanese civic groups had to operate at the higher levels of propaganda to make their case with their target audience. They did so against a background in which critics wondered why activism was even necessary when Taiwan is already a democracy.

Taiwanese authorities, along with outside critics of more confrontational social activists such as Black Island and the Sunflowers, used Taiwan's democracy as a means to counter the *legitimacy* of dissent, as if regular elections alone were sufficient to ensure the quality of a country's democracy. Government mouthpieces and a number of foreign observers also turned to conspiracy theories (e.g. the DPP using protest movements and activists seeking to overthrow the government) and accusations of 'illegality', 'irrationality' and 'violence' to discredit activist groups, especially when the latter exposed inconvenient truths (e.g. relations in the Taiwan Strait were not harmonious) or threatened to undo the artificial stability that much of the international community has chosen to regard as an inevitable future for relations between Taiwan and China.[22] Given this handicap, social movements facing an unresponsive government and neutralized opposition were forced to raise the stakes; the ability to gather large numbers of people was no longer sufficient. In fact, large street protests may have been to the government's advantage, as they provided 'evidence' that the authorities were tolerant of dissent, regardless of whether they had any intent to listen to the public's demands. However, large gatherings often were one-off affairs with no follow-up and therefore were inherently unthreatening to the authorities.

Starting in the second decade of the twenty-first century and intensifying during the second Ma term, Taiwan's civil society realized that if it were to succeed in effecting change it would have to challenge the government in the realm of ideas. And, in order to counter government insistence on narrow democratic processes (e.g. the holding of regular elections), social movements were forced to persevere in the face of harsh criticism and had to rely on well-calibrated use of symbols and occasional escalation to draw attention to their causes. Initially operating in isolation, the groups gradually joined forces and learned from one another, starting a process of cross-pollination and strategic consolidation that eventually gave rise to powerful political forces like the Sunflower Movement. What made the latter a force to be reckoned with was not its ability to bring together close to half a million people on 30 March – by no means an unimpressive feat – but rather the months of local battles that preceded this unprecedented expression of dissent. Besides undermining President Ma's ability to achieve his objectives in cross-strait relations during the two years he had left in office, the movement succeeded in re-energizing people who had given up on Taiwan and reminded the DPP of the issues that should figure in its policy platform. The outcome of the November 2014 'nine-in-one' local elections, in which KMT candidates were defeated across the country, and the 20 January16 presidential and legislative elections, where the DPP gained control of the executive and legislative branches of government and in which many former members of social movements ran and were elected,[23] were in good part influenced by the new environment and discourse generated by social forces in recent years.

The strength of the Sunflower Movement did not lie in numbers, but in the spirit that compelled those 10 or 12 individuals who gathered in front of the Executive Yuan on that excruciatingly hot day on 24 June to protest, when the majority of Taiwanese knew nothing about the CSSTA. To understand their resilience, we must look back at developments in Taiwan's civil society since 2012, at the battles over Dapu, Huaguang, Shilin and Yuanli and the many other causes that served as training grounds for Taiwan's new breed of activists.

Notes

1 According to Ho Ming-sho, the term *zili jiuji* has a broader use and should be used with more caution, having been coined by sympathetic legal scholars to describe the protest activities that emerged in the mid-1980s. A narrow use of that term refers to those spontaneous protests in the mid-1980s when professionalized social movement organizations remained rudimentary (email exchanges with Ho, 20 November 2014).

Fan Yun agrees, stating that, 'Taiwanese social protests went through a wave of professionalization from the mid-1980s. After then, sociologists, political scientists as well as activists started to identify them as "social movements or social forces" instead of "self-relief style."' (email exchanges with Fan, 23 November 2014).
2 Some people would disagree that the Red Shirts played a peripheral role, and indeed the argument could be made that its size, plus the involvement of Shih Ming-teh, a former political prisoner and DPP chairman, may have compounded its impact on government policy and in the undermining of President Chen's legitimacy. Nevertheless, this author maintains that the KMT's majority in the legislature and its hold on media outlets, as well as discontent in China and the US with the DPP administration, played a much larger role in neutralizing Chen, a situation that President Ma would not face given the KMT's solid control of the executive and legislative branches at the time of the Sunflowers.
3 The movement's principal goals were the revoking of the requirement for a permit to hold lawful protests, the abolition of restricted protest areas and a clarification of what law enforcement agencies are allowed to do in order to enforce the law during protests. (http://nvdatabase.swarthmore.edu/content/taiwanese-student-sit-human-rights-wild-strawberry-movement-2008).
4 On many occasions, public hearings were more symbol than substance; key dissenting voices, interest groups and academics were either not invited, informed too late or barred access from the venue by large police deployments. In some cases, as with the controversy over InfraVest Corp's wind turbine project in Yuanli, Miaoli County, police inside a public hearing would turn their cameras on the villagers and activists, but did not do so when company representatives or government officials were making their case, measures that were regarded as intimidating. Repeated complaints by the community of abusive force by a private security company hired by InfraVest to protest the construction sites were ignored by the government, with the National Police Agency (NPA) looking the other way. At one point during the occupation, Ma's approval rate dropped to 9.2 per cent; one month after the occupation, Taiwan Indicators Survey Research (TISR) put his approval rate at 17.9 per cent and his disapproval rate at 71.1 per cent. According to the same poll, public distrust was at an all-time high of 62.2 per cent. Ma's support rate dropped further in June 2014, to 14.8 per cent, while his disapproval rate increased to 74.3 per cent. The same TISR report for June put Ma's credibility at 18 per cent. For the same period, approval rates for the judiciary, law enforcement and legislators were also low, signalling disillusionment with the system as a whole.
5 Known as the Wang Jia (王家) case.
6 Efforts by the DPP to shed its image as being 'anti-business' and 'anti-China', added to the impact of having held office from 2000–08, likely played a role in distancing the party from the 'maximalist' ideals it initially held in the 1980s and 1990s.
7 On 15 August 2013, a small group of activists disguised as Chinese tourists slipped by security outside the Executive Yuan and stormed the compound, spraying the main gate with eggs and paint in protest against home demolitions.
8 As the mass rally concluded on Ketagalan Boulevard, the organizers called upon participants to head for the Executive Yuan, which prompted police to scramble to erect a barricade outside the building. As the crowd headed in the direction of the EY down Zhonghsan South Road, the leadership quickly issued a new directive and the protesters ran for the MOI, where they easily overcame the small police force there. This would not be the first time that the authorities were taken off-guard and deceived by disinformation (author's observation at the site, 18 August 2013).
9 Though a case could be made that the Wild Strawberries Movement served as an ideational precursor to, or an early iteration of, the Black Island Nation Youth Alliance.
10 Private conversation between the author and an academic involved with student movements, 18 May 2014.

11 Based on the author's observations at various protest sites. After the Sunflower Movement, some of the individuals behind Citizen 1985 would claim that the Sunflowers' ability to attract tens of thousands of peaceful participants was in part due to Citizen 1985's success in gathering large crowds the previous year.
12 According to official figures, a total of 7,574 security personnel were deployed around the area during National Day, 323 fewer than the previous year. Twenty-one organizations reportedly held protests on that day; Citizen 1985 was the only group to register. As noted, the police force did not bother with Citizen 1985, but hundreds of police challenged the Black Island early in the morning and confiscated a small vehicle.
13 Similar observations would be made about the Umbrella Movement in Hong Kong, whose leadership and chain of command were for the most part unknown and without a proper structure.
14 In May 2014, the administration announced that the National Police Agency (NPA), the Executive Yuan and the KMT had formed 'new media' units charged with monitoring and countering 'false information' on the Internet.
15 Activists often told this writer that unlike him they did not have a second passport that would make it possible for them to leave if their country were absorbed by China, and therefore they had to fight for their future.
16 For example Tsay Ting-kuei's (蔡丁貴) Taiwan Referendum Alliance (公投護台灣聯盟).
17 One of the lessons learned was the use of English and other languages so as to reach out to the international community. Far too often in the past, Chinese had been the only language used during protests. Throughout the occupation, the Sunflower Movement created websites, Facebook pages and a Reddit site, with translations in dozens of languages.
18 According to a source with direct access to the Sunflower leadership, one of the founders of Citizen 1985 became 'much radicalized' during the occupation.
19 In marked contrast with the Citizen 1985 events outside MND or in front of the Presidential Office, police completely barricaded the area around the Presidential Office and deployed SWAT teams and threatened to use force if protesters did not clear the area by 10 o'clock in the evening.
20 For example, the song 島嶼天光, or *Island's Sunrise* by the Taiwanese rock band Fire Ex, which became an anthem for the movement and was sung by protesters worldwide.
21 More than 1,000 artefacts would be collected by academics following the occupation.
22 Some even unjustly compared Taiwanese activists to Middle Eastern-style 'mobs'.
23 For example, former Sunflower Movement leader Huang Kuo-chang (黃國昌) and Hung Tzu-yung (洪慈庸), sister of deceased army conscript Hung Chung-chiu, were both elected into the legislature as members of the third force New Power Party.

Bibliography

Amnesty International. 2008. *Taiwan: Police should avoid using excessive force at upcoming protests*. Available online at www.amnesty.org/fr/library/asset/ASA38/001/2008/fr/97891491-c13a-11dd-9368-1fd51b1be7bc/asa380012008en.html.
Chen, K. 2014. 'National Day, Protest Day'. *The Participant Observer*. Available online at http://theparticipantobserverblog.blogspot.tw/2013/10/national-day-protest-day.html.
Chuang, Y-C. 2013. *Democracy on Trial: Social Movements and Cultural Politics in Postauthoritarian Taiwan*. Hong Kong: CUHK Press.
Cole, M. 2016. 島嶼無戰事: 不願面對的和平假象. Taipei: 商周出版 (in Chinese).
Cole, M. 2015. 黑色島嶼: 一個外籍資深記者對台灣公民運動的調查性報導, Taipei: 商周出版 (in Chinese).

Cole, M. 2012. 'Taiwan's youth fights for democracy, again'. *Wall Street Journal*. Available online at http://online.wsj.com/news/articles/SB10001424127887323981504578176810391935762.
Cole, M. 2013. 'Forget the PLA, Taiwan's military threatens itself'. *The Diplomat*. Available online at http://thediplomat.com/2013/08/forget-the-pla-taiwans-military-threatens-itself/.
Cole, M. 2013. 'Wind power firm hires thugs to protect site'. *Taipei Times*. Available online at www.taipeitimes.com/News/taiwan/archives/2013/06/10/2003564438.
Cole, M. 2013. 'Professor sues NSB, police over protests'. *Taipei Times*. Available online at www.taipeitimes.com/News/taiwan/archives/2013/08/06/2003569043.
Cole, M. 2014. 'The war over the CSSTA enters a new phase'. *Thinking Taiwan*. Available online at http://thinking-taiwan.com/war-cssta-newphase.
Cole, M. 2014. 'Riot police crack down on Taiwanese protesters'. *The Diplomat*. Available online at http://thediplomat.com/2014/03/riot-police-crack-down-on-taiwanese-protesters.
Cole, M. 2014. 'Was Taiwan's Sunflower Movement successful?' *The Diplomat*. Available online at http://thediplomat.com/2014/07/was-taiwans-sunflower-movement-successful.
Cole, M. 2014. 'In defense of the Sunflower Movement'. *China Policy Institute Blog*. Available online at http://blogs.nottingham.ac.uk/chinapolicyinstitute/2014/04/09/in-defense-of-the-sunflower-movement.
Cole, M. 2014. 'Debunking the myths about Taiwan's Sunflower Movement'. *China Policy Institute Blog*. Available online at http://blogs.nottingham.ac.uk/chinapolicyinstitute/2014/04/04/debunking-the-myths-about-taiwans-sunflower-movement.
Danahar, P. 2013. *The New Middle East: The world after the Arab Spring*, London: Bloomsbury.
Dou, Eva. 2013. 'Soldier's death sparks massive protest in Taiwan'. *Wall Street Journal Chinarealtime*. Available online at http://blogs.wsj.com/chinarealtime/2013/08/05/soldiers-death-sparks-massive-protest-in-taiwan.
Fell, D. 2012. *Government and Politics in Taiwan*, London: Routledge.
Fong, S.-C. 2006. 'Hegemony and identity in the colonial experience of Taiwan, 1895–1945'. In Liao Ping-hui and David Der-wei Wang (eds), *Taiwan Under Japanese Colonial Rule: History, Culture, Memory*. New York, NY: Columbia University Press.
Harrison, M. 2012. 'The anti-media monopoly movement 反媒體壟斷運動 in Taiwan'. *The China Story*. Available online at www.thechinastory.org/2012/12/the-anti-media-monopoly-movement-反媒體壟斷運動-in-taiwan.
Ho, M.-S. 2014. Resisting Naphtha Crackers: A historical survey of environmental politics in Taiwan. *China Perspectives*, 2014/3, 5–14.
Hsu, J. 2014. 'Taiwan government agrees to halt construction on nuclear plant'. *Wall Street Journal*. Available online at http://online.wsj.com/news/articles/SB10001424052702304163604579527072873788850.
Jacobs, B. 2012. *Democratizing Taiwan*. Boston, MA: Brill.
Kerr, G. 1966. *Formosa Betrayed*. London: Eyre & Spottiswoode.
Lin, C.-S. 2014. 'Crisis at the top: Why the presidency is failing us'. *Thinking Taiwan*. Available online at http://thinking-taiwan.com/crisis-at-the-top.
Loa, I.-S. 2013. 'Dapu activists egg executive yuan'. *Taipei Times*. Available online at www.taipeitimes.com/News/front/archives/2013/08/16/2003569805.
Tseng, W.-T. 2013. 「大埔案 農陣出示3年前會議紀錄 … 吳敦義承諾原屋保留 白紙黑字」. *Ziyou Shibao*. Available online at http://news.ltn.com.tw/news/focus/paper/694069 (in Chinese).
Wang, C. 2014. 'DPP's Tsai vows to make changes'. *Taipei Times*. Available online at www.taipeitimes.com/News/taiwan/archives/2014/05/29/2003591497.

3 Virtual ecologies, mobilization and democratic groups without leaders
Impacts of Internet media on the Wild Strawberry Movement

Hsiao Yuan

Introduction

The Wild Strawberry Movement can be seen as the pioneer of a series of social movements since 2008. Many prominent figures in recent social movements had their participation roots in the Wild Strawberry Movement. As this chapter will show later, the Wild Strawberry Movement provided many 'first-timers' with their first taste of civil participation. Another distinctive feature of the Wild Strawberry Movement, which can also be seen in later social movements, was the absence of political parties playing a direct organizing role. While political parties may have supported indirectly, the Wild Strawberry Movement was initiated and organized by citizens, mostly students. The Wild Strawberry Movement provided citizens with an alternative route of political participation without being involved in political parties or even pre-existing organization. Analysis of the Wild Strawberry Movement provides an understanding of the historical roots that enabled a new method of civil participation to emerge.

Examining the Wild Strawberry Movement not only provides context for recent social movements in Taiwan but also sheds light on how the Internet impacts social movements in general. While at the turn of this century scholars showed scepticism of the role that the Internet could play in social movements (Diani 2000; Lin and Cheng 2001), the Internet has unquestionably gained importance in various movements or even revolutions. One can identify the importance of the Internet media, such as Facebook or Twitter, in the Arab Spring Movement, in the Occupy Wall Street Movement and in a substantial number of movements around the world (Caren and Gaby 2011; Hofheinz 2005; Mercea 2011; Zhuo *et al.* 2011). Scholars have pointed out the power of the Internet to mobilize participants effectively and provide new opportunities for social movements (e.g. Harlow 2011; Tufekci and Wilson 2012; Van Laer 2010). In Taiwan, the Internet as a key mobilization tool can be seen in recent large-scale protests such as the protest against the death of Hung Chung-Chiu (洪仲丘) in the military, the Sunflower Movement in 2014 and the protest against the curriculum change. Although it is hard to estimate their direct impact, Internet media, especially Facebook and the Bulletin Board System (BBS), played a large role. For instance, the Sunflower Movement Facebook page received more than 200,000 likes during the protest. Similarly, on the largest board on BBS, the most prominent issue of discussion was about curriculum changes during the period of protest.

Although the Internet has been crucial in increasing the visibility of social movements in Taiwan, underdeveloped questions still linger: what is the impact of the Internet on mobilization structures of social movements? How does Internet mobilization change social movement organizations? This chapter provides preliminary answers to these questions.

Through in-depth analysis of the Wild Strawberry Movement, this chapter proposes the concept of 'virtual ecologies' to depict the unique mobilization structure of Internet social movements. The Internet, such as the BBS in this case, created the ecological basis that supported mobilization power in the absence of pre-existing organizations. However, mobilization through virtual ecologies led to a mobilization structure with 'segmented' social networks, which in turn made it hard to generate the trust needed to create leadership. Consequently, decisions were made through direct democracy, resulting in a flat, power-diverse and low-coordination organizational structure, which can be described as 'democratic groups without leaders'. Internet media may not only provide mobilization power but also fundamentally change mobilization structures as well as organizational structures. While it is beyond the scope of this study, similar phenomena may be seen in recent social movements, and concepts proposed may provide the theoretical lens for analysis. For instance, the Sunflower Movement was also organized by citizens rather than political parties. Similarly, in the protest against curriculum change in 2015 even high school students could initiate protests without prior experience.

Mobilization structures of social movements and the Internet

The mobilization process of social movements contributes to the resources available. Mobilization refers to the process of how a passive individual becomes an active participant (Tilly 1978). Mobilization structure research focuses on the social and organizational structures that affect the process of mobilization (Zhao 2007).

A major obstacle to mobilization is the free-rider problem. Olson's (1965) discussion of the logic of collective action has been widely applied, pointing out that people are not willing to make the effort to protest since benefits made by protesters would be shared by the general populace. To counter this, various theories have provided explanations of why movements successfully mobilize participants. Resource mobilization theory stresses the importance of movement organizations in extracting resources. This line of approach states that resources, including money, organizations, media and party relationship, are the key to success of social movements (McCarthy and Zald 1977; Jenkins 1983). On the other hand, some scholars focus on how social movements create meaning for potential supporters, encouraging them to participate. These scholars contend that in order to successfully mobilize supporters, activists should 'frame' movements appropriately to make citizens concur with goals of the movements (Benford and Snow 2000; McAdam and Snow 1997; Noonan 1997; Snow, Rochford, Worden and Benford 1997).

Many view social networks as the answer to the free-rider problem (Della Porta and Diani 2006). Gould (1997) studies the communities of Paris during World War II and argues that social networks are the key to participation. Social networks composed of private relationships through organizations, such as parties, church and unions, are considered an important factor in encouraging people to participate in social movements (Morris 1997).

In contrast to research stressing the importance of organizations, Zhao (1998) emphasizes the importance of 'place' as the foundation of social network creation. He analyses the 1989 student movements in China and points out that physical places such as dormitories or student restaurants serve as bases to recruit participants. Zhao argues that mobilization based on these places are different from those based on organizations and terms these as 'ecologies'.

The Internet as a relatively independent mobilization base has gained increasing notice. Mele (1999) uses the Jervay region as an example to discuss how residents used the Internet to enhance their movement. Clark and Themudo (2006) show how the anti-globalization movements in the US used the Internet as participants' base of connection. Earl and Kimport (2009) point out that the Internet makes it possible for movement participants to promote and attain diverse goals online. Stein (2009) studies American social movement websites and concludes that the Internet can help gather resources for social movements.

Also, scholars have contended that the Internet can serve as an alternative media to mobilize participants. The Internet may place tools of cultural production in the hands of ordinary people. Movement organizations may use the Internet as a media to better represent themselves (Srinivasan and Fish 2009; Youmans and York 2012). Through the Internet, activists can provide essential information, such as the goals of the movement or how to contribute resources (Biddix and Park 2008). Furthermore, activists may use the Internet to gain attention from mainstream media such as newspapers or television (Lester and Hutchins 2009) or even influence their agendas (Tang and Sampson 2012). Furthermore, the Internet facilitates online users to participate in offline social movements (Brunsting and Postmes 2002; Harlow 2011; Kavada 2010; Petray 2011; Wojcieszak 2009). However, it is debated whether the Internet facilitates trust between users. While Diani (2000) questioned the possibility of online trust generation due to lack of the warmth and intensity compared to face-to-face interaction, Nip (2004) contends that trust and collective identity can be created through the Internet. Furthermore, because of technological advances, Internet users may interact highly with one another more than ever and foster common identities (Petray 2011).

Network analysis has also been important. Many put their focus on multi-network hyperlinks, indicating that websites connecting to one another increases the spread of information and hence resource mobilization (Biddix and Park 2008;

Kropczynski and Nah 2011). Nonetheless, analysis of social networks should not be limited to online communication. Social networks online and offline are not dichotomous (Meek 2012; Mercea 2011; Wellman *et al.* 2001). Scholars have pointed out that mobilization power is at its best when online recruitment is backed by existing social network ties offline (Diani 2000; Van Laer 2010). In other words, those social networks offline may be reproduced online and vice versa.

The discussion above points to ambiguity in how to explain the Internet as a movement mobilization source. Debates range from whether the Internet can spread information effectively and establish trust between users to whether it can mobilize participants in social movements. This chapter argues that changing the perspective of viewing the Internet from a medium to an ecology can shed light on these debates. For instance, when discussing the effectiveness of information transmitting, seeing the Internet as a medium focuses on the technological barriers that impede the process. However, if viewed as an ecology we can incorporate the factor of interacting social networks, which facilitate information spread that may overcome technological barriers. Also, if we see the Internet as a medium whose primary function is transmitting information, it is hard to understand how trust can be established in this process. On the other hand, seeing the Internet as an ecology focuses on the dynamics of multi-user interaction, which help to explain trust formation. Finally, seeing the Internet as an ecology explains not only how offline social networks overlap online but also how these networks converge in an ecology, which in turn may facilitate trust creation and social network generation. This chapter uses the Wild Strawberry Movement as a causal-process observation (Mahoney 2010) to depict the ecological basis of the Internet and how it in turn influences the mobilization structure of the movement.

Organizational structures of social movements and Internet media

How social movements form organizations to manage participants, create strategies, promote themselves and recruit resources has been a main focus of social movement research. As described, resource mobilization theory emphasizes the role of formal and professional organizations. Professional activists play a key role in determining the success of social movements. Resource mobilization theorists argue that social movement participants are not mobs. On the contrary, participants and leaders have structural hierarchical relationships. Formal and power-concentrative organizations are typical of social movements (Jenkins 1983).

However, this perspective is challenged by 'new social movements' theorists. Compared with 'old social movements', which mainly consisted of labour union movements, new social movements include environmental movements, women's movements and anti-war movements, among others. New social movements stress the principle of 'letting participants make decisions that affect their lives'. They allow more participants to make decisions through participatory democracy and develop a decentralized, open and segmented organizational structure (Dalton *et al.* 1990).

Nevertheless, an organizational structure that emphasizes participatory democracy does not imply that leaders do not exist. Polleta (2002) discusses organizational structures of 1960s and 1970s American social movements and points out that, while the movements emphasized decision-making through participatory democracy, they still created leaders. Leaders were created through democratic procedures. Freeman's (1972) investigation of women's rights movements in the US shows that, while formal leaders may not exist, leaders still exist in informal form. Those with stronger network ties with social movement organization members have more power compared with others. In short, in spite of differences in organizational structure, these movements all observe democratic procedures in making decisions. Participatory politics can be implemented in social movement organizations through various forms.

Studies on organizational structures of social movements in Taiwan are relatively few. Gu (2003) points out that after the lifting of martial law in Taiwan social movements started to professionalize to deal with complicated managing issues. Fan (2003) argues that personal experiences of activists of women's rights movements in Taiwan affected their organizational structures, which in turn affected the trajectory of movement actions. Deng (1993) analyses student movements in Taiwan after the 1980s, and contends that student club organizations played a critical role in initiating movements and mobilizing resources. Leaders were often cadre members in the clubs and made important decisions for student movements.

Although much research investigates how social movements are organized, few discuss how the Internet may affect organizational structures of social movements. In her study of movement websites that support or oppose scientology, Peckham (1998) points out that participatory and interactive characteristics of the Internet make it difficult to create leaders for movements. Clark and Themudo (2006) study the websites of the anti-globalization movements and propose that the flat organizational structure of the website encourages democratic participation of website users rather than a hierarchical structure. Some have also analysed the connection between Internet media and offline social movement organizations. Castells (2012) argues that the use of Internet media tends to make movements leaderless, while Gerbaudo (2012) finds that, despite Internet mobilization, soft leaders who conduct key social movement decisions may still exist. In short, the mechanism of how the Internet affects organizational structures of social movements is still underdeveloped, and this chapter aims to contribute to its understanding.

Method

Case description

The Wild Strawberry Movement has its historical meaning in Taiwan. It was not only a pioneer in a series of future social movements but was the first social movement initiated on the Internet, mainly through the BBS, a medium I will describe later in detail. Participants mainly consisted of teachers and students who rallied to protest against acts of the police when the Chinese official Chen Yunlin (陳雲林) visited Taiwan in 2008. Protesters were especially angered by the forceful dispersal of demonstrators who promoted Taiwanese identity and by the prohibition of openly waving the national flag near Chen's residential area. The police actions were seen by protesters as violating freedom of speech. Protesters rallied in front of the Executive Yuan (行政院) and later occupied a space at Liberty Square, a nearby plaza. Supporters also organized Wild Strawberry Movements in other places in Taiwan, such as Taichung or Chiayi. Still, the Taipei site was the centre of attention and would be the focus of discussion in this chapter. As time went by, protest goals eventually moved from protesting against the government to a legislative reform on the Assembly and Parade Act. The movement started on 6 November 2008 and ended on 11 December, lasting for about a month. It eventually ran out of steam and did not receive any direct response from the government. Nevertheless, it inspired many participants to become activists and opened up a new method of mobilization in Taiwanese history.

The use of the BBS is crucial to understand the initiation process. After the controversial acts of the government, a few professors and students attempted to organize a protest. One of them, Lee Ming-Tsung (李明璁), posted the agenda on his personal BBS board. To the surprise of the initiators,[1] the post had a remarkable response on the Internet. Lee's personal board became the online base of the movement, where thousands of articles were discussed. Although Lee left the movement after a few weeks, activists set up a new board to represent the movement. Even to this day, articles related to the freedom of speech are still posted there from time to time.

A simplified description of the Wild Strawberry Movement is listed on Table 3.1.

Research methods

First, content analysis on BBS posts was conducted. All posts on the movement's BBS official site were analysed. The time range of analysis was from 5 November

Table 3.1 Description of the Wild Strawberry Movement

Movement period	6 November 2008 to 11 December 2008
Initiation source	A post on the PTT2 site
Location	Mainly in Taipei but also other areas in Taiwan
Reason of protest	Protest against the abusive use of power by police
Goals	1 Apology by the president and the premier
	2 Resignations of the National Police Agency director-general and National Security Bureau director-general
	3 Amendment of the Assembly and Parade Act
Organizational structure	Leaderless. Decisions made through direct democracy. Groups were formed to perform functions of the movement with minimal coordination

Table 3.2 Categories of posts on the official Wild Strawberry Movement BBS site

Initial mobilization	Issue discussion	News reports	Other
1,285	1,079	188	357

2008 to 10 December 2008, with a total of 2,909 posts. Posts were then sorted according to main purpose, including initial mobilization, news reports, issue discussion and other (see Table 3.2). Primary purpose was coded for those which fitted into more than one category.

Second, in-depth interviews with 21 participants and cadre members were conducted. To diversify interviewee background and obtain a fuller understanding of the movement, three procedures were conducted. To diversify participants by university, an article was posted online asking for participants. Also, through informal social networks, participants from various universities were purposely sampled. In order to create a diverse sample, I interviewed both cadre members and also ordinary movement participants. Finally, another diversification process was undertaken by choosing from those participants who participated throughout the movement and from those who only attended the initial phase. Interviews were recorded and notes were taken.

Third, field note analysis was used. Through author participation in the movement at different times, field notes were taken. The notes helped understand how and why important events appeared during the movement.

From 'virtual ecologies' to 'democratic groups without leaders': how the Internet affected the Wild Strawberry Movement

The BBS as a virtual ecology in daily life

The Wild Strawberry Movement was initiated on the personal PTT2 board of Professor Lee. To understand how a personal board could evolve into the basis of a movement, content analysis was conducted on the BBS media.

The BBS has been used since 1983 in Taiwan (Shen 1995). Although the interface has remained much the same since 1983 and is rather primitive, it is largely used by the younger generation, many of whom are college students. The number of users on PTT, the main site on the BBS, can even now exceed 100,000 simultaneously at its peak. Users use the BBS as their main daily routine of gaining information and socializing. In this chapter, two BBS sites are of particular importance – the PTT and PTT2. The PTT contains boards differentiated by topic (e.g. political issues, news, movies), while in PTT2 boards are mainly posts related to the board owner (e.g. the personal board by Professor Lee). It could be rudimentarily stated that PTT boards are more public while PTT2 boards are more private.

The interface of the BBS is shown in Figures 3.1 and 3.2. Figure 3.1 depicts the interface, where each row represents a board. Users can then choose a board

Internet media and the Wild Strawberries 41

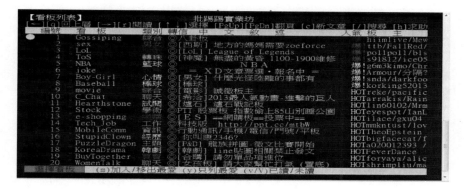

Figure 3.1 The interface of the BBS where users can choose boards.

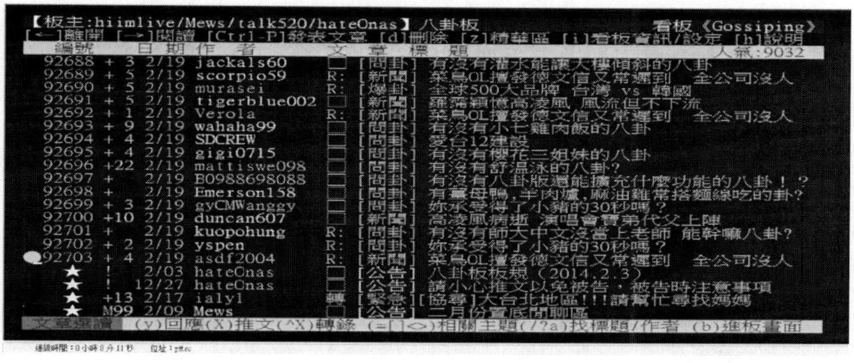

Figure 3.2 The interface of the BBS where users can choose posts.

and enter. For example, one can enter the 'Gossiping' board in the first row. Figure 3.2 depicts what it looks like inside a board. Each row represents a post.

There are many boards on the BBS, differentiated by topic or owner. For instance, many participants of the Wild Strawberry Movement owned PTT2 boards to post articles related to the owner or the movement. The BBS owns the following characteristics that facilitate an ecological environment.

The BBS allows multiple users to interact simultaneously. Since it is a 'board system', the BBS allows all users to post and reply articles, albeit sometimes with restrictions.[2] On some boards, only invited users can view the content of the board. Still, most boards on the BBS allow all users to post and reply to articles as long as content is related to board topic. Also, anyone can create his/her own board and discuss information with friends or even random users. In addition, the BBS allows 'one sentence short replies' beneath the original article. If users want to express quick feelings, they simply reply with one sentence, which encourages between-user participation.

Second, information is transmitted between boards easily. The BBS allows users to forward articles from one board to another by a few commands. Frequently discussed articles are often seen on various boards, especially when board owners are acquainted.

Third, the BBS allows for personal settings adjusted to each individual user. Users can add favourite boards for quick access. Also, users can add friends and blacklists and be notified when friends get online. One can also message or chat with one's friends. These settings are very similar to social media nowadays, such as Facebook.

However, the BBS does not allow users to tag other users, play multiple-player games or share photos. It also does not allow users to trace posts friends have liked or posted. Given these primitive characteristics, the BBS provides an excellent opportunity to analyse which characteristics of the Internet might contribute to the mobilization process of social movements.

The BBS creates an ecological environment where users spend much of their daily lives. It facilitates the daily habit of users producing information collaboratively, even on topics unrelated to public issues. First, users share a variety of information, ranging from personal stories to policy debates. Users express personal interests in a virtual but public space. Second, the collaborative mode may create trust on information generated on the BBS since posts are discussed and even debated. For instance, on 'Gossiping', a board where many share news, a user quoted a lawyer stating that abolishing the death penalty would not increase crime rates. The post created intense debate and spurred 33 posts within two days, with some even comparing the US criminal justice system to Taiwan. At the time of the Wild Strawberry Movement, the movement generated large amounts of debate and information sharing, which can be traced back to the daily habit of BBS users. Third, the BBS not only links personal interests with the public but also facilitates and reinforces personal social networks. This is especially true for PTT2, where boards reflect owners' concerns. These boards allow friends to respond to owners' interests, generating a small ecology centred on the owner. For instance, a user shared how he accomplished his thesis in multiple languages, which received various messages of congratulations and praise. While these events may seem trivial and not related to social movements, it does create the virtual ecology allowing users to transmit information through their personal networks. Users foster social networks through the incorporation of the BBS into daily communication with other users. The importance of the BBS is such that mainstream media often excerpt events on the BBS as reporting material. For instance, ETToday (a mainstream television channel) reported the event of users on the BBS holding an online game tournament, describing the nature of the competition (ETToday, 7 February 2014). The *China Times*, a prominent newspaper in Taiwan, reported how a famous user on the BBS criticized a model girl and the debate between the two (*China Times*, 5 February 2014).

The BBS as an information transmission hub

The Wild Strawberry Movement was officially initiated on the personal board of Professor Lee on the PTT2 site. It started with professors and students discussing organizing a protest on 5 November. They then officially posted an article on PTT2 at 22:58 stating the goals and details of movement participation, which would start at 11:00 the next day. The post was replied to by 674 persons, who spelled out their names and affiliated universities within the 12 hour period, most stating that they would show up the next day. The mobilization power was huge considering the very short time frame. Furthermore, this post was forwarded to at least 698 personal boards on PTT2 within the 12 hours, and it was further forwarded to other boards.

After initiation, the BBS continued to play a prominent role in disseminating information about the movement, inviting others to join. Content analysis shows that, excluding posts when the movement was initiated, 1,624 more posts were posted on the official PTT2 board until the movement ended on 11 December. Of specific interest is the 'summary for lazy people' post, which was located at the bottom of the official PTT2 board. The post was updated from time to time, introducing the goals of the movement, links to the official blog, news reports and other information, which allowed visitors to become familiar with the movement easily. The PTT2 board acted as the online representation of the movement, allowing users to discuss issues, give suggestions, reflect personal experiences and interact with others.

Interview results show that the BBS played a major role in recruiting participants. Over 70 per cent of interviewees came to know the movement through the Internet, especially the BBS. For example, one of the interviewees mentioned why he attended the movement: 'At the time, my classmate messaged me and told me to visit the BBS. I asked him why, and he said that I should go and know about what's going on.'[3] Another interviewee also expressed: 'When I saw a post [on BBS] about a meeting to be held the next day, I decided to join them.'[4]

The BBS enabled users to know about the movement easily, which lowered the barrier for a non-participant to become one. Interactions between users also helped the mobilization process. Users posted questions about the movement and usually got replies quickly. For instance, a user questioned the movement's timing (at the time there were also other protests by the Democratic Progressive Party (DPP), which might make some suspect that the DPP was behind the Wild Strawberry Movement). The post was replied by tens of users within a minute. Similarly, other questions received responses quickly. The interactivity of the BBS allowed users to communicate with each other, which was critical in spreading information. One of the interviewees was originally an online user who debated with others on the official PTT2 board. However, as he participated more he eventually went to the protest site and even became part of the executive group.[5] His case indicates a possible route of how online participation transfers into offline participation.

However, while the BBS was a primary source in spreading information, it played a limited role in influencing the movement's decisions. If one wanted to participate in the decision-making process, one had to go to the protest site. There were many posts questioning or giving suggestions about the goals or strategies of the movement. Nevertheless, while other users replied swiftly, these posts seldom received response from movement cadre members. One cadre member explained:

> Participants had no time to go online and answer questions. However, online users would get infuriated when their questions did not receive responses from participants. There are just too many posts there and it's kind of like an information explosion.[6]

Even if posts did get any response at all, the most common kind of response was asking questioners to come to the site to discuss issues.

Information explosion was one of the reasons why the BBS played a limited role in decision-making. Since there were hundreds of posts online in a day, it was almost impossible to organize those ideas. There was an effort to do so when the movement first started. However, the participant in charge of organizing got exhausted by the workload within a week.[7] Another reason was that participants already had to deal with numerous matters at the site and had no time to answer endless questions online.

The experience of a participant testifies to the point above. Before going to the protest site, this participant posted lots of questions and suggestions on the BBS and was respected for his logic, ability and erudition. However, he insisted on going to the protest site:

> I found out that posting articles on the internet was useless, because you could see that those replying to the posts weren't those actually participating in the movement. At first I posted articles and expected the participants to respond. Then I found out that there were two different worlds.[8]

Although the BBS helped mobilize participants, one could not participate in the decision-making process simply through the BBS.

From daily life to protest mobilization: virtual ecologies as mobilization structure

As mentioned, many studies emphasize the importance of pre-existing organizations in the mobilization process of social movements (e.g. Deng 1993; McCarthy and Zald 1977; Jenkins 1983). However, in the Wild Strawberry Movement the role of pre-existing organizations was relatively small. Even though some participants were members of social organizations, they did not emphasize these identities. The mobilization structure of the movement was mainly through the Internet, which led to a mobilization structure with *segmented social networks*.

The Wild Strawberry Movement was composed of individual participants rather than groups of people from pre-existing organizations. When participants signed names on the initiating post, most of them only posted their names and affiliated department, rather than showing which organization they belonged to. Besides this, none of the participants interviewed was recruited from pre-existing organizations. Most joined because they or friends saw information about the movement online. Many posts on the BBS showed the willingness to join or invite others to participate. In other words, the BBS became an alternative tool to invite individuals to participate. People did not have to be recruited from pre-existing organizations.

Since pre-existing organizations did not play a significant role in the movement's mobilization structure, two characteristics of the movement can be found. First, many participants were 'first-timers' who had never participated in any social movement before. Many interviewees expressed that this was the first time they attended a social movement. Surprisingly, this 'first timer' phenomenon applies to many cadre members as well. Any person who wanted to be a cadre member could volunteer to be one without any prior experience required. Since most participants were recruited from the Internet rather than pre-existing organizations, it is not surprising that they had no experience in social movements. Second, participants were not acquaintances. On the contrary, most were strangers to each other. Since there was no pre-existing organization serving as a mobilizing base, there was no dense pre-existing social network. Many participants said that they had few or no old friends in the movement. This was the case with normal participants as well as cadre members. The social network in the Wild Strawberry Movement can be described as a 'segmented' network, with participants knowing only a segment of other participants before the movement. However, segmentation should not be confused with atomization, which means that participants are individuals with no connection with others. Participants may be connected with a few other participants and form groups, but as a whole the movement was not a dense network. In fact, previous analysis shows that social networks played an important role in mobilizing participants (e.g. users asking personal friends to join after seeing BBS posts).

In short, the mobilization structure of the Wild Strawberry Movement was similar to 'ecologies' discussed by Zhao (2007). Zhao describes the importance of geographical 'ecologies', such as student restaurants or dormitories as bases in mobilizing participants. In ecologies, activists interact with each other and form social network ties. Although it is impossible to know every person in such a large place, trust develops in these ecologies, which can be the base of mobilization. The BBS played a similar role in the Wild Strawberry Movement. On the BBS, users discussed issues, talked about personal experiences and interacted with one another. Also, since there were tens of thousands of users on the BBS, it was impossible to know everyone. When protest issues emerged, the daily ecological roots transformed into mobilization power.

However, when comparing the BBS to the ecologies that Zhao mentioned, BBS users came from much more diverse backgrounds. In the case of the 1989 Beijing Student Movement, most participants came from the same university, while participants of Wild Strawberry Movement came from different ones.

Social networks were even more segmented in the Wild Strawberry Movement compared with the 1989 student protest.

The BBS created a mobilization structure similar to that of geographical 'ecologies', while having the advantage of transgressing geographical boundaries. If ecologies can be conceived as 'particular places' that have mobilizing power, the BBS can be conceived as a 'virtual space' with similar power. Hence, this chapter uses the term 'virtual ecology' to coin such a space with the potential to initiate social movements and mobilize resources.

Democratic groups without leaders: manifestation of segmented networks?

The Wild Strawberry Movement's organizational structure can be best described as 'democratic groups without leaders'. In contrast to previous movements, not only was there no leader or hierarchical organizational structure of any sort, but also little horizontal coordination as well. Daily routines were performed by groups, while important decisions were made through direct democracy.

The movement never successfully created any leadership during the movement. Coordination between groups was loose, with different groups in charge of their own tasks without informing each other. The only legitimate decisions made were those by 'the Grand Assembly'. The Grand Assembly was held every night, allowing any participant on the spot to participate. Any participant could propose motions before the Grand Assembly, which would then be voted on by all. In other words, 'direct democracy' was the only way of making decisions. Although there were cadre members, they could only *execute* decisions rather than make decisions. If they wanted to do something, they had to propose motions just like all other participants.

While there were many efforts to create leaders, all failed. At the beginning of the movement, seven participants were chosen to form a 'decision-making group'. However, the group was questioned by many and did not dare to make any decisions. The only thing they did was set the procedure for proposing motions. The group eventually fell apart and the 'executive group' was formed, meaning that the group would only execute decisions rather than making them. Another example was that, during the movement, many cadre members formed a consensus to end the movement at a certain point. However, one night when the Grand Assembly was held, a participant who learned of the news questioned cadre members why they could end the movement without asking approval of other participants. None of the cadre members admitted that they had reached the consensus and no one ever mentioned the idea of ending the movement afterwards.[9]

Cadre members were not viewed as leaders by other participants either. One participant expressed: 'I don't think cadre members should have the power to make decisions. All decisions should be discussed by everyone before being made.'[10] Another participant also described how participants could oppose cadre members: 'If some cadre members went onstage and said something, they would definitely be booed, no matter what they were saying.'[11] Furthermore, cadre members also viewed themselves as ordinary participants rather than leaders too. Many cadre members in the interviews expressed that this was a movement of every participant; no one should have the right to make decisions for others.

The key organizational structure of the movement was that tasks were organized by factions rather than a centralized and cohesive entity. Groups were responsible for specific tasks, such as the 'executive group', which executed decisions made in the Grand Assembly, or the 'media group', which was in charge of communicating with mass media. Surprisingly, coordination was very loose between groups. First, the formation of groups had nothing to do with existing movement organization. If some participants wanted to form a group, they simply proposed it at the Grand Assembly, got it approved and started to work. Cadre members could not control how the movement organization would evolve. For instance, the 'discourse group' was formulated because some thought there was no one responsible for making discourses to public media. The group was formed without the consent of other cadre members. Similarly, the 'medical group' was spontaneously formed to meet the needs of injured participants. Second, groups did not interfere with one another and often did not inform other groups on what they planned to do. The chief of the 'discourse group', which was responsible for posting articles online, talked about the loose coordination between groups: 'We just did what we wanted to do. The movement was just leaderless. Although the group members got together every night, we did not tell one another what to do. The most we could do was making some suggestions.'[12] Groups formed and disappeared throughout the movement, and even cadre members were not totally aware of which groups existed. One interviewee provided a graph of the organizational structure of the movement.[13] Nevertheless, when asked, other interviewees indicated that they did not know certain groups in the graph even existed. The most representative example of the leaderless structure was the 'funeral hall group', which was formed to represent the death of democracy. They held important activities such as holding a funeral of democracy. Prominent political figures, such as the chairwoman of the DPP, even came to participate in the funeral. However, according to interviews, no cadre member was aware of its formation beforehand. In fact, according to an interview with a member of the funeral hall group, the group was created because they were dissatisfied by lack of activities of the movement. They decided to reinvigorate the movement by holding this event without consulting current cadre members.[14]

To sum up, the organizational structure was a power-diverse structure with loose coordination. There was no leader–subordinate relationship between cadre members and ordinary participants, or between different groups. In this power-diverse organizational structure, the Grand Assembly played a critical role in making decisions. It legitimized actions proposed by different groups. The organizational structure of the movement can be described as 'democratic groups without leaders'. Groups accomplished their goals individually without any leadership. However, they followed the principle of direct democracy and went through the procedures of the Grand Assembly before acting.

While it is difficult to directly verify why the Wild Strawberry Movement opted for 'democratic groups without leaders', its mobilization structure is likely to have played an important role. As discussed, the BBS played the primary role of the initiation and mobilization of the movement. Compared with previous movements in Taiwan, which mainly relied on previous existing organizations in their mobilization process (Deng 1993), the Wild Strawberry Movement was historically unique in its absence of these organizations. While organizations often had strong social network ties, we see no such phenomenon on the BBS. Composition of social networks on the BBS was segmented. While each PTT2 personal board can be viewed as a small ecology with a small cluster of network ties, as a whole the Wild Strawberry Movement was mobilized through many of such boards. Although some users might have known some others personally, it is impossible to have ties with everyone. Lacking a strong network core, it was hard for any individual to legitimately claim to be the leader of the movement. As mentioned, a large portion of the participants had no prior protest experience, let alone forming social movement organizations. Since participants shared no common experience, mutual trust was relatively low. It was therefore hard to create a trusted leader. Hence, cadre members did not view themselves as leaders but merely as one participant, who could not represent the movement. The segmented social network of the virtual ecology may have also played a role in the lack of coordination of groups. Without a strong leader group, segmented social networks could form groups and assume a role in the movement without much opposition. For instance, many core members of the funeral group belonged to the same club in the same university. However, it would be much harder for these segments to coordinate. Since no leader could be created, the only way to make legitimate decisions was through direct democracy.

The form of 'democratic groups without leaders' had significant impact on both the Wild Strawberry Movement and later movements. On the one hand, many criticized its lack of efficiency on decision-making, which may have played a part in its inability to achieve its goals. One interviewee complained: 'In the meetings we wasted so much time on discussing how to discuss things.'[15] Another cadre member stated: 'As cadre members we want to spend time on things that are useful.... However, often the Grand Assembly passes motions that are impractical, then as the cadre members we have to execute them.'[16] Reflecting on the fact that the movement eventually ran out of steam without obtaining its goals, some interviewees saw the outcome as a failure and attributed the reason to the lack of swift decision-making. On the other hand, many interviewees expressed the view that the experience of participating in decision-making in a protest inspired them in seeing how unjust the world is. One interviewee stated: 'I would bring this experience back to my school, and try to do something on campus.'[17] Another indicated that she would definitely attend future social movements.[18] In fact, many prominent activists in future social movements mentioned that the Wild Strawberry Movement was like an enlightenment that motivated them to become activists. The organizational structure of the Wild Strawberry Movement had lasting effects that made its mark on Taiwanese history.

Conclusion

The BBS created a high participatory and interactive 'virtual ecology', which connected people with heterogeneous life experiences in a common virtual space. Daily life connections in turn fuelled the mobilization power during the Wild Strawberry Movement. It allowed initiation and mobilization without the presence of pre-existing organizations. However, in contrast to previous student movements in Taiwan, which originated from daily organizations, participants recruited from such a virtual ecology often had different life experiences, which formed a unique mobilization structure with a segmented social network. Due to network segmentation, it became hard for participants to coordinate, form trust and create leaders. Also, the segmented network produced an organizational structure consisted of independent groups. To facilitate decision-making for the movement, direct democracy was the only way to make legitimate decisions for all participants.

It should be mentioned that democratic organizational structures have appeared in earlier social movements. However, a democratic organizational structure does not imply that leadership would be missing. The 1960s student movements in the US serve as illustrative examples. Leaders of the movements were created through democratic processes, such as voting or consensus (Polleta 2002). Also, a democratic organizational structure does not imply that the members would necessarily have loose coordination. One should ask why the Wild Strawberry Movement had an organizational structure characterized by both the absence of leadership and loose coordination. This chapter argues that the mobilization structure based on the 'virtual ecology' was a critical factor in influencing this particular kind of organizational structure.

The impact of mobilization structure on organizational structure have also been observed in past social movements in Taiwan. For example, during the Wild Lily Movement in 1990 the organizational structure evolved to become more inclusive and participatory as the mobilization scale expanded (for extensive discussion, see Deng 1993). Part of the reason may be that participants were recruited from more diverse universities, forcing the decision group to expand. The Wild Strawberry Movement pushed such a process to an extreme. While providing large mobilization power, virtual ecologies made the mobilization structure composed even more segmented social networks, which in turn led to democratic groups without leaders.

In sum, the examination of the Wild Strawberry Movement in Taiwan shows how media, mobilization structures and organizational structures are deeply related to one another. It provides a 'causal-process observation' (Mahoney 2010), which illustrates a mechanism for further theory building on how the Internet may fundamentally impact social movements. In fact, while beyond the scope of this study, we can speculate that similar mechanisms are also present in recent social movements. For instance, in recent social movements, Facebook created a similar virtual ecology where users could share their daily experiences with others, which in turn could form the mobilization power in times of unrest.

We see that the Anti-Media Monopoly Movement used Facebook as a primary source of mobilization. In other words, the BBS, especially PTT2, could be viewed as a primitive form of Facebook, blurring the boundaries between the public sphere and the private sphere. In the most recent protest against the educational curriculum, even high school students could initiate movements without previous expertise in collective action. Also, while there may be participants who were better known, in the Sunflower Movement it is highly disputed whether these were leaders at all. Rather, participants used the collective term 'co-initiator' to represent the tendency for power equality between participants. The impact of virtual ecologies on mobilization and organizational structures is a fruitful avenue worth investigating in the upcoming decade.

Acknowledgements

This chapter is a rewritten version of 'How the Internet impacts social movements: A case study of the Taiwan Wild Strawberry Movement', published in *Taiwan Democracy Quarterly* (2011), 8(3), 45–85. I sincerely thank the National Science Council, Taiwan (98-2815-C-002-105-H), for funding the original project. I would also like to thank Dr Fan Yun, Dr Lin Kuo-Ming, Dr Lai Shau-Lee and Chiu Ya-wen for providing extensive research feedback.

Notes

1. Interview with Lee indicates that initiators expected only a few friends at the protest site.
2. These are rather minor restrictions such as minimum number of total posts on the whole PTT site, or not posting criminal intent in posts.
3. Interview with cadre member who eventually became participant. Taipei, September 2009.
4. Interview with participant. Taipei, October 2009.
5. Interview with participant who eventually became cadre member. Taipei, November 2009.
6. Interview with cadre member. Taipei, October 2009.
7. Interview with cadre member who eventually became participant. Taipei, October 2009.
8. Interview with participant who eventually became cadre member. Taipei, November 2009.
9. Interview with cadre member. Taipei, October 2009.
10. Interview with participant. Taipei, October 2009.
11. Interview with participant. Taipei, September 2009.
12. Interview with cadre member. Taipei, September 2009.
13. Interview with cadre member. Taipei, October 2009.
14. Interview with cadre member. Taipei, September 2009.
15. Interview with participant. Taipei, September 2009.
16. Interview with cadre member. Taipei, September 2009.
17. Interview with participant. Taipei, October 2009.
18. Interview with cadre member. Taipei, October 2009.

References

Benford, Robert D. and David A. Snow. 2000. 'Framing processes and social movements: An overview and assessment'. *Annual Sociology Review*, 26, 611–39.
Biddix, J. Patrick and Han Woo Park. 2008. 'Online networks of student protest: the case of the living wage campaign'. *New Media and Society*, 10(6), 871–91.
Brunsting, Suzannce and Tom Postmes. 2002. 'Social movement participation in the digital age'. *Small Group Research*, 33(5), 525–54.
Caren, Neal and Sarah Gaby. 2011. *Occupy Online: Facebook and the Spread of Occupy Wall Street*. Available online at http://ssrn.com/abstract=1943168 (accessed 18 July 2013).
Castells, Manuel. 2012. *Networks of Outrage and Hope: Social Movements in the Internet Age*. Cambridge, MA: Polity Press.
China Times. 2014, 5 February. Available online at www.chinatimes.com/real timenews/20140205004562-260404 (accessed 11 August 2015).
Clark, John D. and Nuno S. Themudo. 2006. 'Linking the web and the street: Internet-based "dotcauses" and the "anti-globalization" movement'. *World Development* 34(1), 50–74.
Dalton, Russel J., Manfred Küechler and Wilhelm Burklin. 1990. 'The challenge of new movements'. In Russel J. Dalton and Manfred Küechler (eds), *Challenging the Political Order: New Social and Political Movements in Western Democracies*. Cambridge: Polity Press, pp. 3–20.
Della Porta, Donatella and Mario Diani. 2006. *Social Movements: An Introduction*. Oxford: Blackwell.
Deng, Pi-yun. 1993. *Taiwan's History of Student Movements in the 1980's*. Taipei: Avanguard.
Diani, Mario. 2000. 'Social movement networks virtual and real'. *Information, Communication and Society*, 3(3), 386–401.
Earl, Jennifer and Katrina Kimport. 2009. 'Movement societies and digital protest: Fan activism and other nonpolitical protest online'. *Sociological Theory*, 27(3), 220–43.
ETToday. 2014, 7 February. Available online at www.ettoday.net/news/20140207/323129.htm (accessed 11 August 2015).
Fan, Yun. 2003. 'The women's movement in Taiwan's political transition: An approach focused on the biographical backgrounds of activists'. *Taiwanese Sociology*, 5, 133–94.
Freeman, J. (1975). *The politics of women's liberation: A case study of an emerging social movement and its relation to the policy process*. New York: McKay.
Gerbaudo, Paolo. 2012. *Tweets and the streets: Social media and contemporary activism*. London: Pluto Press.
Gould, Roger V. 1997. 'Multiple networks and mobilization in the Paris Commune, 1871'. In Doug McAdam and David A. Snow (eds), *Social Movements: Readings on Their Emergence, Mobilization and Dynamics*. Los Angeles, CA: Roxbury, pp. 133–44.
Gu, Zhong-hua. 2003. 'Institutionalization of social movements: Also on the role of non-profit organizations in the civil society'. In Mau-kuei Chang and Yung-nien Cheng (eds), *Analysis of Social Movements between Cross Strait*. Taipei: Third Nature Publishing, pp. 1–28.
Harlow, Summer. 2011. 'Social media and social movements: Facebook and an online Guatemalan justice movement that moved offline'. *New Media and Society*, 14(2), 225–43.
Hofheinz, Albrecht. 2005. 'The Internet in the Arab world: Playground for political liberalization'. *International Politics and Society*, 3, 78–96.

Jenkins, J. Craig. 1983. 'Resource mobilization theory and the study of social movements'. *Annual Review of Sociology*, 9, 527–53.

Freeman, Jo. 1972. 'The tyranny of structurelessness'. *Berkeley Journal of Sociology*, 17, 151–64.

Kavada, Anastasia. 2010. 'Email lists and participatory democracy in the European Social Forum'. *Media, Culture and Society*, 32(3), 355–72.

Kropczynski, Jessica and Seungahn Nah. 2011. 'Virtually networked housing movement: Hyperlink network structure of housing social movement organizations'. *New Media & Society*, 13(5), 689–703.

Lester, Libby and Brett Hutchins. 2009. 'Power games: environmental protest, news media and the internet'. *Media, Culture and Society*, 31(4), 579–95.

Lin, Ho-lin and Cheng Lun-lin. 2001. 'Social movement goes online: An exploratory analysis on the internet experience of Taiwan's social movements'. *Taiwan: A Radical Quarterly in Social Studies*, 25, 111–56.

McAdam, Doug and David A. Snow. 1997. 'Motivational factors: Barriers to and correlates of participation'. In Doug McAdam and David A. Snow (eds), *Social Movements: Readings on Their Emergence, Mobilization and Dynamics*. Los Angeles, CA: Roxbury, pp. 172–73.

McCarthy, John David and Mayer N. Zald. 1977. 'Resource mobilization and social movements: A partial theory'. *The American Journal of Sociology*, 82(6), 1212–41.

Mahoney, James. 2010. 'After KKV: The new methodology of qualitative research'. *World Politics*, 62(1), 120–47.

Meek, David. 2012. 'YouTube and social movements: A phenomenological analysis of participation, events and cyberplace'. *Antipode*, 44(4), 1429–48.

Mele, Christopher. 1999. 'Cyberspace and disadvantaged communities: The Internet as a tool for collective action'. In Marc A. Smith and Peter Kollock (eds), *Communities in Cyberspace*. London: Routledge, pp. 290–310.

Mercea, Dan. 2011. 'Digital prefigurative participation: The entwinement of online communication and offline participation in protest events'. *New Media and Society*, 14(1), 153–69.

Morris, Aldon D. 1997. 'Black southern student sit-in movement: An analysis of internal organization'. In Doug McAdam and David A. Snow (eds), *Social Movements: Readings on Their Emergence, Mobilization and Dynamics*. Los Angeles, CA: Roxbury, pp. 90–109.

Nip, Joyce Y. M. 2004. 'The Queer sisters and its electronic bulletin board: A study of the Internet for social movement mobilization'. *Information, Communication and Society*, 7(1), 23–49.

Noonan, Rita K. 1997. 'Women against the state: Political opportunities and collective action frames in Chile's transition to democracy'. In Doug McAdam and David A. Snow (eds), *Social Movements: Readings on Their Emergence, Mobilization and Dynamics*. Los Angeles, CA: Roxbury, 252–67.

Olson, Mancur. 1965. *The Logic of Collective Action*. Cambridge, MA: Harvard University Press.

Peckham, Michael. 1998. 'New dimensions of social movement countermovement interaction: The case of Scientology and its Internet critics'. *Canadian Journal of Sociology*, 23(4), 317–47.

Petray, Theresa Lynn. 2011. 'Protest 2.0: online interactions and Aboriginal activists'. *Media, Culture and Society*, 33(6), 923–40.

Polleta, Francesca. 2002. *Freedom is an Endless Meeting*. Chicago, IL: University of Chicago Press.

Shen, Wen-Chih. 1995. *The applications of internet skills of Internet/Fidonet*. Taipei: Songgang.
Snow, David A., E. Burke Rochford Jr., Steven K. Worden and Robert D. Benford. 1997. 'Frame alignment processes, micromobilization, and movement participation'. In Doug McAdam and David A. Snow (eds), *Social Movements: Readings on Their Emergence, Mobilization and Dynamics*. Los Angeles, CA: Roxbury, pp. 235–51.
Srinivasan, Ramesh and Adam Fish. 2009. 'Internet authorship: Social and political implications within Kyrgyzstan'. *Journal of Computer-Mediated Communication*, 14, 559–80.
Stein, Laura. 2009. 'Social movement web use in theory and practice: A content analysis of US movement websites'. *New Media and Society*, 11(5), 749–71.
Tang, Lijun and Helen Sampson. 2012. 'The interaction between mass media and the internet in non-democratic states: The case of China'. *Media, Culture and Society*, 34(4), 457–71.
Tilly, Charles. 1978. *From Mobilization to Revolution*. Reading, MA: Addison-Wesley.
Tufekci, Zeynep and Christopher Wilson. 2012. 'Social media and the decision to participate in political protest: Observations from Tahrir Square'. *Journal of Communication*, 62(2), 363–79.
Van Laer, Jeroen. 2010. 'Activists online and offline: The internet as an information channel for protest demonstrations'. *Mobilization: An International Quarterly*, *15*(3), 347–66.
Wellman, Barry, Anabel Quan Haase, James Witte and Keith Hampton. 2001. 'Does the Internet increase, decrease, or supplement social capital? Social networks, participation, and community commitment'. *American Behavioral Scientist*, 45(3), 436–55.
Wojcieszak, Magdalena. 2009. 'Carrying online participation offline—Mobilization by radical online groups and politically dissimilar offline ties'. *Journal of Communication*, 59, 564–86.
Youmans, William Lafi and Jillian C. York. 2012. 'Social media and the activist toolkit: User agreements, corporate interests, and the information infrastructure of modern social movements'. *Journal of Communication*, 62, 315–29.
Zhao, Dingxin. 1998. 'Ecologies of social movements: Student mobilization during the 1989 prodemocracy movement in Beijing'. *American Journal of Sociology*, 103(6), 1493–529.
Zhao, Ding-xin. 2007. *Social Movements and Revolution: New Theoretical Perspectives and the Chinese Experience*. Taipei: Chuliu.
Zhuo, Xiaolin, Barry Wellman, and Justine Yu. 2011. 'Egypt: the first Internet revolt?' *Peace Magazine*, 27(3), 6–10.

4 A tale of two offshore islands
Anti-casino movements in Penghu and Mazu

Tsai I-lun and Ho Ming-sho

Introduction

Taiwan witnessed its second power turnover in 2008 as the Kuomintang (KMT) won back the presidency after eight years of Democratic Progressive Party (DPP) governance. The conservatives' comeback triggered a protest wave from Taiwan's civil society (Ho 2014a), with the notable cases of the Wild Strawberry student movement (2008), the Anti-Media Monopoly Movement (2012) and the Sunflower Movement (2014). Among these protests, opposition to developmental projects that brought about pollution and land expropriation was a frequent theme. In the past few years, controversies over the Kuokuang Petrochemical Project, nuclear energy and science park expansion attracted widespread public attention, due to tangible grievances incurred and dogged resistance from the victims (Chiu 2014; Grano 2014; Ho 2014b, 2014c). Less noticed, however, is the fact that even those developmental projects that promised high economic rewards without the accompanying pollution encountered popular resistance. Casino businesses are an example in this regard.

The gambling industry underwent significant global expansion over the past three decades. Beginning in the 1980s, many developed countries in the West legalized gambling products since business leaders were successful in reframing them as a form of modern commercial entertainment rather than a morally questionable activity. Casinos had become a major attraction for tourists, as well as a powerful stimulant to areas struggling economically (Young 2010; Kingma 2004, 2008). South Korea (1999) and Macau (2002) liberalized the regulation of commercial gambling, which paved the way for the international casino industry's expansion into Asia. In 2006, the casino revenue in Macau exceeded that of Las Vegas. Even culturally conservative Singapore followed the trend in 2010, opening the door for the gambling industry in an attempt to revitalize its economy. With the KMT's resumption of power, Taiwan's government added a new clause to the Offshore Islands Development Act, legalizing gambling activities in 2009. From then on casinos could be built on offshore islands as long as the proposal passed a local referendum. In short, betting on the future with casinos has become a popular strategy for economic development in many countries.

Yet, the seeming globalization of the casino industry was a highly uneven process, which brought forth diversified responses and consequences in various places (Bernhard and Frey 2007). Sallaz (2006) showed that a competitive and corporate-dominated gambling industry prevailed in South Africa while Native Americans monopolized casinos in California. The Russian government forbade further casino growth in Moscow in 2009 and decreed that the existing ones be relocated to a designated area (Wu 2011). Analogously, Taiwan's two offshore islands generated different responses when facing the choice. Penghu County (the Pescadores), which is located in the middle of the Taiwan Strait, and Lienchiang County (Mazu), which was actually a part of China's Fujian Province before 1949, held local referendums on the casino project in 2009 and 2012 respectively. The two local governments led the campaign to bring the gambling industry over in order to develop the economically challenged offshore islands, provoking resistance movements in response. On 26 September 2009, 31,095 Penghu citizens cast their ballots (42.2 per cent voter turnout). There were 13,397 votes (43.6 per cent) for the casino and 17,359 votes in opposition (56.4 per cent). The Mazu referendum took place on 7 July 2012. Among the 3,136 votes (40.8 per cent voter turnout), the pro and con votes were 1,795 (57.2 per cent) and 1,341 (42.8 per cent), respectively. As the Offshore Islands Development Act had adopted a simple majority decision rule, the result could be seen as final. Since then, tourist casinos have been rejected in Penghu but legalized in Mazu.[1] The different choices by two of Taiwan's offshore islands require an explanation.

This chapter presents a comparative study of two anti-casino movements, focusing on how local societies responded to politician-led efforts to legalize the gambling industry. Globally, anti-casino movements tended to highlight immorality and addiction issues (Bernhard *et al.* 2010); by contrast, Taiwan's own variant emphasized local identity and framed their campaigns as a defence of their hometowns. While pro-casino leaders argued that the incoming gambling industry would promise 'a bright future' for the host society, opponents retorted that the downsides of a casino economy would be disproportionately shouldered by the offshore island residents (Lin 2009). Moreover, it remained questionable whether the fragile ecology of the tiny offshore islands could sustain more than a million tourists every year. Their carrying capacities were inherently constrained by the lack of sufficient infrastructure and the difficulty in providing enough fresh water, electricity and waste treatment service. As a result, environmental considerations were a prominent issue in the casino debate. In a sense, at the core of the casino disputes was a clash of hometown visions, in which the residents were given an either/or choice of economic prosperity or their older way of life. In particular, the highly visible deployment of local identity arguments by opponents made the anti-casino movements more akin to environmental and community movements (Ho 2005, 2012).

The different outcomes of these two anti-casino movements are intriguing as the two offshore islands share many similarities. As part of the front line during the cold-war era, both Mazu and Penghu used to be highly militarized with a long-term and oversized presence of soldiers. Defence considerations left the two islands chronically weak in infrastructure, thus giving rise to a massive population exodus. The enactment of the Offshore Islands Development Act in 2000 was largely seen as a belated compensation for the relative deprivation of the offshore islanders. In retrospect, Penghu actually pioneered the campaign to promote tourist casinos, as its political leaders were the first to raise the demand in the mid-1990s. Yet, in spite of its early-riser head start, the pro-casino camp suffered a decisive defeat by opponents, whereas the casino proposal for Mazu, which first came on stage only in 2011, managed to secure a victory in its referendum. Moreover, the two offshore islands are characterized as having only small inhabitable areas, where the interpersonal relationships are dense and overlapping because of insular seclusion. Colleagues are oftentimes neighbours or related by kinship systems. In the social movement studies literature, pre-existing social relations are usually seen as conducive to collective mobilization (Snow et al. 1980; Kitts 2000; McAdam 2003). However, there are times when this condition could dampen the willingness to join a protest movement. This chapter will analyse how the dense interpersonal relationships played a role in the anti-casino movements.

This chapter uses the method of comparative case study (Yin 1994), collecting data in various ways. We interviewed anti-casino activists in Taiwan, Penghu and Mazu, as well as local residents and casino promoters. There were 35 interviewees in total. The secondary data came from *United Daily News* (2000–12), *Penghu Times* (2007–09), *Penghu Daily* (2006–09), *Mazu Daily* (2010–12 and the website for Mazu information (www.matsu.idv.tw). Aside from these journalistic sources, we also consulted the proceedings of the Penghu County Council, along with the websites and publications of anti-casino organizations. The data were collected between August 2012 and September 2014.

Penghu and the origin of the pro-casino campaign

Penghu is situated in the middle of the Taiwan Strait, with five townships and one city comprising 126.9 square kilometres of land area. Their geographical location blessed the islands with abundant fishing resources and was the reason why Portuguese sailors in the sixteenth century named them the Pescadores, or fishermen islands. Historically, Penghu was a midway station in the traffic between the Chinese mainland and Taiwan, and as such it was developed and populated much earlier than Taiwan. With the onset of Taiwan's export-oriented industrialization in the 1960s, Penghu saw massive emigration and concomitantly a decline in the local industries. The primary sector, including fishing, dropped to 5.5 per cent of the local economy while the service sector, particularly tourism, saw significant growth (Tsai 2007). For most of the post-war era, Penghu served as a military base. It was not until the lifting of martial law in 1987 that the protracted military rule came to an end. The abolition of the Penghu Command Headquarters in 1992 further decreased the military presence, reducing the number of soldiers stationed in Penghu. While demilitarization restored political freedoms to the people of Penghu, it also dealt a devastating blow to the local economy as many businesspeople made their living by provisioning the needs of soldiers. The lost 'prosperity' of Penghu has been a commonly heard complaint on the islands. Currently around 100,000 people have their household registration in Penghu, but only about 60 per cent of them reside there on a permanent basis (Directorate General of Budget, Accounting and Statistics 2011), the lowest ratio of Taiwan's 22 counties and cities.

To counter the economic decline, political leaders in Penghu raised the casino idea in the mid-1990s. In 2000–07, the locally elected legislator lobbied central government for casino legalization to no avail. Simultaneously, there was also an attempt to open direct transportation links between China and Taiwan's offshore islands (the so-called three mini-links) in Penghu. But the initial policy in 2001 only applied to Kinmen and Mazu, before finally extending to Penghu in 2008. The three islands had previously been sacrificed in the sake of national defence, which justified their privileged treatment. However, with their initial exclusion from the three mini-links scheme, Penghu politicians instead stepped up their casino campaign.

The county magistrate and county council led the lobbying effort to persuade the central government to lift the gambling industry ban. Prior to 2009, two rounds of non-binding 'referendums' had been held, and the supportive voices prevailed twice. The first referendum, in 2002, was initiated by the magistrate, councillors, the chamber of commerce and compatriot societies in Taiwan and took place at the same time as the election for village and ward heads. The result was an 80.0 per cent (26,797 votes) majority in favour of legalizing casinos.[2] In 2003, the county government enacted a by-law to strengthen the legal status of a 'consultative referendum', particularly designed for Penghu. At the end of that year, the second referendum was held, with 57.0 per cent (7,830 votes) supportive of casinos. Although those held were at best large-scale polls, rather than the bona fide 'referendums', whose procedure was strictly prescribed in the Referendum Law passed in 2003, the successful demonstration of pro-casino public opinion nevertheless became a powerful bargaining chip when negotiating with the central government officials.

The early 2000s saw intensive promotional efforts from the pro-casino camp. Local politicians brought gambling industry representatives to visit Penghu and meet President Chen Shui-bian.[3] As casinos became the hottest topic on the offshore island, the subject began to arouse dissenting voices. In 2001, when the gambling clause was under review, an opposition movement emerged. The local bird watching society and environmental groups in Penghu formed the Penghu Anti-Gambling League (Penghu fandu lianmeng), while religious, environmental, and educational reform groups on the main island organized the Taiwan Anti-Gambling League (Taiwan fandu lianmeng). Activists in Taiwan also made efforts to oppose the legal revision by lobbying officials and lawmakers, while the Penghu activists were primarily locally focused. In the consultative referendums of 2002 and 2003 as well as the public hearing in 2004, the Penghu Anti-Gambling League led the protest.

Lin Pin-kuan (林炳坤) was the acknowledged leader in the campaign to legalize casinos. Lin was the only serving legislator who had been locally elected for five straight terms (1996–2011). With a business background in the cement and construction industry, Lin, often called 'the Lord of Penghu', enjoyed strong political and business support locally. Without being a party member, he maintained a good relationship with the KMT and had invited their legislators to visit Penghu many times. At the same time, the Penghu County government was eagerly promoting tourism through a number of BOT (build–operate–transfer) projects. Many private investors applied for these BOT projects with expectations of a future casino economy.[4] In hindsight, the pro-casino camp had successfully mobilized local public opinion in its favour prior to 2008, but ultimately the attempt at decriminalizing gambling failed because the ruling DPP was internally divided over the issue and its incumbents did not adopt a consistent stand on the issue. Twice, in 2002 and 2007, the casino clause came close to being passed. The pro-casino camp was particularly optimistic of its success in 2007, when the DPP government was planning to liberalize gambling products, such as lotteries, horse racing and car racing. However, there was dissent within the DPP[5] and with an upcoming presidential election there were worries about the possible negative impacts.[6] Thus, the DPP government finally decided to abandon the casino idea, even though it had secured the support of KMT legislators.

The stalemate came to an end in 2008 as the KMT not only won the presidential election but also secured a large majority in the Legislative Yuan, taking 81 seats out of 113. Lin Pin-kuan also won his re-election, which allowed him to continue championing the casino legalization campaign. In fact, during his electoral campaign, President Ma Ying-jeou (馬英九) had promised to put the casino question to a referendum. In short, the power turnover in 2008 brought about a drastic shift in political opportunity that favoured the pro-casino camp. Immediately after the KMT's presidential victory in March, it was rumoured that casinos would be legalized before the end of that year (Penghu County Council 2008).

As the morale of the pro-casino camp was boosted by the 2008 regime change, opponents stepped up their own efforts. In 2007, there was an online effort to organize the young Penghu citizens sojourning in Taiwan. Before Ma Ying-jeou (馬英九) assumed the presidency in May 2008, a group of hostel operators in Penghu were so concerned that they set up a blog page[7] and distributed over 10,000 copies of their anti-gambling pamphlet. The local hostel owners reactivated the opposition network that had first been formed in 2002 and enlarged to the Penghu Anti-Gambling League by the end of 2008. They worked closely with activists on Taiwan to resist the imminent threat. A local activist handwrote letters to lawmakers, officials and other celebrities in order to stop the attempt to add the casino clause into the Offshore Islands Development Act.[8]

Their efforts failed in the face of the pro-casino alliance, whose political influence was elevated with the comeback of the conservative KMT. In January 2009, the Legislative Yuan revised the Offshore Islands Development Act with a clause stipulating a referendum process that opened the door for tourist casinos. While regular referendums have a high threshold of 50 per cent voter turnout and acquiring 50 per cent supportive votes, the casino referendum is not constrained by the turnout requirement – a clear victory for the pro-casino camp.

Local identity in the anti-casino movements

With the now-legalized channel of referendum, the battleground for the casino issue shifted to Penghu. Immediately after the amendment, the Penghu County government launched a series of 'public explanation meetings' (*shuominghui*) to publicize its plan to develop 'a tourist resort' and the local chamber of commerce raised the idea of a referendum proposal with a signature-collecting campaign. The Penghu Anti-Gambling League also intensified its activities and attended the official explanation meetings. The opponents were not initially invited by the government, but, after a local prosecutor protested, they were allowed to speak on stage.

As expected, the local media were overwhelmingly pro-casino. In the early 2000s, Lin Pin-kuan owned the only local cable television network, which he maintained substantial control over even during the 2009 referendum, when he was no longer the boss. Local TV was therefore bombarded with pro-casino ads. In addition, the two local newspapers (the *Penghu Times* and the *Penghu Daily*) relied on local government subsidies for their operation and the financial dependence brought about political conformism. During the referendum, the local government earmarked a special grant with which these two newspapers were to publish pro-casino op-ed pieces. Consequently, the pro-casino camp enjoyed a hegemonic position in the local media.

It took three months to complete around 40 public explanation meetings. The government hired scholars and experts to describe how a casino works and its economic benefits. 'The casino brings hope to Penghu' was the core message that pro-casino politicians sought to convince their compatriots of.[9] They argued that the offshore island needed to attract more tourists in order to create economic prosperity and that the only way to do so was to welcome the gambling industry. Most of these public explanation meetings were co-sponsored by village and ward offices; since these grass-roots leaders were often dependent on county-level politicians, they did not welcome the presence of anti-casino activists, whose public speeches were sometimes interrupted. Nevertheless, opponents' persistent efforts to publicize their dissenting voices shattered the illusion of overwhelmingly pro-casino local opinion.

Social protests were not infrequent in Penghu, with the 2000s having witnessed many environmental incidents. In 2003, the local government allowed a gravel company to dredge a beach. However, the contractor paid scant attention to the environmental consequences, leaving the navigation passage silted and the intertidal ecology damaged. After a protest from local environmentalists, the government suspended the dredging operation. From 2003 to 2006, environmentalists also launched a movement opposing the attempt to privatize Jiebeiyu, an offshore island, for tourist development. Environmentalists worked with local residents to fight the Jiebeiyu BOT project and were successful. Activists from these two protests later joined the anti-casino movement.

Being the first casino referendum in Taiwan, the Penghu case attracted considerable national attention because it was believed that a pro-casino success in Penghu would have had a domino effect on other islands. The Taiwan Anti-Gambling League in particular was involved in this issue. Its leader, Master Caohwei (昭慧法師), a Buddhist monk who had been active in environmental and religious movements for more than two decades, mobilized the religious organizations in Penghu to join the opposition camp. Moreover, since the political elites in Penghu exercised a quasi-monopoly over local news channels, the opposition activists had to use their media influence in Taipei to neutralize the pro-casino propaganda offensive. The Taiwan Anti-Gambling League held press conferences, secured the endorsement of celebrities and mobilized rallies to create protest events that were reported by the national media. To the people of Penghu, the coverage of these anti-casino activities gave lie to the claim that a casino was a harmless 'cure-all' to the ailing local economy.[10]

As soon as the referendum date was set for 26 September 2009, the opponents began their mobilization campaign, which lasted around eight months. They targeted different groups of local people. A young man who was serving his alternative military service was responsible for the youth branch, which used the Internet to spread an anti-casino message. There was another group of activists who made door-to-door visits to residents, shop owners and tourist businesspeople in the hope that face-to-face communication could convert them to the opposition camp. The canvassing activists found that Penghu residents actually seldom talked about the casino topic, because it had been championed in public for many years; this meant that people who were disinclined to the idea preferred to keep their personal opposition private so as not to harm their relationships with neighbours. Therefore, the image of unanimous local support for the gambling industry was a false one, pushed by the pro-casino elites. In order to persuade these latent opponents into greater public action, activists utilized the emotional appeal of hometown attachment:

> What is Penghu? It is nothing but us living here and maintaining our precious way of life. It is because of such an environment that we are allowed to keep this lifestyle ... don't forget the importance of our votes. We are now deciding on our own lives as well as the future of our descendants, which is of paramount importance.[11]

These activists paid repeated visits to those residents who seemed to have been persuaded by this argument, and they kept reminding them to cast an opposition vote on referendum day. There was an around-the-island anti-casino 'pilgrimage', or *kuxing* ('suffering procession'), which lasted for four days. Some priests at local churches led their believers in anti-casino prayers on Sunday. One day before the referendum, there was an unprecedented rally in the downtown area, at which 'Tomorrow, when Penghu is no longer Penghu' leaflets were distributed. It is clear that the opponents framed the movement as an effort to preserve their hometown from an incoming threat.

Since the casino proposal had been championed by politicians for a long time, and the strongest argument was its potential economic benefits, those who disagreed were fearful of being negatively labelled as 'obstructing local development'. The movement activists thus understood the importance of public action to help overcome this psychological hurdle. As an activist we interviewed put it, 'I often asked people whether they were afraid of casting their ballots. Many people initially hesitated but then decided to take action because they saw the opposition growing more and more vocal.'[12]

The Penghu casino dispute had a hue of partisanship, as the KMT and the DPP politicians took different attitudes. In the pro-casino camp, the county magistrate and the chair of the local commerce chamber (also vice-speaker of the local council) were KMT members. The county government did not maintain administrative neutrality, instead facilitating the pro-casino mobilization. On the other side, although the DPP's local party branch was disinclined to the casino proposal, it did not publicly participate in the opposition movement. However, some individual DPP members were involved in the anti-casino movement. When police rejected the application for an anti-casino rally, a DPP township representative managed to overcome the hurdle, thereby allowing the protest to go ahead legally. Some activists in the Penghu Anti-Gambling League possessed DPP membership,[13] but they refrained from turning the dispute into a partisan competition. Therefore, the DPP as a whole did not play a significant role in the anti-casino movement.

It is true that many Penghu locals had already made up their minds long before referendum day. Even the activists acknowledged that they were not very successful in converting the determined casino supporters into opponents.[14] But the anti-casino movement worked because it helped stimulate the previously invisible casino sceptics into action. The result was that the pro-casino camp was decisively defeated in the referendum of September 2009, even though its promotional efforts had persisted for over a decade. Immediately after their failure, local politicians vowed to make a comeback three years later, since the law stipulated a minimal interval for referendums on the same issue. Indeed, Penghu held the second casino referendum on 15 October 2016.

The casino dispute in Mazu

While the people of Penghu were engaged in a heated debate over the casino issue, Mazu remained in a state of quietude. But, unlike what had happened in Penghu, the referendum on 7 July 2012 actually produced a pro-casino majority in Mazu, despite the fact that the Mazu pro-casino campaign was relatively brief and the opponents were more vocal (Chung-Hua Institution for Economic Research 2011). While the opponents had to start from scratch to build the anti-casino movement in Penghu, Mazu opponents were facilitated by the previous experience of activists in Penghu and Taiwan, who were willing to share their recipe for success. Yet, the local anti-casino movement collapsed in spite of these favourable conditions.

Similarly, there was a great contrast in the resources of the for and against camps. Supporters controlled the local administrative machinery and emphasized the economic benefits of casinos. The local government hired a professional consultancy company to coordinate the pro-casino propaganda. The American developer Weidner Resort Development Inc set up a local office, which seemed to increase the credibility of a forthcoming casino economy. While the pro-casino camp in Mazu had taken heed of the Penghu lesson and devoted more resources to the battle, the opponents seemed less prepared. In fact, it was only two months before the referendum that the local anti-casino movement came into being. The following section will show that the latter's effort was persistently frustrated by the weakness of local civil society.

Weak civil society in Mazu

Mazu is composed of a string of islands with a total land area of 28.8 square kilometres. The archipelago lies in close proximity to China's Fujian Province, less than 30 kilometres from its provincial capital, Fuzhou, and 205 kilometres from Taiwan. Mazu was initially temporary shelter for fishermen and pirates before it became permanently inhabited. Currently Mazu has four townships, dispersed over the five main islands.

When the Nationalist government withdrew to Taiwan in 1949, Mazu became the frontline in the then ongoing armed confrontation between the Republic of China and the People's Republic of China. The military control imposed on Mazu severed its traditional economic ties with the east of Fujian Province, and the local livelihood of fishing gave way to an economy that catered exclusively to the needs of military servicemen. Since the government lifted the ban on outward migration in 1970, there has been a sharp local population decline and it now has around 10,000 residents. Although Penghu shared a similar historical background of military control, the demilitarization since 1992 was more painful in Mazu. Not only was Mazu much more impoverished and undeveloped, its distance from Taiwan also made it less attractive for tourists. Flights were often cancelled due to weather conditions and the ferry service took up to 10 hours. Thus, it was with similar considerations that local political leaders came to embrace the casino proposal, which they argued could solve the twin problems of transportation and economy at the same time.[15]

The Mazu casino proposal emerged in 2011, first raised by the county magistrate. At the time, the Tourism Bureau under the Ministry of Transportation and Communications was drafting the laws on casinos and held a public hearing in Mazu. The county government rode on that bandwagon and hired a professional consultancy firm to promote the casino project. The contractor was responsible for the site selection, the referendum proposal and the training of civil service personnel. In August, the local chamber of commerce had completed the legal procedure for the referendum. Five public explanation meetings were held in September and October, which were outsourced to the consultancy company. From the proceedings, it was clear that government officials used these occasions to emphasize the advantages of a casino economy. Nevertheless, there were still local dissenters who were willing to voice their reservations. One dissenter mentioned the negative lessons of gambling for children (Chung-Hua Institution for Economic Research 2011: 78). Even in the pro-casino, government-owned *Mazu Daily*, there were reports that individual civil servants and councillors had expressed scepticism at public explanation meetings.[16]

Nevertheless, these dissenting voices did not coalesce into organized activities. While the Taiwan Anti-Gambling League staged a protest at the end of 2011 in Taipei, it failed to elicit a local response. Compared to Penghu, Mazu's civil society remained underdeveloped. The opposition party had never gained a local foothold and Mazu was the only county in which the DPP had yet to establish an office. The DPP had not fielded a candidate in the local magistrate election for many years. In the national election, the DPP obtained less than 5 per cent of the local vote.

The spatial segregation from Taiwan increased Mazu's informational insularity. The only local news agency, the *Mazu Daily*, was operated by the county government, while national newspapers were not widely circulated and TV rarely covered local news. Therefore, living in Mazu meant that one was constantly exposed to pro-casino propaganda without being able to receive more balanced reports or even hear the opposition arguments. Therefore, the strategy of circumventing local elites' control of information by making the national news might have worked in Penghu, but could only have limited effect in Mazu.

Last, civil society means a self-organizing capacity on the part of the citizens who could act independently, if not in defiance, of political incumbents, with well-functioning NGOs often seen as exemplary of that principle. In Taiwan, however, many NGOs are only nominally independent, but actually exist as clientelist networks with which political leaders co-opt their followers (Ho 2010: 454–7). The situation in Mazu appears much worse, as personal experience demonstrates. One of the authors was invited by the Mazu government to lecture on environmental protection in November 2012. Audience participation was below the sponsor's expectations. Upon inquiring, the official in charge explained that local people were particularly busy attending a number of NGO events on that same day. Since it was close to the end of the fiscal year, the county government was eager to use up the approved budget and it gave generous subsidies to local NGOs that could organize free activities more efficiently. In other words, there were a number of local NGOs whose survival depended on redistributing freebies from the public sector. Therefore, it was a reasonable expectation that the more local people were used to the idea of NGOs as government-sponsored gift-givers, the less they would expect that voluntary associations might act contrarily to the government incumbents.

In short, the associated symptoms of weak civil society, such as the absence of an opposition party, the lack of alternative information and the prostrate state of existing NGOs made Mazu a barren land for protest organizing, thus preventing the initial sprouts of sporadic and spontaneous anti-casino voices from taking root there. It was therefore not a surprise that Mazu's first anti-casino press conference was organized by the Taiwan Anti-Gambling League in December 2011. As a matter of fact, Taiwanese activists had searched in vain for a local opponent who would take up the leadership in Mazu.[17]

A cautious anti-casino movement

In early 2012, the Weidner Company unveiled its investment project, which planned to create a 'Mediterranean resort' in Mazu and promised to build a new airport and schools and give out regular cash compensation to residents.[18] According to the county government's pamphlet, which that was distributed in April, 'Whether Mazu can emerge as a new metropolis for international recreational tourism depends on the choice of our compatriots'.[19] Mazu compatriot societies and other cultural associations held several public hearings to highlight the benefits of the forthcoming casino. While Taiwan Anti-Gambling League activists staged protests outside the public hearing room, local opponents chose to not to take part in these meetings.

The first locally initiated protest did not emerge until two months before the referendum. Tsao Ya-ping (曹雅評), a Mazu native and graduate student in Taipei, saw the ubiquitous casino advertisements during a home town visit in May 2012. On learning of the imminent referendum, she contacted the veteran activists from Penghu and Taiwan and then organized an anti-casino youth organization. In late May, Tsao held a two-day anti-casino event in Mazu, inviting activists from Penghu to share their experiences. Around 20 local compatriots came to support her, thus constituting the first public opposition gathering in Mazu.[20]

Like with their comrades in Penghu, local identity was utilized as an ideational resource to counter the gambling industry. In Tsao's anti-casino declaration, she wrote:

> I often introduce my self as 'Little Mazu' because it represents my identification with Mazu.... As a young person from Mazu, I want to tell everyone that we do not want a casino future. We do not want big corporations to take our land and harm it. We do not want to lose our innocent way of life. We do not want to lose our ecology and culture. Big corporations cannot decide the future of the Mazu youth.[21]

Although Mazu activists employed a similar mobilizing frame, they encountered greater difficulties due to the dense interpersonal networks locally, which tended to suppress the public voicing of disagreements. While the first local protest activity attracted 20 persons, the opponents received donation from 35 persons. An interviewed activist explained why donors exceeded participants:

> There are many people who oppose the casino but prefer to keep silent in public because of their personal relationships. For example, employees do

not want to speak their minds if their boss supports the casino. Or a person might find it inconvenient to say anything when his relatives are mostly pro-casino.... Those who give money to us are mostly opponents in private only.²²

Since Mazu is such a tiny place and residents have overlapping relationships, open expression of disagreement is bound to bring about disharmony. Consequently, protest activities had to proceed with extra caution. How anti-casino activists managed their office can be seen as an example. With the help of their parents, young activists from Mazu borrowed a hostel owner's home as their meeting place. It so happened that the county magistrate frequently visited that business owner and anti-casino activists were often asked to leave when that happened so as not to create an embarrassing encounter.²³ Just like the situation in Penghu, those community activists who worked to preserve local history and culture tended to oppose the casino development. However, in Mazu these 'culture workers' (*wenshi gongzuozhe*) chose to keep low profiles, often not joining protest activities because many of them were on good personal terms with the county magistrate, Yang Shui-sheng (楊綏生). These culture workers had often previously worked together with Yang in certain community projects and had served as campaign staff when Yang ran for magistrate in 2009. Although they disagreed with Yang's promotion of the casino industry, they refrained from showing their opposition in public. As a result, they chose to express their personal opposition indirectly, for example by writing anti-casino articles.

Protest mobilization in Mazu was mainly carried out by young people who were sojourning in Taiwan. Since they were mostly students, the mobilization had to wait until the summer vacation, which started in mid-June. Compared to local culture workers, students were less encumbered by existing personal relationships since they tended to be less established in the local community. Their protest activities included the distribution of anti-casino flyers, small-scale explanation meetings, demonstrations and rallies. To emphasize their local roots, they deliberately used a number of cultural elements, such as playing traditional music during demonstrations and speaking the local dialect (the Fuzhou dialect), rather than Mandarin.

Nevertheless, protest mobilization was persistently constrained by local conservatism. It was only on the eve of the July referendum that a number of anti-casino residents finally made up their minds to publicly show their opposition by joining a demonstration. The activists from Taiwan proposed more confrontational protest repertoires, such as a sit-in at the Weidner office or direct action against the county magistrate, but these suggestions were rejected by Mazu activists, who had sufficient reasons to suspect counterproductive results from such actions.²⁴

Compared with Penghu, anti-casino activism in Mazu appeared unprepared and inexperienced as it assumed a less confrontational posture in challenging a mightier pro-casino coalition. Learning the lesson from Penghu, Mazu politicians adopted a more commercial and professional approach to generating pro-casino sentiment. The Weidner Company held a series of explanation meetings between April and June 2012, which emphasized their package of community rewards. Mazu residents who long felt neglected by the central government were particularly attracted by the promise to improve the long complained-about transportation, including a cross-strait bridge linking the two main islands (Nangan and Beigan) and an all-weather international airport.[25] Imitating the door-to-door visits by anti-casino activists, the Weidner president canvassed for support, personally accompanied by local politicians. There was a period of time when the local cable TV station kept running, non-stop, a Weidner public relation film that showcased the company and its commitment to building a Moroccan-style casino in Mazu. The film was originally narrated in Mandarin, but later a Fuzhou-dialect version was played.[26] Furthermore, seeing that opponents had raised the issue of local identity, pro-casino leaders also established the League for Mazu's Future and Hope (Mazu weilai xiwang lianmeng), which claimed to be composed of the local youth.[27] In other words, Mazu's anti-casino activists tried to replicate the experience of their Penghu comrades, but they were fighting an uphill battle against a more adaptive and resourceful rival. In retrospect, the pro-casino camp's victory in the referendum was not particularly unexpected.

Postscript

As a postscript, the pro-casino camp in Penghu did not give up after its 2009 setback. Its leaders had tried to stage another referendum in 2012 without success. Afterwards, the local politics underwent a major change, as the previously anti-casino DPP captured the county executive in 2014 and the presidency in 2016. Nevertheless, rather surprisingly, the DPP executive approved the second casino referendum in 2016. Unlike the first referendum, the members of the pro-casino camp were not local political elites but businessmen. However, the main debate of the pro-and anti-casino campaigns still focused on whether to prioritize economic development or the hometown's ecology. The second referendum on October 15 generated an overwhelming majority (more than eighty-one percent) in opposition to the casino project. On the other hand, while Mazu's casino project was mired in legal technicalities and problems with financial feasibility, the pro-casino leader, county magistrate Yang Shui-sheng, lost his re-election bid in 2014, further casting doubt on the disputed project.

Discussion and conclusion

This chapter compared two anti-casino movements that sought to influence the result of local referendums. True, the KMT's ascendency to power in 2008 brought about a period of conservative hegemony in Taiwan, which favoured the pro-casino camp. But the divergent outcomes in Penghu and Mazu showed that local political conditions remained decisive in shaping the contours of protest movements as well as their consequences.

Both anti-casino movements, in Penghu and Mazu, attempted to mobilize hometown attachment and local identity to resist the influx of the gambling industry. Their campaigns were framed as a defence of traditional culture and the environment, whereas morality was not often mentioned when compared to anti-casino movements in other countries. It is very likely that the prevalence of Taiwan's environmental and community movements since the lifting of martial law in 1987 had provided a powerful template that movement activists found easier to apply to other issues. Nevertheless, there was an inherent dilemma for such locality-based movements, in that local identity was usually stronger in close-knit communities, whose dense interpersonal relationships tended to have the effect of stifling the public expression of disagreement – a strategic disadvantage for protest activists when the established leaders of these communities were promoting the casinos. Moreover, both island societies were insular and inward looking, and much more so in Mazu than in Penghu. With their control over information channels, both formally and informally, elites were more or less able to disseminate the pro-casino discourse effectively.

In the case of Penghu, there emerged a division of labour in that the Taiwan Anti-Gambling League worked on policy lobbying and national news coverage, while local activists were responsible for the groundwork of canvassing and rallying. Environmentalists, religious leaders and hostel owners in Penghu provided the pre-existing civil society network that facilitated protest mobilization. Although the Mazu movement would appear to have enjoyed the advantage of a previous victory, and the activists in Taiwan and Penghu were more than willing to share their experiences, they were crippled by the weaker development of civil society in Mazu. In a place where the opposition party was almost non-existent and NGOs were docile and lacked autonomy, it should not be a surprise that the local anti-casino organization was formed only two months before the referendum. Mazu's young sojourners in Taiwan spearheaded the protest movement. While their lack of an established position in the hometown community allowed them more freedom of action, it was also precisely their junior status that prevented them from influencing the local elders.

The contrasting evolution of anti-casino movements in Penghu and Mazu highlights the unevenness of local conditions in Taiwan. There is a received impression that the conservative KMT regime and a resurgent civil society were on a collision course, as witnessed in the Sunflower Movement during the spring of 2014 (Ho 2015). Indeed, the 2009 success of anti-casino movement in Penghu marked the very beginning of intensified resistance to the KMT's conservative rule, later followed by a string of unanticipated victories for civil society, such as the protest against Kuokuang Petrochemical Project (Grano 2015: 92–117, Ho, 2016), the Anti-Media Monopoly Movement (see Ebswoth's chapter), the anti-nuclear movement (see Grano's chapter) and the Sunflower Movement (see the chapters by Beckershoff and Hsu). However, this characterization cannot be uniformly applied to different localities. After all, if all politics is local, social movements are therefore destined to proceed on the different terrains with various combinations of opportunity and threat.

Notes

1 The Tourist Casino Management Act was drafted in 2011 and sent for legislative review. At the end of 2013, the KMT legislators succeed in finishing the bill's second reading stage. However, the new DPP government withdrew the draft bill in July 2016 and there is no telling when the bill could be enacted. Without that law, no casino permit can be issued. At the time of writing (October 2014), there is still no casino in Mazu because the central government has not finished the relevant regulations. Further complicating the Mazu casino project, the Chinese government indicated its unwillingness to allow the Chinese to visit Mazu for gambling purposes (*Commercial Times*, 1 April 2013). It is highly doubtful that investors would proceed with the original plan without tourists from China.
2 *United Daily*, 9 June 2002, 4.
3 *United Daily*, 9 March 2001, 3.
4 Interview with a casino supporter, 25 September 2013.
5 *United Daily*, 7 April 2007, 2.
6 *United Daily*, 6 December 2007, 14.
7 http://lovepenghu.blogspot.tw (accessed 19 October 2014).
8 Interview with an activist in the Penghu Anti-Gambling League, 14 April 2013.
9 *Penghu Daily*, 5 March 2009. Available online at http://blog.xuite.net/penghu.dialy/blog/22607868 (accessed 20 October 2014).
10 Interview with an activist in Taiwan Anti-Gambling League, 19 September 2014.
11 Interview with an activist in Penghu Anti-Gambling League, 14 April 2013.
12 Interview with an activist in Penghu Anti-Gambling League, 2 April 2013.
13 There was a veteran DPP member who played a leading role in the Penghu Anti-Gambling League. After the referendum, he opted to leave the DPP and took part in the local election as the Green Party nominee.
14 Interview with a Penghu resident, 1 June 2013.
15 *Mazu Daily*, 19 February 2014. Available online at www.matsu-news.gov.tw/2010web/news_detail_101.php?CMD=open&UID=122536 (accessed 20 October 2014).
16 *Mazu Daily*, 14 October 2014. Available online at www.matsu-news.gov.tw/2010web/news_detail_101.php?CMD=open&UID=132852 (accessed 20 October 2014).
17 Interview with a Taiwan Anti-Gambling League activist, 19 September 2014.
18 *Mazu Daily*, 2 March 2012. Available online at www.matsu-news.gov.tw/2010web/news_detail_101.php?CMD=open&UID=137780 (accessed 20 October 2014).
19 *Mazu Daily*, 25 April 2012. Available online at www.matsu-news.gov.tw/2010web/news_detail_101.php?CMD=open&UID=139559 (accessed 20 October 2014).
20 Interview with an activist in Mazu Anti-Gambling League, 1 September 2014.
21 http://matsu.idv.tw/topicdetail.php?f=2&t=102257&p=1 (accessed 20 October 2014).
22 Interview with an activist in Mazu Anti-Gambling League, 1 September 2014.
23 Interview with an activist in Mazu Anti-Gambling League, 1 September 2014.
24 Interview with an activist in Taiwan Anti-Gambling League, 20 September 2014.
25 www.coolloud.org.tw/node/69370 (accessed 4 July 2014).
26 Interview with an activist in Mazu Anti-Gambling League, 1 September 2014.
27 www.matsu-news.gov.tw/2010web/news_detail_101.php?CMD=open&UID=141906 (accessed 22 October 2014).

References

Bernhard, B., R. Futrell and A. Harper. 2010. 'Shots from the pulpit: An ethnographic content analysis of United States anti-gambling social movement documents'. *UNLV Gaming Research & Review Journal*, 14(2), 15–32.
Bernhard, B. and J. Frey. 2007. 'The sociology of gambling'. In C. Bryant and D. Peck (eds), *21st Century Sociology*. Thousand Oaks, CA: SAGE, pp. 399–405.

Chiu, H. 2014. 'The movement against science park expansion and electronics hazards in Taiwan: A review from an environmental justice perspective'. *China Perspectives*, 2014/3, 15–22.
Chung-Hua Institute For Economic Research. 2011. *Mazu juoji guanguang yule boyi chanyeji xianmin gongtou* [*International Tourist Casino Business and County Referendum*]. Lianjian xian zengfu weituo.
Directorate-General of Budget, Accounting and Statistics. 2011. *99nian renkou ji zhuzhai pucha chubu tongji jieguo. Wangzhi* [*General Survey on Population and Housing*]. Available online at www.dgbas.gov.tw/ct.asp?xItem=30081&ctNode=2858 (accessed 21 July 2013).
Grano, S. 2014. 'Change and continuities: Taiwan's post-2008 environmental policies'. *Journal of Current Chinese Affairs*, 43(3), 129–59.
Grano, S. 2015. *Environmental Governance in Taiwan: A new generation of activists and stakeholders*. London: Routledge.
Ho, M. 2005. 'Protest as community revival: Folk religion in a Taiwanese anti-pollution movement'. *African and Asian Studies*, 4(3), 237–69.
Ho, M. 2010. 'Co-opting social ties: How the Taiwanese petrochemical industry neutralized environmental opposition'. *Mobilization*, 15(4), 447–65.
Ho, M. 2012. 'Sponsoring civil society: State and community movement in Taiwan'. *Sociological Inquiry*, 82(3), 404–23.
Ho, M. 2014a. 'The resurgence of social movements under the Ma Ying-jeou government: A political opportunity structure perspective'. In J. Cabastan and J. Delisle (eds), *Political Changes in Taiwan under Ma Ying-jeou: Partisan Conflict, Policy Choices, External Constraints and Security Challenges*. London: Routledge, pp. 100–119.
Ho, M. 2014b. 'Resisting Naphtha Crackers: A historical survey of environmental politics in Taiwan'. *China Perspectives*, 2014/3, 5–14.
Ho, M. 2014c. 'The Fukushima effect: Explaining the recent resurgence of the anti-nuclear movement in Taiwan'. *Environmental Politics*, 23(6), 965–83.
Ho, M. 2015. 'Occupy Congress in Taiwan: Political opportunity, threat and the Sunflower Movement'. *Journal of East Asian Studies* 15(1), 69–97.
Ho, M. 2016. 'Making an opportunity: Strategic bipartisanship in Taiwan's environmental movement'. *Sociological Perspectives* 59(3), 543–60.
Kingma, S. 2004. 'Gambling and the risk society: The liberalisation and legitimation crisis of gambling in the Netherlands'. *International Gambling Studies*, 4(1), 47–67.
Kingma, S. 2008. 'The liberalization and (re) regulation of Dutch gambling markets: National consequences of the changing European context'. *Regulation & Governance*, 2(4), 445–58.
Kitts, J. 2000. 'Mobilizing in black boxes: Social networks and participation in social movement organizations'. *Mobilization: An International Quarterly*, 5(2), 241–57.
Lin. C. 2009. *Penghu fan du yundong jianjie: 2009/9/26 penghu boyi gongtou* [*An Introduction to the Anti-casino Movement in Penghu: The Penghu Casino Referendum in September 26 2009*]. Unpublished manuscript.
McAdam, D. 2003. 'Beyond structural analysis: Toward a more dynamic understanding of social movements'. In M. Diani and D. McAdam (eds), *Social Movements and Networks: Relational Approaches to Collective Action*. Oxford: Oxford University Press, pp. 281–98.
Penghu County Council. 2008. *Penghuxian yihui yishi lu* [*The Proceedings of Penghu County Council*], 16(6), 106–7.

Sallaz, J. 2006. 'The making of the global gambling industry: An application and extension of field theory'. *Theory and Society*, 35(3), 265–297.

Snow, D., L. Zurcher Jr and S. Ekland-Olson. 1980. 'Social networks and social movements: A microstructural approach to differential recruitment'. *American Sociological Review*, 45(5), 787–801.

Tsai, M. 2007. *Penghu de zhengzhi shengtai* [*Politics in Penghu*]. Taipei: Hongye.

Wu, X. 2011. *Xiaoshi de duchang dajie* [*The Disappearing Casino District*]. Shangye zhoukan, 1140, 138.

Yin, R. 1994. *Case Study Research: Design and Methods*. Thousand Oaks, CA: SAGE.

Young, M. 2010. 'Gambling, capitalism and the state: towards a new dialectic of the risk society?' *Journal of Consumer Culture*, 10(2), 254–73.

5 Not wanting Want

The Anti-Media Monopoly Movement in Taiwan

Rowena Ebsworth

Introduction

The Anti-Media Monopoly Movement (反媒體壟斷運動) was a protest led by a coalition of academics, journalists and students that took place in Taiwan between 2012 and 2013. Originally opposed to Want Want China Times Media Group's (旺旺中時媒體集團) monopolization of Taiwan's media, the movement addressed ideas as diverse as freedom of the press, democratic process and national identity. Multidimensional in its practices, the movement ranged from street demonstrations to a global social media campaign before introducing new regulatory proposals to the Legislative Yuan in May 2013. The movement's leaders operated in and used a political style that negotiated the space between their idealism and understanding of political reality. In this way, the Anti-Media Monopoly Movement was indicative of a search for the new sites of power in the changing politics of contemporary Taiwan.

As has often been the tendency when discussing social movements in Taiwan, previous studies of the Anti-Media Monopoly Movement have focused on its place in Taiwan's democratic transition. For example, Ming-yeh Rawnsley and Feng Chien-san have interpreted the movement as part of Taiwan's 'second wave' of democratization. According to this view, the movement is 'an attempt to introduce further political reform in order to reestablish a more responsive political system' (Rawnsley and Feng 2014: 107).

While this assessment is not untrue, it is at risk of treating civil society as a singular entity. It fails to account for the diversity of actors, discourse and protesting strategies that make Taiwan's democracy so dynamic. By focusing upon these elements, this account finds that, beyond pushing for political reform, the Anti-Media Monopoly Movement was driven by generational conflict. The movement's distinctive language and practices emerged as young activists struggled to secure their place in Taiwan's political landscape.

To explore these ideas further, this chapter draws upon the following themes:

Movement roots

The roots of the Anti-Media Monopoly Movement lie in the convergence of debates over freedom of the press, cross-strait relations and distrust of Taiwan's political institutions.

In capitalist societies such as Taiwan, liberty of the press has theoretically been guaranteed through free market economics. According to Milton Friedman (1962), competition and abundance of choice naturally maintain the quality of the media. Even so, in the event of market failure, regulatory mechanisms have been adopted to avoid media monopolies. Protest movements have typically mobilized when these checks and balances are absent or inadequate (Keane 1991).

In the case of Taiwan, a small group of academics and journalists began campaigning for a free press in 2010. At that time, Want Want made a bid to purchase a popular television network, which would place the company in a position of dominance in Taiwan's media market. As interested parties, that is to say, intellectuals who studied the media or industry professionals, this group took it upon themselves to oppose the deal.

In the context of Taiwan's geopolitics, the threat of media monopolies was compounded by Want Want's stance on the People's Republic of China (PRC). Specifically, the company's chairman supported and had a history of using his publications to push for unification.

After government agencies ignored early opposition to Want Want, the movement also began to promote democratic reform. This theme had become increasingly prominent in Taiwan's social movements since the Nationalist government (KMT) returned to power in 2008 and had, many felt, undermined Taiwan's political institutions (Rawnsley and Feng 2014: 106–7).

Movement trajectory

Against this backdrop, the Anti-Media Monopoly Movement developed along a course marked by obstacles and conflict.

In 2012, the defamation of a research fellow by Want Want-owned media provoked students to form an island-wide youth organization. In conjunction with the movement's initiators, they staged a mass rally of a scale unprecedented in media-themed protests in Taiwan.

In organizing the event, however, the students found themselves at the centre of a conflict between media outlets. This led to the utilization of social media and the development of distinctive protest strategies to maintain their independence and integrity.

Meanwhile, the threat of media monopolization had intensified, as Want Want sought to acquire one of Taiwan's largest newspapers. When Taiwanese authorities reacted to street demonstrations in opposition to the new bid with hostility, the students initiated an online global campaign. In doing so, they altered the scale and discourse of the movement and established an international network of support.

In its final phase, the movement attempted to institute new media ownership laws. To the leaders' frustration, this process was marked by partisanship and legislative ineffectiveness. Once again adapting to the political realities of the time, the movement renegotiated the original aim of their campaign in order to enact new media regulations.

Movement success and impact

Overall, this approach proved somewhat successful for the Anti-Media Monopoly Movement. Both of *Want Want's* bids fell through and the immediate threat of media monopolization dissipated.

In addition, the movement had a significant impact on the composition of Taiwan's political sphere. While previously excluded from Taiwan's politics, the young people who mobilized and refined their protesting skills during this time have gone on to become prominent figures in civil society.

Even so, through the duration of the movement it became clear that underlying structural issues continue to threaten the liberty of Taiwan's media. Economic and geopolitical tensions remain, and problems identified within Taiwan's political institutions are yet to be resolved. Thus, participants have turned their attention to other matters. While these protests have been based around disparate themes, they all appertain to the fundamental issues raised by the Anti-Media Monopoly Movement.

Methodology

Data for this project were collected in two stages. It primarily took place in 2013 and involved drawing information from social media websites and the traditional media. The movement was also discussed with several student activists and academics in interviews conducted in late 2014 and early 2015. All interview participants have chosen to remain anonymous.

Origins of the movement: 2010–July 2012

The Anti-Media Monopoly Movement grew out of debate over the ideal relationship between the media and democracy in Taiwan. The traditional leaders of media-themed protests were initially involved, including journalists, academics and NGOs concerned with freedom of the press. As established commentators and experienced protesters, they easily found a public voice. Despite forming the intellectual basis for the movement, however, early campaigns had little success.

The concept of 'liberty of the press' has a long history and was originally part of the bourgeois struggle against the governing class in the late eighteenth century (Keane 1991: 4–5). Since the rise of capitalism, those such as Friedman (1962) have promoted laissez-faire economics to maintain freedom of the press, based on the logic that the market is unbiased and produces an abundance of choice.

Yet market failure has the potential to undermine democracy. For example, in the context of the media market, a free press allows for the 'tyranny of majority', in which minority rights are unrepresented, and those who dominate the media can have an undue influence on public opinion (Keane 1991: 69–83).

As a result, freedom of the press is ultimately an idealized concept, which by its very nature remains largely unrealized in the reality of everyday life. One could argue that the utopian ideals within the institutions of the media themselves, of the media as the guardians of freedom and rationality, have been adverse to their own capacity to address the issues of accountability and bias. According to Keane (1991: 43–6), this has instead fallen to media critics, analysts and activists outside of those institutions.

Media ownership first became a major issue in Taiwan in 2010 when Want Want China Broadband (旺中寬頻) made a NT$70 billion bid to acquire one of Taiwan's largest cable television operators, China Network Systems (中嘉網路, CNS). The parent company of Want Want China Broadband, Want Want Corporation, was originally established as a snack food and beverage company in the 1960s. Under the chairmanship of Tsai Eng-meng (蔡衍明), Want Want launched a mainland Chinese subsidiary food company in 2007. The following year it entered Taiwan's media industry by purchasing the China Times Group, whose assets included the *China Times* (中國時報), one of Taiwan's four major daily newspapers and a series of media corporations previously owned by the KMT. Soon after, Want Want also procured the cable television broadcasters China Television (中視, CTV) and Chung Tien Television (中天新聞台, CtiTV). The purchase of CNS would ensure that Want Want owned media across cable television, newspapers, magazines and Internet services, and would control one-third of Taiwan's media by market share.

When knowledge of Want Want's bid became public, academics and media professionals began lobbying the National Communications Commission (國家通訊傳播委員會, NCC) to reject the deal. To do so, they drew on ideas such as 'protecting press freedom' and 'safeguarding democracy'. For example, in an opinion piece published in the *Apple Daily* (蘋果日報), three journalists remarked that 'it is unbelievable that in 21st century Taiwanese society, if someone has sufficient capital, they can control the transmission of news and information without restraint, and heartlessly trample on the long struggled for democracy and freedom' (Hsu *et al.* 2012). Establishing a free and pluralistic media was therefore imagined as part of Taiwan's process of democratization.

In the context of Taiwan's political history, this evaluation of the role of media had particular ideological implications. It evoked the period of martial law when the KMT government had used censorship and the policy of *baojin* (報禁) to restrict freedom of expression and the possibility of political opposition (Rawnsley and Gong 2012). From the 1970s, several dissident magazines emerged from the 'outside the party' (黨外) movement and played a key role in the 1979 pro-democracy Kaohsiung protests. The ensuing trials and imprisonments of the events' leadership are a founding narrative for the Democratic Progressive Party (DPP). Several key DPP figures, including Annette Lu (呂秀蓮)

and Chen Shui-bian (陳水扁), emerged from the Kaohsiung Incident to become synonymous with opposition to the KMT (Rawnsley 2000). From this perspective, 'protecting press freedom' was being framed as a continuation of the struggle for democracy against oppressive forces.

Indeed, while the media is nominally free from government control, dominant publications of the martial law era laid the basis for what became Taiwan's partisan politics. According to Patricia Batto (2004), publications such as the *United Daily News* and the *China Times* remain sympathetic to the KMT. In contrast, market segmentation meant that the Liberty Times Group (自由時報團體) positioned themselves as pro-Taiwan and supportive of the DPP. In attempting to reform this environment, in 2003 the DPP government compelled the KMT to sell its remaining media stock holdings (Rawnsley and Feng 2014: 113). After the KMT's return to power in 2008, however, the issue of media ownership had disappeared from the political agenda.

Criticism of the deal was also tantamount to the dispute over Taiwan's relationship with mainland China. As Mark Harrison (2006) has argued, the re-emergence of Taiwanese identity and nationalist politics in the 1990s and the increasing belligerence of the PRC in response had structured almost all political debates along a pro-China or pro-Taiwan political divide. Tsai Eng-meng had positioned himself on one side, admitting that the purchase of the *China Times Group* was 'in order to use the power of the press to advance relations between China and Taiwan' (Enav 2012). In November 2010 the Control Yuan found that 69 of the 378 reported incidents of Chinese authorities 'news buying' were in the *China Times*. The publication faced fines for presenting Chinese government paid advertisements as news.

There was therefore concern that Tsai's dominance of Taiwan's media environment would skew public opinion in favour of China and push for unification. As Professor Flora Chang (張錦華) complained in an interview, publications like *China Times* produce news that is 'all about how China's development is thriving [and is] basically there to promote investment and to attract tourists' (Tzou 2011). This issue had become particularly acute since the KMT government, headed by President Ma Ying-jeou (馬英九), had promised economic prosperity through improved cross-strait relations. Since 2008 the two sides had recommenced semi-official dialogue under the 1992 Consensus and instituted a host of policies that could potentially increase the mainland's influence on Taiwan, including allowing Chinese investors to buy shares in Taiwanese companies. According to Chang, the KMT policies and the orientation of Want Want could 'be linked to the basic principles of Chinese propaganda towards Taiwan – entering the country, entering the family, entering the mind and what is called the economic siege' (Tzou 2011). From this perspective, the 'China factor' in the CNS deal could compromise Taiwan's democratic freedom.

As well as its ideological dimension, opposition to the CNS deal addressed the institutional failures of the regulatory processes for Taiwan's media. Professor Jang Show-ling (鄭秀玲 2011) argued that the absence of interested parties undermined the feasibility of the NCC's September 2011 public hearing.

By October 2011, three of the seven NCC review committee members had resigned from the case, after their pictures were published and integrity questioned in the *China Times*. Opposition to the CNS deal was therefore combined with a search for adequate regulation of Taiwan's media.

These events demonstrate that the issue of media ownership in Taiwan was originally addressed using specialized, intellectual knowledge. Established scholars and media professionals campaigned on the issue through the media and political institutions. Yet this approach failed to engage the broader public or spark mass protests. As a result, it was unsuccessful in stopping Want Want's bid. On 25 July 2012, NCC Minister Su Herng (蘇蘅) announced that, providing the Want China Times Group divested itself of CtiTV, CTV ceased to produce news and CTV established an independent editorial system, CNS would become part of the Want Want Group.

Developing into a mass campaign: July–August 2012

After a lethargic beginning, the Anti-Media Monopoly Movement now erupted into a visible protest movement. Although Want Want's actions sparked this shift, pre-established networks were also critical to the process. A nationwide community of youth activists joined the campaign after Want Want used their publications to attack participants. The addition of young people introduced new dimensions and protest strategies to the movement.

Although the NCC considered the decision they announced on 25 July to be a compromise, neither side accepted the outcome. Later that day, Academia Sinica research fellow Huang Kuo-chang (黃國昌) led a small protest outside the NCC and Tsai launched an appeal against the decision. Tsai claimed that he would go ahead with the merger in its original form because the 'NCC [cannot] force rightful owners to sell their properties' (*China Post* 28 July 2012).

Continuing this aggressive approach, between 26 July and 29 publications within the *China Times Group* accused Huang of 'paying' students to be part of his demonstrations. When young Internet users uploaded images suggesting that Lin Chao-xin (林朝鑫) of *Times Weekly* had himself paid the protesters, Want Want-owned media outlets began to attack students. On 30 July, in a Cti News feature nearly 20 minutes long, Lin threatened to sue National Tsing-hua University (NTHU) student Chen Wei-ting (陳為廷) for distributing the image. Although Chen claimed that he was unaware of the picture's origin, the report accused him of falsifying evidence (CtiTV 2012).

This focus on Chen and the actions of young people would prove to be a watershed moment in the development of the movement. Prior to this point, the Student Rights Team at National Taiwan University (NTU) had been following the issue of media monopolies, but now sought to intensify their campaign. To do so, they drew on the community of young activists that had emerged out of the 2008 Wild Strawberry Movement (野草莓運動). At that time, hundreds of students, predominantly from NTU, staged a sit-in at Liberty Square (自由廣場) to seek amendments to the Assembly and Parade Act (集會遊行法). As recounted to me in an interview with an NTU graduate student in sociology on 21 May 2015, this protest failed because there were internal divisions within the core student leadership and a lack of coordination between universities (Participant S 2015, pers.comm., 21 May).

To avoid this happening in the future, students had returned to their universities and founded campus protest groups, while keeping in contact through social media. This had created a network of student activists spanning over 30 universities, who assisted each other in campaigning on student advocacy and general civil rights issues. According to one student from National Chengchi University (NCCU), interviewed on 1 April 2015, most young people would only participate in civil society through these groups because

> if you try to organise anything through, say a magazine or something, it is impossible ... all those institutions, including the NGOs, are controlled by our seniors [and you] can't have a say ... if you try to organise something or you try to provide an idea, you are censored.
> (Participant C 2015, pers.comm., 4 January)

NTU graduate student Lin Fei-fan (林飛帆) was part of this community. He had been interested in coordinating a nationwide youth group since he was an undergraduate student at National Cheng Kung University (NCKU), where he had helped found the 02 Activist Society. As a close friend of Chen's, Lin now drew on this network to form the Youth Alliance Against Media Monsters (反媒體巨獸青年聯盟). It was organized via the 'I am a student and I oppose *Want Want China* (我是學生, 我反旺中)' Facebook page and made its debut at a rally on 31 July (Youth Alliance Against Media Monsters 2012).

From this time, the Youth Alliance skilfully used social media to strengthen and shape the movement. The contours of social media, with their distinctive flow of individual and group interaction, use of text and images and reconfiguration of geographic space, mobilized student activists in new ways. What might have previously been slogans or chants became 'memes' – intertextual references in which the issues of the movement were intersected with a wide range of political tropes, drawn from different settings.

Early memes on the Youth Alliance Facebook page made reference to George Orwell's *1984*. In one, Tsai Eng-meng's face was stencilled onto a red background with the caption 'Yang-ming Tsai is WATCHING YOU' (Youth Alliance Against Media Monsters 2012). Through this image, the students represented Tsai as the incarnation of an omnipresent system of oppression. It suggested that the media no longer existed as a tool for the benefit of society, but that society existed to consume and benefit the media. A boycott would therefore not only send a message to Want Want but also undermine the economic strength that made it threatening.

To stage this boycott, the students drew upon local cultural practices and called on the public to 'Oppose *Want Want China* this 'Ghost Month' (鬼月反旺中)' (Ghost Month is a Daoist festival in which offerings are made to the deceased), using the slogan when you go '"bai bai" [pray] don't buy' (Youth Alliance Against Media Monsters 2012). The meme quickly received over 900 'likes'.

Opposition to Want Want was concurrently building within other circles. On 28 July the Association of Taiwan Journalists (台灣新聞記者協會) posted a statement on their Facebook page highlighting that *'Want Want China Times … violated the profession and ethics of journalism'* (Association of Taiwan Journalists 2012), in their reporting of the Huang scandal. By 10 August 2012, six *China Times* journalists and editors had quit as a result of the incident and three members of the CtiTV ethics committee closely followed.

These events culminated in an official complaint against Want Want, made to the NCC on 14 August. The petition called upon the NCC to investigate whether CtiTV had violated media regulations by publishing accusations against Huang without evidence. The group argued that the resignation of several members of the CtiTV ethics committee demonstrated that the institution's self-disciplinary mechanisms had collapsed and was indicative of the need for the NCC to intervene (Association of Taiwan Journalists 2012). Despite these factors, the NCC maintained that they could not start an investigation because no concrete evidence of wrongdoing had been provided.

Overall, this stage demonstrated both the spontaneous development of the Anti-Media Monopoly Movement and its reliance on pre-existing networks of communication. Although the movement was yet to see a victory, with the inclusion of young people and their new protesting styles it was building momentum. By collectively drafting and presenting the petition on 14 August, the movement had emerged as a coherent force in civil society.

The 901 demonstration: August–September 2012

The next phase of the Anti-Media Monopoly Movement was characterized by the centrality of young people and their use of new political practices. Finding traditional channels closed or dominated by partisan politics, student activists relied on social media and creativity. In comparison to the initial stage of the movement, this approach mobilized a significant support base and led to the successful organization of an unprecedented media-themed rally. Aside from demonstrating the arrival of new protesting strategies into Taiwan's civil society, this outcome suggested that young people were becoming visible in politics. In addition to the issue of media ownership, the movement was now being driven by the students' search for an adequate form of self-representation.

After the failure of the complaint against Want Want, the coalition of groups resolved to hold a march on 1 September, from the *China Times* headquarters in the district of Wanhua (萬華區) to the NCC on Ren'ai Road (仁愛路). It was to be coordinated by the Youth Alliance through a Facebook page entitled 'You're very big but I'm not afraid – Anti-Media Monopoly 901 Demonstration' (「你好大 我不怕」-反媒體壟斷 901 大遊行), which had the Chinese character for 'Big' replaced with the Want Want logo. It would call for 'media professionalism, an apology from *Want Want China*, an NCC investigation and opposition to media monopolies' (Youth Alliance Against Media Monsters 2012).

In the lead-up to the 1 September rally, the editorial lines on the Anti-Media Monopoly Movement were clearly split between competing media outlets. Publications in the Liberty Times Group supported the movement. They published articles that detailed the unfair treatment of individuals in the Want China Times media and several that included a link to the 901 Facebook page (Hu *et al.* 2012).

After having published netizens' accusations against Lin Chaoxin for paying the students in the 25 July rally, Next Media (壹傳媒) continued to target Want Want. Next Media is a Hong Kong-based company owned by Jimmy Lai (黎智英) and is renowned for its publications' politically non-aligned, tabloid-style journalism. In early August, Next Media's *Apple Daily* pointed out that, in response to the 31 July student rally, CtiTV had dedicated an hour to 'allowing *China Times* Chief Editor to defend *Want Want China*' (*Apple Daily* 1 August 2012), while four of the seven major news channels had not covered the incident at all. This was considered evidence of China Times Group's bad intentions towards the movement.

Enmity was further enhanced when Want Want apologized to Professor Huang on 29 August. In a small article on the *China Times* website, Want Want admitted that: 'Academia Sinica professor Huang Kuo-chang was not involved' in paying the students at the 25 July rally. It also said, however, that in response to *Apple Daily*'s insinuation that the *Times Weekly* deputy chief editor, Lin Chaoxin, had been involved in paying the students, Want Want 'expresse[d] the most grave protest and [would] continue to investigate' (*China Times*, 29 August 2012). Next Media defended its coverage and argued that, with the impending 1 September march, Want Want was trying to divert attention away from its company (*NextTV* 29 August 2012). *Apple Daily* was consequently accused of using the movement to damage the reputation of the China Times Group.

This level of mainstream media attention exposed the students to the risk of becoming an instrument for media outlets to discredit one another. With limited resources, the students relied on social media to specify their own understanding of the movement's significance. As Charo Wu expressed on 17 August,

> there are many people who say we students have been used by *Next Media* [to pursue media competition and divisive politics]. [Yet] the whole issue is not that you should choose a side, choose between *Next Media* and *Want Want China*, choose right or wrong, choose blue or green. Rather, regarding the issue of media monopolies, what do you think?
>
> (Wu 2012)

The movement's self-reflexive engagement with the purpose of the media progressively emphasized their central concern as strengthening democracy in Taiwan and positioning themselves as part of a tradition of civil society activity. One banner on the 901 Facebook page included a picture from a protest that had occurred on 1 September 1994, for 'liberty of the press'. It was referred to on 17 August:

> This 'Independent Event' from eighteen years ago is the last time we remember harmoniously calling upon all walks of life to take to the streets ... it would be satirical to suggest that there has been a market place of freedom of expression and freedom of the press in Taiwan in these 25 years since the lifting of martial law ... we believe that if you don't have an independent news media, it's then hard to consolidate and strengthen democracy ... it is our responsibility to supervise the authorities and prevent the abuse of power.
> (Youth Alliance Against Media Monsters 2012)

The Anti-Media Monopoly Movement would continue the struggle of their predecessors and seek to establish a 'liberal press' in Taiwan.

The students themselves had been children at the time of the 1994 protest and were not directly included in this lineage of civil action. In addition, there had long been a perceived lack of political consciousness among their peers, encapsulated in the 'Strawberry Tribe' label given to those born after martial law ended in 1987 (Rigger 2006). To counter this and create solidarity, several Facebook campaigns were launched. For example, over a series of weeks, young people who had only recently become activists uploaded photos of themselves explaining why they supported the movement. A daily meme featuring a different, often comical character and the words '9/1 Come with me to protest' was also produced.

The comparison of 901 to the 1994 protest can therefore be interpreted as a search for legitimacy. As the Youth Alliance was evidently unsure of its own voice, placing the rally in a shared history of civil action enabled them to give 901 shape and justification. While choosing a media-themed protest reflected the focus of their own rally, it also offered a critique of other forms of 'legitimate' political action. Taiwan's history of authoritarianism and resistance has shaped politics in such a way that it is dominated by the two major parties and what has become an acrimoniously divisive politics. By specifically referring to the 1994 protest as an 'independent event' and suggesting that the political activity in the 25 years since the lifting of martial law had failed to maintain media freedom, the students distanced themselves from the repetitive narratives of partisan party politics.

On the same basis, on 30 August 2012 representatives from the movement visited KMT, DPP, Taiwan Solidarity Union (TSU) and the People First Party (PFP) politicians to confirm that anti-media monopoly legislation had universal approval. Political propaganda was also banned at the event to reiterate its neutrality.

In addition to just a refusal to align with either political party, the students were conscious of separating their political style from the dominant forms of party politics in Taiwan. With a lineage of struggle and against the backdrop of the 'China threat', post-martial law politics is often mobilized by political emotions and affect (Hsiao 1990). In contrast, the students sought to distinguish their event by making it well controlled and 'rational'. In the lead-up to the march, posts were made reiterating the itinerary, route map, weather forecast and a checklist of useful items as a way to ensure that participants would be prepared and the action efficient. In addition, seven '901 Anti-Media Monopoly rally items of consideration' (901 反媒體壟斷大遊行注意事項) were provided. Item one read: 'This rally will fundamentally involve a peaceful gathering and a rational expression of opinion. March attendees please always follow the instructions of the leaders and inform a staff member if a spontaneous outburst of emotion seems to be occurring' (Youth Alliance Against Media Monsters 2012).

In the end, on 1 September an estimated 9,000 people participated in the protest. Although it was too soon to determine the impact of the rally, Want Want China Times Group had taken notice. In response, they hung a banner on their headquarters and published a full-page advertisement in the *China Times* defending their actions. The march also made history as the largest ever media-themed demonstration and politically non-aligned rally in Taiwan.

To the students, the protest represented a successful display of their political voice. Not only had the slogans reflected their creativity but young people had also made up over half of all attendees. Their efforts were celebrated in a post on 6 September, which read: the '4,500 who took to the streets erased society's bad impression of young people. The Youth Alliance participated with zeal, using the internet to display creativity and to discuss and formulate a movement with serious demands' (Youth Alliance Against Media Monsters 2012).

The Anti-Media Monopoly Movement had therefore developed into a dynamic mass campaign, capable of mobilizing significant street demonstrations. Student leaders had built on the momentum from dissatisfaction with traditional partisan politics and shaped their political style to fit the climate of the time. With limited capabilities, social media had become a core resource. In light of the 901 rally, these tactics appeared to be more effective than forms of protest used earlier in the movement.

Globalizing the movement: October–December 2012

Even so, the hostility of institutions continued to shape the course of the Anti-Media Monopoly Movement. As the prominence of the movement increased and the issue of media monopolization became more urgent, the authorities became involved. This introduced opportunities but also led to new issues of self-representation for the Youth Alliance. In response, they established an international support base and reshaped the discourse of their arguments to fit the global context. Repositioning the movement in this way ultimately led to an increase in exposure and influence.

Following the 1 September protest, the movement was given renewed urgency. On 18 October the sale of four outlets in the Next Media Group (壹傳媒集團) was announced. Originally, Lai's sale to a consortium headed by

Chinatrust Charity Foundation chairman Jeffrey Koo Jr (辜仲諒) was made with the guarantee that Tsai Eng-meng was not involved. By early November it became clear that Tsai was an 'invisible' investor. Tsai began to attend meetings concerning the sale and claimed to be 'the one who put up the most money' (Liu et al. 2012) for the deal. As *Apple Daily* commanded nearly 30 per cent of Taiwan's market, the deal could have resulted in Tsai having control of half of Taiwan's news media by market share.

By 19 November labour unions covering the employees of Next Media,[1] publicly requested transparency over the sale because they were concerned by Tsai's reputation for editorial interference. When given no response, the *Apple Daily* Employee Union staged a sit-in at the *Apple Daily* headquarters on the night of 26 November.

From mid-November, the 901 and Youth Alliance Facebook pages were plastered with denouncements of the Next Media deal and preparations for a sit-in at the Executive Yuan on Zhongxiao East Road (忠孝東路) in Taipei. Although there were conditions in the proposed business deal that stipulated a guarantee that media 'equity shares not exceed twenty percent', the students would make sure 'the authorities did every final check' (Youth Alliance Against Media Monsters 2012) to uphold the law.

The students assembled outside the Executive Yuan on the afternoon of 26 November in order to present a petition to Premier Sean Chen (陳冲). An announcement was posted on their Facebook page that afternoon explaining that, after 'waiting in heavy rain for nearly three hours', Premier Chen had failed to respond to their request. Now they invited everyone to join them outside the Executive Yuan for an 'overnight vigil for Taiwan's democracy' (Youth Alliance Against Media Monsters 2012). On the morning of 27 November a spokesperson for the government announced that they understood the students' demands but that their interference in the case would be undemocratic. Becoming aggravated, the students tried to enter the Executive Yuan shortly after midday. After failing to do so, they disbanded because 'one person had been sent to hospital ... and another arrested and trampled by police' (Youth Alliance Against Media Monsters 2012).

Towards the end of November, the activities of the Youth Alliance gained the attention of government authorities. On 30 November an email from Taiwan's Ministry for Education was leaked. The email claimed that the 'Head of the Ministry is worried about the health of the students' who had been participating in demonstrations in bad weather. They called on 'Universities to increase understanding and concern for the students' and to 'examine and add to a register the students who had participated in the *Next Media* activity' (*Moemail1 2012*).

The students responded with frustration and anger. They interpreted the actions of the minister as indicative of a lack of respect and tolerance for their political participation. The reference to being 'deeply concerned' (關切) by the state of their health was seen as 'a warning against students participating in student movements'. Student activists throughout the country, such as Chang Fu-shun (張復舜) of the Student Rights Team at Chang Gung University

(CGU),[2] spoke out in support of the Youth Alliance because, in their own experience 'the term 'concern' is often associated with threats and attempts by schools to bar students from taking part in demonstrations' (Loa 2012).

Signifying the impact of the movement on the political process, the students were invited to speak at a meeting at the Legislative Yuan's Education and Culture Committee on 3 December. At the meeting, the minister for education, Chiang Wei-ling (蔣偉寧) argued that he did not have 'the slightest intention of monitoring students' and that 'with empathy toward the students … the ministry will review the methods of expressing concern'. Unconvinced, Chen Wei-ting called the minister 'a liar … hypocritical [and] unknowing of remorse' (Lee 2012).

Chen now came under attack for being 'rude' and demonstrating that political participation by young people was problematic. The first criticism came from NTHU, where Chen was a student. In the days following the committee meeting, the school released a statement to say that it did not support Chen's actions and that: 'Freedom does not represent and allow oneself to behave unscrupulously, especially when it is in relation to an opinion leader' (Lin 2012). Soon after, publications like the *China Times* and the *United Daily News* ran front page articles calling Chen 'ill-mannered' (沒禮貌) (*United Daily News* 5 December 2012).

Several actions were taken to defend Chen. On 6 December NTHU professors launched a petition to criticize the University for apologizing, while civil rights groups initiated a campaign called 'Instead of Reprimanding Students, Let's Protect Democracy' (修理學生, 不如守護民主). However, under the guidance of the president of NTHU, Chen made a public apology to the minister at a rally on 7 December, in order to refocus attention on freedom of the media.

All the same, the political response in Taiwan had encouraged the Youth Alliance to look outside the country for support and deploy contemporary global practices of protest and dissent. From early December, Ling Tzung-kuei (凌宗魁) had used his 'What's Next?' Facebook page to promote the movement. Originally developed as a site for discussing Taiwan's future, Ling suggested that internationally based Taiwanese students upload a picture of themselves holding a sign that read: 'Oppose Media Monopoly, Reject the black hand of China, uphold freedom of the press, I protect Taiwan in ___' (反對媒體壟斷 拒絕中國黑手 捍衛新聞自由 我在___守護台灣) with a blank space left for the participant to add their location (Ling Tzung-kuei 2011). Within a few days, several hundred images had been uploaded from places as diverse as Tiananmen Square, Dusseldorf, Cambridge and Texas. Over time, non-Taiwanese students and prominent figures also contributed, including controversial Beijing artist Ai Weiwei (艾未未) and American public intellectual Noam Chomsky.

This use of a transnational cyber network in the Anti-Media Monopoly Movement is reminiscent of the theories of contemporary social media-based activities put forward in studies of new social movements. In line with Paul Mason's (2012) belief that failure in the global economic system is the ultimate cause of contemporary unrest, the Youth Alliance also began to offer a critique of the way capitalism influences the media. To do so, they explored the ideas of those like Harvard political philosophy professor Michael Sandel, who had addressed the students at NTU on 13 December. They were particularly struck by his claim that in a healthy democracy 'there are some types of things and activities that ought not to be dominated by the logic of the marketplace, including education and the media' (Youth Alliance Against Media Monsters 2012). The students increasingly formulated their actions using this rhetoric. For example, in the lead-up to New Year they posted a statement that read: 'If you only view the issue of media monopolization through the logic of market distribution, you will never be able to break away from the powerful, who through capital monopolise and cast a shadow on public opinion' (Youth Alliance Against Media Monsters 2012).

In conjunction with these types of arguments, the students progressively used symbols that presented the Anti-Media Monopoly Movement as a global political action. From July 2012 the students had made use of the 'Guy Fawkes' mask, taken from the comic *V for Vendetta* and its movie adaptation, which has become identifiable with protests against capitalism and corporate greed (Mason 2012: 603–95). Throughout December the students promoted the international context of the movement by producing numerous memes that represented different 'anti-monopoly stories' from around the world (Youth Alliance Against Media Monsters 2012). They also began the task of collaging the thousands of pictures of support that had been sent in.

The movement remained motivated by ongoing developments in Taiwan's media ownership. In late December, Want China Times made its final application for the purchase of CNS. The Tsai family had placed 75 per cent of their CtiTV shares in the Industrial Bank of Taiwan (台灣工業銀行) so as to disassociate from the television station. The NCC would now determine whether placing shares in a third-party trust fund removed Want Want's control of CtiTV.

Recognizing that the deal still hung in the balance, the students planned a 'New Year's party to oppose media monsters at Liberty Square' (在自由廣場舉辦反巨獸跨年晚會) (Youth Alliance Against Media Monsters 2012). They promoted the event as a criticism of President Ma's unwillingness to address market failure.

On the evening of 31 December, a crowd of nearly 1,000 people gathered in Liberty Square for the annual flag raising ceremony. During the night they relocated to outside the Presidential Office, where they were met by lines of riot police. Images of protesters sitting quietly in front of the well-armed police were circulated around global media and President Ma was criticized for declining to comment on media monopolies. The next day, several prominent publications, including the international version of the *New York Times*, the *International Herald Tribune*, reported on the movement and the Youth Alliance (Tatlow 2013).

Arriving onto the world stage marked the apex of the Anti-Media Monopoly Movement. To reach this point, young people had fought hard to navigate Taiwan's political environment and make their campaign globally relevant. Even so, student leaders remained vulnerable. Despite their achievements, they were unable to direct the progression of events.

Legislative deadlock: 2013–present

Throughout 2012, the issue of media monopolies had been propelled to the forefront of public discussion in Taiwan. Now moving within Taiwan's mainstream political sphere, the Anti-Media Monopoly Movement encountered vying agendas and the ferocity of party politics. This period demonstrates that tangible achievements were only possible through negotiating the movement's original ideological underpinnings.

At the beginning of 2013, Taiwan's politicians commenced discussion of the issue of media monopolies in parliament. In early January, the DPP proposed amendments to the Cable Radio and Television Act, the Radio and Television Act and the Satellite Broadcasting Act, with the intention of instituting a clause to avoid media monopolies. The proposal would be examined in the Transportation and Communications Committee on 9 January. It seemed that this clause had bipartisan support and that changes could be solidified as early as 11 January. Were the bill to pass, the Next Media deal would then officially become illegal.

On 10 January, however, Premier Sean Chen announced that, after consultation with the NCC's Howard Shyr (石世豪), the KMT had resolved not to support the bill. They were concerned it would inhibit investment and, if applied retroactively, have an unpredictable effect on the market. The KMT would wait until the NCC had unveiled their own legislation before passing amendments.

Determined to see the 'KMT stick to their word' over media monopolies, the Youth Alliance organized a sit-in at the Legislative Yuan on 13 January (Youth Alliance Against Media Monsters 2013). At the same time, the DPP, largely absent from the media issue up to this point, deployed its well-practised resources to hold a mass anti-Ma rally. The premise of the 'Fury Mass Rally' (火大) was the DPP's claim that the president was 'incompetent' and had not fulfilled his promise to produce economic prosperity. Appropriating the anger against the KMT's failure to legislate on media ownership, the 100,000 participants demanded that Ma instigate a cabinet reshuffle, reject the Next Media sale and organize a national affairs conference (Lee and Hung 2013).

The DPP now became the dominant representative of opposition to media monopolies. This allowed it to frame the movement within the party's broader agenda of pushing for Taiwanese self-determination. DPP legislators announced that anti-media monopoly reform was needed because the movement was worried about 'Chinese interference in Taiwanese media' (Lee and Hung 2013) and that they believed that the Chinese government could be financing the purchase.

Despite the issue of media monopolies gaining visibility through the DPP, the Youth Alliance did not actively support its actions. Yet a series of announcements throughout February revealed that the movement had begun to achieve real outcomes in Taiwan's media regulation mechanisms. On 20 February, Shyr announced that Want Want had not met the NCC's conditions, so the CNS acquisition would not go ahead. According to the Trust Act, '*Want Want's* handing of the shares to a third party does not change the nature of its ownership of CtiTV' (Li 2013). The company was welcome to reapply but not by placing their shares in a third party.

The NCC had also felt it necessary to draft a 'Prevention of Broadcasting and Television Monopoly and the Maintenance of Diversity Act' (Rawnsley 2013). The bill posed a threat to the Next Media deal by prohibiting cross-media ownership of outlets that held more than 15 per cent of audience share. Indeed, one official interviewed for the *New York Times* admitted that, in regards to Want China Times, 'whether or not a group is leaning too much towards China would affect the extent of the health of the market' (Jim and Lee 2013). Public hearings would be held on 18 and 21 March to gather comments on the legislation before it was passed to the Executive Yuan and the Legislative Yuan in June.

Despite the role that the Anti-Media Monopoly Movement had clearly played in forcing politicians and regulators to confront the issue, celebration was subdued. In response to the announcement, the Youth Alliance made a post on Facebook attributing this quick decision by the NCC 'to the spirited resistance of citizens' (Youth Alliance Against Media Monsters 2013). Yet they added that, since 'if the court finds that the NCC's disciplinary action [against Want China] is invalid then the whole [outcome of the merger and acquisition] case [would] have to change', they must continue to put pressure on the NCC.

Then, on 26 March, newspapers reported that the Next Media transaction was about to fall through. Next Media spokesman Mark Simon publicly announced that the deal was off, while other reports declared that Want China Times planned to withdraw because 'Tsai Eng-meng ... sought to pare the purchase back to avoid antitrust queries into his family's media ownership' (Chen 2013).

The following day it was confirmed that the China Times Group was withdrawing from the deal. Want Want did not concede ideological defeat but complained that the movement had damaged the market value of the deal. They reported that 'the group predicts Taiwan's regulatory authorities will set hurdles for the deal to proceed in response to public opposition [and] Taiwan's Fair Trade Commission may humiliate the group again by imposing more conditions' (Want China Times 27 March 2013). Want Want's Wu Ken-cheng (吳根成) also reiterated that the firm thought that the NCC was behaving illegally and that there was political involvement over the issue of media ownership.

Activists in the Anti-Media Monopoly Movement now focused on the details of the legislation and hoped that it would be passed by the legislature. Yet, in January, the DPP had decided to set up a 'task force' to establish its own version of the Act after their proposed amendments were rejected. The DPP's bill sought to regulate market share rather than viewer ratings. As the two parties were unable to agree on this element, the legislation was delayed.

The movement grew frustrated with both sides of politics. Academia Sinica fellow Chiu Hei-yuan (瞿海源) publicly complained that, 'despite many politicians across party lines promising that they would push for legislation against media monopolization, they have been rather unenthusiastic about turning their words into action' (Loa and Wang 2013). The issue would be 'pretty much decided by the attitude of the Chinese Nationalist Party caucus', but the DPP had pledged to legislate on the issue and was not, the movement believed, doing everything possible to fulfil this promise. In response, the movement drafted its own, simplified legislation. The group's proposal sought to only control news outlets, because focusing on entertainment or sports channels was seen as a waste of resources.

The numerous draft acts finally made it to the review process of the Transportation and Communications Committee at the end of May 2013, but parliamentary debate was delayed for over a year. Within this time, the Anti-Media Monopoly Movement had dissolved into the coalition of groups who occupied the Legislative Yuan on 18 March 2014 in opposition to a Cross-Strait Service Trade Agreement and the issue of media ownership was incorporated into a campaign for general political reform. Since then, movement participants have become part of the 'third force' in Taiwan's political sphere, joining minor parties that do not align themselves along the traditional blue/green divide (Harrison 2014). For example, Huang Kuo-chang went on to win a legislative seat in the January 2016 elections as chairperson of the New Power Party (NPP) and currently sits on the Legislative Yuan Finance Committee. He has expressed disappointment with not having been assigned to the committee responsible for the NCC and therefore being able to continue to push for media reform.

In its final stage, the Ant-Media Monopoly Movement became a secondary actor in the debate over media ownership in Taiwan. While participants were frustrated with their role and the lethargy of progress, this phase proved necessary to the campaign's success. The failure of Want Want's bids and the introduction of legislation were tangible victories, only made possible through working within legislative procedure. This process also revealed, however, the limits of Taiwan's political institutions.

Conclusion

A series of media takeovers in 2012 sparked debate over the ideal relationship between the media, capitalism and democracy in Taiwan. The Anti-Media Monopoly Movement emerged in response and began campaigning for a regulated media that promoted vibrancy and pluralism. The marketization of the industry had threatened these principles by producing media monopolies. In the context of cross-straits relations and the complexity of Taiwanese identity, Want Want Corporation was viewed with particular anxiety because of Chairman Tsai Eng-meng's pro-China stance.

The Anti-Media Monopoly Movement had to negotiate the space between ideals and legislative practice. The movement's strength was based around the ability of leaders, particularly the Youth Alliance, to adapt and compromise. In its initial phase, the movement's complex arguments and limited engagement with the general population hindered its impact. Yet through building on pre-established networks and harnessing momentum from disaffected elements of civil society, the movement found a political presence. Finding localized practices and entrenched power structures unaccommodating, student leaders developed solidarity and political action outside traditional avenues. They established a distinctive style of protest that deployed social media and transnational communities. Then, to secure concrete results, they moderated this approach to work within Taiwan's political institutions.

If the movement is to be understood as a single-issue campaign, then it was successful. Want Want's acquisition bids failed and media legislation was introduced to parliament. In doing so, the campaign's fundamental objectives had been realized. CNS and *Next Media* were temporarily excluded from Tsai's corporate influence, while their future security could be legislatively guaranteed *ad interim*.

Yet the movement's achievements exposed the strength of the structural conditions that had produced the original threat of media monopolies. As seen during the failure of the Next Media deal, market forces continue to shape the media environment in Taiwan and will only be tempered by legislation. Based on Want Want's comments in March 2013, the movement influenced the outcome by disturbing the media market and undermining buyer confidence. As Next Media's popularity rests on its independent reporting, the criticism of Want Want's proposed takeover damaged Next Media's brand value. Recognizing that Next Media was losing market value, Want Want withdrew from the deal. The opinion piece in the *Apple Daily* reiterated that business growth and profit remained the central concern in Taiwan's media, while market competition is the focus of the new media regulation legislation.

Even so, the movement's impact on Taiwan's civil society transcends the issue of media ownership. Through the actions of the students, power was shown to coalesce around the institutions of capitalism, with no real resistance from Taiwan's dominant political parties. Dissatisfied with the ensuing media environment, the movement sought to challenge the central pro-capitalist libertarian ideology that underpins the contemporary system. They concurrently revealed that, without political reform, any attempts to alter this environment would be limited.

These ideologies, along with the movement's campaign strategies and networks of participants have been utilized to great effect several times since. In this sense, the Anti-Media Monopoly Movement was a sign of things to come, while its legacy continues.

Notes

1 Until martial law was lifted in 1987, labour unions were predominantly affiliated with the government in Taiwan. From 1987 amid a climate of liberalization, groups of workers organized and campaigned on specific issues relating to their working conditions, despite unions being illegal under the Trade Union Law. The perceived need for independent labour unions increased in 1996 when the government developed a

plan to privatize industry. The ad hoc company-based groups that already existed laid the foundation for the independent unions that arose. Consequently, as in the case of the Next Media labour unions, labour unions in Taiwan tend to be company-, rather than industry-based. For more information on industrial relations in Taiwan, see Lee, Joseph S. 2004. 'Political and workplace democracy in Taiwan'. *The Industrial Relations Research Association*, 56, 72–80.

2 As previously mentioned, student activists in Taiwan are familiar through the Wild Strawberry Movement of 2008, and have since developed a national network of student rights teams and government bodies. While this network was drawn upon to form the core of the Youth Alliance Against Media Monsters, other activists outside of the Youth Alliance, such as Chang Fu-shun, supported the movement at various times. For more information on student mobilization in Taiwan during the time of the Anti-Media Monopoly Movement see Jeffcoat, Kyle. 2012. 'College kids come together to fight media monopolization'. *Taipei Times*, 17 December. Available online at www.taipeitimes.com/News/lang/archives/2012/12/17/2003550302.

Bibliography

Apple Daily. 2012, 1 August. '學生抗議中天 4新聞台不報導'. Available online at www.appledaily.com.tw/appledaily/article/headline/20120801/34408560 (accessed 4 June 2013).

Association of Taiwan Journalists. 2012. *Social networking group*. Facebook, 27 July. Available online at www.facebook.com/TaiwanJournalists/posts/452802598074869 (accessed 6 May 2013).

Batto, Patricia R. S. 2004. 'The consequences of democratisation on Taiwan's daily press'. *China Perspectives*, 51. Available online at http://chinaperspectives.revues.org/791 (accessed 9 September 2013).

Chen, Lulu Yilun. 2013. 'Next media says $536 million Taiwan asset sale falls through'. *Bloomberg*, 26 March. Available online at www.bloomberg.com/news/2013-03-26/next-media-says-taiwan-print-asset-sale-plan-falls-through.html (accessed 27 June 2013).

China Post. 2012, 28 July. 'Want Want rejects terms set by NCC'. Available online at www.chinapost.com.tw/taiwan/national/national-news/2012/07/28/349111/Want-Want.htm (accessed 23 April 2013).

China Times. 2012, 29 August. '旺旺中時媒體集團聲明'. Available online at http://news.chinatimes.com/politics/11050202/112012082900083.html (accessed 24 May 2013).

CtiTV [中天新聞台]. 2012, 30 July. '時周副總林朝鑫現場採訪 被網友惡意抹黑栽贓'. Available online at http://tv.fanswong.com/play.php?mid=7201 (accessed 6 June 2013).

Enav, Peter. 2012. 'Taiwan media kingpin pushes hard on China ties'. *The Big Story*, 22 February. Available online at http://bigstory.ap.org/article/taiwan-media-kingpin-pushes-hard-china-ties (accessed 16 March 2013).

Friedman, Milton. 1962. *Capitalism and Freedom*. Chicago, IL: University of Chicago Press.

Harrison, Mark. 2006. *Legitimacy, Meaning and Knowledge in the Making of Taiwanese Identity*. Basingstoke: Palgrave Macmillan.

Harrison, Mark. 2014. 'The Sunflower Movement in Taiwan'. *The China Story Blog*, 18 April. Available online at www.thechinastory.org/2014/04/the-sunflower-movement-in-taiwan (accessed 20 April 2014).

Hsiao, Hsin-Huang Michael. 1990. 'Emerging social movements and the rise of a demanding civil society in Taiwan', *The Australian Journal of Chinese Affairs*, 24, 163–80.

Hsu Yu-li, Chen Chia-en and Su Sheng-yi. 2012. '台灣不能只剩一種聲音 旺旺'. *Apple Daily*, 18 April. Available online at www.appledaily.com.tw/appledaily/article/headline/20120418/34167962/ (accessed 15 March 2013).

Hu Qinghui, Huang Zhenyin and Liu Liren. 2012. '傳播科系學生 發起拒進旺中工作'. 自由時報, 15 August. Available online at www.libertytimes.com.tw/2012/new/aug/15/today-life1.htm (accessed 23 May 2013).

Jang, Show-ling. 2011. 'The public is left out of public hearings'. *Taipei Times*, 13 September. Available online at www.taipeitimes.com/News/editorials/archives/2011/09/13/2003513137 (accessed 13 April 2013).

Jeffcoat, Kyle. 2012. 'College kids come together to fight media monopolization'. *Taipei Times*, 17 December. Available online at www.taipeitimes.com/News/lang/archives/2012/12/17/2003550302 (accessed 6 June 2013).

Jim, Clare and Lee Yimou. 2013. 'Tough talk in Taiwan on media deals'. *New York Times*, 11 March. Available online at www.nytimes.com/2013/03/12/business/global/tough-talk-in-taiwan-on-media-deals.html?pagewanted=all&_r=0 (accessed 8 August 2013).

Keane, John. 1991. *The Media and Democracy*. Cambridge: Polity Press.

Lee, I-chia. 2012. 'Minister backtracks over e-mail'. *Taipei Times*, 4 December. Available online at www.taipeitimes.com/News/front/archives/2012/12/04/2003549297 (accessed 18 June 2013).

Lee, Joseph S. 2004. 'Political and Workplace Democracy in Taiwan'. *The Industrial Relations Research Association*, 56, 72–80.

Lee, Yimou and Hung Faith. 2013. 'Taiwan blocks anti-media monopoly bill, raising fears for press freedom'. *Reuters UK Edition*, 11 January. Available online at http://uk.reuters.com/article/2013/01/11/uk-taiwan-media-idUKBRE90A0DF20130111 (accessed 5 August 2013).

Li, Lauly. 2013. 'Want Want bid to buy CNS rejected by NCC'. *China Post*, 21 February. Available online at www.chinapost.com.tw/taiwan/national/national-news/2013/02/21/370878/Want-Want.htm (accessed 6 August 2013).

Lin Zhicheng. 2012. '清大：自由不代表允許恣意妄為'. 中時電子報, 5 December. Available online at http://news.chinatimes.com/focus/501012419/112012120500082.html (accessed 26 July 2013).

Ling Tzung-kuei. 2011. *Social networking group*. Facebook, 1 October. Available online at www.facebook.com/TaiwanWhatsNext (accessed 26 June 2013).

Liu, Li-jen, Chen Yi-ching and Jason Pan. 2012. 'Want Want's Tsai behind next media bid: report'. *Taipei Times*, 8 November. Available online at www.taipeitimes.com/News/front/archives/2012/11/08/2003547154 (accessed 9 April 2013).

Loa, Lok-sin. 2012. 'Policies needed, not 'concern': Students'. *Taipei Times*, 2 December. Available online at www.taipeitimes.com/News/taiwan/archives/2012/12/02/2003549147/1 (accessed 23 July 2013).

Loa, Lok-sin and Chris Wang. 2013. 'Groups draft act on media monopolies'. *Taipei Times*, 16 May. Available online at www.taipeitimes.com/News/taiwan/archives/2013/05/16/2003562407/2 (accessed 7 August 2013).

Mason, Paul. 2012. *Why It's Kicking Off Everywhere: The New Global Revolutions*. London: Verso.

Moemail1. 2012. Available online at www.flickr.com/photos/michaelturton/8232203524 (accessed 17 July 2013).

NextTV. 2012, 29 August. '旺中集團針對「走路工」事件發表聲明'. Available online at www.nexttv.com.tw/news/realtime/latest/10387888 (accessed 22 May 2013).
Participant C. Personal Interview. 4 January 2015.
Participant S. Personal Interview. 21 May 2015.
Rawnsley, Gary D. 2000. 'The media and popular protest in pre-democratic Taiwan'. *Historical Journal of Film, Radio and Television*, 20(4), 565–80.
Rawnsley, Gary D. and Gong Qian. 2012. 'The media and the vitality of democratic Taiwan'. In Steve Tsang (ed.), *The Vitality of Taiwan: Politics, Economics, Society and Culture*. Basingstoke: Palgrave Macmillan, pp. 98–118.
Rawnsley, Ming-yeh. 2013. 'Anti-media monopoly policies in Taiwan'. *University of Nottingham China Policy Institute Blog*, 25 March. Available online at http://blogs.nottingham.ac.uk/chinapolicyinstitute/2013/03/25/anti-media-monopoly-policies-in-taiwan (accessed 3 April 2013).
Rawnsley, Ming-yeh and Feng Chien-san. 2014. 'Anti–media-monopoly policies and further democratisation in Taiwan'. *Journal of Current Chinese Affairs*, 43(3), 105–28.
Rigger, Shelley. 2006. 'Strawberry jam: National identity, cross-strait relations and Taiwan's youth'. In Yi Yuan (ed.), *Is There a Greater China Identity? Security and Economic Dilemma*. Institute of International Relations English Series 53, National Chengchi University, Taipei, pp. 117–35.
Tatlow, Didi Kirsten. 2013. 'As Taiwan's links with mainland grow, so do concerns'. *IHT Rendezvous*, 1 January. Available online at http://rendezvous.blogs.nytimes.com/2013/01/01/as-taiwans-links-with-mainland-grow-so-do-concerns (accessed 5 January 2013).
Tzou Jiing-wen. 2011. '《星期專訪》台大新研所教授張錦華：早就超過媒體集中度的標準了 / 旺中併購案 NCC應駁回 立即停審'. *Liberty Times*, 24 October. Available online at www.libertytimes.com.tw/2011/new/oct/24/today-p20.htm (accessed 12 June 2013).
United Daily News. 2012, 5 December. 'A Commentary: Disability to Exercise Freedom'. Available online at www.kmt.org.tw/english/page.aspx?type=article&mnum=112&anum=12258 (accessed 26 July 2013).
Want China Times. 2013, 27 March. 'Want Want pulls out of next media deal'. Available online at www.wantchinatimes.com/news-subclass-cnt.aspx?id=20130327000100&cid=1104 (accessed 5 August 2013).
Wu, Charo. 2012. *Social networking group*. Facebook, 17 August. Available online at www.facebook.com/notes/charo-wu/誰的涉己事務/479867015365259 (accessed 3 April 2013).
Youth Alliance Against Media Monsters. 2012. *Social networking group*. Facebook, 15 August. Available online at www.facebook.com/antimonopoly (accessed 12 April 2013).
Youth Alliance Against Media Monsters. 2012. *Social networking group*. Facebook, 31 July. Available online at www.facebook.com/idontwantwant (accessed 5 May 2013).

6 This land is your land? This land is *MY* land

Land expropriation during the Ma Ying-jeou administration and implications for social movements

Ketty W. Chen

Introduction

On 31 March 2014, half a million Taiwanese citizens came out on the streets of Taipei to demonstrate their support for the young activists who had climbed over the gates of Taiwan's parliament, the Legislative Yuan. They had entered its main chamber two weeks earlier, to protest against a trade agreement the Taiwanese government had signed with China.[1] The demonstrators crowded Ketagalan Boulevard, an open road in front of the Presidential Office, and permeated the surrounding streets extending north to the Legislative Yuan and south to Liberty Square and the National Central Library. The occupation of the Legislative Yuan by students and activists, mostly youths and young professionals in their twenties and thirties, would ultimately last 23 days. Known as the 'Sunflower Movement', the event signalled a new stage of urban resistance movement and citizen nationalism in Taiwan.

If one examines the modern political history of Taiwan, one would find that it was not short of protests, street marches and political rallies. Political dissidents often defied martial law and took to the streets to advocate political reform and political rights.[2] Protesters would often march or conduct sit-ins without the application of permits. Such behaviour was even more prevalent in the second Ma administration (2012–16), as protesters began engaging in behaviour similar to what Sheehan Moore (2013) described in his article 'Taking up Space' – using their bodies to 'fill in' the space in and around government buildings and refusing to leave in order to protest a variety of issues ranging from environmental pollution and energy policy to labour rights and land expropriation (Moore 2013: 6–16).

As the largest protest in the country's recent history, the Sunflower Movement marked the critical juncture of Taiwan's democracy in many ways that deserve research and scrutiny. Specifically, it was significant in Taiwan's democratic consolidation in two ways. First, the Sunflower Movement inspired a much-needed societal and political debate on the constitution of 'democracy' and 'citizen participation' in Taiwan. Second, the Sunflower Movement signifies the ripening of a distinct Taiwan-centric identity. In other words, the Sunflower

Movement solidified the fact that citizen nationalism is very much alive and vibrant in Taiwan and the bottom line for most Taiwanese, especially the young, is the preservation of Taiwan's democracy. This is also the 'status quo' most Taiwanese expected the government to safeguard with regards to the relationship with China. The movement, therefore, obligated the decision makers in Taipei, Washington and Beijing to re-evaluate their policies towards Taiwan.

Even more significantly, the Sunflower Movement reinvigorated and reanimated Taiwan's civil society groups and non-governmental organizations, which during the last decade had been dormant, dishevelled, pessimistic and combative with one another in competition for limited resources. The Sunflower Movement essentially created an overarching platform for civil society groups to communicate, cooperate with and, at least, to get to know about each other. In general, the movement also renewed hopes for those who seemed to have given up on Taiwan in terms of its democratic consolidation and autonomous future. Many had mistakenly come to believe that the young in Taiwan were apathetic to politics. The movement also managed to keep alive the related issues involving Taiwan's trade relations with China and facilitated them into subjects of debate and discussion, in both the public and the private spheres. That is, the contribution of the Sunflower Movement was also in the education of constituents and brought to focus an issue that otherwise had been ignored for more than a year.

As mentioned at the outset, the Sunflower Movement defined the occupation of government buildings as one method of protest in Taiwan. However, it is imperative for researchers of social movements and Taiwanese politics to note that the Sunflower Movement was not the first instance in recent years where activists occupied a government building in demonstration. The Sunflower Movement, now an emblem of Taiwan's social movements, was orchestrated by young activists who had already been actively participating and engaging in social issues such as protests against eviction and land expropriation by the government. The social movement surrounding the advocacy for land justice, as this chapter argues, served as a training ground for the Sunflower Movement. The main student advocate groups, such as the 'Lost Wanderers of the Golden Block' (華光, 金磚上的遺民) and the 'Safeguard Miaoli Youth Alliance' (捍衛苗栗青年聯盟), not only have overlapping members and leaderships with earlier student movements, such as the Wild Strawberry Movement and the Anti-Media Monopoly Movement; their members and leaders would become those who took over the legislature in March 2014. Therefore, this chapter also asserts that the Sunflower Movement would not have been as effective if it had not been for the series of social activism in the previous two years (2012–14).

The purpose of this chapter is manifold. First, this chapter will examine and investigate social movements surrounding the issue of land expropriation in Taiwan during the second Ma Ying-jeou administration. Through the examination of the history of Taiwan's land expropriation and the legal framework permitting such governmental action, the chapter elucidates the result of land expropriation in Taiwan and the accumulated discontent among ordinary citizens and their advocates. The chapter will then explore the extent to which land and residential justice became the centre of persistent, and occasionally massive, demonstrations through the examples of the demolition of the Huaguang Community in Taipei and land incident in the Dapu Borough of Miaoli County. This chapter will also scrutinize the extent to which the two protests not only cross-pollinated one another but also influenced the subsequent Sunflower Movement. This chapter argues the nature of Huaguang Community and Dapu Borough as incidents of government land-grabbing are quite different; however, the similarity of the two cases was the intense fury such eviction generated and the invoked methods of demonstration. That is to say, the government was ultimately seen by society as praying on the weakest segment of society. And, after extended periods protesting under legal means, that is, petitioning, requests for public hearing and peaceful sit-ins without avail or clear proposals of solution from the government, the activists ultimately escalated their means of protest by occupying public spaces; in the cases of land expropriation, the compound of the Ministry of Interior. Approximately a year later, the Sunflower Movement would follow a similar path.

Land expropriation and the Kuomintang regime

Land-related protests are among the fiercest and most persistent and emotionally charged forms of activism in Taiwan. In recent years, activists from non-governmental organizations such as the Taiwan Rural Front (台灣農村陣線), the Alliance of Anti-Forced Eviction (反迫遷連線), Covenant and Conventions Watch (人權公約施行監督聯盟), the Taiwan Alliance for Victims of Urban Renewal (台灣都市更新受害者聯盟) and other self-help groups associated with similar causes often utilized their bodies as a means of demonstration.[3] The typical protest often involved protesters lying on the ground, chanting slogans, locking arms and sometimes chaining their bodies to the soon-to-be demolished structures to prevent government enforcers and construction workers from demolishing the targeted structures. Often, such methods delayed demolition for hours, as law enforcement removed and relocated all protesters from the premises. At times, the removal of protesters took so long that the demolition became delayed for days. In addition, demonstrations as such created sensational images that fed the media, and the distribution of those images on the television gave attention to the particular demolition cases and, subsequently, the cause. Setha Low and Neil Smith (2006) predicted that now is the pivotal moment for examining the politics of public space, as the frequency of protesters' occupation of public spaces began to increase.[4] In Taiwan, the occupation of government buildings and public spaces has become the norm of protest and expression. As Jeff Hou contends in *Insurgent Public Space*, the protesters in Taiwan redefined their own public urban space of protest into spaces and areas, temporary and impromptu events. There are even 'flash mob' spaces (Hou 2010).

While occupying public spaces has become the preferred method of recent protests, land issues in Taiwan have been a major subject of contention since the

Chinese Nationalist Party (Kuomintang, KMT) retreated to Taiwan after losing the Chinese Civil War in 1949. History textbooks in Taiwan usually portrayed land reform policies implemented by the KMT regime as the essential foundation of Taiwan's modernization and economic development (Bristow 2010, 21–2).[5] The existing research and scholarship on Taiwan's land reform also largely focused on the documentation of administrative procedures and the historical legal texts. The existing writings on land expropriation, according to Hsu Shih-jung (徐世榮), professor at National Chengchi University and land rights activist, often neglect providing analysis and scrutiny on the extent to which the KMT regime managed to obtain the land or implement the 'reforms' (Hsu 2013). Moreover, land in Taiwan has tremendous potential for profit, and those rights to land have almost always been obtained through political forces or those who are closely associated with the powers that be (Bristow 2010: 23). From historical polices such as the '37.5% Arable Rent Reduction Act'[6] and the 'Land to the Tiller Act'[7] to the 'Land Expropriation Act',[8] the 'Zone Expropriation Act'[9] and the 'Urban Renewal Act', these aforesaid tenets were and still are frequently exercised by the government to obtain land, often through forceful means, from owners who retained ownership of the land for generations.

During the authoritarian era, discontent and complaints often went unnoticed. Disgruntled citizens would also self-censor for fear of the legal and political repercussions. Although the KMT regime vaunted its land reform policy as the exemplar of equality and fair redistribution, land reform policies and their implementation were, in actuality, riddled with inconsistencies and nepotism.[10] Landowners and farmers were inadequately defined, and, frequently, those who lost their land were never sufficiently compensated.[11] Some claim they were never compensated at all.[12] Since democratization, the right to residence and property has become one of the focuses of Taiwan's democratic consolidation and the country's endeavour to become a liberal democracy. Land justice also became one of the issues associated closely with the push for transitional justice. Nonetheless, the Taiwanese government, including former Democratic Progressive Party (DPP) president Chen Shui-bian's administration, was less than satisfactory in compensating and rendering justice to the victims of land grabs under the KMT authoritarian regime (Hsu 2007).

In 2009, President Ma Ying-jeou signed the 'International Covenant on Civil and Political Rights' and the 'International Covenant on Economic, Social and Cultural Rights'.[13] The same year, the Legislative Yuan passed the two covenants into law. Land expropriation issues thus became a prominent subject for social movements and activism. Activists often invoke Article 10 of the Republic of China Constitution, which gives its citizens the right to residence and freedom of movement, and the two UN Covenants, during protests.[14] In addition, land-related protests occurred frequently and confrontationally under President Ma Ying-jeou, as the administration ramped up the utilization of courts to take legal actions against the residents, while imposing substantial fines to evict and acquire the land desired. Moreover, and more importantly, the violent nature of eviction, for example dispatching law enforcement personnel who substantially outnumbered residents to intimidate and remove the mostly elderly residents, also generated tremendously negative public opinion and sparked harsh protests from activists.

Land politics in Taiwan

Land reform was one of the first policies implemented by the KMT regime after arriving Taiwan. In the 1940s and 50s, reforms such as the '37.5% Arable Rent Reduction Act', the 'Land to the Tiller Act' and the 'Public Land Release Act' were said to improve the lives of tenant farmers by allowing them to own farmland and provided a platform for Taiwan's economic progress. On the other hand, land reform policies were also the KMT's method of control over Taiwanese society and to purge the influence of the land-owning class. In the 1960s, in order to boost the island's economy, the government passed guidelines providing rewards for investment and entrepreneurship. The government also provided tax cuts and land to those who were willing to invest in the dedicated economic sectors and crops. Subsequently, the government utilized the obtained land for building industrial areas and factories, and it also allowed the new landowners to change the purpose of the land from farming to industrial use. Over time, buying, selling and manipulating land usage became the way by which the government managed land and garnered funds for itself in Taiwan.

As the KMT proactively increased and extended influence in Taiwan at the local and grass-roots levels, land also became the means for the governing elites to solidify their power and influence. Land expropriation provided the necessary leverage the local elites needed to stay politically and financially afloat. Both the national and local governments sold the expropriated land for profit when they encountered financial difficulties. According to Hsu, the abuse of land did not change much over the years and it explains the extent to which land-related controversies still occurred more than two decades into Taiwan's democratization.[15] Such was the case of the Miaoli County government's expropriation in Dapu township for the purpose of building an extension to a science park. And, the Huaguang Community in Taipei was razed for the purpose of erecting glitzy hotels, strip malls and night clubs to entice tourists, most of them from China.

In 1969, the KMT regime passed the Zone Expropriation Act. The Ministry of Interior began cornering off plots of land for developmental purposes in Taiwan.[16] According to Hsu and Frida Pei-hui Tsai (蔡培慧) of the Graduate Institute for Social Transformation Studies at Shih Hsin University,[17] the Zone Expropriation Act was the principal cause for rampant and excessive land expropriation in Taiwan. Lack of oversight and planning allowed local governments to expropriate whichever land they desired in the name of progress and modernity, while offering less than satisfactory compensation to land owners. For example, as one tours the Miaoli County today, one would notice numerous advertisements from development companies selling expropriated or about-to-be expropriated land. A former Miaoli County commissioner, Liu

Cheng-hung (劉政鴻), was even caught on video stating that he would be able to resolve the debt problem for the county by selling the land expropriated in Dapu township.[18] Liu's comment came after the owner of the Chang Pharmacy in the said township collapsed from stress and long-term exhaustion and was sent to the hospital. The timing of Liu's comment generated a tremendous backlash; however, the Miaoli County government refused to back down and the homes of the four Dapu residents would be demolished in the days after.

The following sections provide the background of two high-profile land expropriation cases under President Ma Ying-jeou's second term and their impact on the subsequent social movements such as the Sunflower Movement and methods of modern day protest in Taiwan. As mentioned at the outset, even though there are some fundamental differences in the nature and the eventual court ruling of the cases, a closer examination would reveal similarities in the progression, escalation and methods of advocacy among the demonstrators. That is, residents and their supporters would petition through legal means via appropriate government agencies for an extended period of time, in both cases for years. Then, as the residents' pleas fell on deaf ears, the advocates would change the venue of protest to the court of public opinion by organizing marches and public events. And in both cases, and as with the Sunflower Movement against the trade pact Taiwan signed with China, the responsible government agencies would again refuse to acknowledge and provide any solutions to the protesters' demands. The results of such behaviour was the escalation of methods of protest to throwing paints, spray painting, applying stickers on government buildings and then the occupation of government buildings.

The 'Golden Brick' and the Agrestic Borough

The Huaguang Community and the baggage from history

The Huaguang Community is located on Hangzhou S. Road and Jihua Road, next to the Chiang Kai-shek Memorial Hall. This vibrant area of Taipei is also known as 'The Golden Brick'. Taiwan's Ministry of Justice claims ownership of the land, as the area was Taipei Prison during the Japanese colonial era. The majority of the residents of Huaguang were employees of the Ministry of Justice, civil servants and low-ranking KMT military personnel who fled to Taiwan after the Nationalist government was defeated in China in the Chinese Civil War in 1949,[19] though some of the residents established their homes before the arrival of the KMT troops. The third group of residents was from southern Taiwan. They came to Taipei for work and either rented or bought the dwelling place in the community from owners of the houses.

The Ministry of Justice took over Taipei Prison and surrounding area following the conclusion of World War II. More specifically, it is the ministry's Taipei Correctional Facility that bears the right to the land. During the Chen Shui-bian administration, between 2000 and 2008, the government signalled its intention to retrieve the land from the residents. Although there were court cases filed by the government against some of the residents, the administration did not act on such signals. On 7 June 2013, the Ministry of Justice temporarily suspended the demolition of Huaguang Community pending evaluation of the remains of the Taipei Prison within the community by the city's Department of Cultural Affairs. The Department's Cultural Assets Review Committee decreed that the southern wall of Taipei Prison, the residence of the prison director and the public bathing house, as well as 20 additional Japanese-style houses eastward of the bathing house, were historical sites and should not be demolished.[20] In addition to the historic value, the Huaguang Community is said to have had over 50 different kinds of plants, including trees more than 80 years old. More importantly, the community also served as a habitat for 20 species of birds. Advocates of the community had been working with legislators and their staff in an attempt to save the old trees and plants.

Consequently, as soon as President Ma Ying-jeou was inaugurated for his second term, the Ministry of Justice filed lawsuits against all the residents of Huaguang, as well as those whose names were listed under the household, making some of the defendants in those suits children. All seven members of Huaguang resident Lin Ya-chi's (林雅琪) family were sued by the government.[21] The Lin family had owned a small automotive shop on the property of the community for the past six decades. Father Lin was a mechanic who worked on cars belonging to the ministry. Even that did not save Mr Lin from being the target of a lawsuit by the government. To make matters worse, the ministry then accused residents like Lin of illegally occupying and profiting from the land, tagging a six million dollar fine on all members of the Lin family.[22]

According to the Ministry of Justice, such government action stemmed for its endeavour to demolish the community to make space for the government's bid to create a district that resembled Tokyo's Roppongi neighbourhood. In fact, the government named the project 'Taipei Roppongi' (台北六本木). The name Roppongi originated from Japan's Edo period. Tokugawa Shogun insisted to have the clan leaders of the six *daimyo* relocate to the area that would later be referred to as Roppongi for the purpose of distancing them from their home turf in order to prevent them from revolting. As Roppongi prospered, the feudal lords eventually sought expansion of the area and forcibly took land from their neighbours. Today's Roppongi in Tokyo is filled with nightclubs, hostess bars, cabarets, strip bars and restaurants. However, it is also riddled with crime and is known for the presence of *yakuza* members, both as patrons or business operators.

Ironically, most residents of the Huaguang Community were also victims of exile. After the end of the Chinese Civil War, many Huaguang residents escaped to Taiwan from China with the KMT troops. Those who were employees of the Ministry of Justice received housing in the community; however, those who did not receive a home began building houses and dwellings near their colleagues and friends' homes. As the residents of Huaguang settled, many families grew; therefore, additional structures were built as extensions to existing houses, making Huaguang a close community in a literal sense. It is also important to note that, in the initial establishment of the Huaguang Community and the building of additional housing structures, there was no government intervention. Contrarily, door numbers and street signs were created, the post office began delivering mail to the households and utility companies began sending out bills to residents. In other words, residents of the Huaguang Community had been paying bills to government-owned enterprises for decades.

The Ministry of Justice began evicting the community residents and demolishing their houses in early February 2013. In total there were six major waves of demolitions, accompanied by isolated demolitions. The two demolitions in March and April 2013 received the largest resistance from residents and their young supporters and the most attention from the public. The ministry also proposed no relocation plan and did not offer any assistance to the residents, mostly elderly. According to Premier Jiang Yi-huah (江宜樺),

> Illegal residents do not have the rights to be protected under the law. The government is also not responsible for the aftermath of the eviction and demolition for relocation and rent subsidies, as the government cannot be responsible for illegal activities of citizens.[23]

The Taipei City government begrudgingly offered a few public housing units; however, the public housing units for the residents were scattered through Taipei on a first-come-first-serve basis and contingent on the evicted residents signing a promissory note. The agreement was to promise that resident would not apply for any rent assistance and to be solely responsible for the rent of the housing. Rent of the public housing was NT$13,000 (US$433) per month. In addition, the residents who accepted the public housing unit were only promised a two-year contract with a one-year extension. What prompted yet another wave of discontent was that the notice to apply for such public housing was made public to the community on 13 April 2013 and the residents had to finish applying by 17 April. Most residents of Huaguang – and many of them were elderly and of failing health – caved under the financial and legal pressure. Some decided to demolish their houses on their own to avoid paying the demolition fees demanded by the government; others settled with the government for lesser fines.

Methods of protest and advocacy

At the end of July 2013, the remaining residents of Huaguang received a notice from the Ministry of Justice stating that the final round of demolitions and evictions would be executed from 27 to 29 August 2013. By that time, the community area had only approximately 20 residents left. The residents and their supporters were determined to protest until the end. The last bid to bring public attention to the Huaguang Community came in the form of a long march, with a surprise. For almost three years, the residents of Huaguang Community were a familiar sight at the Ministry of Justice, the Executive Yuan and the Taipei City government. The residents and their advocates took turns pleading with government officials to at least provide a solution to prevent them from becoming homeless. The residents were met with police officers with shields and batons, or low-ranking government officials who were merely present to receive the plea letter but without any authority to propose a resolution.

During the evictions and demolitions of March and April 2013, the advocates of Huaguang Community began adopting a different and more drastic method of protest. The young protesters chained themselves to the structure about to be demolished by the government. The protesters distributed themselves throughout the designated areas. Some were chained to the roofs of the houses. Some were chained to the side beams. Some positioned themselves inside the homes and the majority of them lay on the ground, locking arms and legs in order to block the excavators and other machines from entering the area. One would later see the same strategy at the Miaoli Dapu protest and, subsequently, the occupation of the Legislative chamber by the Sunflower Movement activists. During the March 2013 protest, it took more than 100 police officers and several hours to remove all protesters from the premises, causing massive delay. The images of young protesters being dragged away by police officers also permeated the airwaves on most channels and for several news cycles, invoking discussions on nightly talk shows and among netizens and reinvigorating the issue of transitional and generational justice. Lin Fei-fan (林飛帆), who later became one of the most recognizable leaders of the Sunflower Movement, participated in the March 2013 protest. Lin was reportedly slapped by a police officer after Lin argued with the police over their methods of eviction.[24]

It is also important to note that the ethnic composition of the young protesters ranged from Hoklo and Hakka to second- and third-generation mainlander, whose parents or grandparents fled to Taiwan after 1949. To the protesters, evicting the elderly residents of Huaguang Community constituted an assault to the most basic democratic value and human right, the right to residence. The case of Huaguang was also an elucidation of the mature democracy that Taiwan had become, that the ethnic divide that plagued the older generation no longer existed among the younger generation in Taiwan.

The farewell event for the Huaguang Community took the form of a march in August 2013, with an unexpected surprise for the Ministry of Justice. The public event started at the premise of the Huaguang Community with a commemoration ceremony at a shrine of the 'Land God'. The participants then tied small white ghosts of the community, made of tissue paper and napkins, around the community. The marchers walked all the way to the Executive Yuan to stop for a skit featuring a snail having its shell taken away and a young man dressed in ghost money. As the group marched in front of the Ministry of Justice, the 200 protesters turned towards the compound, pushed through the guards and occupied the courtyard and front steps of the ministry.

The occupation of the ministry's courtyard and front steps were the protesters' last attempt to bring attention to the public on the unjust nature of eviction and demolition. The protesters sat on the ground and locked arms while demanding to be let inside to file a complaint against the ministry. The duration of the occupation of the Ministry of Justice was shorter than the Miaoli Dapu and the Sunflower Protests; however, this occupation signified what was to come in the subsequent months and year.

The disturbance and destruction of a humble borough named Dapu

On 28 June 2010, Miaoli County Commissioner Liu Cheng-hung ordered the excavation of farmland in Dapu Borough without prior notice. The Miaoli County government claimed that it had completed the legal process to acquire the land, even though there were farmers who had never surrendered their deeds to the government. Residents of Dapu Borough thus formed the Dapu Self-Help Organization (大埔自救會) to campaign against the county government's plan to take over their farmland to make space for the Jhunan (竹南) Science Park expansion project.

The plan to expropriate land in Dapu township, Miaoli County, was set in 2001. In 2008, Innolux Corporation applied to invest NT$500 billion (US$16 billion) in the Jhunan Science Park. Within a year, the Miaoli County government raced through administrative procedures, acquiring more than 800 plots of farm land in the Dapu Jhunan area, including Dapu Borough.[25] In June 2010, without notice, the county government began blocking off entry and exits to plots of land and moved in with excavators and law enforcement to raze the farms in Jhunan. A documentary film-maker, who desired to be known only as 'Tyrannosaurus Rex' (大暴龍), was in Miaoli for another filming project and filmed the excavators unearthing crops that were almost ready for harvest. The images of the excavators turning over rice paddies, the heavy police presence and the screaming and pleading farmers shocked the nation. The society, which was agricultural at heart, found it difficult to tolerate such a waste of food and County Commissioner Liu was heavily criticized.

To add insult to injury, on 3 August 2010 one of the elderly farmers, the 73-year-old Chu Feng-min (朱馮敏), committed suicide by drinking herbicide, owing to depression and hopelessness caused by the destruction of her ancestral land. Upon hearing the news, Premier Wu Den-yih (吳敦義) was forced to comment, 'I understand this woman suffers from chronic diseases, maybe even depression, so I don't know the reason for her suicide ... regardless, I am very sorry'.[26] The backlash from the destruction of the farm and suicide of the elderly woman was tremendous. County Commissioner Liu was heavily criticized and he apologized for his government's action. Premier Wu Den-yih invited the residents and advocates to the Executive Yuan for arbitration. The result of the arbitration was that the Dapu residents who refused to turn over their land to the government were allowed to keep their homes and property.[27]

The relief of the Dapu Borough residents was short-lived. At the end of June 2013, the Miaoli County government delivered renewed demolition orders to the remaining households in Dapu Borough. The demolition order set 5 July 2013 as the deadline for the residents to move out of their homes and demolish the houses on their own. If the residents failed to do so by 5 July, the government would forcibly acquire the land. When the demolition order was issued, the four families named in the order were still in the middle of administrative suits with the county government.

On 18 July 2013, as hundreds of protesters gathered outside the Presidential Office in Taipei, the county's demolition team moved in and destroyed the houses in Dapu Borough. According to Commissioner Liu, the protest in Taipei was a 'gift from God' as it had created an opportunity to order the demolitions.[28] One of the four households that were demolished was a small and humble pharmacy, the Chang Pharmacy, manned by a middle-aged couple with the surname Chang. The demolished structure served as both home and business for the Chang family. The video of the Chang family's despair quickly filled the television channels, as well as the protesters, most of whom were young students from prestigious universities, being dragged away by police officers. The suddenness of the demolition, and the demolition victims' obvious distress, sparked outrage and propelled the case onto the national scene and angered many, including those from civil society, which gave birth of the 'Today Demolish Dapu, Tomorrow Demolish the Government' (今天拆大埔，明天拆政府) movement.

Years of advocacy and persistent demonstrations

The case of Dapu Borough bears a resemblance to Huaguang Community, as the victims of both cases all lost their houses and were evicted from their homes. Nevertheless, the Dapu Borough generated much greater backlash and anger within society and much stronger pushback due to public perception of the demolition victims. Mr and Mrs Chang's life story resonated with a large portion of the society in Taiwan. Soft-spoken, frugal and humble, the Changs were the poster child of the hard-working Taiwanese family story. The Changs purchased the piece of land where they built their small pharmacy, which served the community, and lived their lives upstairs from their work. The same story applied to another resident, Chu Bing-kun, the owner of a small family store, whose mother committed suicide after the expropriation of his family's farm land.

The journey of the Dapu Borough incident, which led to the occupation of the Ministry of Interior for 48 hours, began years beforehand. Where the residents of Dapu Borough would visit the responsible government agencies and met with officials to plead their case and provide reasons for their lack of interest to move elsewhere. In all, since President Ma Ying-jeou assumed office in 2008, the Dapu residents regularly visited the Ministry of Interior, the Executive Yuan, the legislature and the Miaoli County government with hopes of resolving the endeavour to drive them from their homes. The residents were readily disappointed by both the government's lack of attentiveness to hear their pleas and the downright denial of their request to meet. The residents of Dapu and their supporters began taking their anguish to the streets.

On 2 July 2013, residents of Dapu and their supporters gathered outside the Executive Yuan in Taipei to stage yet another demonstration, pleading with Premier Jiang Yi-huah to honour his predecessor's promise and to step in to halt the demolitions. Many students and professors from Taiwan's prestigious universities participated in the protest,[29] which came to be known as the 'July 5th, Save Dapu' (七月五, 救大埔) event. It should be important to note that, during this event, several students managed to climb over the fence of the Executive Yuan and made it to the courtyard before being subdued by the police. On 5 July 2013, more than 1,000 supporters drove, chartered buses and took trains to Miaoli County for yet another demonstration at the home that the government was set demolish. Individuals came from as far as Kaohsiung and Taitung to lend their support.

The argument to halt demolition was simple. For example, in July 2013 the size of the Changs' home was six ping (one ping = $3.3\,\text{m}^2$) after the government had already expropriated 14 ping of their home to make way for a road leading to the science park. If the Miaoli government succeeded in taking what it wanted this time, the Changs would only have 0.6 ping of their home left, which was about the size of half a bed.

After three days of protest in July 2013, the central government suddenly announced it would halt demolition. Media reported that Vice President Wu Den-yih asked Miaoli County Commissioner Liu Cheng-hung not to demolish the homes on 5 July and to have yet another round of negotiations to resolve the issue with the residents, as the protest garnered sympathetic attention from the public and was generating negative perception of the government.

As a response, the Miaoli County government placed half-page adverts titled 'The county government has the obligation to its residents to provide a safe road' in Taiwan's major newspapers, the *Liberty Times*, *United News Daily*, the *China Times* and *Apple Daily*. The adverts reportedly cost NT$4 million. Furthermore, the ads accused the Changs of disregarding public road safety with their refusal to vacate their home. The ad also included a photograph of an 18-wheeler making a U-turn, crossing several lanes of traffic, as evidence of the Changs' home preventing smooth traffic flow. However, young supporters of Dapu and netizens friendly to the self-help organization quickly found facts to counter the county government's argument. They found that, three days earlier, the Miaoli County government had sent another 18-wheeler to test that same corner and the vehicle had made a U-turn with no problem. Video of the U-turn was shot by student supporters, who formed a watch group to guard the homes of the residents.

In the meantime, another video surfaced of County Commissioner Liu, which further tarnished the commissioner's argument that the expropriation of land was for the propose of bringing the Dapu Borough to modernity and for economic prosperity of all involved. In the video, Commissioner Liu was answering questions from a Miaoli County legislator. Liu made a comment that the acquisition of the land in Dapu would generate NT$200 billion (US$666 million) for the county, and that the entire Jhunan Township project would help generate

NT$150 billion (US$5 billion). Commissioner Liu said that he planned to sell the land he acquired, including the land surrounding the High Speed Rail (HSR) area, and that after the construction of the HSR station in Miaoli was completed the price of the land in the surrounding area would rise, making the area more profitable. In another video, Commissioner Liu was heard telling another legislator not to worry, because he would 'give birth to a lot more land'.[30] It was said that during Commissioner Liu's administration he acquired and developed more than 30 plots of land for industrial and factory use. Most remained unused and unoccupied.

Dapu residents and their supporters also held demonstrations in front of the Presidential Office. The protests drew mostly young people, students and academics. They took over Ketagalan Boulevard, held all-night vigils, 'planted crops' on the boulevard and demanded that the government halt the demolition and return the farmland to the farmers.

Escalation and guerrilla protests

The peaceful sit-ins and visits to the responsible government agencies were met with not only contempt but also neglect. Government agencies refused to take responsibility for providing a solution to the issue. Premier Jiang Yi-huah, who had been somewhat silent on Dapu, now said that the Dapu matter should be dealt with at the discretion of the local government. The Executive Yuan, said Jiang, would give the county government a free hand to carry out what was necessary. Also, to make matters worse, the Miaoli County government refused to soften its stance.

On 8 July 2013, politicians of Commissioner Liu's party in Miaoli organized a counter-protest, in which they mobilized more than a thousand people to attend a press conference to support the county commissioner. The press conference felt more like an election rally than an occasion for the Miaoli County government to explain its position to the press. Some of the press conference attendees wore the KMT 'battle' vest. During the counter-protest, Miaoli County Council speaker Yu Chung-tien (游忠鈿) led the chant, 'Go Commissioner Liu!' (縣長加油!) to encourage the county commissioner. Yu said that it was the county council's responsibility to mobilize those who supported the demolitions and that, to him, it did not make sense that the government would halt demolition simply because some people were protesting. Both Yu and the head of the Jhunan residents' representative council, Lin Shu-wen (林樹文), said that they planned to bring 50 busloads of people to Taipei for another counter-demonstration. Lin said the reason he decided to speak up was because Taiwan had become 'too democratic'.[31]

After the destruction of the Chang Pharmacy and other residences, small, guerrilla-style protests began to emerge. In the evening of 19 July 2013, young protesters went to the KMT headquarters, where they threw eggs at the building. President Ma's campaign office for his bid for the KMT chairmanship was also egged the same night. Days later, a young mother decided to confront President

Ma Ying-jeou as the president toured a paper factory near her home in Taichung. Carrying her small child while holding on to another, the young mother approached the president while exclaiming, 'Today you tore down Dapu, Tomorrow we tear down the government!'[32] A stunned President Ma was quickly whisked away by security. The young mother later posted an entry on social media saying she sincerely hoped others could join her. Subsequently, dozens of protests followed suit across Taiwan, targeting the president, the vice president, the premier and the county commissioner. The Taiwan Rural Front, The Safeguard Miaoli Youth Alliance and supporters of the residents of Dapu vowed that the protests would continue until the issue was resolved. They were joined by other social movement organization, such as the Laid-Off Workers Alliance (關廠工人陣線), celebrities, film directors, singers and even rappers. With the – now seminal – slogan 'Today's Dapu, Tomorrow's Government' (今天拆大埔, 明天拆政府), the social movement's endeavour to not only resolve the issue of Dapu Borough but also to reform the Land Expropriation Act garnered increasing strength, assisted by the collaborative efforts of other social movement activists. The Dapu advocates promised for their protests to bloom like wild flowers (遍地開花), and they kept their promise. The protesters also demanded government action on four issues. They are:

1 Apologies from President Ma, Vice President Wu, Premier Jiang and County Commissioner Liu and to compensate the victims of expropriation;
2 Return the acquired land to the residents and assist the rebuilding of their houses;
3 Investigate the legality and possible corruption involving County Commissioner Liu's development projects;
4 Amend the Land Expropriation Act.

In one incident, young protesters pretended to be tourists from China as they made their way to the Executive Yuan. The protesters then pushed through security to enter the Executive Yuan's courtyard and began throwing balloons filled with red paint at the Executive Yuan building. As security called for backup, the protesters sat on the ground, locking arms and chanting the Dapu slogan. The faux Chinese tourist protest was one of the most inventive of all protest strategies in recent years.[33]

Occupation of public space

The highest point of Dapu Borough Movement took place at a massive rally at Ketagalan Boulevard on 18 August 2013 and the succeeding occupation of the Ministry of Interior. Similar to previous demonstration, the theme and the name of the rally was 'Return the Country to the People'. Fire Ex, the band that would later create the anthem for the Sunflower Movement, *Island Sunrise*, opened the rally. Participants took turns taking the stage to articulate their plight and their causes. Self-help groups including the Huaguang Community, Victims of Urban

Renewal and Eviction (都更受害者聯盟), the San-ying Aboriginal Community (三鶯部落自救會), the Shaoxing Community (紹興學程), the Taiwan Rural Front (台灣農村陣線), the Yuanli Self-Help Group against Wind Turbines (苑裡反瘋車自救會), the Self-Help Group Against Eviction for Railroad Relocation in Tainan (反台南鐵路東移自救會), the Safeguard East Coast Alliance (不要告別東海岸) and the Chi-ting Self-Help Group (崎頂自救會) all participated in the rally, lending support to their comrades in Dapu. During this particular rally, it was not difficult to observe the cross-pollination of the social movements, the self-help groups and their associated members. As the groups often state, 'the plight of one is the plight of all'.

As the rally drew to an end, Frida Tsai of the Taiwan Rural Front encouraged rally participants to march down Zhongshan South Road and to relocate to the Executive Yuan for an overnight sit-in. As the marchers approached Xuzhou Road (徐州路), the side street leading to the Ministry of Interior, the leading students ran towards the ministry and began climbing over the fence. The students also prepared blankets to cover the blades and barbed wire to prevent injuries. In the matter of minutes, hundreds of youths had taken over the ministry's courtyard. Security and police officers on the premises were outnumbered by the 2,000 protesters who eventually entered the ministry.

The protesters surrounded the government building and started placing stickers with the Dapu slogan on the windows and walls of the building. Some students began to use spray paint to produce graffiti on the ministry's ground. Chen Wei-ting (陳為廷), another leader of the Sunflower Movement, was also on the premises, as he was originally from Miaoli County. Chen directed the students towards the centre of the courtyard and then read newspaper articles to the protesters. Chen later threw his shoe at County Commissioner Liu, hitting him on his head, when Liu attempted to enter the Changs' household to pay respect after the suicide of Mr Chang.

The young protesters followed directions from the organizers and did almost no damage to the ministry building. They also did not enter the building or cause any damage to the offices. As dawn approached, Deputy Minister of the Interior Hsiao Chia-chi (蕭家淇) met with the protesters but offered no promise or solution. Hsiao left under heavy police protection and the protesters successfully inconvenienced the operation of the government for the next 48 hours. Declaring the protest as successful, the protesters left the ministry with the promise to keep lobbying for their four demands.

As Jeff Hou elucidates in *Insurgent of Public Space*, the city premises became the venue for the social movement groups to negotiate with the government for their demands (Hou 2010). The escalation of city protests and the occupation of government buildings became the representative phenomenon of protests during President Ma Ying-jeou's second term in office. The duration of occupation increased with different social issues and paved the way for the 21-day occupation of the Legislative Yuan by the Sunflower Movement activists. Comparatively, occupations in Taiwan are relatively peaceful, with minimal damage to buildings. The occupations almost always involved sit-ins, while protesters utilized their bodies to inconvenience government operations. The two years of land expropriation protests not only brought to the forefront the archaic nature of Taiwan's land-grabbing law; the protests also allowed the young activists to advance their methods of organization and their creativity to outsmart law enforcement and to perfect their decision-making mechanism and practise negotiation with government officials. It is safe to say that the cases of Huaguang Community and Miaoli Dapu paved the way for the successful result of the Sunflower Movement a year later.

The new frontier for social movements in Taiwan

Social movements in Taiwan in the past had been organized to demand democracy and human rights. During Taiwan's democratic transition, social movements flourished under conditions of prosperity rather than economic hardship. Street protests were nothing new in Taiwan's political history. They served as an educator for later social movements and activists of a wide range of causes. For example, in May 1986, a few months prior to the official establishment of the Democratic Progressive Party, democracy activists Nylon Cheng (鄭南榕), Jiang Peng-chien (江鵬堅) and Yu Chin (尤清) occupied the courtyard of the popular Longshan Temple with a sit-in to demand the lifting of martial law. The occupation lasted more than 10 hours, as the protesters were surrounded by riot police. Supporters, concerned that the protesters would become hungry, threw meat buns inside the closed gates of Longshan Temple. During the Farmers' Movement in 1988, protesters stormed the Legislative Yuan and took down the Legislative Yuan's plaque. Street protests have been a common sight in Taiwan's political history; however, occupation of government buildings and public space for an extended period is a more recent trend. From the Anti-Media Monopoly Movement (discussed in the Ebsworth chapter) to the Sunflower Movement, the activists warned about the consequences of having too close a relationship with China, which to today still claims Taiwan as its 'unalienable territory'. During the Sunflower Movement, young activists were seen declaring their support for Taiwan's independence using democracy activist Nylon Cheng's last words, 'I am [the name of the activist], I support Taiwan Independence' (我叫 _____, 我支持台灣獨立). Blurred ethnic lines is another trend one can observe in recent protests. Such camaraderie was seen in the other social movements in the past two years – during the protest against the forced demolition of the Huaguang Community and during the land expropriation case of Dapu township in Miaoli County. The residents in the latter case are mostly comprised of ethnic Hakkas. One observed youths from all ethnic backgrounds coming together to preserve the community members' right to residence and property, as they believe that what qualifies one as Taiwanese does not and should not include one's ethnic background. To the youths, democratic values and one's identification with the land reign supreme.

Conclusion

Despite the different legal outcomes of Dapu and Huaguang, the level of activism in the last years of the Ma administration was a demonstration of the thriving civil society in Taiwan and the consolidation of the country's liberal democracy. More importantly, the cases of Huaguang and Dapu are prime examples of the current state of Taiwan's identity, especially among the young Taiwanese. In both cases, young Taiwanese from all ethnic backgrounds came to support, protest and advocate for the victims of land expropriation. Through protest and collaboration, the young activists obtained and perfected the necessary methods and strategies to make later social movements more effective. Political and social rivalries are no longer between political parties, or, in other words, between the blue and the green; it is over upholding what Taiwanese believe to be a citizen's natural right versus those who want to obliterate them.

Civil organizations and NGOs found themselves also working together on both cases of the Huaguang Community and Dapu Borough, as well as the subsequent cases of expropriation, to mobilize and inform their respective members on the various issues relating to land justice. The cross-pollination of these civic organizations also furthered the momentum of land-related social movements and in turn generated more media coverage and created additional pressure on government agencies and politicians, including the premier, the vice president and the president.

In all, the land-related social movements not only highlighted the archaic nature of Taiwan's land laws; they also explicated the entrenchment and tremendous influence of the KMT over local politics. Protests relating to land expropriation during President Ma Ying-jeou's administration ultimately aided in making salient the core values of modern Taiwan and its democracy.

Notes

1 Cross-Strait Service Trade Agreement (CSSTA), a sub-agreement to the Economic Cooperative Framework Agreement (ECFA) signed between Taiwan and China in 2010.
2 The Chungli Incident (1977) and the Formosa Incident (1979) were two major street protests in Taiwan that marked Taiwan's liberalization process. The Chungli Incident was sparked by rigged electoral results of opposition candidates in a local election, and the Formosa Incident was over the government's crackdown of the *Formosa Magazine*, which was highly critical of the government.
3 Self-help groups relating to the land expropriation cases such as the 'Lost Wanderers of the Golden Block' (華光, 金磚上的遺民), the Shaoxing Community Education group (紹興學程@紹興社區) and the Chi-ting Self-Help Group (崎頂自救會) are groups that would often travel to assist fellow protesters and victims of land expropriation.
4 Setha Low and Neil Smith made the prediction in their seminal book *The Politics of Public Space*.
5 Textbooks were also the focus of protests under the President Ma Ying-jeou administration from 2013. High school students, teachers, parents and academics took to the streets to protest against what the government claimed were 'minor adjustments' to

Taiwanese high school students' history and civic education textbooks and the extent to which the adjustments were passed, as well as the members of the textbook evaluation committee. For more information on the textbook protests in Taiwan, see: Chen, Ketty W. 'Party-state reemerges through education in Taiwan', Available online at https://blogs.nottingham.ac.uk/chinapolicyinstitute/2014/02/23/party-state-reemerges-through-education-in-taiwan.

6 The 37.5% Arable Rent Reduction Act (三七五減租條例) was introduced on 14 April 1949 as part of the Taiwan Provincial Arable Land Rent Policy (臺灣省私有耕地租用辦法).
7 Sometimes commonly referred to simply as the 'Land Reform Act' (耕者有其田條例). This reform act was implemented in 1953.
8 The Land Expropriation Act (土地徵收法) was last amended in 1986. According to Professor Hsu Shih-jung, the law has not been adjusted since, leaving the methods of evaluating citizens' land outdated.
9 According to land rights activists and experts Professor Hsu Shih-jung and Professor Frida Tsai, the Zone Expropriation Act (區段徵收法) is one of the most controversial land expropriation acts in existence.
10 The inconsistencies included proper compensation and the categorization of landowners and farmers and those who were in poverty and needed assistance.
11 The author's grandmother's family was categorized as a landowner; however, the government never compensated her family on the land in Chiayi County that was expropriated. The Ku family finally received some compensation during the Chen Shui-bian administration.
12 For example, my maternal grandmother did not receive any compensation for the land her family lost to the KMT regime until after the Chen Shui-bian administration.
13 Ko, S. 2009. Ma Signed UN Rights Convenants. *The Taipei Times*. Available online at www.taipeitimes.com/News/front/archives/2009/05/15/2003443649 (accessed 30 May 2016).
14 More specifically, the International Covenant on Economic, Social and Cultural Rights (ICESCR) general comment, No. 4 and No. 7. *No. 7*: In the committee's view, the right to housing should not be interpreted in a narrow or restrictive sense which equates it with, for example, the shelter provided by merely having a roof over one's head or views shelter exclusively as a commodity. Rather, it should be seen as the right to live somewhere in security, peace and dignity. This is appropriate for at least two reasons. In the first place, the right to housing is integrally linked to other human rights and to the fundamental principles upon which the Covenant is premised. Thus 'the inherent dignity of the human person', from which the rights in the Covenant are said to derive, requires that the term 'housing' be interpreted so as to take account of a variety of other considerations, most importantly that the right to housing should be ensured to all persons irrespective of income or access to economic resources. Second, the reference in article 11(1) must be read as referring not just to housing but to adequate housing. As both the Commission on Human Settlements and the Global Strategy for Shelter to the Year 2000 have stated, 'Adequate shelter means ... adequate privacy, adequate space, adequate security, adequate lighting and ventilation, adequate basic infrastructure and adequate location with regard to work and basic facilities – all at a reasonable cost'.
15 Conversation with Professor Hsu Shih-jung of National Chengchi University's Land Politics Department and the Taiwan Rural Front on 29 August 2013 over land issues in Taiwan.
16 Department of Land Administration at the Ministry of Interior. Available online at www.land.moi.gov.tw/chhtml/content.asp?cid=86.
17 Tsai, F. 2004. 'The Free Economic Pilot Zone and land expropriation', 23 May. Available online at www.slideshare.net/wayne930242/05-140523.
18 Formosa Television News. 2013. TV News. Available online at www.youtube.com/watch?v=tXjHJQihooY.

19 The Huaguang Community Petition (守護華光, 為居住正義聯署). Available online at http://campaign.tw-npo.org/sign.php?id=201302808594300.
20 Central News Agency. 'Taipei City request Demolition of Huaguang to be delayed' (北市要求緩拆華光社區). Available online at www.cna.com.tw/news/aloc/201304120346-1.aspx.
21 Public News Network (PNN), 2013. 'The six million dollar mansion', 29 January. Available online at http://pnn.pts.org.tw/main/2013/01/29. The Court decided that the Lin family owed the government over six million dollars for 'illegally residing and profiting from the land'.
22 Conversation with the Lin family on 28 June 2013.
23 Jiang made the comment on 15 March 2013. Edd J. 2013. 'Jiang Yi-huan: Illegal residents are not protected by law on their rights to residence' (江宜樺: 違建戶居住權不受保障 華光居民激憤抗爭). PTS News Network. Available online at http://pnn.pts.org.tw/main/2013/03/15/ 江宜樺: 違建戶居住權不受保障-華光居民激憤抗爭 (accessed 14 August 2015).
24 Liberty Times editor (2013) 聲援華光民眾 驚傳遭警察賞巴掌. Liberty Times. Available online at http://news.ltn.com.tw/news/society/breakingnews/784331 (accessed 7 July 2016).
25 Weng, S. 2016. 'Dapu Chang Pharmacy Lost Lawsuit again' (大埔案張藥房討地再敗訴). The News Lens. Available online at www.thenewslens.com/article/28121 (accessed 8 May 2016).
26 SET TV News. 2010. 'Dapu grandma committed suicide. Premier Wu: the woman had mental issues' (2010/08/03三立新聞~大埔阿嬤自殺身亡.吳敦義: 這婦女平時就有病痛), 3 August 2010.
27 Chiu, Y. and Peng, C. 2013. 'Wu Den-yih reneged on promise' (大埔「原屋原地」保留 吳敦義承諾跳票). Liberty Times. Available online at http://news.ltn.com.tw/news/focus/paper/692113 (accessed 28 June 2015).
28 Apple Daily Editorial Staff. 2013. 'Forced demolition of Dapu. Liu: A chance from God' (強拆大埔4屋 劉政鴻: 天賜良機). Apple Daily. Available online at www.appledaily.com.tw/realtimenews/article/new/20130719/227520 (accessed 8 August 2015).
29 Kuan-yu. 2013. 'Wu Den-yih reneged on promise. Crowd gathered in protest' (吳敦義唬弄全台灣, 民眾怒罵垃圾縣長). Taiwan Good Life, 5 July.
30 Kuan Y. 2013. 'Miaoli Dapu: The truth about the government officials' role in corruption and death' (苗栗大埔: 官僚謀財害命的真相), Taiwan Good Life. Available online at www.taiwangoodlife.org/story/20130706/5084 (accessed 8 August 2015).
31 Liberty Times Editorial Staff. 2013. 'Three gangsters responsible for Chang Senwen's Death? Family members suspect being monitored' (3惡霸逼死張森文? 家屬質疑遭監聽). Available online at http://news.ltn.com.tw/news/politics/breakingnews/874265 (accessed 7 August 2015).
32 Chen, H. 2013. The First Step to Demolish the Government. Saying Hi to the President. Facebook. Available online at www.facebook.com/permalink.php?story_fbid=427676427346099&id=100003112373762 (accessed 4 September 2015).
33 Apple Daily Editorial Staff. 2013. 'Students pretend to be Chinese tourists. Throwing paint in support of Dapu' (直擊 學子扮陸客攻政院: 提名產袋突圍 丟漆彈挺大埔) Available online at www.appledaily.com.tw/appledaily/article/headline/20130816/35225485 (accessed 4 September 2015).

Bibliography

Apple Daily Editorial Staff. 2013. 'Forced demolition of Dapu. Liu: A chance from God' ['強拆大埔4屋 劉政鴻: 天賜良機']. The Apple Daily. Available online at www.appledaily.com.tw/realtimenews/article/new/20130719/227520 (accessed 8 August 2015).

Apple Daily Editorial Staff. 2013. 'Students pretend to be Chinese tourists. Throwing paint in support of Dapu' ['直擊 學子扮陸客攻政院: 提名產袋突圍 丟漆彈挺大埔']. *The Apple Daily*. Available online at www.appledaily.com.tw/appledaily/article/headline/20130816/35225485 (accessed 4 September 2015).

Bristow, Roger (ed.). 2010. *Planning in Taiwan: Spatial Planning in the Twenty-First Century*. London: Routledge.

Chen, H. 2013. *The first step to demolish the government. Saying Hi to the president.* Facebook. Available online at www.facebook.com/permalink.php?story_fbid=427676427346099&id=100003112373762 (accessed 4 September 2015).

Chiu, Y. and C. Peng. 2013. 'Premier Wu reneged on promise to let Dapu residents to keep their land and homes' ['大埔「原屋原地」保留 吳敦義承諾跳票']. *The Liberty Times*. Available online at http://news.ltn.com.tw/news/focus/paper/692113 (accessed 28 June 2015).

Edd J. 2013. 'Jiang Yi-huan: Illegal residents are not protected by law on their rights to residence' ['江宜樺: 違建戶居住權不受保障 華光居民激憤抗爭']. *PTS News Network*. Available online at http://pnn.pts.org.tw/main/2013/03/15/ 江宜樺: 違建戶居住權不受保障-華光居民激憤抗爭 (accessed 14 August 2015).

Formosa Television News. 2013. *TV News*. Available online at www.youtube.com/watch?v=tXjHJQihooY.

Hou, Jeffrey (ed.). 2010. *Insurgent Public Space: Guerrilla Urbanism and the Remaking of Contemporary Cities*. London: Routledge.

Hsu, S. J. 2007. 'Victims of KMT land reform still seek justice'. *Taipei Times*, 8. Available online at www.taipeitimes.com/News/editorials/archives/2007/02/01/2003347250/1 (accessed 15 April 2015).

Hsu, S. J. 2013. 'Land rights can come from death'. *Taipei Times*, 8. Available online at www.taipeitimes.com/News/editorials/archives/2013/09/26/2003573009 (accessed 28 July 2016).

Ko. S. 2009. 'Ma signed UN rights covenants'. *The Taipei Times*. Available online at www.taipeitimes.com/News/front/archives/2009/05/15/2003443649 (accessed 30 May 2016).

Kuan Y. 2013. 'Miaoli Dapu: The truth about the government officials' role in corruption and death' ['苗栗大埔: 官僚謀財害命的真相']. *Taiwan Good Life*. Available online at www.taiwangoodlife.org/story/20130706/5084 (accessed 8 August 2015).

Kuan-yu. 2013. 'Wu Den-yih reneged on promise. Crowd gathered in protest' ['吳敦義唬弄全台灣, 民眾怒罵垃圾縣長']. *Taiwan Good Life*, 5 July 2013.

Liberty Times editor. 2013. 'Supporting Huaguang resident: Police slapped protesters' ['聲援華光民眾 驚傳遭警察賞巴掌']. *Liberty Times*. Available online at http://news.ltn.com.tw/news/society/breakingnews/784331 (accessed 7 July 2016).

Liberty Times Editorial Staff. 2013. 3惡霸逼死張森文? 家屬質疑遭監聽. Available online at http://news.ltn.com.tw/news/politics/breakingnews/874265 (accessed 7 August 2015).

Low, Setha M. and Neil Smith (eds). 2006. *The Politics of Public Space*. New York, NY: Routledge.

Moore, Sheehan. 2013. 'Taking up space: Anthropology and embodied protest'. *Radical Anthropology*, 7, 6–16.

Public News Network (PNN) Editors. 2013. 'The Six Million Dollar "Mansion"'. *PNN*. Available online at http://pnn.pts.org.tw/main/2013/01/29.

SET TV News. 2010. 'Dapu grandma committed suicide. Premier Wu: the woman had mental issues' ['2010/08/03三立新聞~大埔阿嬤自殺身亡.吳敦義: 這婦女平時就有病痛'].

Tsai, F. 2014. 'The free economic pilot zone and land expropriation. Available online at www.slideshare.net/wayne930242/05-140523.

Weng, S. 2016. 'Dapu Chang pharmacy lost lawsuit' ['大埔案張藥房討地再敗訴']. *The News Lens*. Available online at www.thenewslens.com/article/28121 (accessed 8 May 2016).

7 The Sunflower Movement

Origins, structures, and strategies of Taiwan's resistance against the 'Black Box'

André Beckershoff

1 Introduction

What became Taiwan's largest social movement in two decades began in a rather modest fashion. On the evening of 18 March 2014, about 200 to 300 protesters gathered around Taiwan's parliament, the Legislative Yuan, in order to listen to speeches and concerts. The occasion for this gathering was a trade pact between China and Taiwan that had been rushed through a review committee the previous day. Kuomintang (KMT) legislator Chang Ching-chung (張慶忠) had declared the review period for the Cross-Strait Service Trade Agreement (CSSTA) to be over and passed the pact on to the plenary session of the Legislative Yuan, where, given the KMT's firm majority at the time, it was expected to be ratified.

After the CSSTA's signing in June 2013 in Shanghai, the ratification process had been accompanied by protests in Taiwan. However, the actual participation at these protests was rather low, ranging from a few dozen to the low hundreds. This also held true for the gathering on 18 March. As the crowds assembled around the Legislative Yuan that night, nothing indicated that this protest would soon expand far beyond the scope of the previous demonstrations. How could the issue of the cross-strait pact, which for half a year had only mobilized a few dozen activists, evolve into the Sunflower Movement, which was supported by demonstrations with 350,000 participants and which arguably not only had profound impacts on the elections in November 2014 and January 2016 but could also be said to have thoroughly and lastingly rejuvenated the vibrancy of Taiwan's civil society?

The trade pact itself and the expected real impact that its ratification would have had can only partly account for this degree of mobilization. Rather, the movement's strength rests on the fact that the CSSTA served as the focal point for a broad range of grievances that had accumulated within Taiwan's civil society over the previous years. The present chapter[1] aims to show how the organization and strategies that characterized the Sunflower Movement reflect the organic growth of Taiwan's protest movements in general over the past years. It will be argued that both its strengths and the weaknesses lie in the variety of the participating groups. Through the lens of Bourdieu's notion of synchronization, the movement will be understood as the result of an '*integration* rather than a simple *addition*' (Bourdieu 1988: 162, my emphasis) of crises and their respective social movements. The CSSTA, rather than being the immediate cause of the various grievances, was successfully defined as the central node to which various social crises in Taiwan, such as land justice, labour and the democratic system, could be related. The movement could therefore rely on grown structures, which made it possible not only to resort to and refine previously developed protest repertoires, but also to activate social networks within a very short time. These provided the skills and resources that made it possible to transform the occupation into a broad social movement, which ultimately challenged the KMT-led government in a profound way.

For the purpose of this analysis, the Sunflower Movement will be divided into four distinct phases, each of which was characterized by certain forms of organization, tactical challenges, strategic considerations, internal tensions and crises. The first section will deal with the emergence of the movement and the early stages of the occupation. The focus lies on the various grievances and protest themes, the groups and networks that sustained the movement and the initial emergence of organizational structures in and around the Legislative Yuan. The second section covers the developments that resulted in its major crisis, the attempted occupation of the Executive Yuan on 23 March. The third section, covering the ground up to the mass demonstration of 30 March, examines the consolidation of the decision-making process as well as the media strategy, two processes that were crucial for the continuation of the movement. The fourth and final phase was characterized by the movement's struggle to convert the public support into a tangible result. The concluding section will assess the Sunflower Movement's impact on Taiwan's political landscape and civil society.

2 From discontent to action

Visitors who approached the Legislative Yuan in late March 2014 witnessed a contradictory scene of orderly clutter. The streets around the parliament compound, usually reserved for traffic, were occupied by stages, tents and booths. In between, activists distributed flyers, attached posters or engaged passers-by in discussions. On some stages, bands played concerts; elsewhere, artists performed or presented their works. Some spaces were reserved for lectures by university professors and speeches by activists, while others hosted open discussion forums, where people of all ages discussed issues of economy, democracy, human rights or culture. At a first glance, the atmosphere resembled that of a fair. But, in the middle of these activities and separated from the surroundings by a cordon of police, lay the meeting hall of the Legislative Yuan, where between 200 and 300 protesters had been holding out since the evening of 18 March.

This spatial configuration was by no means accidental. On a first level, it was the consequence of the events that surrounded the occupation and therefore the result of a series of tactical decisions taken in the heat of the moment. But, as will become clear as this analysis progresses, the major structural characteristics of the Legislative Yuan occupation, particularly the division of labour between the inside and the outside, also reflect the social organization that sustained the movement and which had emerged over the previous years. The stages and booths that surrounded the parliament were set up and operated by several dozen non-governmental organizations (NGOs), covering a wide range of issues such as labour, environment, nuclear power, feminism, Taiwan independence, rural development and others. The occupation inside the Legislative Yuan was conceived, put into practice and managed by student groups, such as the Black Island Nation Youth Front (BIY). Their key members had been active in protests and social movements for several years prior to 18 March and had cooperated with scholars and NGOs previously. The Sunflower Movement can therefore only be understood as the culmination of a longer development made up of two closely related processes. On the one hand, Taiwan's civil society under President Ma Ying-jeou (馬英九) had experienced an accumulation of grievances over various social fields. On the other hand, and closely related, the groups that had formed around these issues gradually increased cooperation and together developed 'routine ways of acting collectively' (Barker *et al.* 2013: 4). This ensemble of social networks, alliances, overlapping goals and common activities – including activist training workshops – not only was the foundation of what would become the Sunflower Movement, but also structured its emergence, dynamic and conclusion profoundly.

Hence, it is necessary to understand the three highly intertwined, but analytically separate, sources of discontent. First is the theme against the neo-liberal transformation, that is, Ma Ying-jeou's project to increase Taiwan's integration into the global economy. Liberalization through trade agreements, the official argument goes, will consolidate Taiwan's position in the world economy and bring benefits for the whole country. As the People's Republic of China is Taiwan's major trading partner, reducing trade barriers across the Taiwan Strait is a priority for the government. However, the push by the KMT, the Chinese Communist Party (CCP) and business groups to advance the deepening of cross-strait relations coincided with the perceived relative decline in prosperity of large parts of Taiwan's society, particularly the younger generation. The signing of the Economic Cooperation Framework Agreement (ECFA) in 2010 could have provided an opportunity similar to the CSSTA three years later. Yet, despite a series of protests against the agreement, these did not transform into a general crisis. This is because ECFA, as the first part of a broader project for deepening economic exchanges across the Taiwan Strait, still had a degree of plausibility to it that closer economic relations between China and Taiwan would actually benefit broad strata of Taiwan's society. By summer 2013, however, the younger generation had come under the impression that this promise had been broken. The so-called '22,000 NT$ generation', referring to the monthly US$700 that a university student can expect after graduation, had been promised '10 Golden Years' by President Ma. Instead, rising housing prices compelled them to live with their parents, they experienced difficulties in finding a job after graduation and they became concerned by the urban and rural redevelopment that had taken place in their neighbourhood and was often accompanied by the display of police force. Particularly in Taipei, the rising housing and living costs meant that young people continued to live with their parents, unable to afford moving into an apartment on their own and deferring plans of marriage or parenthood (Respondent 14). 'Hard work,' a respondent summarized the students' disillusionment with the promised golden age, 'does not guarantee rewards' (Respondent 1).

The political elites failed to respond to this growing scepticism beyond repeating the mantra of portraying them as beneficiaries of the rapprochement.[2] On the contrary, students were specifically targeted as multipliers of a process that is supposed to lead to a better understanding across the Taiwan Strait:

> Among the various forms of exchanges, it is cultural and educational exchanges that help enhance mutual understanding between the peoples on both sides of the Strait, and are favorable to the exchange of experiences, that are complementary and mutually beneficial, and that are conducive to social prosperity.
>
> (Mainland Affairs Council 2013b)

Due to their young age, their high level of education and their relative mobility, students have been assigned a key role in fostering a common identity that can consolidate the social base of the rapprochement: 'Students are more innocent and zealous, and so it is easier for them to establish friendships and widen their horizons through the exchanges' (Mainland Affairs Council 2013a).

Second, and closely related, is what has been termed the China factor in Taiwan's society (see Hsu, this volume). Opening up Taiwan's economy to China has particular implications, given the Communist Party's openly declared goal of unification. In the years preceding the Sunflower Movement, activists became convinced that the cross-strait rapprochement could not be contained to economic transactions. Rather, the transformation permeated all sectors of Taiwan's society and made Taiwan's civil society both a terrain and a stake of cross-strait relations. A case in point is the events that triggered the Anti-Media Monopoly Movement (see Ebsworth, this volume), which made it clear that closer economic relations with China and the functioning of democratic institutions could not be separated (Respondents 2, 4 and 5). In this sense, the rapprochement had a profound impact on everyday life in Taiwan that was often perceived as negatively affecting the middle and lower classes, and leading to alienation with not only Chinese visitors but also the political forces that encouraged those transformations:

> We can see Chinese programme on TV, and lots of China in the news.... Chinese tourism has changed the environment in the South. Hotels have been bought by Chinese businessmen, and people notice the difference with the tourists. There are stores that sell their products especially to Chinese!
>
> (Respondent 10)

This impact on everyday life is closely related to the domestic political repercussions the cross-strait rapprochement had. The third theme that drives activism is concerned with democratic justice. A major turning point was the year 2012, when several business leaders came out before the 2012 elections to publicly support the 1992 consensus, and as such effectively endorsing the KMT. Activists perceived this development as a negative spill-over of economics into politics (Respondents 5 and 12). The situation was aggravated by the fact that negotiations between the KMT government and the Communist Party took place in a web of various official, semi-official and non-official channels, an arrangement that the Sunflower Movement would go on to call the 'Black Box'. Taiwan's democratically elected legislators would, at best, only see the final product of those negotiations (Beckershoff 2014). The 'Black Box' was criticized as exclusive, not only because deals were made in an opaque manner but also because these deals were perceived to benefit only a small elite within Taiwan.

The CSSTA exemplified all these issues. As a trade agreement with China, it linked the China factor to the liberalization project. And while ECFA failed to stimulate economic growth in Taiwan, activists pointed out the negative social impact that opening Taiwan further might have. Civic groups warned that the cross-strait liberalization of trade in services, a result of 'Black Box' negotiations, might pull Taiwan even closer to China, especially if PRC state-owned enterprises were to gain access to sensitive sectors such as publishing, banking and telecommunications. When KMT legislator Chang pushed the CSSTA through the review committee in a mere 30 seconds, this was said to show the KMT's willingness to use all possible means to implement the pact.

After the signing of the CSSTA in the summer of 2013, student and civic groups emerged with the aim of preventing the ratification of the pact. The activists condensed around two centres of gravity. The student groups built on networks that had emerged and consolidated since the 2008 Wild Strawberry Movement.[3] Several student leaders, such as Lin Fei-fan (林飛帆) and Chen Wei-ting (陳為廷), had become veterans of activism, particularly during the two years that preceded 18 March. In summer 2013, Lin and other students formed the Black Island Nation Youth Front, a group that fought against the CSSTA and consisted to a large degree of veteran student activists of the Anti-Media Monopoly Movement.

The NGOs convened around the Democratic Front Against the Cross-Strait Trade in Services Agreement, an umbrella organization that united groups from various sectors such as labour, human rights and the environment (see Hsu, this volume). The central figure of the Democratic Front was Lai Chung-chiang (賴中強), a lawyer-activist and principal networker among the NGOs and student groups (Respondent 8). He invited about 30 NGOs and several student organizations, such as the BIY, to become members of the coalition (Respondents 5 and 11). Although both the student groups and the Democratic Front cooperated closely, their approaches differed. The Democratic Front concentrated on bundling research around the impact of the trade as well as organizing press conferences and demonstrations. They also closely monitored the public hearings that were held during the ratification process as the result of a compromise between the KMT and the opposition parties Democratic Progressive Party (DPP) and Taiwan Solidarity Union. The student groups, on the other hand, also prepared direct actions.

The unfolding of events on 18 March reflects this broad range of protest repertoire. On the surface, it was a matter of quick and decisive action, both radical and risky. But this surface appearance masks the degree to which the protest repertoire, the occupation and the initial strategies built on years of previous experience, even including the occupation itself: at a previous demonstration against the CSSTA at the Legislative Yuan in July 2013, protesters had attempted to enter the gates (*Taipei Times* 2013b).

Only a few weeks later, protesters succeeded in entering the compound of the Ministry of Interior during a protest against land-grabbing in Dapu (*Taipei Times* 2013a). At the time, the activists were surprised by their success, but they were neither equipped nor prepared for sustaining the occupation, and they could not agree on whether or not to break the windows in order to enter the ministry itself. The occupation of the grounds ended the next morning but the event made movement leaders aware of the feasibility of occupying a political space, if preparations were made accordingly (Respondents 1 and 7).

In mid-March, the public hearings were concluded, and the KMT planned to make the CSSTA pass the review committee. While student groups were considering attempting to enter the Legislative Yuan, the NGOs advised against radical actions. Instead, the Democratic Front was preparing for a 120-hour marathon of public lectures and speeches to cover the whole week during which the CSSTA was to be discussed in the review committee. These plans were frustrated when legislator Chang declared the review period over on 17 March, earlier than the activists had expected. On that evening and during the next day, several meetings were held to discuss a response to the 30-second review, but these were ultimately inconclusive.

The next day, several hundred protesters convened around the parliament to participate in the activities organized by the NGOs. Most of the people were surprised when at nine o'clock a first group attempted to enter through the main gate of the compound. Once this attempt had drawn the police force that was present at the scene to the front of the parliament, two student groups climbed over the rear gates, where they quickly gained access to the meeting chamber of the Legislative Yuan (Respondents 1, 4, 6 and 8). The operation bears witness to the degree of organization, communication and timing with which the plan was put into action. And, yet, the fact that the occupation could be sustained beyond the first night came at a surprise: during the early stages, the police unsuccessfully attempted to raid the meeting chamber four times. The situation inside was described as chaotic and the activists were preoccupied with resisting the police raids by blocking the gates and obtaining water (Respondent 10). During the night, people who had learned about the occupation (mostly via social media) came to support the students by gathering outside. In the morning of 19 March, around 10,000 people surrounded the Legislative Yuan.

When it was clear that the police refrained from further action, working groups emerged as a response to problems that arose one after another: who should guard the doors? Who should speak to the press? Who should organize food? How should supplies that were donated be administered and distributed? Among the first groups that formed around specific sets of tasks were the security team that organized the blockage of the entry doors, as well as the medical and communication teams. Over the coming days, several other working groups followed: one team was tasked with administering and distributing donated material (such as sleeping bags), an art group made posters, the computer team set up the infrastructure for communication and a group of attorneys provided legal aid.

These groups did not form out of thin air. Rather, the organizational structures condensed around personal relationships that had formed over the past years. Many seasoned activists of various movements since the Wild Strawberry Movement had entered the Legislative Yuan during the first night, and others followed soon. The past experience had not only made the occupation possible; it had also facilitated the allocation of specific tasks to persons that were known to possess the necessary expertise. These networks also served as recruitment channels and further participants were mobilized systematically to fill gaps of particular skills, such as languages or information technology.

In addition to this division of labour within the Legislative Yuan, there was also a division of labour between the inside of the chamber and the outside. On the inside, students assumed all tasks that were essential to sustain the occupation of the Legislative Yuan from a logistical point of view. The outside was mostly run by civic groups and saw the emergence of various activities, such as street classes, discussion forums and speeches by activists. These played a crucial role in attracting the crowds that would provide support for the students holding out on the inside of the meeting chamber.

Due to the unexpected success of the occupation, no plans were in place for a long-term strategy. But the tactical situation encouraged close cooperation and coordination between all the parties. Hence, the occupation was not only a major token to be held against the government; the situation also served as a catalyst among the activists. While until 18 March the NGOs and the student groups could not agree to a common strategy, the *fait accompli* took the place of long discussions: faced with the unique situation, all participants mobilized their resources to maintain the occupation. Moreover, this also affected their narratives. This is what Bourdieu refers to as a synchronization during an immediate crisis:

> The principal effect of this synchronization is to compel people to introduce into positions adopted a relative coherence which is not required in ordinary circumstances.
>
> (Bourdieu 1988: 180)

In other words, despite the varying goals and interpretations of the groups that constitute the Sunflower Movement, the immediacy of the occupation pushed the various groups to take position on their demands, what Bourdieu (ibid.: 187) calls a 'generalized unveiling of public opinion', and then subscribe to one set of demands. These demands were made public during a press conference on 20 March. The activists urged the government to withdraw the CSSTA and to halt all negotiations with China until a monitoring mechanism had been passed into law. On that day, the movement had already adopted the sunflower as its symbol, when a florist donated a large number of sunflowers to decorate the speaker's desk in the Legislative Yuan. The sunflower image, though accidental, nevertheless conveyed a fitting narrative to the goal of the movement, as the central demand of an oversight mechanism can be equated with the request to shed light into the 'Black Box'.

3 Crisis

Together with the public statement of demands on 20 March the movement leaders issued an ultimatum. They demanded a response from the government as well as an apology from Ma Ying-jeou by noon the following day. However, the ultimatum passed without any reaction from the government branch. Students hoped to initiate a dialogue on 22 March, when Premier Jiang Yi-huah (江宜樺) visited the Legislative Yuan and was received by Lin Fei-fan. Lin offered negotiations in the event that the premier agree to reject the CSSTA and halt all negotiations with China until the establishment of a cross-strait oversight mechanism. As Jiang saw himself unable to agree to these terms, the meeting ended abruptly.

The lack of responsiveness to the occupation alarmed the movement leaders:

> When Ma and Jiang did not respond, we knew that they wanted to sit it out. We had to plan the next step very soon, because people would go home.
> (Respondent 6)

Although the movement had been able to sustain the occupation and the support outside was growing, it failed to convert this increasing support into a strong position for negotiations. Movement leaders feared a repetition of the KMT's strategy during the Wild Strawberry Movement (see Hsiao, this volume). Back in late 2008 and early 2009, students had occupied Liberty Square in Taipei, demanding the government to apologize for the violation of human rights during demonstrations against the first visit of Chen Yunlin (陈云林), the chairman of the Association for Relations across the Taiwan Strait (ARATS), to Taipei. The Ma government did not react to the students' demands and over the following weeks participation and support slowly faded and the movement dissipated.

In comparison to the Wild Strawberry Movement, the Sunflower Movement was in a stronger, yet more complex position. First, it had successfully occupied a political space rather than a public space.[4] This created a new quality of urgency for the government. In order to ensure the functioning of the legislature, the time frame during which the Legislative Yuan had to be reclaimed – either by negotiation or by forceful eviction – was significantly shorter than in the case of the Liberty Square, which only had symbolic value. Second, Taiwan's social movements had drawn lessons from the Wild Strawberry Movement, resulting in the formation of social networks. Sunflower leader Lin Fei-fan, for example, established the '02 Group' at National Cheng Kung University in Tainan, while Chen Wei-ting, who had still been a high school student at the time of the Wild Strawberry Movement, became central to the student magazine *Radical* at National Tsinghua University in Hsinchu (Respondent 4). These and similar groups gave future activists a platform to establish connections, exchange views and plan protests. Consequently, in 2014 the leaders were better trained, had more experience in dealing with public representatives and media and could rely on the cooperation of NGOs. This allowed the rapid establishment of an apparatus inside and around the Legislative Yuan that encompassed aspects ranging from logistics to public relations (see the following section for details on the media work). Therefore, the Sunflower Movement could rely on a broader, more stable and proven social foundation.

At the same time, these characteristics introduced new complexities into the internal dynamics of the movement. First, a larger variety of perspectives had to be accommodated by the movement leaders. Unlike the rather homogeneous Wild Strawberry Movement, the Sunflower Movement consisted of a broad range of civic groups, many of which feared that radical action would hurt their reputation. As the decision-making became more centralized and formalized, several groups felt that they were cut out from the core. This dissatisfaction among some of the groups provided potential for internal tensions. Second, the occupation of a political space came at a price. Occupying the Legislative Yuan made the movement vulnerable to the criticism of obstructing the work of a democratically elected parliament, and the KMT in particular did not miss a single occasion to raise this point.[5] The legitimacy of blocking the formal democratic process on the inside of the parliament depended on demonstrating that a new grass-roots democratic culture could be put into practice on the outside. It therefore relied to a large degree on the activities that were organized around the Legislative Yuan by NGOs, university professors who relocated their classes to the streets and similar activities. Third, this made the Sunflower Movement far more costly to sustain. Should the crowd diminish or the occupation drag out over several weeks, the NGOs would not be able to justify their costly operations, nor could university professors or other volunteers stay away from their workplace for a longer time. This would leave the students inside the chamber cut off not only from logistical support but also from the essential grass-roots counter-legitimacy.

Consequently, the architecture of the Sunflower Movement was sensitive to stalling in quite a different way than the Wild Strawberry Movement had been. Its continuation depended not only on the individual stamina and willingness of students to hold out under demanding and both physically and psychologically exhausting conditions but also on the prospect of creating a perspective of converting collective action into social and political change. Given the silence by the government, creating this perspective became a critical priority within the leadership.

Hence, student groups proposed the escalation of the Sunflower Movement, hoping that increasing the pressure on the government would evoke a reaction. To this end, several options were discussed. One group favoured the expansion of the occupation to the whole compound (Respondents 6 and 7). After the night of 18 March, the meeting chamber had been successfully occupied but the other buildings on the compound had not been taken under control. Another proposal envisaged the occupation of the offices of Taiwan's executive branch, the Executive Yuan. However, the NGOs, as well as some student leaders, feared that a violent escalation of the movement would undermine public support and ultimately prove self-defeating (Respondents 3, 4, 9 and 10). It proved problematic that no formal decision-making process was in place: proposals for escalating the movement were made in different meetings, and the variation in how these meetings were composed meant that the proposals were met with different reactions at different times, precluding the formation of a clear consensus (Respondent 6).

The crisis turned acute when, on 23 March, Ma Ying-jeou reiterated his view on the CSSTA. Urging the students to end the occupation, he called for a quick ratification of the trade agreement, virtually dismissing all potential for negotiation (Ministry of Foreign Affairs, ROC 2014). Although the students had previously threatened to escalate should the ultimatum pass without a response, the leading groups could not decide on a common course of action. At this critical juncture, ineffective lines of communication, an opaque decision-making process as well as disagreements on goals and the means to attain them, contributed to the re-emergence of underlying frictions between various groups. When the key leaders decided against plans to occupy the Executive Yuan, a student group planned and executed the Executive Yuan action semi-independently. On the evening of 23 March, several hundred people forced their way into the Executive Yuan, located only 100 metres away from the Legislative Yuan. Premier Jiang immediately ordered the police to clear the building and through the following night the protesters were forcefully evicted from the compound. Several activists were put under arrest but, more crucially, the images of the police action and bleeding students would dominate the various social media platforms over the coming days.

This critical juncture marks the end of the second phase. During the first days, the Sunflower Movement demonstrated that Taiwan's civil society was able to sustain the occupation of the Legislative Yuan beyond the rapid and unexpected success of 18 March. Despite the high degree of cooperation between NGOs and student groups, the protesters had failed to trigger a response from the government, which in turn put the synchronization at risk. The movement had reached its moment of crisis.

4 Consolidation and mass mobilization

After the 23 March incident, the organizers realized that they had to find a strategy that would pressure the government before public support started to decrease (Respondent 10). In order to prepare the movement for a longer campaign, the internal structures had to be optimized. The leadership concluded that several factors had contributed to the initiative of the attempted Executive Yuan occupation. Among those were unclear communication structures, the problem of balancing the internal groups to produce a coherent strategy, and the failure to provide a perspective for a successful outcome of the movement. The consolidation of the decision-making mechanism therefore became a priority (Respondent 13). The mechanism that was established at the end of the first week of the occupation was not an ad hoc arrangement. Rather, it has to be understood as the formalization of the structures that had organically emerged during the occupation. These, in turn, were an expression of the social network and the power relations that had formed over the previous years. The structure, furthermore, took into account the particular spatial configuration of the Legislative Yuan and its surroundings, integrating both inside/outside and the already grown division of labour within and around the parliament. As the students had undertaken the actual occupation of the Legislative Yuan and held the ground inside the meeting chamber, they were given a numerical majority in the decision-making bodies, with the NGOs and other civic representatives taking fewer seats (Respondent 4).

The apparatus consisted of three committees. Inside the Legislative Yuan, a daily *Work Congress* (工作會議) was held to coordinate the various work groups that had been set up to maintain the occupation. Each group, such as the supply group, the security group and the media group, sent delegates that reported on the state of their tasks. Whenever an initiative demanded the cooperation of several teams, the cooperation could be planned in the Work Congress. After each meeting, the delegates reported back to their respective groups.

The main decision-making body was the *Joint Congress* (聯席會議), which convened on a daily basis outside the parliament. It held 10 seats for NGO representatives and 20 seats for student delegates.[6] While the Work Congress dealt with day-to-day matters of sustaining the occupation, the Joint Congress discussed the direction of the movement and the general strategy. The delegates were chosen in a way to represent as closely as possible the whole range of NGOs at the various stages around the compound. Whenever a pressing decision had to be made before the Joint Congress would convene again, the third body, a nine-person committee, met. It comprised five student and four NGO representatives, all of whom were part of the Joint Congress, and could convene without much preparation on an ad hoc basis. Consequently, it was able to make quick decisions in emergency situations with certain degree of legitimacy, as it represented the core of the Joint Congress.

This organization had important consequences for the internal power relations. In the Joint Congress and its emergency committee, all decisions were made by reaching a consensus. Although the architecture and composition of the committees acknowledged the fact that the movement was led by students, the practice of unanimous decisions meant that the numerical majority was secondary. Rather, the professors' experience, eloquence and personal authority proved more decisive, strengthening the relative weight of the NGOs (Respondents 2, 8 and 13). In the words of one student, 'Some of the students [in the congress] were freshmen, for many it was their first experience – how could young students stand against professors?' (Respondent 2). As a consequence, the NGOs' rather moderate concerns tended to prevail over the more radical views of the students.

The second priority was a better coordination within the working groups in order to ensure the effective implementation of the decisions that were taken by the leaders. This twofold reconfiguration had an appeasing effect on the movement. This was not because it was able to integrate all the currents within the movement, but because it allowed the core group to effectively set a moderate agenda in the Joint Congress and mobilize the movement's resources to realize it through the Work Congress.

The high degree of coordination and professionalism that characterized the working groups, particularly from the second week onwards, is best exemplified by the effort to project the movement's narrative into national and international media. The relative importance of the media group to the movement is demonstrated by the fact that the group had a delegate in the nine-person emergency group. Although the media had been identified as a key terrain for the struggle over the legitimacy of the movement from the beginning, the events at the Executive Yuan triggered a process towards systematization. Surveys published in the Taiwanese media in the aftermath of 23 March showed that more than two-thirds of the public supported the demands of the Sunflower Movement (*Taipei Times* 2014e). The immediate aim of the media group was to counter attempts to portray the movement as violent and illegal, and to uphold or increase public support. In the absence of direct negotiations with the government, projecting a positive image of the Sunflower Movement into the media and converting *declared* public support into *actual* supporters in the streets became the key strategy to pressure the government.

The media group and the international media group had several tasks. All around the clock they had to monitor and digest the various media. In the morning, the group screened the major daily newspapers, in the evening the major evening news on television, while online media were scanned continuously (Respondent 13). Based on the analysis of the collected data, the groups then briefed the movement leaders on media coverage concerning the Sunflower Movement. After the leaders had agreed on a response to the coverage, the media groups prepared speeches and press releases and scheduled press conferences.

Reducing the complexity of the narrative came at the cost of increasing internal tensions. The various themes of the movement were weighted differently by particular groups within the movement. The media group, however, faced mainly pragmatic choices, thereby alienating some of the groups that wanted to put the China factor or the neo-liberal character of the CSSTA at the centre of the narrative (Respondent 13). As the media coordinator of the Sunflower Movement explained,

When the government or the KMT said something, we needed to find the best story we were going to tell among all the possible routes.... Each day we had three to four people go to TV shows, and we had to react to events or stories in the same way. Producing the common story was our main task.... Different groups had different agendas: democracy, free trade, independence. We took the strategy to focus on procedures, because this was the one everybody could accept. But it was highly criticised.... Our response to criticism: we have to be concerned with the reality of the Taiwanese people. We are either successful or not, and this is measured by the support: we have to mobilise as many people as possible, then this is a sacrifice we have to make.

(Respondent 15)

The focus on the procedural question was motivated by the attempt to evade potential pitfalls of the other themes. The theme of Taiwan independence was seen as too risky, as it was deemed to play into the hands of those who tried to brand the occupation as a plot by the opposition party DPP (Respondents 8 and 15). The issue of free trade was avoided due to its complexity: against the background of Taiwan's history as an export-oriented economy, the idea that trade was closely related to prosperity is deeply engrained in Taiwan's self-perception, and this common sense was deemed too rigid to be evaluated critically (Respondent 14). The Sunflower Movement's narrative was therefore boiled down to the issue of democracy, which encompassed both the way the Taiwanese government negotiated with China in general and the procedural issue of reviewing and ratifying the CSSTA domestically in particular.

A growing challenge was the media's appetite for first-hand information. All major Taiwanese television stations inquired to interview movement organizers live during their prime-time evening news. To meet the large number of requests, the media groups had to train and prepare young and inexperienced people in addition to the more experienced leaders. To ensure that all readers and viewers would encounter a coherent vision irrespective of their chosen channel or newspaper, the spokespersons were meticulously briefed by the media group (Respondent 15). The key focus of these briefings was to translate a complex situation of legitimate civil disobedience during a situation of emergency into an easy language.

The use of social media had been expanded through the previous movements. During the Anti-Media Monopoly Movement (see Ebsworth, this volume; also Rawnsley and Feng 2014), a Facebook campaign had successfully contributed to internationalizing the movement and to counter Taiwanese mass media, some of which were thought to be strong supporters of Ma Ying-jeou's China-course (Respondent 4). The use of social media was expanded by the international media group during the Sunflower Movement. First, it aimed at broadening the languages to spread first-hand information about the movement globally. To this end, press releases were published in several languages (ultimately the group prepared translations in 14 different languages, including sign language), accompanied by blogs.

Second, they aimed at further reducing the complexity of the story. As the international audience was not familiar with the dynamics of cross-strait relations or Taiwan's civil society, international press releases included fewer details and aimed to make one concise point. Activists also crowdfunded a project to publish full-page advertisements in the *New York Times* and *Apple Daily*. The advertisement included images of protesters being hit by water cannons during the night of 23/24 March. The images were accompanied by a text that put the police brutality and the violation of human rights, such as the freedom of assembly and the freedom of press, to the fore:

> After the President and ruling party failed to respond, the students expanded their protest at 4am on March 24th. The authorities sent police to remove the peaceful protesters with batons, riot shields, belts and water cannons, beating them into submission. Police brutality resulted in multiple injuries to the protesters, who only had their bodies to shield themselves. The media, too, were removed from the scene.
> (Original test print of the advertisement, obtained from the organizers)

This ad campaign exemplifies that the events at the Executive Yuan, rather than harming the public support of the Sunflower Movement, were transformed into a narrative that intensified the mobilization process. After narrowing down the Sunflower narrative to the issue of democratic justice, the 23 March events allowed them to broaden the theme of democracy beyond the procedures of the Black Box and the review committee to also include human rights more abstractly, as previously done during the Wild Strawberry Movement. This was reflected by the announcement of the movement's major demonstration on 27 March. The organizers called for a six-hour event close to the president's office on 30 March, the motto of which was 'Defend the democracy! Send back the CSSTA!' It was during the preparation for the demonstration that the theme of democracy finally prevailed over the other themes.

On 30 March, large crowds followed the call by the Sunflower Movement. The estimates concerning the number of demonstrators varied between 116,000 (the official number provided by the police) to 500,000 (given by the organizers), making it the largest demonstration in Taiwan's recent history. Compared to the demonstrations against the media monopoly two years earlier, where the largest demonstrations attracted around 10,000 participants, the 30 March event represented not only a quantitative, but a qualitative leap. The CSSTA was not a broader topic than the media monopoly per se, but it was successfully made into a canvas for all kinds of discontent. The large attendance was the result of a successful synchronization and a matured organizational apparatus.

5 Decision and denouement

To the participants, it was obvious that the demonstration on 30 March was the high point of mobilization, and therefore of the whole movement. Although the various media companies in Taiwan chose higher or lower numbers across the range of estimates, it was hard to deny that the Sunflower Movement was a broad movement rather than a small handful of supposedly violent students. The decision to mobilize the people's voice had succeeded, but in the end everything boiled down to the same question: 'What if we have 500,000 people, but the government still does not react?' (Respondent 3).

The students and NGO representatives, who had been holding out in and around the Legislative Yuan for nearly two weeks, were physically and mentally exhausted.

The final push to mobilize the masses for the demonstration had drained their strength even further. The decline in the number of participants in the activities around the compound suggests that the public also considered the demonstration to be the movement's culmination (Respondents 10 and 15). The NGOs faced additional constraints: the activities around the Legislative Yuan tied up personnel and resources that could not be put to use for the NGOs' respective causes, such as protests against nuclear power or for land justice. The booths and stages also posed a financial burden. To cover at least a part of these costs, a donation box had been set up in Qingdao East Road. But, mirroring the decreasing turnout in supporters, the cash donations also declined from the end of March, resulting in a rising pressure to conclude the occupation (Respondent 5).

The terms and modalities of what such a conclusion might look like, however, were widely disputed. Although the set of demands had consolidated, it was unlikely that the government would respond positively soon. The terms of success had to be defined in another way. As both President Ma Ying-jeou and Premier Jiang Yi-huah had failed to respond to overtures from the movement, the Sunflower leaders shifted their attention to the speaker of the Legislative Yuan, Wang Jin-Pyng (王金平):

> When we occupied the Legislative Yuan, we knew there were two choices: Ma and Wang. We knew that they had a bad relationship, and that Ma would never accept our demands. So we negotiated with Wang.
>
> (Respondent 10)

The movement leaders hoped to exploit a feud between President Ma, who also served as the KMT chairman, and Wang Jin-Pyng (Respondent 3). The conflict between the two KMT politicians had built up over a period of several months. In 2013, the KMT's Central Evaluation and Discipline Committee had revoked Wang's party membership, accusing him of influencing the outcome of a legal procedure against DPP caucus whip Ker Chien-ming (柯建銘) (*Taipei Times* 2013c). Losing the party membership would have also resulted in losing his position as a speaker of the parliament, a position that came with the privilege of deciding on any police action on the grounds of the Legislative Yuan. Wang's position was strengthened when the party's decision was overturned by the Taipei District Court on 19 March, the second day of the occupation (*Taipei Times* 2014a). The same day, Wang failed to appear at an inter-Yuan meeting that had been called by Ma in order to discuss the situation at the Legislative Yuan, which was to include the president himself, Legislative Speaker Wang, Vice President Wu Den-Yih (吳敦義) and Premier Jiang Yi-huah. This development signalled that the split within the KMT had been transposed into the strategic environment of the Sunflower Movement. Wang's power to decide on a potential police action on the grounds of the Legislative Yuan gave him a token in the controversy with Ma and also made him a logical negotiating partner for the activists. Strengthened by the court decision, Wang deepened the wedge between himself and the president when he declared on the evening of 20 March that he had heard the students' voices and would negotiate in response to concerns from the students and the public. From this point onwards, the movement's strategy focused on this split. In the words of one Black Island Youth spokesperson,

> When Ma said something, we replied that we were against what he said. When Wang said something, we said, 'maybe we can talk about it'. Ma had often failed his promises, but we had more confidence in Wang. He seemed available to make an arrangement. As Ma wanted to exclude Wang, talking to Wang would strengthen him against Ma. It would be an insult for Ma if we negotiated with Wang.
>
> (Respondent 3)

Exploiting the Ma–Wang schism proved to be an effective tactical decision, particularly after the successful mobilization of 30 March. On 6 April, Wang came to the Legislative Yuan. In a press conference outside the parliament, he declared that he would ensure that inter-party negotiations concerning the trade agreement would not resume until an oversight bill had been passed, therefore effectively accepting the movement's demand of 'legislate before review' (*Taipei Times* 2014f). He then appealed to the students to consider leaving the compound in order to enable the democratic process to resume. This announcement opened a window of opportunity for the movement. With Wang being the only responsive voice inside of the KMT, groups within the movement pushed towards a decision, fearing that the occupation would enter an impasse if this opportunity was foregone:

> Wang had a fight with Ma. If we do not seize the opportunity with Wang, and the support declines further, then it will be worse. If we stay longer, [the movement] might be a complete failure. If we retreat now, at least the public support is still high.
>
> (Respondent 15)

Proponents of a continuation of the occupation raised concerns that none of the demands had been met: the CSSTA had not been officially withdrawn, none of the oversight bills had entered parliamentary review, Ma Ying-jeou had not apologized and a national conference was only vaguely on the agenda (Respondent 13). Those in favour of seizing the window of opportunity argued that the executive branch was still not available for negotiation and that the activists could not expect a better offer. Furthermore, the demand of passing an oversight law could not be met unless the students liberated parliament; the pressure therefore had to be upheld from civil society (Respondent 10). It is this view that ultimately prevailed after long discussions in several meetings. The decisive meeting in the Joint Conference resulted in a decision to end the occupation after 10 hours (Respondent 13). On 7 April, student leaders announced that they would leave the parliament three days later.

While the decision was taken unanimously within the core group, it was not taken without objections. Several of the leaders objected the decision but decided to accept it in order to keep the movement unified. On 10 April, the students left the Legislative Yuan, leaving the meeting chamber behind in a tidy state.

6 Conclusion: Taiwan after the 'Big Bang'[7]

The exodus from the Legislative Yuan concluded the Sunflower Movement. Some groups from the anti-neo-liberal current left the Legislative Yuan earlier to protest against the decision to leave, while a few pro-independence groups – united as the Free Taiwan Front – stayed outside the compound for a few days after 10 April for the same reason (*Taipei Times* 2014b). Observers and participants alike are divided on whether the end of the occupation marked the end of the Sunflower Movement or the beginning of something new.

The impact of the Sunflower Movement can be assessed on three levels. First, on a strictly political level, the CSSTA has been stalled and the change in political and social power relations makes it unlikely that it will be ratified in the near future. In addition, eight different cross-strait oversight bills were proposed to allow the monitoring of negotiations with China and are under legislative review, although at the time of writing none has yet been passed into law. And, while negotiations for the complementary pact for trade in goods continued after the Sunflower Movement, they were not concluded before Ma Ying-jeou and the KMT lost the general elections in January 2016. Already, in November 2014, Taiwan held local elections that resulted in huge losses for the party, and even previously solid KMT strongholds in Taiwan's industrial north were won by independent or DPP candidates. For his last year in office, President Ma was therefore a lame duck and unable to substantially further the rapprochement with China. Although Ma was able to arrange a highly symbolic meeting with PRC President Xi Jinping (習近平) on the neutral ground of Singapore in November 2015 (the first meeting of leaders of the two sides of the Taiwan Strait since the Chinese Civil War), the KMT was unable to overturn the trend before the presidential elections in January 2016. Ma lost the presidential elections against DPP candidate Tsai Ing-wen (蔡英文) and, for the first time in Taiwan's history, the DPP was able to secure the majority of seats in the Legislative Yuan. Furthermore, the political spectrum in Taiwan saw the arrival of new parties. Law scholar and Sunflower leader Huang Kuo-chang (黃國昌) was directly elected as one of five legislators who entered parliament for the newly founded New Power

Party. This election result cannot be separated from Taiwan's social movements over the past years. Therefore, the Sunflower Movement has directly contributed to lasting repercussions for the relations between China and Taiwan that must surprise all who see China's rise, and therefore cross-strait relations, as a unidirectional and crisis-free path towards integration (e.g. Mearsheimer 2014). However, the ultimate criterion for assessing the Sunflower Movement's political impact has to be the potential implementation of an oversight mechanism, because only this would mark a first step towards shedding light into the Black Box.

Second, Taiwan's civil society has experienced a thorough revitalization, building on the experience of strength during the Sunflower Movement. The post-occupation phase is characterized by a proliferation of groups, and views differ on whether this should be interpreted as split or as different paths in pursuit of the same goal (Respondent 11). In addition to the Black Island Youth, other groups such as Taiwan March, Formoshock, Democracy Tautin and the Appendectomy Project, to only name a few, have been formed by Sunflower leaders. Their activities range from local discussion groups and rapid street protests in reaction to current events to large-scale events, as in the case of Taiwan March. The groups pursue various paths, which range from training future activists to constitutional reform, usually showing that the capacity to mobilize support has been strong since the conclusion of the Sunflower Movement. A few groups, such as Formoshock, ran candidates in the 2014 local elections, and the formation of both the New Power Party and the Social Democratic Party can be traced back to the Sunflower Movement. Taiwan March, organized by the Sunflower Movement leaders Lin Fei-fan, Chen Wei-ting and Huang Kuo-chang, has more than 1,000 volunteers (Respondent 10), while the Appendectomy Project succeeded in sustaining a campaign to recall KMT legislator Alex Tsai (蔡正元), which only failed in the third and final phase (*Taipei Times* 2015). The youth's continuous interest in public affairs can also be felt in places such as the Café Philo. This café in Taipei has been organizing events on political, cultural and economic issues for several years. But the attendance has never been higher than since the events in spring 2014. More than 100 mostly young people come to the weekly presentations and discussions. The format was even expanded to other cities all over Taiwan, in order to provide a node for all kinds of social movements to present their issues. The student groups also continue to cooperate with NGOs, as was the case, for example, with the anti-nuclear movement directly after the conclusion of the Sunflower Movement (see Grano, this volume; also Rowen 2015: 16). The NGOs, on their side, continue to support the Democratic Front against the CSSTA, which has been reformed into the Economic Democracy Union to emphasize its broader focus after the occupation.

The synchronization not only intensified the cooperation between those groups but also established a strong link between civic groups and the general public. The quest for legitimacy for the occupation meant that convincing the public was more crucial than ever, and for this a common narrative had to be forged. But the high-profile 'state of emergency' of the legitimation crisis also meant that the general public was open to receive new narratives. The occupation therefore worked as a catalyst to transform the relations both among the groups and between the groups and Taiwan's society. In the words of a leading member of the media group,

> in the NGOs, we cooperate with each other more closely. Before, people promoted their own things, now – also with society – we vibrate with each other.... Before, people ignored NGOs, but step by step, they listen.... Taiwan's movements finally have a common language with society. [Before we] focused on what we wanted to say, not what society wanted to hear.
> (Respondent 14)

But only the coming years will show whether the dynamics of Taiwan's civil society can be sustained under a DPP government or whether the presidency of Tsai Ing-wen will lead to a decline of social movement activism, as was the case under the first DPP government between 2000 and 2008 (Ho 2010).

Third, and much harder evaluate, are the effects that the movement had on a personal level. Respondents have repeatedly declared that the Sunflower Movement has raised new questions for them, and that it had become possible to discuss subjects in the family that had previously been taboo. Participating in or simply witnessing the Sunflower Movement has influenced the life choices of many young Taiwanese, including voting behaviour, the choice of subject to study at university, the country to spend time abroad in and from which source to get news and information on social and political issues. For many, the Sunflower Movement has also brought the question of what makes them Taiwanese or Chinese back to the fore. 'We want to find out who we are,' as a young participant at an event at the Café Philo, who said he had not been interested in politics before March 2014, aptly summed up this personal quest. The consequences of those choices will only unfold in the course of the years and decades to come.

Taiwan's social movements during the administration of Ma Ying-jeou have come a long way. And while the Sunflower Movement is most adequately understood as the culmination of the previous struggles, it is probably also the starting point of a lasting transformation of Taiwan's civil society.

Notes

1 This chapter is the revised version of a paper originally prepared for the Joint International Conference by the 'Governance in China' research network and the Association for Social Science Research on China (ASC), held in Berlin, (21–22 November 2014). The research has been undertaken on a field research grant by the French Centre for Research on Contemporary China (CEFC). The author would like to thank all involved for valuable feedback and comments.
2 This went beyond economic benefits. For instance, one document by the Mainland Affairs Council outlining the benefits of cross-strait agreements mentioned Taiwanese students in China as having a 'greater peace of mind' as a consequence of a nuclear safety agreement with China (Mainland Affairs Council 2012: 29).

3 For the trajectory of the main groups and key individuals involved in these protests, see Hsiao, Ebsworth, Chen and Cole, this volume.
4 This was brought to my attention by Igor Rogelja.
5 President Ma stated that the students 'illegally occupy the Legislative Yuan building, paralyzing our legislature' (Ministry of Foreign Affairs, ROC 2014), while Premier Jiang lamented the 'disorderly manner' (*Taipei Times* 2014c) in which the students behaved. Other KMT legislators referred to the protesters as 'bandits' (*Taipei Times* 2014d) who should 'respect the rule of law in a democracy' (ibid.).
6 It was possible that each seat that represented one group was occupied by several individuals, meaning that some meetings were made up of 40 or even 50 individuals, although the number of seats, and therefore votes, remained at 30.
7 Respondent 14.

Interview data

Respondent 1, *Student activist*, interviewed in Taipei, 25 September 2014.

Respondent 2, *Sunflower Movement Spokesperson*, interviewed in Taipei, 25 September 2014.

Respondent 3, *Black Island Youth Spokesperson*, interviewed in Taipei, 26 September 2014.

Respondent 4, *Professor, Sunflower Movement core group*, interviewed in Taipei, 30 September 2014.

Respondent 5, *Taiwan Labor Front representative*, interviewed in Taipei, 1 October 2014.

Respondent 6, *Student activist, Formoshock*, interviewed in Taipei, 2 October 2014.

Respondent 7, *Student activist*, interviewed in Taipei, 4 October 2014.

Respondent 8, *Student activist*, interviewed in Taipei, 6 October 2014.

Respondent 9, *Student activist, Formoshock*, interviewed in Taipei, 7 October 2014.

Respondent 10, *Sunflower student leader, Taiwan March*, interviewed in Taipei, 7 October 2014.

Respondent 11, *Taiwan Association of University Professors representative*, interviewed in Taipei, 8 October 2014.

Respondent 12, *Student activist, Radical Wing*, interviewed in Taipei, 10 October 2014.

Respondent 13, *Sunflower group coordinator, Democracy Tautin*, interviewed in Taipei, 12 October 2014.

Respondent 14, *Sunflower international media coordinator, Democracy Tautin*, interviewed in Taipei, 13 October 2014.

Respondent 15, *Sunflower media group, Black Island Youth representative*, interviewed in Taipei, 21 October 2014.

References

Barker, Colin, Laurence Cox, John Krinsky and Alf Gunvald Nilsen. 2013. 'Marxism and social movements: An introduction'. In Colin Barker, Laurence Cox, John Krinsky and Alf Gunvald Nilsen (eds), *Marxism and Social Movements*. Leiden: Brill, pp. 1–37.

Beckershoff, André. 2014. 'The KMT–CCP forum: Securing consent for CrossStrait rapprochement'. *Journal of Current Chinese Affairs*, 43(1), 213–41.

Bourdieu, Pierre. 1988. *Homo academicus*. Stanford, CA: Stanford University Press.

Ho, Ming-sho. 2010. 'Understanding the trajectory of social movements in Taiwan (1980–2010)'. *Journal of Current Chinese Affairs*, 39(3), 3–22.

Mainland Affairs Council. 2012. *Opening Up and Guarding the Country. Benefits of the 16 Cross-Strait Agreements*. Available online at www.mac.gov.tw/public/Data/ 2101911582271.pdf (accessed 18 July 2014).

Mainland Affairs Council. 2013a. *What are the Concrete Effects of Cross-Strait Cultural and Educational Exchanges?* Available online at www.mac.gov.tw/ct.asp?xItem=64419 &ctNode=5944& mp=3 (accessed 18 July 2014).

Mainland Affairs Council. 2013b. *What Assistance or Incentives Does the Government Have on Cross-Strait Cultural and Educational Activities?* Available online at www. mac.gov.tw/ct.asp?xItem= 64420&ctNode=5944&mp=3 (accessed 18 July 2014).

Mearsheimer, John J. 2014. 'Taiwan's dire straits'. *The National Interest*, 130 (March–April), 29–39.

Ministry of Foreign Affairs, ROC. 2014. *President Ma News Briefing on the CrossStrait Trade in Services Agreement*. Available online at www.mofa.gov.tw/EnMobile/ News_ Content.aspx?s=47CD44F4B19DAA56 (accessed 29 March 2015).

Rawnsley, Ming-yeh T. and Chien-san Feng. 2014. 'Anti–media-monopoly policies and further democratisation in Taiwan'. *Journal of Current Chinese Affairs*, 43(3), 105–28.

Rowen, Ian. 2015. 'Inside Taiwan's Sunflower Movement: Twenty-four days in a student-occupied parliament, and the future of the region'. *The Journal of Asian Studies*, 74(01), 5–21.

Taipei Times. 2013a. *Protesters Occupy Government Building*. Available online at www. taipeitimes.com/News/front/archives/2013/08/20/2003570116 (accessed 26 August 2014).

Taipei Times. 2013b. *Students, Police Clash in Front of Legislature*. Available online at www.taipeitimes.com/News/front/archives/2013/08/01/2003568649 (accessed 30 March 2015).

Taipei Times. 2013c. *Wang's KMT Membership Revoked as per Ma Request*. Available online at www.taipeitimes.com/News/front/archives/2013/09/12/2003571929 (accessed 29 March 2015).

Taipei Times. 2014a. *Court Rules for Wang in KMT Membership Fight*. Available online at www.taipeitimes.com/News/front/archives/2014/03/20/2003586091 (accessed 29 March 2015).

Taipei Times. 2014b. *Hawks' Coalition to Stay Outside Legislative Yuan*. Available online at www.taipeitimes.com/News/front/archives/2014/04/09/2003587609 (accessed 2 April 2015).

Taipei Times. 2014c. *Jiang–Protester Talks Fail Before They Start*. Available online at www.taipeitimes.com/News/front/archives/2014/03/23/2003586322 (accessed 29 March 2015).

Taipei Times. 2014d. *Protest Hindering Crucial Bills: KMT*. Available online at www. taipeitimes.com/News/taiwan/archives/2014/04/06/2003587402 (accessed 29 March 2015).

Taipei Times. 2014e. *Survey Shows Public Favors Students' Demands*. Available online at www.taipeitimes.com/News/taiwan/archives/2014/03/27/2003586646 (accessed 29 March 2015).

Taipei Times. 2014f. *Wang Vows Monitoring Law Before Pact*. Available online at www. taipeitimes.com/News/front/archives/2014/04/07/2003587457 (accessed 30 March 2015).

Taipei Times. 2015. *Alex Tsai Survives Appendectomy Project*. Available online at www. taipeitimes.com/News/front/archives/2015/02/15/2003611602 (accessed 30 March 2015).

8 The China factor and Taiwan's civil society organizations in the Sunflower Movement

The case of the Democratic Front Against the Cross-Strait Service Trade Agreement

Hsu Szu-chien

Introduction and research question

On 18 March of 2014, a group of students and civil society organization (CSO) activists broke into the building of the Legislative Yuan (LY) in Taiwan and then occupied the assembly hall for more than three weeks to protest against the passing of the Cross-Strait Service Trade Agreement (CSSTA) in the legislature. This is the famous 318 Sunflower Movement, better known as the Sunflower Movement. This chapter argues that the occupation of the LY, which was dominated by the action of students, was not merely a student movement (Wright 2014: 193) or a student-led movement (Romberg 2014: 2). Actually, and more importantly, it was a culmination of a long series of contentions and a confluence of diverse streams of many CSOs in the past few years. These CSOs that flocked together in the Sunflower Movement were originally of very different backgrounds, both in terms of the issues they were concerned with and in the major ideas or ideology that drove them. It was the multiple impacts of the 'China factor' that actually brought them eventually together and made the Sunflower Movement possible. The Sunflower Movement, therefore, should be understood as a collective self-defence by Taiwan's civil society against the multiple impacts of the 'China factor', and the Janus-faced 'China factor' in the Sunflower Movement has allowed the CSOs to develop a wider and closer solidarity network.

Some of the existing literature studying the Sunflower Movement follows the convention of social movement studies in emphasizing elite disunity as a political opportunity (Ho 2015; Smith and Yu 2014), the mobilization processes (Ho 2015; Chen and Liao 2014; Chen *et al.* 2014) and public perceptions (Kuan 2014; Liu 2014; Wu and Hsieh 2014), while other studies emphasize the significance of the impact of China (Jieh-min Wu 2014, 2015; Chien-huei Wu 2015). The former analyse the movement with the framework of general theories, whereas the latter employ a more contextualized approach. This chapter adopts a mixed analytical strategy, that is, it contextualizes the theoretical explanation with the China factor and focuses on CSOs as the unit of analysis. This chapter thus asks the following questions:

1 When and how did the CSOs get involved in the Democratic Front Against the Cross-Strait Service Trade Agreement (DFACSSTA) and the Sunflower Movement? (Time, event, connection, purpose)
2 What was the major context under which the CSOs became involved in the DFACSSTA?
3 How and to what extent did the China factor in the movement against CSSTA change these CSOs in their ideas, organization and activities?
4 Has the participation in DFACSSTA changed the CSOs' attitudes towards or perception of cross-strait relations and China?

By answering these questions, this chapter argues that it was the 'China factor' that brought CSOs of different backgrounds together, forming overlapping movement purpose and identity and thus pooling together the resources they had to make the Sunflower Movement possible. For such an argument, the 'China factor' plays a crucial role. In this chapter, the 'China factor' in Taiwan is defined as follows:

> The China Factor refers to the direct or indirect effects that China generates in various public domains in Taiwan. The effects may be the results of intentional measures that the Chinese government, firms, or social actors take toward Taiwan. But they may also be unintended consequences of the mere existence of China as an objective structure for Taiwan's state, economy, or society. The China factor is not merely reflected in the attitudes of Taiwan's citizens and society toward unification or independence as in the context of traditional Taiwanese politics. The China factor is mirrored in an integrated perception of China given its impacts in various dimensions, such as security, sovereignty, economy, social equality, culture, national identity, and so on. The impact of China is perceived and interpreted by various agents in Taiwan with their own social, economic, and political predispositions and prejudices. The manifestation of the China factor is thus also a social construction in Taiwan.[1]

The qualitative data in this chapter draw from both the author's personal participatory observations in the Sunflower Movement and a series of interviews with leaders of CSOs that were heavily involved in the Sunflower Movement conducted in May 2014, less than two months after the movement ended. These CSOs were all members of the anti-CSSTA coalition and the Democratic Front against Cross-Strait Service Trade Agreement (DFACSSTA),[2] and each of them had their own context through which they were involved in the movement and played their own distinctive role. Some of the CSOs were well-established organizations with rich experiences in highly politicized events such as the Sunflower Movement, but some of them were previously less politicized and more focused on their own specialized issues. Some of these groups were of a larger scale, with many members and a more complicated internal structure, whereas some others were of a small scale and composed of a few key activists. The interviews conducted for this chapter can only cover one representative for each CSO, which may not perfectly reflect the diversity and complexity of the positions and perceptions within the group. But all of them hold important positions within their group, either as the most prominent leader or one of the leading figures within their organization, and were personally very involved in the movement.[3]

This chapter therefore intends to provide an account of how the impact of China has been gradually perceived by these CSOs in their own contexts and how these seemingly different contexts of the China factor eventually brought the CSOs together in the movement. The chapter is organized in the following sequence. After the introduction, the second section will examine the multiple waves of social movement prior to the Sunflower Movement, with analytical emphasis focused on how the overlapping mobilization and the common movement tactics led to their involvement in the DFACSSTA and how the China factor was relevant to each context for the movement. The third section then discusses different ways in which the CSOs' perceptions of the China factor changed in the movement. Last, the concluding discussion provides some general observations of the China factor and the CSOs in the movement.

Waves of previous movements and cross-sectional mobilization networks

Intertwined mobilization

The Sunflower Movement cannot be fully understood without tracing back to a prolonged and gradually escalated process of social movements and social mobilization. Some studies have already identified the relevance of previous social protests and the Sunflower Movement, but their analyses were either incomplete or without the context of the concrete actors (Yuen 2014: 74; Rowen 2015: 9–10). There were at least five to six important waves of social movement in 2012 and 2013, which paved the way for the Sunflower Movement. (1) In July 2012, the 'Anti-Media Monopoly Movement' was probably the most conspicuous social reaction to the China factor. (2) In February 2013 the 'National Alliance of the Laid-off Workers from the Shut-down Factories' (NALWSF, 全國關廠工人連線) organized a raid to block the railway to register their protest against the government's neglect of their demands. (3) Environmental groups such as the Green Citizens Action Alliance (GCAA綠色公民行動聯盟) and Citizen of the Earth (CET) then organized a huge anti-nuclear demonstration in March, with more than 150 CSOs and roughly 220,000 people participating. (4) In July and August, a group of netizens unacquainted to each other, taking everyone by surprise, was able to form a group, the Citizen 1985 Action Alliance, and mobilize more than 250,000 citizens to a mass gathering in front of the Presidential Palace protesting against the death of an abused soldier, Hong.

(5) Right after the incident, another shocking movement took place in August 2013, the '818 Land Justice (and Government Demolishment) Movements', protesting the Miaoli County government tearing down citizens' houses in the name of industrial park development in Dapu. On 18 August 2013, the Taiwan Rural Front organized a protest in front of the Ministry of Interior and then occupied the external entrance until the next day. (6) In September, a 929 Citizen Action Alliance (九二九公民行動聯盟), composed of around 20 groups and led by the National Alliance of the Laid-off Workers, assembled to protest against President Ma, who was supposed to show up at the Nineteenth Party Congress of the KMT. The KMT was forced to cancel the congress and delayed it to October. In each of these movements, some CSOs played a central role, while other CSOs were mobilized to provide support.

These waves of movement were initiated by different CSOs and aimed at different public issues. There might be overlapping participants of CSOs in different waves of movement, but there was no overarching coordinator behind the scenes throughout all these waves. Quite on the contrary, many CSOs were either not acquainted with each other as they spent most of the time focusing on their own concerned issue, or they joined a movement initiated by another organization merely as supporters. In the past, CSOs in Taiwan were either divided by their position on the independence versus unification issue, or by politicized versus non-politicized issue. But, in these waves of movements, the CSOs shared one common enemy, that is, the Ma administration. It was their frustration with the Ma administration that led them to join each other, which in turn led to the development of a mobilization network that made the Sunflower Movement possible.

For example, in the Anti-Media Monopoly Movement student organizations developed cooperative relations with a group of CSOs such as the Taiwan Association for Human Rights (TAHR) (台灣人權促進會), Taiwan Democracy Watch (TDW) (台灣守護民主平台), and a group of scholars, who organized the '901 Anti-Monopoly Alliance' (九零一反壟斷聯盟). In the protest of the laid-off workers, it was pretty much a one-organization action. Other CSOs did not really join the protests but rendered their moral support through public opinions expressed on social media. For example, in its annual press conference the TDW listed the event as one of the 10 most significant events of the year.[4] It is worth noting that the political tendency of the NALWSF, the leading group for the laid-off workers' protest, was seen as a non-green group, whereas groups such as TDW that lent support were seen as more pro-independence ones. This cross-ideological alliance was reproduced again in the protests against the KMT National Congress in September and October 2013. In that wave of movement, more than 50 groups joined, including not only pro-left (which is also seen as non-green) groups such as GCAA but also groups such as the student organizations and other organizations such as TAHR, Citizen of the Earth (CET, 地球公民基金會) and Black Island Nation Youth, which were seen as pro-green. Even the pro-green labour organizations such as the Taiwan Labor Front (TLF, 台灣勞工陣線) also joined the action.[5] Although NALWSF was not a member of DFACSSTA and was not involved in the occupation of the LY during the

Sunflower Movement, it still took part in the movement in an alternative manner by setting up its own tent on the street fringe around the LY. According to one interviewee, NALWSF was not willing to be perceived as 'anti-China' but it was absolutely against the Ma administration.[6]

The 'Citizens' Agenda' (公民議程) movement was also a typical case, in which a cross-sectional horizontal mobilization network among CSOs was developed. In the aftermath of the 818 Government Demolishment Movement, the TDW proposed an initiation to invite some partner CSOs to discuss some important common policy agendas that would need joint collaboration to push forward new legislation or prevent certain legislation proposed by the government, including issues such as the Free Trade and Economic Zone (FTEZ), the CSSTA, the Fourth Nuclear Power Station and so on. In this joint effort, DFAC-SSTA, TLF, the Taiwan Rural Front (TRF, 台灣農村陣線), the Awakening Foundation (AF, 婦女新知基金會), TAHR, CET and GCAA were involved. They held four meetings together from August 2013 to the dawn of the Sunflower Movement in 2014. In that interaction, these groups were already aware that the nature of the challenges that they faced was not merely about positions in each policy but that there were major problems in the dysfunction of the LY, the blockage of citizens' rights such as the restrictive Referendum Law, and, furthermore, the deep problem in the constitutional framework that allows the government to be non-accountable and non-responsive.[7]

The birth of movement tactics

The multiple waves of social movement from 2012 to 2013 not only helped the CSOs of different issues and backgrounds to develop cross-sectional interaction and cooperation; they also helped the CSOs to learn the experiences of movement tactics from each other, which in turn contributed to the gradual development of the general strategy of 'occupation' and 'peaceful resistance' and the discourse of 'civil disobedience', which became dominant in the Sunflower Movement. The anti-nuclear movement and the land justice movement are good cases in which radical tactics were gradually developed.

The tactics of occupation or blockage of public space have been adopted many times in the history of Taiwan's social movement and contentious politics. The occupation of the Taipei Station in the protest of the 'Independent Taiwan Study Group' in 1991 and the occupation of the Ketagalan Boulevard of the 'Red Shirt movement' protest against President Chen in 2006 were only two conspicuous cases.

In February 2013, the 'Laid-off Workers' Movement', organized by NALWSF, occupied Platform 4 of the Taipei Main Railway Station, and some protesters lay on the railway tracks to paralyse the train traffic. These protesting workers were sued by the government but were later found not guilty in court. It was understandable why such a radical move was taken given that their demand to the government for unpaid funds and pension had not been properly dealt with for more than 17 years.

The same tactic was copied one month later by the anti-nuclear movement. In April 2013, environmental organizations such as GCAA and CET mobilized a large number of citizens in the anti-nuclear demonstration. Such an anti-nuclear demonstration has been regularly organized in recent years in Taiwan, but the number of protesters increased tremendously in the one in 2013. One of the main reasons of such an expanding mobilization was that the Ma Ying-jeou administration insisted on the construction of the Fourth Nuclear Power Station, even after the accident of Fukushima, when the opposition to such a policy kept increasing. The major leader of the movement, the GCAA, expressed in the interview that the efforts of the environmental groups to persuade both the executive and the legislative branch to have a public and substantial policy discussion on the nuclear power issue in recent years had all been futile in recent years. Thus they became very frustrated and saw no sign that the Ma administration was willing to communicate with them. Such a disappointment in the intransigent government and despair at the closed participatory channel in the existing political institutions led them to think that taking more radical action was necessary and justified. After the street demonstration, a small group of people occupied the main road of the downtown Central Business District (Zhongxiao West Road).[8]

In the land justice movement, the Miaoli County government's action of tearing down the house of the Chang Pharmacy on 18 July infuriated many CSOs. The rage from the civil society was expressed in the '818 Government Demolishment Movement', in which more than 20,000 people went to Ketagalan Boulevard in front of the Presidential Palace. Environmental groups (the Anti-nuclear Platform) and the laid-off workers (NALWSF) also joined in to support. In this event, the CSOs clearly raised the ideas of 'civil disobedience' and 'peaceful resistance'. After the demonstration, around 2,000 volunteers, led by the Taiwan Rural Front (TRF), occupied the entrance of the Ministry of Interior in the late afternoon of 18 August. The occupation lasted until six o'clock in the afternoon the next day, blocking the entrance of the building the whole day. This rare occupation of a government building by TRF set a precedent for the occupation of LY by the Sunflower Movement seven months later.

Contextualizing the China factor from different involvement paths

In the multiple waves of social movements prior to the Sunflower Movement, CSOs of originally different backgrounds were gradually involved together through cross-sectional mobilization. Four contexts can be identified for this process of gradual integration: the cross-strait-centred path, the anti-globalization path, the pro-democracy path and the movement partnership path.

The cross-strait-centred path

The first path through which the China factor is perceived and the CSOs became involved in the Sunflower Movement was the 'cross-strait-centred path'. CSOs that were involved into the movement through this path were either concerned with the China factor due to their pursuit and defence of democracy and human rights, such as with Cross-Strait Agreement Watch (CSWA, 兩岸協議監督聯盟) and Taiwan Democracy Watch (TDW), or because of their worries that the development of economic ties might undermine Taiwan's independent status and sovereignty, such as with the Taiwan Association of University Professors (TAUP, 台灣教授協會).

Since late 2012, many CSOs had already stressed the impact of China on the public issues that they were concerned with. Three groups are typical examples: CSAW, TDW and TAUP. As this chapter has argued, the Anti-Media Monopoly Movement led by the student group was a conspicuous case. But, regarding cross-strait trade relations, DFACSSTA was actually not the first. After the ECFA was signed, Cross-Strait Agreement Watch (CSAW) was established in June 2010 as a civil society organization to monitor the negotiation of all the cross-strait agreements. The key person of this organization was lawyer Lai, who was also the key person in DFACSSTA. On the day after the ECFA was signed, 30 June 2010, a group of 18 CSOs held a press conference to announce the establishment of the Cross-Strait Agreement Watch to monitor the negotiation and implementation of the cross-strait agreements from the perspective of civil society. In October 2010, two DPP legislators became the chairpersons of the Committee for Interior Affairs. During the review of the 'Cross-strait Bilateral Investment Protection and Promotion Agreement' and the 'Cross-strait Medical and Healthcare Cooperation Agreement', the committee was able to establish precedents for administrative officials to make reports to the Legislative Committee (chaired by these DPP legislators) before the agreement was signed. From then on, the CSAW (and later the DFACSSTA) was able to bring supervision of the cross-strait agreements by civil society into the LY with the support of the DPP legislators.[9] Table 8.1 shows the important events that CSAW held from 2010 to 2012.

The second example in this path was TDW. TDW was established by a group of university professors to join and to protect the protesting students in the Wild Strawberry Movement after the visit of Chen Yunlin in 2008. From its very beginning, TDW was deeply concerned about the impact of the China factor. After its establishment, it became involved in many events dealing with the China factor. From late 2010 it started to advocate granting Chinese students rights to health care treatment equal to those of other foreign students. In April 2013, six members of TDW co-authored and promulgated a document, *The Manifesto of the Free*, to advocate developing a partnership with Chinese civil society organizations across the strait and oppose a formal political settlement before both sides became totally free societies. In May 2013, a delegation from TDW visited the Mainland Affairs Council and demanded the Council include the 'humanitarian visitation rights' when negotiating with China on the representative offices across the strait. In short, TDW has been one of the closest partners of CSAW since the ECFA in monitoring the cross-strait policies and agreements of the Ma administration. TDW was also one of the first two major

Table 8.1 Important events of the Cross-Strait Agreement Watch (CSAW) 2010–12*

Date	Event
30 June 2010	Press conference reacting to ECFA
10 July 2010	Formally established
September 2010	Protesting the opening of imports of blood serum from China
October 2010	Two DPP legislators became committee chairpersons
2 December 2010	Supporting Liu Xiaobo
February 2011	14 Taiwanese citizens 'repatriated' to China by the Philippines
May 2011	The credit information centre (Chinese bank access)
July 2011	Two Taiwanese citizens face death penalty in China
October 2011	Presenting 'human rights lists' to SEF
May 2012	Investor Protection Agreement – 'human rights article'
August 2012	Reacting to the SEF-ARATS meeting – raising human rights issue list
September 2012	Opposing opening the Taiwan market to China's lawyers
December 2012	Opposing media merging and monopoly

Note
* Data acquired from author's interview and website records.

organizations, together with CSAW, to raise the idea of 'cross-strait agreement supervision legislation'.[10]

These two groups raised their opposition to or suspicion of the cross-strait policies or agreements mainly based on the principles of democracy or human rights, and sometimes on the principle of social equality or justice. In comparison, TAUP was concerned about the cross-strait issue, mainly from the perspective of defending Taiwan's independent status of sovereignty. According to the TAUP interviewee, TAUP was already concerned with China's impact through the cross-strait economic ties after ECFA. When the CSSTA was signed and publicized in June 2013, TAUP members were all appalled by the content of the agreement. They thought the agreement was not only democratically illegitimate and socially unjust but also opened the gates for the Chinese Trojan Horse to dominate Taiwan's economy. They therefore had an extremely strong sense of crisis and urgency. After approaching the DPP, they came to understand that the DPP had too many pragmatic considerations and constraints in political operation and was not likely to take prompt and decisive action in the LY. The TAUP decision-making body (the chairperson and the executive committee) decided that TAUP should take action on its own. They decided to hold a mass rally on 27 July 2013 on Ketagalan Boulevard. TAUP tried to invite other active groups such as CSAW and TDW, but did not get any clear response. The TAUP then found that TDW and CSAW were about to hold another rally on 28 July. TAUP did not cancel the event but they recommended to their own mobilized supporters that they join the event held by TDW and CSAW the next day, and this paved the way for further cooperation between TAUP and the CSAW/TDW team in the later efforts of opposing CSSTA.[11]

The anti-globalization path

The second path through which the CSOs became involved in the Sunflower Movement was through the anti-globalization context. Groups such as TLF, TRF, GCAA and the Taiwan Alliance for Advancement of Youth Rights and Welfare (TAAYRW, 台灣少年權益與福利促進聯盟) were typical examples.

The Taiwan Labour Front (TLF) was one of the most important CSOs on labour-related issues in Taiwan. It is well known that labour-related CSOs in Taiwan have been very divided owing to their political positions on pro-independence versus pro-unification, or their attitudes towards China. TLF has been a major labour CSO on the pro-independence side since TLF started its activities with the *dangwai* as early as under authoritarian rule in the 1980s.[12] Its involvement in the Sunflower Movement was due to its concern about the potential impact of CSSTA on Taiwan's labour market and economic inequality. In fact, TLF was probably the first CSO that paid attention to the impact of cross-strait economic ties on Taiwan's labour market. According to the TLF interviewee, the laid-off workers from the shut-down factories, who moved to China in the late 1990s, reflected the first wave of the China impact. As early as 2007, even before ECFA was passed, the TLF had already held many public meetings discussing the potential negative impact of ECFA on Taiwan's labour market. It made that judgement according to the conditions of Hong Kong after the Closer Economic Partnership Agreement (CEPA, 內地與香港關於建立更緊密經貿關係安排). TLF therefore became the core partner, alongside CSAW once the latter had been established. The TLF interviewee also criticized the pro-independence camp and DPP for not having consistent positions on the trade issue. The interviewee claimed that, on many public occasions when he was with the green camp people opposing either trade with China or the import of American beef, those green camp people always emphasized that they were not opposing trade with the US or opposing the US per se. He basically thought that such a position held by the green camp could only weaken their own argument if challenged by the logic of globalization.[13]

Taiwan Rural Front (TRF), in a similar way to TLF, is also a left-wing organization holding an ideology against globalization. However, it was not a pro-independence group. When talking about the Sunflower Movement, the interviewee of TRL talked about the close relationship that TRF had with social organizations in China and interviewees' personal experiences and observations in China. The TRF interviewee held that it was too short-sighted to talk about the Sunflower Movement merely within the political context of Taiwan. It should be understood within the global context of capitalism and how the societies in each country resisted the concentration of capital around the world. As for Taiwan's relationship with the global capital, the TRF interviewee traced it back to Taiwan's entry to the WTO. By comparing how the Lee Teng-hui administration dealt with the potential impact on Taiwan's agriculture and how the Ma administration dealt with the potential impact on Taiwan's service sectors, the TRF interviewee said that both political leaders were determined to move forward in the direction of globalization, but the Lee administration did much more in coping with potential impact, particularly in communicating with the possible affected social sectors, than the Ma administration. The interviewee did not deny the fact that globalization could bring about economic development in GDP. However, while the GDP in Taiwan has been growing every year, the average wage is the same as 16 years ago. This proved, the interviewee pointed out, that there was a big problem in distribution. Therefore, the interviewee emphasized, that is the reason why so many young people came out to the streets in recent years, not only in the Sunflower Movement. The China factor, in the analysis of the TRF interviewee, was merely a surrogate for globalization. It was undeniable that further globalization through deeper economic ties and more trade agreements would inevitably wreak further havoc on the unequal distribution of Taiwan's society, but it would have the same effect on China's society. In short, the interviewee opposed interpreting the Sunflower Movement merely as an anti-China movement.[14]

GCAA was very similar to TRF, in that it was against globalization and was internationalist and left-wing in ideological background. As described earlier in this chapter, many CSOs became partners with GCAA through the anti-nuclear movement, and GCAA also supported many other movements. It developed a closer partnership with groups such as TDW and TAHR in discussing 'referendum' as a strategy of opposing the Fourth Nuclear Power Station. GCAA was one of the founding members of the DFACSSTA and also joined the 'Citizens' Agenda' hosted by the TDW. The GCAA interviewee, when talking about the China factor in the Sunflower Movement, criticized the mobilization strategies adopted by other CSOs by appealing to nationalistic and purely democratic logics. Appealing to the nationalistic logic could be exhausted if the DPP were in power to negotiate with China on trade agreements, whereas the democratic logic could also lose steam if all democratic procedures were observed. As far as the GCAA is concerned, trade agreements are nothing but the international rich class exploiting the poor in all the countries involved in free trade. Nevertheless, on the other hand, there was also an important difference between GCAA and many other left-oriented CSOs in Taiwan: many, if not most, of the left-oriented CSOs were politically anti-independence or pro-unification. More concretely, many left-oriented CSOs intentionally refrained from criticizing China lest they be perceived as aligned with the pro-independence groups. As stated earlier, this was also the reason why groups such as NALWSF were not willing to directly participate in or were not directly mobilized to join the Sunflower Movement. GCAA was not afraid of criticizing China, although not in a nationalistic manner. For them, Chinese investment in Taiwan is no different from any foreign other investment as an agent of globalized capitalism. Chinese capitalism is also a part of global capitalism. The GCAA interviewee informed me that he had a debate with other civil society colleagues in the left circle in Taiwan and criticized them in that they saw Chinese investment as less evil than Western capitalism.[15]

There are also CSOs that are involved in the movement through the anti-globalization context without so ideological tendencies as the previous three groups. The debate on the impact of China on the hair and beauty salon industry is a good example to illustrate such a contrast. When talking about the issue, the GCAA interviewee raised his disagreement at accusing Chinese investment of being the potential exploiter of Taiwan's labour. For him, the Taiwanese hair and beauty salon businesses are the real exploiters, given the existing system of utilizing their cooperation with schools for the cheap labour of the students. However, organizations such as the Taiwan Alliance for Advancement of Youth Rights and Welfare (TAAYRW) and the Awakening Foundation (AF) had different views. For TAAYRW, which was specialized in protecting the rights of the young, the interviewee pointed out that the CSSTA was not clear about whether the same labour regulations would be applied to the Chinese investors in this industry in Taiwan. The local companies worried that, if the average pay or the working hours were further limited, as advocated by the CSOs but the same regulations could not be applied to the Chinese investors, then there would be unfair competition. Thus, TAAYRW opposed the CSSTA because the Ma administration kept a very vague attitude on issues like this. The TAAYRW interviewee thought the government intentionally kept this vague when the CSSTA was signed.[16] For the interviewee of the AF, she also admitted that the Taiwanese businesses in the hair and beauty salon industry were themselves notorious for exploiting student workers, but she also emphasized that the business cultures of Chinese firms were equally bad, if not worse. The Chinese companies not only were well known for exploiting workers but also had bad names for sexual discrimination, which was to the major concern of organizations such as AF.[17] For organizations such as TAAYRW and AF, the concern was about the possible negative impacts of Chinese investment in the service trade, not out of ideological grounds or nationalism but out of very concrete and pragmatic concerns. For them, the Taiwanese firms as well as the Chinese firms were equally responsible as an agent of globalization for aggravating labour conditions in Taiwan. Those Taiwanese firms with investment or business interests in China may also play the transmitting or facilitating role for lowering the labour rights standards in Taiwan. These Taiwanese firms were deemed the surrogates of the China factor under such a context.[18]

The pro-democracy/human rights path

The fact that certain KMT legislators and the KMT caucus had seriously violated democratic procedures, not only in the hasty passing of CSSTA in the LY committee but also in signing the agreement without consulting society in advance, has been widely seen as the fuse that inflamed the wrath of the CSOs and the students. But their dissatisfaction with the degeneration of Taiwan's democratic institutions, particularly during the second Ma administration, can already be observed in the many previous waves of social protests prior to the Sunflower Movement, as discussed earlier in this chapter. The China factor was blended into these events. There were several ways through which defending democracy or human rights motivated these CSOs to be involved in the movement, and the China factor was contextualized as: (1) frustration with the irresponsive Ma administration and LY in general and the undemocratic procedure to pass CSSTA in particular; (2) anti-authoritarianism against KMT and CCP; (3) frustration with human rights violations implied in CSSTA.

The first motivation was the most common one, that is, the frustration with the LY and the undemocratic passing of CSSTA in the committee by the KMT legislators. There are several phenomena worth our notice. First, it was interesting that many CSO interviewees from different backgrounds, without any question leading them during the interview, all held a similar observation that there had long been a deep frustration with the political institutions, particularly the LY, on their irresponsiveness, unrepresentativeness and lack of checks and balances under the Ma administration. Interestingly, both groups like GCAA, which was not pro-independence, and groups like TLF, which was pro-independence, expressed the same sentiment. Even TAUP, which was strongly motivated towards Taiwan nationalism, had a similar feeling in losing confidence in the DPP's ability to properly defend what they perceive as Taiwan's interests in the LY. Other groups such as Citizen 1985 had parallel views.

The second interesting phenomenon was that many groups, again without any question leading them, came up with similar views that Taiwan's civil society had been 'pushed to the edge of the cliff' by the Ma administration by the eve of the Sunflower Movement, particularly by the hasty and illicit passing of the CSSTA in the LY committee. They all thought that the Ma administration was determined to disregard the most basic democratic principles to carry out its policy agenda, which, if not promptly and effectively obstructed, would cause Taiwan's democracy or civil society to pass the point of no return, heading to irreversible damage. Interviewees such as those from CSAW, TDW and Citizen 1985 were the most representative cases. Taking Citizen 1985, for example, the interviewee said:

> On the eve of the 318, we had come to a very clear understanding that the Ma administration was going to exhaust every possible means [to push forward its policy agenda], and had pushed people to the edge of the precipice. We citizens had also exhausted every possible channel within the institutions to stop it, yet it was obviously useless. The government officials were either pretending they don't hear us, or they only take superficial measures ...
>
> When CSOs met together in the evening of 17 March, we all had a strong feeling that we were already at a dead end. Therefore, we knew we were left with only two choices: either to give in or we have to fight to the end. Otherwise, there was no other way out.
>
> And except for the total disappointment in the government, there was also a long shadow of China looming behind the Ma administration. That shadow of China was suffocating to us, making us fear that we could once and for

all lose the life style we had taken for granted in Taiwan for so many years.[19]

Such a desperate feeling reoccurred in many interviewees' descriptions. It was therefore not difficult to see why the Sunflower Movement in a certain sense was inevitable. In fact, the citation above also reflected CSOs' deep dissatisfaction with and total disappointment at the irresponsiveness of the Ma administration.

Another line of argument is at a more abstract level, though extracted from concrete experiences. Another interviewee was an activist in the LGBT rights circle. She reflected that, through the contact with their counterpart groups in Hong Kong and China, they learned that gender rights, particular LGBT rights, were very heavily suppressed in China, owing to the authoritarian culture. Discrimination was rampant and the space for advocacy was extremely curtailed and limited. Such experiences alarmed many activists in the circle about the authoritarian tendency of the KMT regime. The perception that the Ma administration promoted closer ties with China by sacrificing democracy and people's interests was for them a signal of the coming back of an authoritarian culture under the coalition of the KMT and CCP. Such an attitude of anti-authoritarianism was a very important motivation for people like her to get involved in the Sunflower Movement.[20] These feelings of the coming loss of democracy were vividly felt not only during the movement but also long before the movement. For example, in September 2013, during the political storm of the power struggle wielded by President Ma against the LY Speaker Wang Jin-ping (王金平), TDW held a press conference with seven other CSOs to raise a warning to the Ma administration not to further ruin the checks and balances mechanism of the legislative branch against the executive branch.[21] But, of course, it was to no avail. Dozens of press conferences and demonstrations like this were organized by various CSOs but led to no response from the Ma administration.

Last, the signing of CSSTA through an opaque process alarmed CSOs with respect not only to the procedures but also to the contents, which contained articles perceived as threats and encroachment to human rights. For example, organizations such as TAHR and CSAW raised concerns about the negative impact on human rights if Taiwan's financial market were opened to the Chinese banks without proper regulations. The TAHR interviewee reported that the organization started to include the China factor into their major concern because they gradually felt the Chinese investment could have very concrete effects of encroaching on Taiwan's human rights. For example, if the Chinese banks were allowed to be established in Taiwan and conduct business in the same way as Taiwanese ones, they would also be allowed to have access to individuals' personal information in the 'Joint Credit Information Center', which is a semi-official entity holding national credit records. CSOs such as TAHR and CSAW worried that, since the Chinese banks were all controlled by the Chinese government, once they acquired the individual credit information of Taiwanese citizens no one would know how that information would be utilized and whether personal rights could be well protected. They therefore opposed the unconditional opening to the Chinese banking industry in the CSSTA.[22]

CSOs' changing epistemology and perception of the China factor

Through the analyses above, it appears that the China factor was basically perceived by various CSOs in quite different ways. It has to do with their original specialty, their ideological predisposition, their social connections and their own contact experiences with China. Each CSO has its own original epistemology of the China factor. However, in the process of multiple waves of social movement prior to the Sunflower Movement and the process of the Sunflower Movement itself, through involvement in DFACSSTA and in supporting and networking with other CSOs, their epistemology and perception of China factor may also have changed. From the interviews, this chapter found four types of change: first, from not being conscious of the China factor to being conscious (such as TAAYRW); second, from being potentially suspicious to explicitly opposing (such as AF, TAHR, CET, Citizen 1985 and CCW); third, from not opposing to a divided epistemology between politics and economy (such as GCAA and TRF); fourth, not much change as they had always opposed the China factor (such as CSAW, TDW, TLF and TAUP).

For the first group, the China factor was relatively irrelevant to or remote from their original concerned issues. For example, TAAYRW paid attention to the rights of the young and children. But when it understood that the service trade agreement would be relevant for student workers in the hair and beauty salon industry, it immediately found that the China factor was closely related and thus it was willing to work together with other CSOs on that highly politicized policy agenda, such as anti-CSSTA, and support other groups in a politicized contention. The transition, according to the TAAYRW interviewee, was not natural and smooth. The organization itself was a coalition of many smaller grass-roots groups. Therefore, it had to go through a process of internal debate, communication and persuasion.[23]

A similar situation occurred to the CET, which represents the second group, whose perception of the China factor went from potentially suspicious to explicitly opposing. According to the CET interviewee, as an environmental group CET was very much preoccupied by local issues such as pollution or community environmental rights. These are relatively grass-roots or local issues. Members of the group were not used to taking interests in highly political issues. But, when it was involved into the anti-nuclear issue, it found that it was not able to resist being sucked into a strong vortex of national politics. It was soon pushed to the centre of the anti-CSSTA movement by becoming a member of DFACSSTA and it immediately found that the group members were pretty unfamiliar with this impact of China. According to the CET interviewee, they invited specialists such as Wu Jieh-min (吳介民) or Professor Chen Chi-chung (陳吉仲) to give them training lectures. Together with the intensity of mobilization and confrontation in the movement, CET has now become a steady core member of the anti-CCSTA coalition in civil society. But the CET interviewee also emphasized that they were against the Chinese government but not Chinese civil society. They had good exchange experiences with Chinese environmental groups and admired what they had achieved. They are still open to future opportunities of collaboration and exchange with them.[24]

The third group can be best illustrated by GCAA, which is a CSO with a left-oriented ideological background and reservations about supporting anti-China sentiment in general. However, in the context of the Sunflower Movement and the anti-CSSTA movement, GCAA was very clear that capitalism by the Chinese state is still a kind of capitalism, which no doubt should also be objected to. Unlike other left-wing CSOs in Taiwan, GCAA thus is firmly opposing the negative impact of capitalism from China (as well as from the rest of the world) through CSSTA. However, it is still critical of appealing to Taiwanese nationalism or to purely democratic arguments in opposing CSSTA. Its left-wing ideological foundation has not been modified. But it was very flexible in joining other CSOs as an alliance in the movement. Therefore, its perception of China is divided.

The last group is one that has held the same perception all the way through, and perhaps the perception has been further strengthened by the movement. Groups such as CSAW, TDW, TLF and TAUP are of this group. However, we can see that there is also a difference or even division in the epistemology of the China factor within this group. For example, the TLF has been critical of the neutral position of the pro-independence group (such as TAUP) in not criticizing developing trade relations with other Western countries such as the US. Although CSAW and TDW have had a very solid partnership with the TAUP in waves of movement and in the Sunflower Movement, they still intentionally kept a distance from other pro-independence political forces. For groups of this category, the China factor is relevant to them through all three contexts.

Concluding discussions

By examining how the major CSO members of DFACSSTA became involved in the Sunflower Movement, and how they perceived the China factor, this chapter has acquired the following general observations.

First, the Sunflower Movement is not merely a student movement but also a movement contributed to by a prolonged and intensive period of mobilization of Taiwan's civil society organizations. The Sunflower Movement is better characterized as a comprehensive self-defence of Taiwan's civil society against an irresponsible and irresponsive administration with policies that amplified the negative impact of the China factor in many ways.

Second, multiple waves of social movements and contentions prior to the Sunflower Movement have paved the paths. CSOs are involved through three major contexts: the cross-strait or sovereignty-centred context, anti-globalization and democracy/human rights. Each context embodies the China factor in its particular manner and presents diffuse and different perceptions of what the

China factor is and how it impacts on Taiwan's politics. Among the 13 groups the author interviewed, the China factor was relevant in all three contexts for three CSOs (CSAW, TDW and TFL); for another three CSOs (TAUP, TAHR and CCW) the China factor was mainly relevant to the sovereignty and democracy/human rights contexts; and among the remaining six CSOs, for three (CET, AF and TAAYRW) the China factor became relevant mainly through the democracy/human rights and anti-globalization context, for Citizen 1985 the democracy/human-rights context was the most obvious context, and for GCAA and TRF the anti-globalization context was solely relevant (See Table 8.2).

CSOs holding one epistemology or perception may not agree with those holding another.

Third, despite such a division in their perception of the China factor, this chapter finds that CSOs of very different ideological backgrounds, or concerned with very different issues, were able to join each other in the battle fighting against the CSSTA under the banner of DFACSSTA. Even groups with pro-independence positions could work with groups with strong reservations about Taiwanese nationalism in the movement and prior to the movement. It may not be the China factor per se that brought all the groups together in the Sunflower Movement. Their common enemy, more often than not, was the Ma administration and its unpopular policies and undemocratic style of decision-making, instead of China in a direct way. Not all the CSOs in the movement held an anti-China position, nor were all of them really anti-globalization.

Table 8.2 China factor and the three contexts of the Sunflower Movement

CSO title	I Taiwan nationalism −2 – +2	II Democracy/human rights nature	III Anti-globalization nature	China factor context
CSAW	1	Both	Moderate	I, <u>II</u>, III
TDW	1	Both	Moderate	I, <u>II</u>, III
TLF	2	Rights (left)	Strong/left	I, II, <u>III</u>
TAUP	2	Democracy	Neutral	<u>I</u>, II
TAHR	1	HR/Dem	Neutral	I, <u>II</u>
CCW	1	HR > Dem	Neutral	I, <u>II</u>
CET	0	Rights (Env.)	Moderate	II, <u>III</u>
AF	0	Rights (gender)	Strong/pragmatic	<u>II</u>, III
TAAYRW	0	Rights	Strong/pragmatic	<u>II</u>, III
1985	1	Democracy	Neutral	II
GCAA	−2	Rights (Env./left)/referendum	Strong/left	<u>III</u>
TRF	−1	Rights (left)	Strong/left	<u>III</u>

Note
In the right-hand column, the underlined number refers to the major China factor context for the referred CSO. For example, the major China factor context for CSAW is 'democracy/human rights', and for TRF it is 'anti-globalization'.

Fourth, in spite of that, the China factor in one way or another has been more clearly perceived by more CSOs through the movement, and its complex relevance, indirect as it may be, to the domestic issues concerned by these CSOs has also been more keenly perceived, acknowledged and reflected upon. It will definitely affect the agenda and actions of these CSOs in the future.

Last, echoing the observation of Michael Cole, this chapter also finds that the Sunflower Movement has reanimated Taiwan's civil society, broadened its network and strengthened its solidarity (Cole 2014). Nevertheless, as the China factor itself is perceived differently by different CSOs involved in the movement, the fact that they were able to come together as a coalition in the battle of fighting against CSSTA in the movement cannot naturally guarantee the endurance of such an alliance in the battles to come.

Appendix 8.1 Membership of DFACSSTA

Chinese title	English title	English abbreviation
兩岸協議監督聯盟	Cross-Strait Agreement Watch	CSAW
台灣守護民主平台	Taiwan Democracy Watch	TDW
台灣人權促進會	Taiwan Association for Human Rights	TAHR
台灣勞工陣線	Taiwan Labor Front	TLF
婦女新知基金會	Awakening Foundation	AF
台灣教授協會	Taiwan Association of University Professors	TAUP
地球公民基金會	Citizen of the Earth, Taiwan	CET
綠色公民行動聯盟	Green Citizen's Action Alliance	GCAA
反媒體巨獸青年聯盟	Anti-Media Monopoly Youth Alliance	AMMYA
台灣環境資訊協會	Taiwan Environmental Information Association	TEIA
文化元年基金會	Culture Year One Foundation	CY1
中華民國殘障聯盟	Disability Alliance of Republic of China	DARC
中華民國老人福利推動聯盟	Federation for the Welfare of the Elderly	FWE
民間監督健保聯盟	Alliance of Health Insurance Watch	AHIW
台灣少年權益與福利促進聯盟	Taiwan Alliance for Advancement of Youth Rights and Welfare	TAAYRW
建教生權益促進聯盟	Taiwan Advocacy for Rights of Cooperative Education Students	TARWCE
勵馨社會福利事業基金會	The Garden of Hope Foundation	GHF
社區大學全國促進會	National Association for the Promotion of the Community Universities	NAPCU
台南市社區大學研究發展學會	Tainan Community University Research & Development Association	TNCOMU
台灣農村陣線	Taiwan Rural Front	TRF
人權公約施行監督聯盟	Covenants and Conventions Watch	CCW
公民1985行動聯盟	Citizen 1985 Action Alliance	1985

Appendix 8.2 Interview list

No.	Date time	Location	Organization	Interviewee's position
1	2014/05/12 16:00	Taipei	TDW	Chairperson
2	2014/05/12 19:30	Taipei	TRF	Secretary General
3	2014/05/13 17:30	Hsinchu	TAUP	Chairman
4	2014/05/14 13:50	Taipei	TAHR	Previous Chairperson
5	2014/05/14 15:30	Taipei	CET	Secretary General
6	2014/05/14 17:00	Taipei	CSAW	Secretary General
7	2014/05/15 10:00	Taipei	CCW	Secretary General
8	2014/05/16 10:00	Taipei	TLF	Secretary General
9	2014/05/16 18:00	Taipei	AF	Previous Board Chairperson
10	2014/05/19 19:00	Taipei	GCAA	Deputy Executive Secretary
11	2014/05/21 17:00	Taipei	1985	Secretary General
12	2014/05/21 19:30	Taipei	LGBT*	Core member
13	2014/06/04 15:00	Taipei	TAAYRW	Secretary General

Note
* The interviewee was not authorized to represent the organization (a LGBT group), therefore its genuine title is not reported here.

Notes

1 My definition of the China factor differs from that of Wu Jieh-min. Wu's definition is more a result of the intentional actions of the Chinese party-state with specific strategic purposes towards Taiwan. He adopts a political economy analysis. (See Wu 2014, 2015) My definition approaches the issue from a political sociology perspective by emphasizing the social network, perception and political context through which China's impact takes place in Taiwan.
2 Appendix 8.1 shows the membership of the DFACSSTA. The core groups among the membership are: CSAW (兩督盟), TDW (民主平台), TAHR (台權會), TLF (勞陣), AF (新知) and TAUP (台教會).
3 See Appendix 8.2 for the list of interviews.
4 See http://newtalk.tw/news/view/2013-05-20/36626 (accessed 19 May 2015).
5 See the report at the Coolloud Net: www.coolloud.org.tw/node/75714 (accessed 19 May 2015).
6 Interview no. 1.
7 Interview no. 1.
8 Interview no. 10.
9 Interview no. 6.
10 Interview no. 1.
11 Interview no. 3.
12 Chiu Yi-ren (邱義仁) was the first secretary general of the TLF.
13 Interview no. 8.
14 Interview no. 2.
15 Interview no. 10.
16 Interview no. 13.
17 Interview no. 9.
18 Interview no. 13.
19 Interview no. 11.
20 Interview no. 12.
21 The participants in this press conference included: Taipei Society (澄社), the Anti-Media Monster Youth League (反媒體巨獸青年聯盟召), the Black Island Nation

Youth Front (黑色島國青年陣線), Citizen Congress Watch (公民監督國會聯盟), DFACSSTA (反黑箱服貿民主陣線), GCAA (綠色公民行動聯盟) and ETC (地球公民基金會); see the website record of TWD: www.twdem.org/search?updated-min=2013-01-01T00:00:00%2B08:00&updated-max=2014-01-01T00:00:00%2B08:00&max-results=5 (accessed 19 May 2015).
22 Interview no. 4.
23 Interview no. 13.
24 Interview no. 5.

Bibliography

Chen, Boyu and Da-chi Liao. 2014. *Social Media, Social Movements and the Challenge of Democratic Governability*. Available online at http://fsi.stanford.edu/sites/default/files/chen_boyu.stanford_2014_oct_10.pdf (accessed 18 May 2015).

Chen, Boyu, Da-chi Liao, Hsin-Che Wu and San-Yih Hwan. 2014. *The Logic of Communitive Action: A Case Study of Taiwan's Sunflower Movement*. Available online at http://ipp.oii.ox.ac.uk/sites/ipp/files/documents/IPP2014_Chen.pdf (accessed 18 May 2015).

Cole, Michael. 2014. 'Was Taiwan's Sunflower Movement successful?' *The Diplomat*, 1 July. Available online at http://thediplomat.com/2014/07/was-taiwans-sunflower-movement-successful (accessed 18 May 2015).

Ho, Ming-sho. 2010. 'Understanding the trajectory of social movements in Taiwan (1980–2010)'. *Journal of Current Chinese Affairs*, 39(3), 3–22.

Ho, Ming-sho. 2015. 'Occupy Congress in Taiwan: Political Opportunity, Threat, and the Sunflower Movement'. *Journal of East Asian Studies*, 15(1), 69–97.

Jones, Brian Christopher and Yen-Tu Su. (Forthcoming). 'Confrontational contestation and democratic compromise: The Sunflower Movement and its aftermath'. *Hong Kong Law Journal* (Spring 2015). Available online at http://ssrn.com/abstract=2563434 (accessed 18 May 2015).

Kuan, Ping-Yin. 2014. *Generational Differences in Attitudes towards Cross-Straits Trade*. Available online at http://fsi.stanford.edu/sites/default/files/kuan.gen_diffs.20141011.pdf (accessed 18 May 2015).

Liu, Li Yin. 2014. *Individuals' Cultural Biases and Their Reaction on the Cross-Strait Issues: A Case Study on the Sunflower Movement in Taiwan*. Available online at http://aacs.ccny.cuny.edu/2014conference/Papers/Li%20Yin%20Liu.pdf (accessed 18 May 2015).

Philion, Stephen. 2010. 'The impact of social movements on Taiwan's democracy'. *Journal of Current Chinese Affairs*, 39(3), 149–63.

Romberg, Alan D. 2014. 'Sunshine Heats Up Taiwan Politics, Affects PRC Tactics'. *China Leadership Monitor*, 44, 1–20.

Rowen, Ian. 2015. 'Inside Taiwan's Sunflower Movement: Twenty-four days in a student-occupied parliament, and the future of the region'. *The Journal of Asian Studies*, 74(1), 5–21.

Smith, Stephen and Ching-hsin Yu. 2014. *Wild Lilies and Sunflowers: Political Actors' Responses to Student Movements in Taiwan*. Available online at http://aacs.ccny.cuny.edu/2014conference/Papers/Stephen%20Smith.pdf (accessed 18 May 2015).

Wang, James W. Y. 2010. 'The Political Economy of Collective Labour Legislation in Taiwan'. *Journal of Current Chinese Affairs*, 39(3), 51–85.

Wright, David Curtis. 2014. 'Chasing Sunflowers: Personal Firsthand Observations of the

Student Occupation of the Legislative Yuan and Popular Protests in Taiwan, 18 March – 10 April 2014'. *Journal of Military and Strategic Studies*, 15(4), 134–200.

Wu, Chien-huei. 2015. 'Dance with the dragon: Closer economic integration with China and deteriorating democracy and rule of law in Taiwan and Hong Kong?' *Hong Kong Law Journal*, 45(1), 275–94.

Wu, Jieh-min. 2014. 'Civic resistance movements in Taiwan and Hong Kong under the China factor'. In C.-y. Hsieh, N. Takahashi and H. Ying-che (eds), *Cooperation and Peace in East Asia*. Taipei: Avanguard, pp. 130–144 (in Chinese).

Wu Jieh-min. 2015. 'The path to the Sunflower Movement: How the Taiwanese civil society has resisted the China factor'. *Nihon Taiwan Gakkaihou*, 17 (forthcoming) (in Japanese).

Wu, Yi-an and Shu-kai Hsieh. 2014. 'Public opinion toward CSSTA: A text mining approach'. *International Journal of Computational Linguistics and Chinese Language Processing*, 19(4), 19–28.

Yuen, Samson. 2014. 'Under the shadow of China: Beijing's policy towards Hong Kong and Taiwan in comparative perspective'. *China Perspectives*, 2, 69–76.

9 The evolution of the anti-nuclear movement in Taiwan since 2008

Simona Grano

Introduction

On 27 April 2014, barely three weeks after the end of the Sunflower Student Movement,[1] the Ma Ying-jeou (馬英九) administration announced that it was halting work on the Lungmen nuclear power plant (the country's Fourth Nuclear Power Station, construction of which is basically completed), pending a referendum on its future (Hsu 2014). The historic decision was taken in light of several periodic protests over the past few years, which have put the government under great pressure (Yuen 2014: 74; Cole 2014), a topic which is studied in detail in Chapter 2 of this book with Cole's comparison of two new social movements and the different impacts these have had on the political scene.

Since nuclear awareness started to spread in Taiwan, towards the end of the 1980s, anti-nuclear concerns have been at times influential and at times forgotten under more pressing affairs; this chapter is particularly interested in the post-2008 resurgence of the anti-nuclear movement and in the possible reasons for why such a powerful comeback did indeed take place.

The analysis begins by depicting the origins of the anti-nuclear movement in Taiwan, right at the time when the martial law period was coming to an end. The second section attempts to sketch the organizational structure of the movement, its main strategies and its relationship with political parties and society at large from the 1980s until 2008. The third and main section focuses on the most significant post-2008 events for the anti-nuclear movement, such as the KMT-led proposal of holding a referendum on the island's Fourth Nuclear Power Plant (hence, NPP-4) and describes how the movement has changed in its organization, tactics and alliances with other social movements, with political organs and with society at large. Furthermore, a paragraph will investigate how public opinion in regards to nuclear energy has been transformed throughout the past few years, especially in light of the Fukushima nuclear disaster and, two years later in 2013, of the government's proposal to hold a public referendum on NPP-4. Last, this section will analyse the significance of the Sunflower Student Movement for the anti-nuclear cause and the ultimate decision to halt NPP-4's construction. The fourth section will try to gauge the political motivations, which have compelled the former KMT government to reach the decision to stop

NPP-4 from becoming operational and then analyse the newly elected DPP government's positioning towards nuclear energy.

Finally, in the conclusions, the chapter will try to pinpoint how the anti-nuclear movement changed its strategies and why it has become more successful and impact-oriented since 2008.

Origins of the anti-nuclear movement in Taiwan

In the aftermath of World War II, nuclear power seemed to be the most promising form of energy, because it guaranteed clean, low-cost supplies, thus helping power-hungry nations recover from the disasters of the war. In Taiwan, massive propaganda on part of the government and its state-owned energy provider, Taiwan Power Company (Taipower),[2] ensured high support in academic circles all throughout the 1980s;[3] things began to change after the Chernobyl incident in 1986 and the lifting of martial law one year later, which loosened one-party control over Taiwan, creating several outlets to criticize the state.

Construction of the island's first nuclear plant began in 1971 in Shimen (石門), Taipei County (currently New Taipei City); the second plant was started in 1974 in Wanli (萬里), also in Taipei County, while construction of NPP-3, set in Hengchun (恆春), Kending (墾丁), began in 1978. The three plants are all operated by Taipower – under the Ministry of Economic Affairs – and were projected to have a 40-year lifespan. They have been operational since 1978 (NPP-1), 1981 (NPP-2) and 1984 (NPP-3) (Ho *et al.* 2013: 775). All of Taiwan's three functioning nuclear plants are near the ocean and located by the side of geological faults, which has prompted the World Nuclear Association to list them among the world's most dangerous (Chan and Chen 2011: 4); the same is true for the fourth facility, currently under construction.

A real anti-nuclear power movement arose out of the dispute surrounding the idea of building a fourth nuclear power station in the country, even though a few sparse protests had already taken place when the construction of NPP-3 had started. In fact, we can date back the history of the anti-nuclear movement in Taiwan to the 1980s, as the government proposed Kongliao (貢寮), also in New Taipei City, as the chosen location for the island's fourth nuclear facility. The plant was planned during the tail end of the oil crises of the 1970s to diversify the nation's energy sources, but the project was then suspended after mounting opposition following the Chernobyl incident in 1986, which prompted many individuals to begin questioning the safety and sustainability of nuclear power.

In any case, in those years environmental issues were beginning to attract more attention among politicians; back in 1985 a joint petition against the construction of NPP-4 was signed by both KMT and *Tangwai* (黨外) legislators (Ho 2003: 692).

In 1988, Taiwan Environmental Protection Union (TEPU), one of the island's earliest environmental movements, ranking among its members several university professors and scholars, started a series of anti-nuclear events, ranging from public lectures to street protests (Hsiao 1999: 38; Fell 2011: 186). In those early stages the core of the environmental movement was made of scholars and intellectuals. Whether they really opposed the KMT's energy policies or whether the anti-nuclear banner was just a 'safer' valve to express discontent towards an oppressive political regime, the nuclear energy problem played a prominent role in their activism (Ho 2006: 74). From that same year onward, anti-nuclear intellectuals were joined by the active participation of residents of Kongliao, who feared the negative impact of the future power facility on their livelihood; thus, with outside help, they established the Yanliao Anti-Nuclear Self-Help Association (鹽寮反核自救會, *yanliao fanhe zijiuhui*) (Shih F. L. 2012: 297); barely one year after the lifting of martial law, the fierce battle between the state and those opposed to NPP-4 had begun. In Professor Chou Kuei-tien's words,

> Since Taiwan's first three power plants were all built previous to the lifting of martial law there was nothing that concerned citizens nor anti-nuclear activists could do. The fourth one, however, became activists' cause célèbre.
> (Chou Kuei-tien, 14 October 2011)

Furthermore, with the political liberalization process, which culminated in the lifting of martial law in 1987, street protests erupted and discontent towards the ruling party became increasingly vocal. Several previously repressed individuals and groups were finally free to express their anger without fear. In December 1987 several representatives of the indigenous people of Orchid Island (蘭嶼島, Lanyu dao) protested for the first time against the KMT's past policy of dumping nuclear waste on their land (Ho 2014: 8).

Nuclear waste has been shipped to Orchid Island since 1982, when construction of what was initially supposed to be a temporary deposit, was finally completed. Initially, the KMT had told locals that a fish-canning factory was being built on their land, which would bring with it new job opportunities (Huang *et al.* 2013: 1559). Once an NGO found out the truth, that nuclear waste was being sent to Orchid Island without previous consent from locals, a long and still ongoing controversy between the state and locals, and among local residents themselves, began. Even though opinions among the inhabitants of Lanyu are not uniform, some valuing the improved infrastructure and lifestyle opportunities that the new facility has created and some utterly opposed to it (Enn 2015), in the past few years, and especially since the Fukushima disaster in 2011, locals have upped their requests to have the repository moved elsewhere (Loa 2012).

Once protest erupted and gained status as a lawful way to express discontent towards the KMT's one-party rule (Lyons 2009: 60), the anti-nuclear cause, and specifically the battle to have construction of NPP-4 shelved, became the stronghold to attack the state and had the effect of bringing several individuals opposed to the KMT's authoritarian behaviour closer together. Nevertheless this convergence of positions between anti-KMT groups, which saw the DPP fully embracing the anti-nuclear cause, also symbolizes the beginning of what Taiwanese scholar Ho Ming-sho (2003) has termed a 'party-dependent' movement; in fact, nuclear issues gradually came to be seen as politically and ideologically identified with the green camp. While this union initially assisted activists in finding new outlets to disseminate their ideas, especially after the DPP won more than one-third of seats in the Legislative Yuan in 1992, in the long run it transformed nuclear issues into partisan topics, attributed almost solely to the opposition party. This, in turn, meant that many KMT legislators who were not supporters of nuclear energy did not dare to admit so in public, for fear of being ascribed to the DPP sympathizers' camp. While anti-nuclear voices were quite vocal all throughout the first half of the 1990s, protests quietened down in the second half of the decade and the anti-nuclear movement lost its salience, so that fewer voices against NPP-4 could be heard.

Actual construction of the plant began in 1999, only to be suspended for 110 days under the DPP government in 2000. At that moment, albeit for a brief time, the anti-nuclear power movement seemed to have scored a major goal in halting the construction of NPP-4. However, after the DPP's 'awkward' attempt at scrapping the facility, subsequently deemed unconstitutional by the Council of Grand Justice (Ho 2005: 412; Lyons 2009: 65), the government resumed construction in 2001 in what would become a thorn in the eye for anti-nuclear activists for years to come, as we shall see in the next section, which will sketch the organizational structure of the anti-nuclear movement, its main strategies and its relationship with political parties and society at large and how these have changed throughout the years, until 2008.

Anti-nuclear movement's organizational structure and early political alliances (1980–2008)

As mentioned above, the initial relationship between the anti-nuclear power movement and the DPP was symbiotic and of one sided-dependence on the part of activists (Ho 2003), who needed the contacts and organizational strength of its far more established political ally; however, over the years this relationship has become more distant and anti-nuclear activists have repeatedly struggled to break free from what had become, in their eyes, a burdensome affiliation. This gradual change has come about for two reasons: first, the ambiguous attitude of the DPP towards nuclear energy and NPP-4, which activists consider a betrayal of its original commitment and of its nuclear-free clause of the party's 1986 charter; second, the arrival of a newer and more radical generation of activists, less ready to compromise and to forgive the DPP's ambivalent behaviour towards the environment over the past years. The first cracks in this alliance started to appear from the mid- to late 1990s. In May 1996 the DPP joined forces with the New Party and a few KMT anti-nuclear voices trying to pass a bill, which would terminate all nuclear plants under construction. However, a few months later this anti-nuclear alliance inside the Legislative Yuan had weakened and it appears that the anti-nuclear cause was traded in for some other concession from the KMT (Ho 2003: 702). When protesters and anti-nuclear activists discovered this betrayal they blamed the DPP, whose behaviour they dubbed opportunistic. In fact, its initial anti-nuclear positioning had been instrumental for the party to gain in visibility and popularity. Perhaps the best sign of the growing disappointment towards the DPP's changing environmental stance is the establishment of a Green Party, by anti-nuclear advocate Kao Cheng-yan (高成炎) in 1996.

Anti-nuclear activists' desire to distance themselves from their former political ally took a slow and difficult path, which lasted more than a decade. While anti-nuclear concerns were a relevant topic of social concern until the first half of the 1990s (Ho 2014: 8), afterwards they gradually lost salience until the year 2000, when the DPP won the presidency and announced the termination of NPP-4 in October of that year, a decision that was briefly regarded as the final victory of Taiwan's anti-nuclear power movement against NPP-4. The KMT, though, opposed to the choice of scrapping the facility, tried to have President Chen impeached; already confronted with several major political and economic concerns, the DPP administration backtracked and resumed construction in February 2001. Furthermore, after it gained the presidency the DPP had to face urgent matters such as lethargic economic growth and gradually assumed a more careful attitude in regards to ecological safeguarding, deemed of secondary importance vis-à-vis the country's economic development (Ho 2005; Ho 2010: 14–15; Williams and Chang 2008: 88; Jobin 2010: 48). In 2004 and in 2006 the DPP government twice approved the supplementary budget for NPP-4, supported by KMT legislators, who controlled the parliament (Ho 2014: 9).

At the same time the party gradually changed its attitude towards social activists, who came to be considered a 'liability', and towards those regulations in place for protecting the environment; the Environmental Impact Assessment (EIA), which constitutes the backbone of this system of regulations, was defined by President Chen himself as roadblock to economic development (Ho 2005b: 350). By the year 2004, when Chen Shui-bian won his second electoral term, the cancellation of NPP-4 seemed like a distant memory.

After the DPP's betrayal of its pro-environmental commitments, anti-nuclear activists had to reorganize themselves and had to find new strategies as well as potential allies. In that moment, a schism among the anti-nuclear community took place between those who would rather remain cooperative towards the DPP without severing ties (TEPU, for example) and those who resolutely wanted to distance themselves from the ambivalent behaviour of the mainstream party. As stated by Ho (2014: 10), this second current represented the newer fringe of Taiwan's environmentalism, with several groups and organizations clustering underneath its broad roof.[4] The leading role in this newer stream of Taiwan's environmental movement is played by Green Citizens Action Alliance (GCAA), which was originally TEPU's Taipei Branch from 1992 to 2000; its members left the mother organization and established GCAA in 2000 (Tsui Shu-hsin, interview, 24 March 2011). Deprived of 'official channels' after having cut all ties with both the DPP and its former organization, the better-established TEPU, GCAA's activists were compelled to conceive of new ways to rebuild a wide anti-nuclear consensus among the general public. Therefore, they sought to rekindle old alliances, for example with Kongliao residents, who had suffered the most due to the DPP's unexpected 'betrayal' in 2001. Three years later, Tsui

The anti-nuclear movement since 2008 159

Figure 9.1 Anti-nuclear rock concert in Gongguan, Taipei, 5 November 2011.
Source: Simona Grano.

Shu-hsin (崔愫欣), the secretary general of GCAA, produced a critically acclaimed documentary on the lives of Kongliao fishermen, shattered by the incident that had taken place in 1991,[5] which attracted widespread sympathy for their plight.

Under the lead of this newer generation of activists, films, documentary, music – rock concerts in particular – and online campaigns have become valuable tools to win new supporters to the anti-nuclear cause.

Generally, though, in the eight years when the DPP ruled the country, nuclear activists were at loss in regards to finding political partners with whom to forge useful alliances. The ambivalence of the DPP and its anti-nuclear commitment disillusioned several militants and pushed nuclear awareness and related concerns into second place. The division between activists who refrained from distancing themselves from the more powerful political ally and those who openly criticized the DPP has become more deeply entrenched throughout the past years.

Most significant anti-nuclear trends since 2008

Since 2008 social movements have enjoyed a phase of resurgence, which has allowed activists to become more independent and less ready to compromise with political parties. This resurgence has been facilitated by a series of external events. According to some Taiwan watchers, experts and scholars, after more than three decades since Taiwan's democratic turn, starting from 2008 the country has experienced a partial return to certain intimidating behaviours vis-à-vis scholars and regressive policies (Ho 2010: 17).[6] This trend has coincided with the KMT's return to power after eight years. Nevertheless, as mentioned by Ho Ming-sho (2010: 16–17), rather than pressuring civil society into silence, 2008 seems to mark the beginning of a renaissance period for social movements, which had its symbolical birth with the Wild Strawberry (野草莓, *ye caomei*) series of protests in November of that same year.

However, it will be useful to pinpoint the main factors, which have to be credited with reactivating anti-nuclear concerns, prompting such a powerful and vigorous come back.

First, during the eight years in which the party in opposition, the KMT's had not changed its attitude towards social issues, remaining quite conservative on a variety of matters. Thus, when it regained the presidency in 2008 many social activists feared for their cause and saw many of the previously available official channels closing down (Ho 2014: 12). For instance, the Nuclear-Free Homeland Communication Committee, established by the DPP as a gesture of goodwill towards activists after its 2001 turnaround on NPP-4, was abolished soon after Ma became president. Fearing that their role in society was gradually being eroded, social movements shifted back to more 'impact-oriented' and attention-seeking techniques, such as mass protests. Second, the Fukushima disaster of 2011 gave rise to a series of anti-nuclear events and rallies, riding on the renewed visibility enjoyed by nuclear concerns. Third, in January 2013, the DPP and, later, the KMT unveiled their respective plans for a nuclear referendum, which will be the subject of the next section and, last, in 2014, the three-week-long Sunflower Student Movement's occupation of the Legislative and Executive Yuan had far-reaching secondary effects, which relaunched anti-nuclear feelings.

Seemingly different in their scope, the anti-nuclear movement and the Sunflower Movement have joined forces, so that a clear-cut demarcation between them is no more possible, with numerous anti-nuclear activists being part of the Sunflower Movement and vice versa.

Let us now examine through which methods and tactics activists have tried to increase the visibility of anti-nuclear issues since 2008, to fully exploit this favourable convergence of events.

Starting from August 2009, GCAA stepped up its anti-nuclear campaigns by planning a series of concerts in Kongliao and Fulong (福隆) beach together with the No Nuke Street Band. The intention behind these actions was to expose young people to the dangers of nuclear energy and in particular to the construction of the Fourth Nuclear Power Station, around which the two organizations planned a symbolic human chain event. As mentioned by Ho in his latest article on nuclear energy (2014), it is events such as these that played a pivotal role in distancing anti-nuclear opposition from politics, lending it a more easy-going image, which would later on enable the movement to cross the partisanship divide.

One year later, in 2010, the same two organizations, the No Nuke Street Band and Green Citizens Action Alliance, aided by a few smaller anti-nuclear groups, attempted to simulate a nuclear radiation contamination accident on the streets of downtown Taipei, using a fake barrel of nuclear waste, to see how the people would react (Tsui Shu-hsin, interview, 20 September 2011). They were stopped while trying to load the barrel onto the train from Kongliao to Taipei. Police forces were called in and eventually determined that the barrel was not dangerous; GCAA was thus allowed to bring back the barrel on the train with the condition that they would keep it covered and invisible to other passengers and as long as rail staff would escort it all the way back.

Another activity undertaken was the direct result of the increasing use of new social media among younger generations, for both online as well as offline activities. In fact, social media such as Twitter and Facebook are used both for actions that remain at the virtual level (e.g. online petitions or online campaigns) and to garner support for the organization of actual street protests that will then take place offline.[7]

The No Nuke Street Band used a more radical and aggressive cyber method: it hijacked the Ho Hai Yan Rock Festival website. With the help of some hacker friends, it filled this website with information on the Fourth Nuclear Power Station and on nuclear issues in general.

As we have seen, some anti-nuclear protests were taking place prior to the Fukushima nuclear incident; however, after the nuclear meltdown in Japan anti-nuclear activities and efforts were taken to a whole new level of visibility. In fact, for the anti-nuclear movement the importance of 2011 is twofold: first, the Fukushima incident gave Taiwanese anti-nuclear activists renewed vigour to organize countless protests, relying on the emotional fears created by the nuclear accident in Japan; and, second, being fully aware of the strategic political fallout of such an event taking place in the year preceding a national election, activists sought to exploit the nuclear meltdown to their own advantage.

Right after the nuclear disaster, in March 2011, 2,000 anti-nuclear activists protested all over Taiwan for an immediate end to the construction of the island's Fourth Nuclear Power Station. Protesters were also opposed to any lifespan extension for the three other, already functioning, nuclear plants (Asia One News 2011). Barely one month later, on 30 April 2011, 5,000 people joined an anti-nuclear protest in Taipei City, holding yellow banners and waving sunflowers[8] as part of a nationwide 'No Nuke Action' campaign against the construction of NPP-4 and in favour of a more renewable energy-oriented policy (Lee 2011); participants were so numerous that a new term was coined to describe the parade: 'the 430 movement' (430 行動, 430 *xindong*).

With the occasion of the World Environment Day in June of that same year, environmental groups protested, once again, against Taiwan's nuclear power policy. On this occasion, TEPU, aided by other environmental movements,

Figure 9.2 National 'No-Nuke Action Campaign', Taipei, 30 April 2011.
Source: Simona Grano.

organized a big gathering in Taipei to complain against the nation's nuclear power facilities.

In 2012, rather than declining, the number of protests increased. As shown by Cole in Chapter 2 of this volume, when President Ma was elected for a second term in that same year social forces that would eventually challenge its non-responsive behaviour vis-à-vis dissenters, started to emerge. The various protests, which culminated in the above-mentioned Sunflower Student Movement, put the government under pressure and influenced its policies, for instance in the decision reached in regards to the future of NPP-4, as we shall see towards the end of this chapter. The building up of social discontent was a gradual but relentless process.

On 9 March 2013, 200,000 people took to the streets in Taipei and three other major cities, again requesting that the construction on the Fourth Nuclear Power Station be halted. The protest in Taipei is to this day the largest ever anti-nuclear demonstration held in Taiwan (Taiwan Insights 2013).

Afterwards a series of anti-nuclear events was organized by the cultural community with several film directors marching at Liberty Square in Taipei, under the banner of the 'Movement to say no to a fourth, fifth or sixth nuclear plant' (不要核四, 五六運動). This anti-nuclear campaign, which began on 15 March

2013, included in its ranks several cultural heavyweights, including film director Ko I-chen (柯一正) and writer Hsiao Yeh (小野) (Tseng *et al.* 2013). The campaign, which aimed at bringing together individuals opposed to nuclear energy and to the construction of NPP-4, took place every Friday on Liberty Square, where activists and intellectuals held anti-nuclear speeches trying to raise awareness of the underlying risks connected to nuclear power and, more specifically, of the flaws and risks of NPP-4. Such anti-nuclear speeches and parades by cultural heavyweights are somewhat reminiscent of the early stages of the anti-nuclear movement in Taiwan, when scholars and intellectuals would travel to rural areas (下鄉) and impart their knowledge on uninformed villagers (Ho 2006: 54).

Furthermore, the Fukushima nuclear meltdown had several political consequences, which had diverse repercussions on various stakeholders and agents in Taiwan, ranging from political parties to social activists, all trying to fully exploit such 'real-life' dramatic events to their own advantage. In the case of anti-nuclear activists, it made the schism among the different factions become even more profound. While the TEPU once again chose to renew its cooperation with the DPP, GCAA and its newer allies opted to reach a wider audience, which would in no way be 'related to' or be 'part of' the KMT–DPP political rivalry. They were convinced that, by piggybacking on real-life issues (Japanese losses and dramas), they would be able to fully exploit the nuclear disaster to gain support for their cause and so they saw no need for compromise.

Political parties, realizing the growing significance of anti-nuclear issues for their electoral platforms, tried to jump on the anti-nuclear wagon themselves, the DPP by reverting to its early anti-nuclear stance and the KMT by supporting a gradual phase-out of nuclear energy.

In fact, as anti-nuclear activists organized a first protest parade against NPP-4's construction on 20 March 2011, the DPP immediately tried to relaunch its visibility by organizing banners of support for the protest in light of the upcoming presidential election of 2012. Activists became enraged at what they perceived to be a clear attempt to gain votes; hence they coined the slogan '核四是藍綠共業' (*hesi shi lan lü gongye*, NPP-4 is a joint venture of the green and blue camp) (Tsui Shu-hsin, personal email communication, 6 July 2012) to signal their distance from both of the two main parties, KMT and DPP, which were deemed equally guilty for the protraction of this controversial project. Former president Ma Ying-jeou, while not declaring outright opposition to nuclear energy, which would have been perceived as a downright denial of the party's past pro-nuclear stance, nevertheless softened the KMT's position and openly declared that Taiwan would gradually phase out nuclear energy by not renewing the shelf life of the already three existing facilities, provided that construction of NPP-4 would go on as planned.

At the same time, a shift in the public's perception of nuclear energy was gradually taking place, influenced by several popular figures, such as movie stars, directors, singers, writers and even some KMT legislators, openly voicing their own opposition towards NPP-4.

A further motivation for this shift throughout these past years has been the direct result of the allowance of independent energy providers in the power generation industry. As noted by Ho (2014: 4–5), while Taipower and AEC initially had an easy game swaying big businesses' support behind the nuclear cause, after the liberalization of the energy market took place power generation became a lucrative business and NPP-4 came to be considered, by some of these independent energy providers, a potential threat since it would lead to a loss of their own sales to Taipower, which would be able to rely further on the new plant. Formosa Plastic Group, which owns a power plant in Changhua (彰化), was the first to voice a negative opinion in regards to NPP-4 back in 1999. The Fukushima nuclear incident led to more widespread and open opposition towards the project, thus depriving the government of the support of one of its traditional allies, namely the business community (Ho 2014: 6).

These slow changes were also reflected among the general public. In a survey of public perceptions of technological risks conducted by Chen Dung-Sheng in 2009, 74.5 per cent of respondents thought that nuclear waste affected the health of humans, and 71 per cent agreed that nuclear technologies posed unknown risks to both the environment and to mankind (Chen 2011: 570).

A few opinion polls carried out after Fukushima showed a clear division reflecting political orientations. While the *Liberty Times* suggested that anti-nuclear feelings were predominant among its readership – with more than 92 per cent of respondents fearing the risks posed by nuclear plants – the *China Times*, sympathetic to the KMT, reflected opinion on the other side of the political spectrum, with 57 per cent of the people agreeing with President Ma's stance on nuclear energy (as quoted in Jobin 2012: 12). This percentage has steadily decreased since 2011. In fact, three different opinion polls, conducted in 2013 by both the DPP and pro-KMT polling agencies, showed that between 58 per cent and 69 per cent of the citizens were opposed to NPP-4. Its share of supporters was between 18 per cent and 25 per cent (*Liberty Times*, 12 March 2013: 4). Later on, in a poll led by Commonwealth magazine at the end of April 2014, right after the students' occupation of the Legislative Yuan, 58.7 per cent of respondents said that they were in favour of scrapping the power plant project entirely, while 27.2 per cent were in favour of suspending the project and 14.1 per cent did not provide an answer (Wang 2014b).

Last but not least, trust in Taipower's (and in the government's) capacity to handle a nuclear facility is at an all-time low. A survey carried out by the Atomic Energy Council in 2010 discovered that more than half of the people residing in the vicinity of NPP-1/2/3 displayed similar levels of trust towards nuclear plants' safety (between 58 per cent and 66 per cent), with a much lower percentage if the question shifted on the level of trust in the capability of the government to effectively handle a nuclear emergency (between 37 per cent and 46 per cent) (Atomic Energy Council 2010). A survey by Ho *et al.* (2013) discovered that 56 per cent of respondents were opposed to NPP-4; this percentage became higher among local Kongliao residents, with almost 94 per cent opposed to NPP-4 and displaying a high level of distrust (also 94 per cent) towards the safety management capability of Taipower and the government (Ho *et al.* 2013: 782). A sample of 2,819 individuals responded to the survey, with 66 per cent perceiving that Taiwan's safety management of NPPs was inferior to Japan's, while 40 per cent perceived a higher possibility of nuclear accidents like that in Japan.

Given the high degree of visibility enjoyed by nuclear issues in the aftermath of Fukushima and the mounting tide of discontent against NPP-4, this section has tried, among other things, to show how politicians have jumped on the anti-nuclear and pro-environment bandwagons in the hope of attracting votes. In dissent with the traditional pro-nuclear orientation of the party, a few KMT politicians, as well as some influential businessmen, openly expressed their opposition to NPP-4. In light of this internal party strife, in early 2013 the KMT government came up with the idea of a legal referendum to settle the plant's fate (Fell 2013; Chung 2013).

The nuclear referendum issue: to be or not to be

In reality, the party that first came up with the idea to launch a referendum on NPP-4 was the DPP, which in January 2013 launched a signature campaign to hold a referendum on the facility in conjunction with the national municipal election of November 2014; the idea to hold the plebiscite concomitantly with a national election, so as to mobilize more voters, was directly related to the high threshold set for referendums to have validity. However, since the DPP launched the idea without previously consulting anti-nuclear activists, the move alienated a good share of otherwise supportive individuals, increasing concerns that the DPP was merely trying to exploit the anti-nuclear issue for electoral purposes (Tsui Shu-hsin, email communication, 20 April 2013). Confronted with fierce criticism, Su Tseng-chang (蘇貞昌), DPP chairperson after the 2012 loss of the presidency, withdrew the plan.

Barely one month later, eyebrows were raised as in February 2013 the KMT's unveiled its own plan to hold a popular referendum over the summer to settle the fate of the controversial NPP-4. The KMT's proposal was soon followed by a large-scale protest, which brought more than 200,000 people onto the streets of Taiwan's major cities.

After a months-long debate, in which the DPP and the KMT disagreed on several issues, among these the way the referendum question had been phrased by the proponent (KMT), the plan was postponed indefinitely in the September of that same year by the very same KMT legislator, Lee Ching-hua (李慶華), who had first launched the idea, largely due to the resistance put up by the opposition party and several NGOs (Shih 2013). Afterwards, the nuclear referendum issue lay forgotten in the midst of more pressing concerns and protests, such as those towards the Cross-Strait Service Trade Agreement, until April 2014.

Building on the high degree of popular support towards the Sunflower Student Movement, activists criticized the government for what they considered a hypocritical stance in regards to the quorum for a referendum to have validity. In fact, while the KMT continues to uphold the 50 per cent threshold in regards to NPP-4, Chapter 4 of this book, by Ho and Tsai, will show how the party has nevertheless allowed a casino referendum held on Mazu in 2012 to be declared valid with a 40 per cent turnout of voters, thus with a simple majority of votes (Shih 2014b). Since none of the six earlier national referendums held in Taiwan has managed to reach the threshold, protesters argue that the requirement for more than 50 per cent of eligible voters to cast a ballot for a referendum to be declared valid is too high.

The significance of the Sunflower Movement for anti-nuclear activists: a commonality of targets

As mentioned above, the Sunflower Student Movement protest took place between March and April 2014 in Taiwan and was mainly focused on requesting a clause-by-clause review of the controversial CSSTA.

Barely two weeks after the end of the Sunflower Movement's occupation, on 22 April, DPP former chairman Lin I-hsiung (林義雄) started a hunger strike to protest against the construction of NPP-4 (Chen and Hsu 2014). Lin, a former head of the DPP sadly famous for the brutal murder of his mother and twin daughters in 1980, de facto inspired with his action a series of anti-nuclear rallies across the island. In fact, on 27 April thousands of protesters took to the streets (Lee 2014a), presenting the government with a series of demands, voiced for them during the parade by Tsui Shu-hsin:

> We have two demands for this government: that it stop construction of the Fourth Nuclear Power Plant while decommissioning the other operating plants as soon as possible and that it amend the 'bird-cage' Referendum Act (公民投票法 *gongmin toupiao fa*). Yet officials in power still neglect our demands, stall and evade their responsibilities with several excuses.
> (Tsui Shu-hsin, email communication, 26 May 2014)

Clashes with the police took place on that same day as anti-nuclear activists protested outside the Legislative Yuan in support of Lin (Loa 2014).

What is clearly visible from the latest flurry of civil activism in Taiwan is that, no matter whether a protest focuses on the abolition of nuclear energy or on requesting a clause-by-clause review of the Cross-Strait Service Trade Agreement, as in the case of the Sunflower Movement, the common thread linking various activists is firmly rooted in the upholding of Taiwan's democratic principles and the protection of its citizens' independence and right to self-determination, both from the government and from external interferences. In this regard, I contend that all the main social protests that have taken place in Taiwan since 2008 have a common denominator and cause: they were invigorated by what activists perceived to be an authoritarian turn on the part of the government, which affects an important decision for the future and the well-being of the Taiwanese populace, without consulting the public. Activists believe this to be the case both for the construction of NPP-4 and for the various trade agreements passed between mainland China and Taiwan under the KMT's first and second administrations.

In fact, according to Wang Chung-ming, former Green Party candidate and green activist,

> Governmental handling of the service trade agreement and the nuclear power issue reflect a superficial understanding of public values and clearly illustrate the government's controlling behaviour in denying the public access to policy making, by holding closed-door meetings to discuss issues that concern the country's future as well as its economic and political independence.
>
> (Wang Chung-ming, email communication, 2 May 2014)

Therefore protesters try to act as 'watchdogs', joining forces with like-minded activists, with the common goal of requesting more transparency and accountability from the government, no matter the formal cause they stand for.

That there is a direct link between the Sunflower Student Movement and the anti-nuclear power movement is also clear by the open declaration of student leaders, such as Chen Wei-ting (陳為廷), who was very active on social media in defending an anti-nuclear rally where activists (including himself) occupied Zhongxiao West Road, blocking the traffic for hours, and were criticized by many annoyed citizens who had to be re-routed owing to the parade (Tsai and Chung 2014: 3).[9]

In this regard, some scholars believe that the return to certain forms of dissent of the past, such as mass protests and occupation of public spaces, are necessary means, given that protesters perceive the state as indifferent towards their pleas. In Rawnsley's words,

> However, governmental indifference to popular sentiment is commonplace in all political systems. While breaking into and occupying the Legislative Yuan is illegal, such forms of protest are often a weapon wielded by the weak, an instrument of activism used by groups of people frustrated that their voices are not being heard through any other channel.
>
> (Rawnsley 2014: 8)

NPP-4 in mothballs: the political component

As mentioned above, under pressure owing to the rising popular discontent directed at several issues, on 27 April 2014 the Taiwanese government announced that it was halting work on the Lungmen nuclear power plant (NPP-4's official name), pending a referendum on its future, and that fuel rods would not be inserted before the referendum. Specifically, the KMT agreed to seal off the plant's No. 1 reactor after it had passed its safety tests and halt all work on No. 2 reactor, while suspending all other construction at the plant except for contracted and safety-related projects (Hsu 2014). So far, the plant has cost more than US$9 billion (Ho 2014: 5). The announcement was made after several thousand protesters, asking for the plant to be cancelled, organized an island-wide series of anti-nuclear rallies, tallying on the wave of popular participation generated by the Sunflower Movement protests and in support of Lin's hunger strike at the end of April.

In Linda Arrigo's words, NPP-4's cancellation is 'An outfall of the student movement, and also supposedly [linked] to the fact that Taipower internally is fearful that it was not safely constructed, such a boondoggle of stolen money' (Linda Arrigo, email communication, 14 May 2014).

In regards to the rumours raised by Arrigo – and circulating on several media outlets – concerning Taipower's own fears in regards to the facility, the *Liberty Times* reported on 12 April 2014 an anonymous comment, from a person who identified himself as a worker at NPP-4, who claimed that during the integrated leak rate test (ILRT) and structure integral test (SIT), conducted at the plant's No. 1 reactor from 26 February to 5 March 2014, leakage rates were found to be too high (Lee 2014b: 1).[10]

However, on the very same day of the announcement, Premier Jiang Yi-hua also specified two things: that suspending work on the project did not mean that the government was giving up the possibility of restarting it at a later date (Ramzy 2014); and that the referendum was likely to be pushed back to an indefinite date, in light of the disagreement in regards to the lowering of the threshold of voters (Shih 2014a).

A general observation that we can draw from tailing the anti-nuclear trajectory in Taiwan since 2008 is that, even though protesters have been 'successful' in preventing NPP-4 from becoming operational, by spreading awareness and pressuring the authorities governmental decisions have been reached almost certainly out of political concerns. Such was the case in 2011, when electoral interests on the part of politicians for the upcoming 2012 presidential election caused President Ma Ying-jeou to publicly announce that Taiwan would gradually phase out nuclear energy, while not renewing the life of the already three existing facilities, provided that construction and operation of NPP-4 would go on. This scenario, which seemed the most plausible in store for the future until 2013 has by now radically changed, since Taiwan will not be able to rely on the share of electric output generated by NPP-4.

Political motivations were again crucial in 2014, with nuclear safety and related concerns once again a hot topic in the run-up to the nine-in-one (九合一選舉, *jiu he yi xuanju*) municipal elections, which were held in November 2014[11] and which each candidate sought to take advantage of: Tsai Ing-wen (蔡英文), with her claim that the party has to grow nearer to civil society since the Sunflower Movement had radically changed Taiwanese politics (Wang 2014a), and the two KMT candidates Hung Hsiu-chu (洪秀柱) and, later, Eric Chu (朱立倫) insisting on ensuring nuclear safety.

Social activists, aware of the significance of the leverage that could be exerted, also attempted to turn environmental and nuclear-related issues into electoral topics. In an editorial in the *Taipei Times*, Tu Wen-ling 杜文苓, a member of the board of Taiwan Democracy Watch, urged the public to challenge all the candidates in the municipal elections of November 2014 by asking them several nuclear-related questions (Tu 2014). These elections were clearly a prelude to the presidential and parliamentary elections of 2016 and therefore of extreme importance for both camps. In fact, it was most probably the fear of losing votes and sympathy from the public, in what was quickly becoming an increasingly anti-establishment Taiwan, that pressured the KMT into reaching the decision to 'freeze' NPP-4. The growing dissatisfaction among the people has actually greatly impacted on the country's political life; the municipal elections have in fact awarded small parties such as the Green Party (2 seats), the Tree Party (1 mayoralty in Nantou County) and the Labour Party (2 citizen representatives seats), with the KMT losing several of its posts around Taiwan (Wen 2014); the most significant loss being the mayoralty of Taipei City, which had for 16 years been firmly in the hands of the KMT.

Professor Hsu Yung-ming (徐永明) of Soochow University has predicted that the 'post-Ma Ying-jeou era' scenario is quite clear. In regards to the referendum quarrel he said, 'The future scenario is that the current Referendum Act, also known as the "birdcage referendum act," will be amended' (Hsu, as quoted in Wang 2014c: 3).

His statement was made upon learning the results of a nuclear poll conducted by the Taiwan Think Tank, in which 64.8 per cent of those polled expressed a favourable opinion towards the amendment of the Referendum Act.

Furthermore, a survey carried out by Taiwan Indicators Survey Research found that support for a nuclear-free Taiwan had risen by 5 per cent from March 2014 to 55 per cent at the end of April, while another 29.6 per cent backed atomic power (as quoted in Wang 2014b: 3).

In regards to the plausible scenarios in store for the future, after the DPP's presidential victory in January 2016 it will be interesting to see the diplomatic fallout and implications of the political change for international powers such as Beijing and Washington. In the environmental arena, the transfer of ruling power back to the DPP could also represent a variation in the country's ecological route, towards more eco-friendly approaches and a detour from nuclear energy. At any rate, the newly elected Taiwanese government, led by President Tsai Ing-wen and the Democratic Progressive Party (DPP), are faced with significant challenges in regards to the country's energy provision. Most urgently, viable replacements for Taiwan's ageing fleet of nuclear reactors must be found, considering that NPP-1 is likely to be decommissioned in 2019 and that the DPP government will never dare resume the construction of NPP-4. In fact, Tsai, who assumed the presidency in May 2016, has officially committed to phasing out nuclear energy by promoting energy efficiency and adjusting the current energy mix (SCMP 2016). The DPP should therefore conduct an intensive review of national energy policy in order to find a viable alternative to the 18 per cent of electricity output currently derived from nuclear (Grano 2015: 62; Ho *et al.* 2013: 775).

Whether this supporting and cooperative attitude towards the anti-nuclear movement will turn out to have positive effects for activists, or whether it will once again make the movement less proactive and more ready to compromise as in the early days of cooperation between the DPP and the anti-nuclear movement, it is too early to say. However as stated by long-term environmental activist, lawyer and naturalized Taiwanese politician Robin Winkler (文魯彬),

> My main reason for optimism is the presence of many 'green politicians' in the new legislature including two former Green Party co-chairs, the five New Power Party members and a number of other activist friendly list candidates from the DPP and at least one from the KMT. There are a lot of opportunities for dialogue and good prospects for the environment.
> (Robin Winkler, email communication, 28 January 2016)

Conclusions

Although it is quite safe to assume that Taiwan will not radically depart from its nuclear trajectory in the near future, most probably following a path of gradual and slow nuclear dismantling of the three functioning power plants, soon nearing the end of their operative life, the Fukushima incident and the most recent protests and dissatisfactions towards the KMT government have had two effects: they forced many previously indifferent citizens in Taiwan to be confronted with the risks the country would face in the event of a nuclear catastrophe; and, second, they ignited strong social protests and concerns that the KMT could no longer ignore.

Second, on top of the extraordinary vibrancy of Taiwan's civil society participation, a distinctive feature and direct outcome of the Sunflower Student Movement was its usefulness in relaunching anti-nuclear feelings inside Taiwan, already ignited by the Fukushima nuclear meltdown in 2011 and reinvigorated by the 24-day occupation of the country's legislature, which paralysed the island, three years after the incident in Japan.

The crucial importance of timing has to be emphasized. Timing was critical in the early phases of the development of an anti-nuclear movement in Taiwan, when the formation of an opposition that was gradually expanding its scope under Taiwan's collapsing authoritarian regime presented activists with a ready-made ally. Later on, timing was again essential in reviving anti-nuclear awareness among the population in 2011, when activists were able to exploit the Fukushima incident as well as the pre-electoral concerns regarding the 2012 elections; and, finally, timing was again critical in 2014 both for the Sunflower Student Movement and for anti-nuclear activists to fully exploit the rising tide of discontent against the Ma administration, once again in a year preceding a big election (the 29 November municipal elections), considered a prelude to the national election in 2016, and thus of extreme importance for all parties.

To summarize, the key events that have shaped the anti-nuclear power movement since its inception were: *democratization*, when suddenly protest was allowed; the *DPP's first electoral victory*, which brought along the hope for anti-nuclear activists to see NPP-4 shelved; the return to power of the KMT, which pushed social movements towards a rising wave of social discontent; the *Fukushima incident*, which reignited nuclear concerns empowering activists with renewed vigour; and, finally, the *Sunflower Student Movement*.

In light of this chapter's findings, it is quite clear that the halting of the construction of NPP-4 is the direct outcome of the Sunflower protest and its international visibility, which triggered another series of events, such as the Lin I-hsiung hunger strike, which in turn rode on the wave of heightened awareness generated by the students' activism. Such events put more pressure on the former administration, which felt compelled to reach a 'compromise' in halting NPP-4's project until a referendum is held for fear of mounting social discontent in the light of the elections.

Starting in 2013, an anti-nuclear majority that crossed the partisan political divide has gradually established itself. This shift in the public's mentality has taken place due to several factors: first, President Ma's second mandate in 2012, which has had the secondary effect of giving rise to the return of active social mobilization; second, the coming along of a newer generation of anti-nuclear activists, able to lend a new image to the anti-nuclear cause, to attract new supporters and to cross the political divide; and, third, a shift that fractured the previous cohesiveness of the pro-nuclear faction, with several businessmen and KMT politicians openly declaring their opposition to NPP-4.

The conclusions that can be drawn is that civil society in Taiwan has experienced a favourable convergence of events, which it has been able to skilfully exploit in its favour. The recent protests and social upheavals have been much more successful than those of the past because activists have increasingly distanced themselves from political organs by becoming united in their issues and crossing previous boundaries tied to ethnic and political identifications.

It will be interesting to see the future course of the relationship between anti-nuclear activists and the newly elected president, Tsai Ing-wen, and the DPP. Considering the difficult challenges faced by Tsai in foreign policy and particularly cross-strait relations, anti-nuclear and environmental concerns risk once again taking a back seat, as happened during the first two presidential terms of the DPP (2000–08).

However, the fact that Tsai based her presidential campaign on transitional justice issues, that she has vowed to phase out nuclear energy usage by 2025 and that she has included in the DPP party's list several former Green Party and environmental activists make many in the environmental community hopeful.

At any rate, the change in ruling party has already had an effect in the number of people that participated to the annual anti-nuclear parade in March; in fact, the 2016 commemoration of the Fukushima incident in Taipei generated a much lower turnout of participants than in previous years (SCMP 2016).

Notes

1 The Sunflower Student Movement (*taiyanghua xueyun*, 太陽花學運) was a 24-day occupation (18 March – 10 April 2014) of Taiwan's legislature, to protest against the attempt on part of the ruling Kuomintang (KMT) to pass a service trade agreement with China, titled the Cross-Strait Service Trade Agreement (CSSTA), for which protesters maintained a 'clause-by-clause' review was needed. The treaty, signed between China and Taiwan in June 2013, was one of the follow-up agreements to controversial Economic Cooperation Framework Agreement (EFCA), signed in 2010. The movement is also known as the 'March 18 Student Movement' (318 學運) or 'Occupy Taiwan Legislature Incident' (佔領國會事件). The protest was so named by the media after a florist sent bunches of sunflowers to the protesters, in reference to the sunlight and transparency that protesters wished to obtain from the government. The term 'Sunflower Student Movement' might possibly also be referred to the use of sunflowers as a symbol of clean energy as the flower is heliotropic (moves towards the sun); most certainly though, it is an allusion to the Wild Lily Movement of 1990, which set a milestone in the democratization of Taiwan.
2 The Taiwan Power Company (台灣電力公司, *Taiwan dianli gongsi*, generally known as Taipower) is a state-owned electric power company providing electric power to Taiwan's main island and to the offshore islands of the Republic of China.
3 With a few notable exceptions, such as Edgar Lin (林俊毅), widely regarded as the 'Father of the anti-nuclear movement' in Taiwan, who openly expressed his distrust and criticism towards Taipower and the government's energetic policies by writing scathing articles as early as 1979. Because of his outward opinion, Lin was forced to leave the country so as to avoid being arrested and blacklisted in the mid-1980s (Fell 2011: 185).
4 These groups have recently formed the National Nuclear Abolition Action Platform, an alliance of more than 100 civic groups who fight for the complete acquittal of nuclear energy on Taiwanese soil.
5 In 1991 local residents and activists took to the streets in Gongliao to mark their opposition to the construction of the controversial NPP-4, known as '*he si*, 核四', inside Taiwan. During the conflict, one policeman was accidentally killed, driven over by a lorry; the young officer responsible for his death was later convicted for life. In her film, Tsui addresses several questions to this officer (in the form of an epistolary conversation), who, like herself, is an outsider who came to Kongliao in order to help locals in their struggle towards anti-nuclear lobbies.
6 See also an open letter signed by several influential professors and scholars of Taiwan in 2009, sent to the *Taipei Times* on 13 November (available online at www.taipeitimes.com/News/editorials/archives/2009/11/13/2003458289), in which the signatories renew their hopes that President Ma Ying-jeou will safeguard Taiwan's future and sovereignty and uphold the country's democratic principles.
7 The author herself is a subscriber to two newsletters, a more official one (環境資訊電子報, e-info.org.tw) and a more unofficial and semi-private one (環境培力群組, Peli.net), through which she receives several emails calling for the signing of petitions or for joining actual protests or rallies in favour of several environmental campaigns all over Taiwan.
8 This photograph was taken by the author in 2011. As can be seen from the picture, sunflowers, as symbols to oppose the government's energetic policies, were already being used by anti-nuclear activists in 2011, thus clearly illustrating the relationship between the various social movements and their members, which go way beyond issue-related boundaries.
9 In regards to the occupation of Zhongxiao West Road, the Anti-Nuclear Abolition Platform, which includes several anti-nuclear groups, announced on 9 June 2014 that many of its members had been requested to report to their nearest police station for

questioning in regards to their actions on 27 April. Among them, the Green Citizens Action Alliance secretary general, Tsui Shu-hsin (崔愫欣), and Citizen of the Earth Taiwan's Taipei Office director, Tsai Chung-yueh (蔡中岳), have both been told that they risk being charged with violating the Assembly and Parade Act (集會遊行法, *jihui youxingfa*) and endangering public safety (Lee 2014c: 3). Wang Chun-ming was handed a three-month (finally reduced to two) jail term for violating the Assembly and Parade Act and was thus unable to take part in the latest round of national elections as a candidate for the Green Party (Wang Chung-ming, email communication, 9 February 2016).

10 The ILRT and SIT are just two of 307 tests that must be conducted before fuel rods can be installed in the reactor of a nuclear power plant.

11 The 'nine-in-one' elections were held on 29 November 2014 for all directly elected local government positions, such as the mayors and councillors of the special municipalities; county commissioners and councillors; city mayors and city councillors; township administrators and councillors; and, finally, borough village wardens. In short, nine categories of office were up for election. The Democratic People's Progressive Party (DPP) defeated the ruling KMT in most of the key races, winning 13 of the 22 cities and counties. Thus, the number of cities and counties under KMT control dropped from 15 to six. The remaining three were won by independent candidates, among these the mayoralty of Taipei City.

References

Asia One News. 2011, 20 March. *Over 2,000 Rally against Nuclear Plants in Taiwan*. Available online at http://news.asiaone.com/News/Latest+News/Asia/Story/A1Story 20110320-269104.html (accessed 2 November 2014).

Arrigo, Linda. 2014. Email communication, 14 May 2014.

Atomic Energy Council. 2010. *The Technology Report of Opinion Poll of Emergency Plan on Nuclear Accidents in 2006–2009*. Available online at www.aec.gov.tw/english/index.html.

Chan, Chang-chuan and Chen Ya-mei. 2011. 'A Fukushima-like nuclear crisis in Taiwan or a non-nuclear Taiwan?' *East Asian Science, Technology and Society*, 5(3), 403–7.

Chen Hui-ping and Hsu Stacey. 2014. 'Lin's daughter sends support in letter'. *Taipei Times*, 24 April. Available online at www.taipeitimes.com/News/taiwan/archives/2014/04/24/2003588766.

Chen, Du-sheng. 2011. 'Taiwan's antinuclear movement in the wake of the Fukushima disaster, viewed from an STS perspective'. *East Asian Science, Technology and Society*, 5, 567–72.

Chou, Kuei-tien [周桂田]. 2011. Interview with the author, 14 October 2011.

Chung, Lawrence. 2013. 'Taiwan's ruling Kuomintang seeks referendum on nuclear power plant'. *South China Morning Post*, 8 March. Available online at www.scmp.com/news/china/article/1185793/taiwans-ruling-kuomintang-seeks-referendum-nuclear-power-plant.

Cole, Michael J. 2014. *Civic Activism and Protests in Taiwan: Why Size Doesn't (Always) Matter*. Draft paper presented at the Conference on Social Movements in Taiwan after 2008, SOAS Centre of Taiwan Studies, 16–18 June 2014. Courtesy of the author.

Enn, Rosa. 2015. *Orchid Island and the nuclear waste deposit*. Lecture at Zürich University, 18 November 2015.

Fell, Dafydd. 2011. *Government and Politics in Taiwan*. London: Routledge.

Fell, Dafydd. 2013. 'The Nuclear Referendum Issue in Taiwan'. *China Policy Institute Blog*,

27 March. Available online at http://blogs.nottingham.ac.uk/chinapolicyinstitute/2013/03/27/the-nuclear-referendum-issue-in-taiwan.

Grano, Simona. 2015. *Environmental Governance in Taiwan: A new generation of activists and stakeholders*. London: Routledge.

Ho Jung-chun, Kao Shu-fen, Wang Jung-der, Su Chien-tien, Lee Chiao-tzu Patricia, Chen Ruey-yu, Chang Hung-lun, Leong Marco C. F. and Chang Peter Wushou. 2013. 'Risk perception, trust, and factors related to a planned new nuclear power plant in Taiwan after the 2011 Fukushima disaster'. *Journal of Radiological Protection*, 33(4), 773–89.

Ho, Ming-sho. 2003. 'The politics of the anti-nuclear movement in Taiwan: Case of party dependant movement (1988–2000)'. *Modern Asian Studies*, 37(3), 683–708.

Ho, Ming-sho. 2005. 'Taiwan's state and social movements under the DPP government, 2000–2004'. *Journal of East Asian Studies*, 5(3), 401–25.

Ho, Ming-sho. 2005b. 'Weakened state and social movement: The paradox of the Taiwanese environmental movement after the power transfer'. *Journal of Contemporary China*, 14(43), 339–52.

Ho, Ming-sho. 2006. 綠色民主: 台灣環境運動的研究 [*Lüse Minzhu, Taiwan Huanjing yundong de yanjiu, Green Democracy: A research on Taiwan's environmental movements*]. Taipei: Qunxue.

Ho, Ming-sho. 2010. 'Understanding the Trajectory of Social Movements in Taiwan (1980–2010)'. *Journal of Current Chinese Affairs*, 39(3), 3–22.

Ho, Ming-sho. 2014. 'The Fukushima effect: explaining the resurgence of the anti-nuclear movement in Taiwan'. *Environmental Politics*. doi: 10.1080/09644016.2014.918303.

Hsiao, Alison. 2014. 'Jiang nuclear report needless: KMT whip'. *Taipei Times*, 29 April, 3. Available online at www.taipeitimes.com/News/taiwan/archives/2014/04/29/2003589158.

Hsiao, Michael Hsin-huang. 1999. 'Environmental movements in Taiwan'. In Y. S. Lee and Y. So (eds), *Asia's Environmental Movements: Comparative Perspectives*. Armonk, NY, and London: M. E. Sharpe, pp. 31–54.

Hsu, Jenny W. 2014. 'Taiwan Government Agrees to Halt Construction on Nuclear Plant'. *The Wall Street Journal*, 27 April. Available online at http://online.wsj.com/news/articles/SB10001424052702304163604579527072873788850.

Huang Gillan Chi-Lun, Tim Gray, Derek Bell Environment. 2013. 'Environmental justice of nuclear waste policy in Taiwan: Taipower, government, and local community'. *Development and Sustainability*, 15(6), 1555–71.

Jobin, Paul. 2010. 'Hazards and protest in the "Green Silicon Island". The struggle for visibility of industrial hazards in contemporary Taiwan'. *China Perspectives*, 83(3), 46–62.

Lee, I-Chia. 2011. 'Anti-nuclear rally draws legions'. *Taipei Times*, 1 May.

Lee, I-Chia. 2014a. 'Antinuclear protest to continue: groups'. *Taipei Times*, 28 April. Available online at www.taipeitimes.com/News/front/archives/2014/04/28/2003589062.

Lee, I-Chia. 2014b. 'Officials downplay nuclear plant flaws'. *Taipei Times*, 12 May, 1. Available online at www.taipeitimes.com/News/front/archives/2014/05/13/2003590217.

Lee, I-Chia. 2014c. 'Group pans police summons over anti-nuclear rally'. *Taipei Times*, 10 June, 3. Available online at www.taipeitimes.com/News/taiwan/archives/2014/06/10/2003592416.

Liberty Times. 2013, 12 March. P A4.

Loa, Lok-sin. 2012. 'Tao protest against nuclear waste'. *Taipei Times*, 2 March. Available online at www.taipeitimes.com/News/front/archives/2012/03/02/2003526783 (accessed 15 October 2012).

Loa, Lok-sin. 2014. 'Police clash with activists rallying for Lin in Taipei'. *Taipei Times*, 24 April. Available online at www.taipeitimes.com/News/taiwan/archives/2014/04/24/2003588767.

Lyons, David. 2009. 'The two-headed dragon: Environmental policy and progress under rising democracy in Taiwan'. *East Asia*, 26(1), 57–76.

Ramzy Austin. 2014. 'Hunger striker ends fast, but not fight, against nuclear power in Taiwan'. *New York Times*, 1 May. Available online at http://sinosphere.blogs.nytimes.com/2014/05/01/hunger-striker-ends-fast-but-not-fight-against-nuclear-power-in-taiwan/?ref=asia.

Rawnsley, Ming Yeh T. [蔡明燁]. 2014. 'Protests boost democratic growth'. *Taipei Times*, 2 May. Available online at www.taipeitimes.com/News/editorials/archives/2014/05/02/2003589360/2.

Shih, Fang-Long. 2012. 'Generating power in Taiwan: Nuclear, political and religious power'. *Culture and Religion*, 13(3), 295–313.

Shih, Hsiu-chuan. 2013. 'Nuclear referendum on ice: KMT caucus'. *Taipei Times*, 27 September. Available online at www.taipeitimes.com/News/taiwan/archives/2013/09/27/2003573128.

Shih, Hsiu-chuan. 2014a. 'Government will never axe plant: Jiang'. *Taipei Times*, 29 April, 1. Available online at www.taipeitimes.com/News/front/archives/2014/04/29/2003589140.

Shih, Hsiu-chuan. 2014b. 'Matsu casino referendum invalid on turnout: critics'. *Taipei Times*, 30 April, 3. Available online at www.taipeitimes.com/News/taiwan/archives/2014/04/30/2003589242.

SCMP (South China Morning Post). 2016, 13 March. 'Low turnout at anti-nuclear rally as Taiwan banks on new leader Tsai Ing-wen's wow to abolish atomic energy use by 2025'. Available online at www.scmp.com/news/china/policies-politics/article/1924093/low-turnout-anti-nuclear-rally-taiwan-banks-new-leader (accessed 12 April 2016).

Taiwan Insights. 2013. 'Amid massive anti-nuclear protests, Taiwanese rethink their desired lifestyle'. Available online at www.taiwaninsights.com/tag/green-citizens-action-alliance (accessed 27 December 2013).

Tseng Te-jung, Ling Mei-hsueh and Stacy Hsu. 2013. 'Actor Joseph Cheng makes first anti-nuclear film'. *Taipei Times*, 11 August, 3. Available online at www.taipeitimes.com/News/taiwan/print/2013/08/11/2003569435.

Tsai Chang-sheng and Chung Jake. 2014. 'Zhongxiao W Road occupation sparks huge online debate'. *Taipei Times*, 29 April, 3. Available online at www.taipeitimes.com/News/taiwan/archives/2014/04/29/2003589162.

Tsui Shu-hsin [崔愫欣]. Interview with the author on 24 March and 20 September 2011; email communication, 20 April 2013 and 26 May 2014.

Tu, Wen-ling. 2014. 'Nuclear safety plan is in question'. *Taipei Times*, 24 April, 8. Available online at www.taipeitimes.com/News/editorials/archives/2014/04/24/2003588736.

Wang, Chris. 2014a. 'DPP's Tsai calls for fuel rod moratorium at Gongliao plant'. *Taipei Times*, 24 April. Available online at www.taipeitimes.com/News/taiwan/archives/2014/04/24/2003588770.

Wang, Chris. 2014b. 'Polls say majority favor suspending or aborting plant'. *Taipei Times*, 29 April. Available online at www.taipeitimes.com/News/taiwan/archives/2014/04/29/2003589159/2.

Wang, Chris. 2014c. 'Majority wants no plebiscite threshold'. *Taipei Times*, 30 April. Available online at www.taipeitimes.com/News/taiwan/archives/2014/04/30/2003589235.

Wang Chung-ming [王鐘銘]. Email communication, 2 May 2014 and 9 February 2016.
Wen, Lii 2014. 'Elections 2014: Smaller parties clinch big victories'. *Taipei Times*, 1 December Available online at www.taipeitimes.com/News/taiwan/archives/2014/12/01/2003605715.
Williams, Jack and Ch'ang-yi David Chang. 2008. *Taiwan's Environmental Struggle: Toward a Green Silicon Island*. London: Routledge.
Winkler, Robin. 2016. Email communication, 28 January 2016.
Yuen Samson. 2014. 'Under the shadow of China'. *China Perspectives*, 2, 69–76.

10 The revival of Taiwan's Green Party after 2008

Dafydd Fell and Peng Yen-wen

In January 2008, Taiwan held its first election under the new predominantly single member district (SMD) electoral system.[1] That year, the Green Party Taiwan (GPT) was just one of a group of small parties gaining under 1 per cent of the party list vote. In contrast, four years later the GPT came fifth, with 1.7 per cent and over a quarter of a million votes. Then, in 2014, the party made a breakthrough in local elections, winning assembly seats in Taoyuan City and Hsinchu County. The party continued to expand its support base, as in an alliance with the Social Democratic Party (SDP) it won 2.52 per cent in the 2016 legislative elections. The GPT has shown that it has the potential to become Taiwan's first relevant alternative political party.[2]

Despite currently not holding any national seats, the GPT represents an important case both from the perspective of social movements and party politics. Formed in 1996, the GPT is the second-oldest and arguably the most vibrant Asian green party. While most other small alternative parties in Taiwan contested one or two elections before disappearing, the GPT has consistently joined elections for almost two decades (Fell and Peng 2016). The majority of relevant challenger parties, such as the New Party (NP), and Taiwan Solidarity Union (TSU), are splinters from Taiwan's two largest political parties, the Kuomintang (KMT) and the Democratic Progressive Party (DPP). In other words, they base their issue appeals on those of the mainstream parties, particularly over the China versus Taiwan identity, relations with China and the unification versus independence (*Tongdu*) debates. They are what Lucardie (2000: 176) calls 'purifier parties', which cling 'to an existing ideology, which it feels are diluted or betrayed by one (or more) of the established parties.' In contrast, the GPT tends to stress new issues that 'established parties appear to ignore or neglect' (Lucardie 2000: 177). Lucardie terms such parties 'prophetic parties'. The GPT has been the most successful of Taiwan's prophetic parties, steering clear of the identity politics that have so dominated the party scene. The literature on Taiwan's party politics has been overwhelmingly dominated by studies of the KMT and DPP (Rigger 2001; Hood 1996; Fell 2005a), while very little scholarly work exists on smaller challenger parties, such as the GPT (Copper 1993, Fell 2005b; Fell 2006; Fell 2014).

The pattern of the GPT's electoral performances also makes it an interesting case. It virtually disappeared during the peak period of multiparty politics between 2000 and 2005, when the environment seemed quite favourable for new parties. In contrast, while other challenger parties went into what seemed like terminal decline between 2006 and 2010, the GPT began its revival and enjoyed a gradual growth in support levels. This improvement came after Taiwan adopted the predominantly SMD electoral system, which was designed to squeeze the space for smaller parties (Cabestan 2008: 29–47). At a time when there is such a high level of distrust with mainstream Taiwanese parties, it is important to examine the potential for alternative political forces to enter the party system.

Generally, political parties and social movements are studied separately. However, in the case of ecological parties the dividing lines are often blurred. In many cases, including Taiwan, green parties emerged out of the environmental, particularly anti-nuclear movements. Carter (2007: 100) notes that the German 'Die Grünen was rooted in social movement activity dating from the late 1960s and 1970s'. A core factor in the formation of the GPT was the environmental movement's growing dissatisfaction with its mainstream ally, the DPP (Ho 2003: 683–708). Green parties (including the GPT) aim to serve as a political tool and spokesperson for a range of social movements whose core issues have been neglected by mainstream parties. The main source of GPT election candidates and activists has also been social movements. However, there are also often tensions between social movements and green parties, especially once the parties begin to professionalize and enter government office. This was particularly apparent when the German Greens entered a coalition government with the Social Democratic Party in 1998 and compromised on its pledge to close down the country's nuclear power stations within 100 days of coming to power (Doyle 2005: 138–60).

In this chapter we examine the development of the GPT after 2008 through to the most recent election, in January 2016. The KMT's return to power in 2008 represents a suitable time to consider the GPT's development alongside those of other social movements. After tracking the key patterns in the party's post-2008 electoral performance, we offer some analysis of how best to explain its growth and the limits to its development. We do this using a framework proposed by Lucardie (2000), which examines the development of small parties by considering their political project, mobilization of resources and political opportunity structure. We last consider the prospects for the party in the aftermath of the 2016 elections.

GPT's electoral fortunes

We have summarized the GPT's electoral performance in two tables. Table 10.1 shows the GPT's performance in national-level parliamentary elections, while Table 10.2 covers local city council elections. These tables suggest that the GPT has gone through three broad phases. The first was its initial impressive performance in 1996 and, to a lesser extent, in 1998. The party managed to win a seat in the 1996 National Assembly and received 1.1 per cent of the vote (almost 3 per

Table 10.1 Green Taiwan Party performance in national-level elections (National Assembly: NA and Legislative Yuan: LY)

	1996 NA	1998 LY	2001 LY	2008 LY District	2008 LY Party List	2012 LY District	2012 LY Party List	2016 LY District	2016 Party List
Total votes	113,949	8,089	1,045	14,767	58,473	79,729	229,566	203,658	308,106
Vote share	1.1%	0.1%	0%	0.15%	0.6%	0.62%	1.74%	1.7%	2.52%
Candidates	13 district and 3 party list	1 district	1 district	10 district	4 party list	10 district	2 party list	11 district	6 party list

Table 10.2 Green Taiwan Party performance in local-level elections

	1998 County Council	1998 Taipei City Council	2002 Taipei City Council TPCC	2006 Taipei City Council TPCC	2009 County Council	2010 Taipei City Council	2010 New Taipei City Council	2014 New Taipei City Council	2014 Taoyuan City Council
Total votes	5,721	22,274	1,807	5,381	843	18,329	8,321	14,125	25,913
and Vote share	0.1%	1.5%	0.1%	0.42%	0.01%	1.15%	0.4%	0.74%	2.29%
Candidates	4	4	1	2	1	4	1	2	3

cent where it nominated candidates). However, in the period from 2000 through to 2005 the party went through a period whereby it barely functioned in elections. It appeared that the party was following the pattern shown by previous small parties such as the Labour Party of giving up elections after failing to make an initial breakthrough. In this dormant phase, the GPT either only nominated a single token candidate or simply did not nominate any candidates, such as in the 2004 legislative elections. The start of the revival period can be dated from 2006, when the GPT nominated two experienced social movement activists for the Taipei City Council election. The growth accelerated after 2008. This was visible from its return to similar levels of vote share in Taipei City Council in 2010 to those last seen in 1998. Then, in 2012 it enjoyed its best ever vote share, 1.7 per cent (229,566 votes) on the Legislative Yuan party list and in Taipei City district 7 GPT candidate Pan Han-sheng (潘翰聲) gained 43,449 votes, the highest ever number of votes received by a single GPT candidate. By coming fifth on the party list vote, the GPT had outpolled the resource-rich NP.

It is difficult to gauge the GPT's strength through the standard methods of survey data, as even in 2015 the National Chengchi University (NCCU) Election Study Center and TVBS Poll Center party identification trends still do not include the GPT (but do list the NP). There are signs, however, that the GPT has continued the momentum from 2012. For instance, for the November 2014 local elections it nominated extensively, with 10 local council candidates, a record number for the party, and nominated much earlier than its common past practice of last-minute nominations. As mentioned earlier, two of these candidates were elected. In terms of seats it was the fifth largest party and enjoyed the third largest vote share in Taoyuan City (2.89 per cent). When the party established an alliance with the newly formed Social Democratic Party (SDP), there were hopes that it could make its breakthrough at the national level in 2016. The party did increase its number of votes and vote share (2.52 per cent) and had much stronger candidates at the district level. However, the party alliance was still well short of gaining party list seats; it was beaten into sixth place and instead another party recruiting from social movements, the New Power Party (NPP), made the breakthrough into the party system.[3]

In line with the theme of the book, our chapter will focus on the latter part of the third phase in the GPT's development. In other words, we will analyse the party's development after the KMT returned to power in 2008.

Data and methodology

This study is part of a larger project designed to analyse the development of the GPT since its establishment in the mid-1990s. We carried out a series of fieldwork activities between 2012 and 2016. This included interviews and focus groups with party leaders, candidates, activists, party supporters and party members.

Political science studies of green parties tend to be located in the literature on small parties (Spoon 2011; Meguid 2008; Müller-Rommel 1998). There is also much debate on which is the most appropriate term for such parties. Should it be new, small, niche or anti-system party (Adams *et al.* 2006)? The kinds of parties associated with this sub-field include green parties, radical right, far left and ethno-regional parties. Key approaches for explaining the impact of small parties consider sociological variables (Inglehart 1997), small party agency (Spoon 2011), the impact of mainstream party strategies (Meguid 2008) and the mechanical effect of political institutions, such as the electoral system (Duverger 1954; Müller-Rommel 1998).

In this chapter we have adopted Lucardie's hybrid framework, which allows us to bring in elements of a number of the approaches mentioned above. He proposes that the success or failure of new parties can best be explained with reference to their political project, resources and the political opportunity structure. The first variable is summarized as the need to articulate 'a clear and convincing *political project* which addresses social problems considered urgent by a significant number of voters' (Lucardie 2000: 176). Second, a party requires sufficient resources to compete against mainstream parties. This element of the framework borrows from the resource mobilization approach, which is commonly used in social movement studies (McCarthy and Zald 2001). It is particularly important when we consider just how expensive Taiwanese election campaigns are. Moreover, in addition to financial resources, a new party needs strong human and organizational resources to have an impact on elections. In the 1990s a key factor in the NP's ability to make its early breakthrough was its rich supply of politicians with extensive electoral and government experience (Fell 2006). In contrast, Ho (2003: 701–6) has noted the inability of the GPT to recruit leading figures from the environmental movement as a factor in its limited impact in the late 1990s. Third, even if new parties have an attractive policy package and ample resources they remain dependent on the political opportunity structure. In essence we can think of this factor as being whether or not the overall political environment is favourable for the emergence and development of new political parties. Lucardie suggest giving particular attention to dimensions such as the institutional structure (especially electoral system), the party system, political culture, salient issue cleavages and political or economic events. One way we can view this effect is by comparing the GPT's fortunes under the new national, predominantly SMD, electoral system and under the more favourable multiple member district (MMD) system used in local council elections.

Political project

A perennial challenge for almost all green parties is to deal with the stereotype that they are single-issue parties solely concerned with environmental issues. The GPT has attempted to develop a wide range of policy appeals since 2008. These have tended to address issues that have either been neglected by the mainstream parties or place the GPT in direct opposition to at least one of the two dominant parties.

Naturally, environmental issues have been at the heart of the GPT's campaigns. This was clear from the GPT's 2012 election television advertisement, in which the majority of its candidates discussed environmental issues.[4] The most central environmental issue over the last two decades in Taiwan has been surrounding nuclear energy, particularly relating to the Fourth Nuclear Power Station. While the KMT has always taken an unashamedly pro-nuclear position, the DPP's nuclear credentials were seriously undermined by its time in office (Arrigo and Puleston 2006). The DPP failed in both its major pledges of stopping construction of the Fourth Nuclear Power Station and of removing nuclear waste stored on the island of Lanyu. The GPT has taken a consistently anti-nuclear position and its leading figures have been prominent in the anti-nuclear movement. Party founder Kao Cheng-yan (高成炎) has been a leading figure in the campaign for a national referendum on the Fourth Nuclear Power Station for over two decades. A similar figure is a GPT Central Executive Committee (CEC) member, the film-maker and secretary general of the Green Citizens Action Alliance Tsui Shu-hsin (崔愫欣). She brought the issue to international audiences through her award winning documentary film *Gongliao, How are you?* (貢寮你好嗎?).

The party was able to benefit from this appeal as the nuclear issue rose in salience after 2008. Three events were critical in heightening the salience of the nuclear power station issue to unprecedented levels. These were the nuclear disaster in Japan at Fukushima of 2011, the debate over a national referendum over the Fourth Nuclear Power Station in 2013 and the drive to terminate the Fourth Nuclear Power Station in April 2014, associated with Lin I-hsiung's (林義雄) hunger strike. This meant that environmental issues reached record levels of attention on the political agenda and thus benefitted the most consistently anti-nuclear party. The party is also likely to have benefitted from the shift in public opinion towards a more anti-nuclear position. In 2001, surveys (TVBS 2001) showed 49 per cent supporting construction of the Fourth Nuclear Power Station and only 32 per cent against. In contrast, in the 2013 and 2014 surveys (TVBS 2014), 73 and 60 per cent respectively expressed a preference for ceasing construction of the project. The GPT also addressed the issue of nuclear waste on Lanyu by nominating the local anti-nuclear campaigner Sinan Mavivo (希婻 瑪飛洑) as one of its party list candidates in 2012.

In addition to anti-nuclear campaigning, the GPT and its leading figures were also actively involved in opposition to a number of land development and industrial projects strongly backed by local and/or national KMT governments, which had the potential to deliver high environmental costs. One such example was the role played by Wild at Heart Legal Defence Lawyers Association and other NGOs in challenging the Miramar resort project in Taitung. In this case, the local KMT administration worked together with developers to disregard the Environmental Impact Assessment process, indigenous rights and legal rulings against the project.[5] The GPT again reminded voters of the Miramar controversy by showing images of the location before and after construction in its 2016 *Change* election advertisement.[6] In addition, campaigns to protect old trees from being uprooted in major construction projects have featured prominent GPT figures. For example, a treetop protest was the most memorable campaign event in GPT candidate Calvin Wen's (溫炳原) involvement in the 2009 Ta An legislative by-election. This tree protection campaign theme again received extensive media coverage in the case of the Farglory Construction Group's redevelopment of the Sungshan Tobacco Factory and was a core appeal during GPT legislative candidate Pan Han-sheng's 2012 campaign.

In a recent study of the German Green Party, Rüdig (2012: 108) argued that 'Despite the party's effort to emphasize economic and social and issues in its campaigning, the chief factors explaining Green Party voting remain environmental concerns and opposition to nuclear energy'. We can see a similar positive impact of the GPT's environmental campaigning on its performances since 2008. For instance, out of our interviewed party supporters almost all listed concern for environmental issues, particularly anti-nuclear sentiment, as their main reason for voting GPT. Among party members there was a more diverse range of critical issues, but environmental issues were again prominent in why they chose to join the party. The impact can also be seen in the quite remarkable voting results in the 2012 party list on Lanyu island, where the GPT received 35.76 per cent of the vote (its national vote share was 1.7 per cent), coming a close second behind the KMT.[7] Similarly, we found that the experience of involvement with environmental NGOs and their campaigns served to bring in GPT members and supporters. As one supporter explained, 'Later I went there [Green Citizens Action Alliance] as a volunteer and since the GP has had a longstanding cooperative relationship with social movements and environmental movement, I got to know more about it [GPT].'[8]

Nevertheless, there has been some potential for negative effects from some more radical environmental campaigns. For instance, one party supporter we interviewed questioned the campaigns to protect old trees: 'The developers want to move the trees elsewhere, but now the GPT is saying protect the trees! I don't know and want to understand, is it really such a serious threat to the environment?'[9] In addition, a number of supporters questioned whether environmentalists were adopting too radical strategies in some protests. For instance, another distinguished between moderate and extreme environmental protection groups, commenting 'You must not directly throw eggs or use violence, I cannot accept that.'[10] Another more recent challenge has been the way that the newly formed NPP has competed for environmental protection-oriented voters. For instance, in 2016 the NPP included images of anti-nuclear protests in its election advertisements and nominated the film director and well known anti-nuclear campaigner Ko I-chen (柯一正) on its party list.

The GPT has made highly distinctive appeals on a number of issues either ignored by mainstream parties or on which they take ambiguous positions. One such issue has been animal rights, as the GPT is the only party in Taiwan with an animal branch. It was prominent in the animal rights demonstration in May 2014 and also in the campaign to protect the leopard cat against a development project in Miaoli in April 2014.[11] In the November 2014 local elections, GPT candidates in Taoyuan gave particular emphasis to animal rights protection. For instance, the successfully elected Xavier Wang (王浩宇) included calls for better protection of stray dogs in his election gazette policy proposals.[12] In fact, one of our interviewed supporters noted this was the issue that first attracted her to the party.[13] However, in this policy realm supporter views were also mixed, with one calling the GPT's animal rights proposals 'a joke'.[14]

The GPT, like other green parties, has attempted to take progressive stances on a range of social issues such as decriminalizing adultery, gay and lesbian rights and the death sentence. Such appeals appear to have mixed results. A case described by GPT CEC member Chiu Hua-mei (邱花妹) reflects the challenges the party faces on such issues:

> Many of our candidates are from environment protection groups and they are very knowledgeable in their fields but do not necessarily have the same progressive thinking in other areas. One of the GPT candidates was asked by the Awakening Foundation [婦女新知基金會] about his/her stance regarding 'Should we get rid of legal punishment for adulterous women?' and his/her stand was 'No.' This was rather embarrassing.[15]

The issue of the death penalty, though, has been more salient and controversial from the perspective of the GPT. The KMT drew international criticism as a result of its decision to resume carrying out death sentences after 2010, while the previous DPP administration had failed to formally end capital punishment.[16] The GPT has been alone among political parties in taking an open position calling for the abolition of the death sentence.[17] This has its risks as surveys have shown between 75 and 85 per cent of respondents oppose ending capital punishment (TVBS Poll Center 2010). In fact, this issue was one frequently used to attack the GPT on social media. For instance, a Facebook site was established during the 2012 campaign titled 'Oppose the Anti-Death Penalty GPT, Don't Vote 8 on the Party List' (抵制廢死綠黨 政黨票不投 '8').[18] Even among our interviewed GPT supporters, we found some disquiet about this policy. Even where they agreed with the policy, they suggested the party avoid this advocacy in campaigns. As one supporter explained,

> Don't touch this kind of issue. Because there are only a few people shouting 'abolish the death sentence'. Do those officials in office dare say end the death sentence? Who dares say abolish the death sentence? It's not the right time for this kind of thing.[19]

Globally, green parties are associated with the promotion of gender equality. The emphasis on gay and lesbian issues has been an important feature in GPT campaigns since the 2010 local council elections. This new approach is closely related to the changing and more diverse internal makeup of the party in the post-2008 period. This issue has developed into one of the party's most distinctive appeals as the two mainstream parties have sent mixed signals on the issue. In contrast, the GPT has been unambiguous in its call for legal reforms to promote gay rights on issues such as marriage and adoption.[20] At the individual candidate level, LGBT issues received extensive attention in the 2010 campaigns and also in the build-up to 2014 local elections. It has shown this in a number of symbolic ways as well, such as its inclusion of the LGBT pride (rainbow flag) into the GPT's party flag. Similarly, the GPT is the only party to nominate openly gay candidates in multiple elections. This image was reinforced in the 2016 election, when the party nominated Victoria Hsu (許秀雯), the CEO of the Taiwan Alliance to Promote Civil Partnership Rights, to the party list. Moreover, the GPT's 2016 *Change* election advert ended with the image of a lesbian wedding.[21]

We do not yet have hard evidence on the overall effect of this LGBT appeal on GPT support. Public opinion appears quite divided on issues such as gay marriage (45 per cent opposing versus 40 per cent supporting) and a number of religious, especially Christian, churches have come out strongly against such reforms (TVBS Poll Center 2013). For instance, in the 2016 elections the Faith and Hope Alliance was widely viewed as a single-issue party solely focused on undermining the LGBT rights movement. However, we did find more support for the GPT promoting gay rights in our supporter interviews (compared to the death sentence) and it is likely that the nomination of openly gay candidates will benefit the party win the pink vote. The survey data, though, show growing support for gay marriage, finding that support was particularly strong in the 20–29 and 30–39 age groups, which the GPT has tended to target most (TVBS Poll Center 2013). We also found the issue to be a major factor in motivating a number of interviewed party members and also campaign activists to support the party. One sign of the growing impact of this new advocacy was that GPT candidate and gay rights activist Liang Yi-chih (梁益誌) was the highest vote winner in the GPT's 2015 CEC election.[22] However, a number of our supporter respondents did urge caution on this. One noted, 'It would not affect my voting intensions, but it would (negatively) influence your votes.'[23] Another supporter described how she had been questioned on her support for the GPT at her church as a result of the party's advocacy of gay rights. She went on to explain that, on understanding this GPT policy, 'I did begin to hesitate [in my support].'[24] With Taiwan hosting the largest gay pride parade in Asia and having an increasingly tolerant public opinion, there clearly is a market for a party taking a clearly pro-LGBT stance.

A core appeal of European green parties is that they aim to be neither left nor right but ahead. However, standard analysis techniques such as Manifesto Research Group and Laver's elite survey studies tend to locate ecological parties to the left of mainstream social democratic parties on the left–right spectrum (Budge and Klingemann 2001: 39). This image is reinforced by coalition governments between green parties and social democratic parties in Germany and France. In the past, left-wing parties have failed to have an impact in Taiwan's elections. Thus, it was noteworthy that the GPT's 2016 campaign gave the impression of its most left-wing approach to date. One factor was its electoral alliance with the SDP. More importantly, the party placed much emphasis on workers' rights in its advertising.

In the Taiwanese context, most political scientists view China–Taiwan relations and questions of national identity as the most salient issues in electoral politics (Hsieh 2002: 38). The GPT has tried to steer clear of this most divisive issue. This has meant that the party includes activists and supporters who stand on both ends of the national identity spectrum. For instance, many of the early generation of the GPT are closer to the DPP and its identity positions, while others even support unification. As a former GPT convenor explained about a potential candidate,

> He did many things that made him look green, for instance he opposed the cable car project. So we thought he was qualified. But when we saw on his resume: member of Promoting Chinese Unification Alliance [中國統一聯盟], some of us thought we can't nominate this kind of person.[25]

Similarly, an example of this alternative perspective on China is former CEC member Lin Cheng-hsiu (林正修), someone who had previously worked as a department director in Ma Ying-jeou's Taipei City government. In our focus group discussion he argued that 'the GPT should do something in China'.[26] In other words, he called for greater interaction with environmental movements in China.

Our supporter interviews suggested that the party is taking the right approach in staying above the national identity battle. In fact many of the younger generation are bored of the national identity appeals of the mainstream parties. Thus, one middle-aged supporter offered these commented,

> Let me tell you, young people in Taiwan today, they have a good life. Young people today don't say I want to be independent. They don't think about that as much as before. We have a good life now. Do you believe it? If you keep shouting independence, unification all day, people will feel annoyed. We are a country now, why do you need to keep repeating those things?[27]

In short, the GPT has made this non-engagement with the identity debate one of its distinctive features. However, with the GPT taking a stance supportive of the Sunflower Movement and its opposition to the Cross-Strait Service Trade Agreement, it may be harder for the party to maintain its non-engagement with identity politics. In an interview, the 2014 GPT candidate Liang Yi-chih explained that 'In Kaohsiung, you only need to join the Taiwan Independence Alliance and can get a substantial number of votes.'[28] However, he preferred to focus on other more pressing issues such as nuclear power and gay rights.

Political resources

Raising sufficient resources is a challenge for political parties in all democracies. However, this is a particularly serious problem for smaller parties in Taiwan, as campaigns are just so expensive. One of the reasons for the costly campaigns is that there is essentially a US-style free market in purchasing media election advertisements. Moreover, smaller parties must compete against the spending powers of the two largest parties, one of which, the KMT, has long been known as the richest party in the world.[29] Even before the campaign starts, a major challenge is raising the candidate deposit. As former GPT co-convenor Karen Yu (余宛如) explained, 'the deposit required for participating in elections is very high, the second highest in Asia, just below Japan'.[30] In most cases, the GPT would lose its deposit where its candidates failed to pass the set vote share threshold. As Yu explained, 'we did not get anything from those 230,000 votes [in 2012], our financial situation got worse after the election'.[31]

Unsurprisingly, problems of fundraising came up repeatedly in our party leader and candidate focus groups. Without reliable funding sources, the party often even struggled to pay for a full-time administrator and until recently shared its office with two other NGOs. The co-convenor in 2011–12, Yang Chang-ling (楊長苓), explained the resource challenges: 'Though I was the Convenor of the GPT, I was more like an unpaid secretary.'[32] With only about 200–400 fee-paying members in past years, the party has tended to be highly reliant on the fundraising abilities of a small number of individuals. Chiu Hua-mei described the state of the affairs when she first joined: '[we] reviewed the party's finances, and we noticed it still owed some people money. There were messy financial records, such as some money was classified as donations but later we found it was a loan from someone.'[33]

An equally and highly related challenge for the GPT, though, has been human resources. This is important because many Taiwanese voters are candidate- rather than party-oriented in their voting behaviour (Rigger 1999: 43). Moreover, the most reliable source of fundraising in Taiwanese politics is established politicians. This partly explains why the splinter parties such as the NP, PFP and, to a lesser extent, the TSU have been more successful than the new prophetic parties. In other words, when these parties split off from the KMT and the DPP they already had pools of incumbent and/or electorally and government-experienced politicians. Such politicians are naturally better able to raise campaign funds and have their own support organizations. The splinter parties were often able to attract politicians who failed to gain nomination from the mainstream parties. In contrast, a review of GPT candidates reveals that almost none had previously stood for other established parties (including splinters).[34] The GPT has just not been viewed as an attractive venue for established politicians. As former GPT Co-Convenor Chen Man-li (陳曼麗) explained,

> We know some legislators that pay more attention to environmental protection, later when they were not re-elected, we tried to invite them to come to the GPT. But they were unwilling. They know we do not have a big enough stage for them.[35]

Even if such mainstream politicians were willing to join, the distrust of mainstream political parties among GPT members and supporters would be a further barrier. Karen Yu explained that

We are clear that we have our way of thinking and they have theirs. It's completely different. Even if they wanted to switch over to us, I feel our GPT members would not necessarily be able to accept them. They would regard them as politicians [政客].[36]

Therefore, one of the biggest problems facing the party has been to find candidates willing to stand. As Yang Chang-ling recalled,

Until July [2011], because of the election in the end of the year, we had to find out some candidates. Time was running out, so I participated in the activities very hard since August and also detected it's hard to find the candidates. We tried to convince others but were always rejected.[37]

Moreover, because it was so hard to find candidates, this tended to result in late nominations, which naturally put GPT candidates at a further disadvantage. As Chiu Hua-mei commented, 'The last minute approach. They selected the candidate for election and often the candidates did not even know the GPT very well.'[38]

A common pattern that undermined the party's human resource base has been that the vast majority of GPT candidates only stood once. At times this was partly because of the poorly run campaign, a lack of resources or where serious inner party disputes led to a falling out. For example, many involved in the 2010 Taipei City Council elections fell out with the party headquarters and not only left the party but took out a legal case due to unpaid wages. Karen Yu's comment after the 2012 election reflects this pattern: 'The others [candidates] have disappeared, and it's not that we're not trying to seek them out, but that they no longer have any interest in political activities. So we do not think they will stand again in 2014.'[39] Despite 2012 being a relatively successful campaign, Yang's comment reflects the post-campaign frustrations: 'those who really join will be filled with setbacks and argument. All the messes lead to an unhappy group, everyone wants to leave.'[40]

In the last two campaigns, in 2014 and 2016, there has been a mixed picture when it comes to the GPT's human resources. Overall, its district and party list candidates have been much stronger and the party has nominated earlier. However, in 2014 the closest the party had to a star, Pan Han-sheng, left the party to form the Tree Party. Even more damaging for the GPT's prospects has been the fact that its main rival challenger party, the NPP, was able to attract more political stars from social movement circles.

The final resource constraint on the party is what the former co-convenor in 2008, Chen Man-li, calls 'loose organization'.[41] Coming from the well-established NGO the Homemakers Union, Chen recalled how on, joining the party,

I discovered that the GPT's organization was not tight [yanjin]. Everyone wanted to extensively discuss their topics of concern systematically, they called for setting up the environment branch, the women's branch, animal welfare branch, but then later no one really followed up on these proposals. So I say its [organization] seemed looser [than NGOs].[42]

Yang was less polite in her appraisal: 'The first time I visited the GPT's office I was surprised – it's a mess and lack of organization.'[43]

Naturally, the GPT has tried to deal with this impression of not being a serious party. Chiu Hua-mei recalled how a DPP politician had suggested they instead join the DPP, as the GPT was more like 'running movements on quicksand'.[44] There was a clear attempt to establish its organizational structure after Li Ken-cheng (李根政), the CEO of the Citizen of the Earth Foundation (地球公民基金會), joined as co-convenor in 2013. As Chiu explained,

Li wanted to build up a structure to begin with. He even reviewed the party's financial books and noticed faults in its financial system. He wanted to set up a proper office and an organized structure for the party first.[45]

Perhaps one of the most significant reforms introduced by Li has been a systematic nomination system that requires candidates to receive the formal support of local NGOs and the signatures of a proportion of the constituency electorate. Another sign of organizational change has been the establishment of genuine party branches, which played an important role in the 2016 campaign. Nevertheless, as Harmel and Janda (1994: 261) warn, reforming a party will 'face a wall of resistance common to large organizations.' This is especially the case in a movement party such as the GPT, which has been accustomed to being a loosely organized party. Chiu reflects the uncertainty, 'we are still not sure if we made a good decision [to reform the party]'.[46] However, these organizational reforms meant that by 2016 the GPT looked on the surface more like a political party than at any time in its history.

Political opportunity structure

The first element of the political opportunity structure we need to consider is the electoral system. In theory, the GPT should have the best opportunity in the MMD national legislative and local council elections, while the predominantly SMD national election system should hold little space for the party. However, the GPT made almost no impact in the MMD Legislative Yuan elections prior to the reforms of 2005. Even though in the MMD Taipei City Council elections in 2010 the GPT showed growth in support, the party was still not yet competitive. In contrast, the party's best performance came in the 2012 and 2016 legislative elections. Apart from the high candidate deposits, another major institutional constraint has been the requirement that parties need to have 10 district candidates in order to be able to be listed on the party list. Although the Taiwanese election system is very similar to the Japanese post-1993 one, Taiwan's seems to offer less space for small parties. This is partly because, unlike in Japan, there is a 5 per cent threshold in the party list and also the number and proportion of party list seats is far lower in Taiwan. Clearly, the electoral system cannot tell us the whole story as the GPT actually recovers under a system designed to squeeze small parties out of the system. Thus the GPT's significant vote share growth in 2012 and 2016 compared to 2008 challenges theoretical expectations.

Clearly the GPT has been trying to find a way to survive within the existing system. The number of successful and nearly successful candidates in 2014 elections showed that a well-run campaign in a local MMD setting can potentially be successful. However, a lesson from 2014 was that the GPT's national campaign struggled to have an impact at the local district level, where candidate voting seemed to predominate over national issues. There is an agreement among GPT figures that there is more space for the party in national-level elections. In early 2014, Chiu Hua-mei noted, 'Actually we have higher hopes for 2016 [than 2014] and one of the targets is to pass the 5 percent threshold.'[47]

In recent years the GPT has been increasingly vocal in calling for reform to the electoral system. For instance, it has challenged the constitutionality of the current election system and its 5 per cent threshold and high candidate deposit regulations.[48] Another key reform the party is advocating is to reduce the voting age to 18, as Taiwan is one of the only democracies where voting age is 20. Such reforms have once again returned to the political agenda in the advent of the Sunflower Movement and its core demand for a constitutional convention.

Another crucial dimension of the political opportunity structure is the party system. Taiwan has the most stable party system of any Asian democracy. Although there have been periods when challenger parties have gained a foothold in parliament, the two largest parties, the KMT and DPP, have dominated the party system since the first multiparty election, in 1986. Two party domination reached its climax between 2008 and 2010, when the smaller parties were largely wiped out from national and local legislatures. These dominant parties present a number of challenges to the GPT's development.

First, many voters either do not know about the existence of the GPT and even if they do they often confuse it with the DPP, as it is common to talk about the green camp as the DPP and its allies. As former GPT candidate Tsai Chi-hao (蔡志豪) explained, 'In south and central Taiwan, if you ask people about the GPT, nine out of ten won't have heard about it'.[49] A related problem is that other voters see the GPT as a DPP ally or faction. Therefore, in our focus groups one of the most commonly raised problems was how to make a clear distinction from the DPP. According to Pan Han-sheng, this problem became more severe in the post-2000 period: 'Once Taiwan began talking about the Blue–Green divide, it became very difficult for the GPT Greens to distinguish ourselves [from the DPP].'[50] In the GPT's early years it had tended to be much closer to the DPP, however the post-2008 party is much more diverse and suspicious of the DPP. This explains why the Pan Han-sheng's cooperation with the DPP in 2012 created such controversy and so many of our interviewees were critical of this deal.

A second major challenge that the mainstream parties pose to challenger parties is their very extensive personal and party support networks. One key element in this is local factional politics. Tsai Chih-hao explained,

> Because of higher levels of mobility, they can only control about 50–60 per cent in Taipei, the rest they cannot control. As soon as you leave Taipei, these control networks have 80–90 per cent of the votes under their control.[51]

For Tsai, key elements of this control system include businesses, community development associations, administrative networks such as Lichang (里長), civic groups such as farmer and fishermen associations, and even gangster groups. He argued that even the GPT would be in danger of being bought off or infiltrated.

Nevertheless, the unpopularity of mainstream parties represents a significant opportunity for small parties such as the GPT. This is due to the growing alienation of voters with mainstream parties. One of the most common reasons supporters and members gave for voting GPT was their dislike of mainstream parties. As one interviewee explained, 'In fact you can't say the GPT particularly attracts me, but that the other parties hold no attraction at all to me.'[52] Thus, the advantage was that the GPT was the only real alternative party on the voting ticket. While there are KMT and DPP splinters, their issue agendas are quite similar to that of their mother parties. Thus, many of those voting GPT in 2012 may not have been especially aware or impressed with the party but viewed it as the best form of protest voting. As former CEC member Hsu Wen-yen (徐文彥) explained,

> It was because we had the right to be voted for. I am sure many people were not satisfied [with the GPT]. But we had spent the two million for those votes, the deposit. That two million allowed us to be chosen.[53]

The experience of the 2014 and 2016 elections reveals that the party system offers challenges and opportunities for the GPT. After 2012, competition for social movement-oriented voters and movement activists became much more intense. We can see this for instance in the case of Li Yi-chieh (李宜潔), who was formerly GPT office manager but in 2014 stood for the TSU in New Taipei City. More damaging, though, was the DPP's attempt to contest the social movement appeal by nominating a number of prominent social movement activists, including three former GPT candidates, in 2016.[54]

Another potential threat is that rather than being the main voice of Taiwan's social movements, the GPT will be sidelined by new political forces. In the 2014 local elections the Tree Party emerged, led by the former GPT figure Pan Han-sheng. This party and the leftist People's Democratic Front (人民民主陣線) nominated quite extensively in the 2014 elections, particularly in the GPT's traditional base of Taipei City. In the aftermath of the Sunflower Movement, the Citizen's Union was created as the first step towards bringing civil society actors together as an alternative political force. This grouping later splintered into two new parties, the NPP and SDP, which intended to contest the 2016 legislative elections. Although the GPT was able to expand its vote share in alliance with the SDP in 2016, it was still far from the 5 per cent threshold to enter parliament.

In contrast, the NPP's electoral success will make it much harder for the GPT to frame itself as the best representative of civil society.

The media environment is also a major structural issue for smaller parties. Our focus groups often heard complaints over the lack of coverage in traditional print and electronic media. For instance, Karen Yu complained how 'In every election journalists deliberately ignore us small parties'.[55] In fact, the problem appears to have got worse as the changes in ownership have led to a media system with clear alliances with the mainstream parties. As discussed in the Ebsworth chapter, some media groups such as Want Want (旺旺) actually take a highly hostile line towards social movements. The political news coverage has become highly partisan. We can see this for instance in the main politics talk shows, where the vast majority of guests are politicians, academics or media commentators with clear partisan allegiances. However, the media environment offers opportunities for the GPT as well because most of the voters the GPT is targeting have abandoned traditional media by now. Instead, their main sources of political information are now the Internet and social media. The Internet naturally has its challenges, however it serves to reduce campaigning costs significantly. Thus, for instance, while the GPT cannot afford to buy TV advertising time, since 2010 it has placed its ads onto YouTube and then they are widely shared on social media. Karen Yu explained how the party is now investing more in its website and social media operations.[56] In our supporter interviews we found that many of them first heard about the GPT or gained their information mainly from social media. This also is a factor in why in 2012 the party was able to expand its support base beyond Taipei compared to 2008 (when Facebook was not yet widely used), even in areas where the party does not have active networks and activists operating.

Often the most effective use of the Internet and social media has been conducted by candidates and party supporters rather than the party official websites. For instance, Pan Han-sheng has long made use of his blog as a campaign tool. One of Pan's 2012 campaigners, Hsiao Yuan (蕭遠), explained the Internet effect:

> Overall the Internet helps the GPT because too many people do not know about the GPT … because I feel the first step is to make people aware of the GPT and then you can talk about what's good about the GPT. No one is going to vote for the GPT if they don't know about the party. So I feel it's essential to use the Internet to raise awareness of the GPT, as the awareness of the party is low in Taiwan, especially in the South and Central Taiwan.[57]

A review of the 2014 campaign revealed that all nine GPT candidates had both websites and campaign Facebook sites with page likes ranging from a few hundred to 225,000.[58] However, there may be limits to the effects of social media campaigning. Tsai Chih-hao's comments reflect this perspective:

> Your Facebook community are already your own people, don't think that is the whole world. It's not. When you go into the market, stand on the front

line, then you'll see people have not even heard of [GPT]. What are you going to do then?[59]

The final element of the political opportunity structure that we consider is the overall strength of social movements. Since the GPT is an integral component of Taiwanese civil society, we can hypothesize that a strong social movement scene should provide a better environment for the GPT to develop. Here the most influential development has been the rise of Taiwan's social movements after the KMT returned to power in 2008, which is the focus of this volume. Moreover, many of these movements share the GPT's core party values, such as gay rights, land justice, environmental protection and democratic political reforms. These movements raised the visibility of the GPT's owned issues. We found that many of the interviewed supporters and activists had first got to know about the GPT through involvement, often as volunteers, in various environmental NGOs. The GPT has been highly supportive of most of these movements, either on the party level or in terms of members taking prominent roles in these campaigns. This at least was the view of Tsai Chih-hao, who stated, 'The GPT's vote share this time [2012] was the result of the combined support of all the environmental groups, this was not only the GPT's achievement.'[60] The GPT was highly supportive of the Sunflower Movement and its core demands. The NGO led by Li Ken-cheng, Citizen of the Earth, was an active part of the alliance against the Cross-Strait Service Trade Agreement, discussed in the chapter by Hsu Szu-chien. Although the Sunflower Movement has served to strengthen Taiwan's social movements, it is possible that the GPT will not be the main beneficiary of this development. In other words, the emergence of a number of civil society parties (discussed earlier) in the aftermath of the Sunflower Movement might actually dilute the political strength of the social movements.

Conclusions

In this chapter we have examined the electoral development of the GPT after the KMT returned to power in 2008. The party's development reveals the blurred boundaries between political and civil society. We showed how the party grew in popularity through to its fine electoral performance in 2012, local breakthrough in 2014 and continued growth in 2016.

Applying a framework suggested by Lucardie, we showed how we can understand the GPT's growth and its limits with reference to its political project, resources and political opportunity structure. In addition to environmental issues, the party has developed a unique range of distinctive niche policy appeals. As has been the case in European green parties, environmental issues remain the core basis of the GPT's support. However, our data suggest that newer appeals, particularly gay rights, have contributed to the GPT's expanded support.

The GPT has struggled with financial, organizational and human resources since its foundation. The expense of campaigning means fundraising remains a severe challenge for small parties in Taiwan. However, the GPT appears to have developed a stronger organizational structure since 2013 and expanded its human resource network. In other words, it appears to have its strongest resource base to date.

Last, the GPT faces a mixed political opportunity structure. The party faces institutional barriers such as high candidate deposit costs, the SMD electoral system and the high voting age. In addition, the party system is quite institutionalized, with two large parties and up to five competitive small parties. Overall, the anti-KMT wing of the party system has become more crowded and competitive. The way that the DPP and NPP have competed for environmental and social movement causes has increasingly posed a major challenge for the GPT. However, some elements of the political environment are quite positive for the GPT. These include the high salience of environmental issues and the growing alienation of many voters from traditional parties; there are elements of the electoral system such as MMD local and party list voting that offer some space for smaller parties. The GPT has benefitted from the growing strength of Taiwan's civil society since the KMT returned to power. Thus the Sunflower Movement represented a major opportunity for the GPT, as it gave many of its core policy objectives greater attention on the political agenda.

When we wrote the early drafts of this chapter in mid-2014 and into 2015, we argued that the GPT had a historic window of opportunity to become Taiwan's first genuine alternative party. However, its failure to make a national-level breakthrough in 2016 and the rise of the NPP mean that the prospects for the party appear much bleaker. It remains to be seen how the party will recover from the disappointment of 2016 and face the challenge of the next round of elections in 2018.

Notes

1 Under the new electoral system there are 113 seats. Voters have two votes. The first vote is for candidates in 73 single member districts. The second vote is for a political party. The party list votes are used to proportionally allocate a further 34 seats to parties that gained more than 5 per cent of the vote. The final six seats are for indigenous voters.
2 The newly formed New Power Party (NPP) is a hybrid party that has combined both alternative and traditional appeals. Thus, we do not view it as a genuine alternative party. For discussion of the NPP's issue appeals, see Fell 2016.
3 In addition to the KMT and DPP, the GPT was outpolled by the PFP, NPP and NP in 2016.
4 www.youtube.com/watch?v=hYYEytLDbjo.
5 http://en.wildatheart.org.tw/story/109/7194.
6 www.youtube.com/watch?v=C9z6iaXqNao.
7 The nomination of Sinan Mavivo, however, did not bring lasting benefits for the GPT. Four years later, the GPT's vote on Lanyu fell to only 19 votes.
8 Supporter Interview 9, 10 August 2013.
9 Supporter Interview 7, 27 July 2013.
10 Supporter Interview 1, 3 April 2013.
11 Lee I-chia. 2014. 'Protestors rally over leopard cat habitat'. *Taipei Times*, 17 April, 1.
12 See CEC database: http://103bulletin.cec.gov.tw/103/%E6%A1%83%E5%9C%92%E

13 Supporter Interview 7, 27 July 2013.
14 Supporter Interview 1, 3 April 2013.
15 Interview, Kaohsiung, 4 January 2014.
16 Shih Hsiu-chuan. 2011. 'Amnesty International urges abolition of death penalty'. *Taipei Times*, 14 May, 3.
17 Although it did not take a clear stance on the death sentence in 2016, the NPP was also attacked by the KMT on the death sentence issue.
18 https://zh-tw.facebook.com/events/325972060766995.
19 Supporter Interview 6, 26 July 2013.
20 www.greenparty.org.tw/news/20131203/85.
21 www.youtube.com/watch?v=C9z6iaXqNao.
22 www.greenparty.org.tw/news/20150214/245.
23 Supporter Interview 6, 26 July 2013.
24 Supporter Interview 1, 3 April 2013.
25 Interview, 2 January 2014.
26 Focus Group, 20 December 2012.
27 Supporter Interview 6, 26 July 2013.
28 www.facebook.com/video.php?v=324894497702625&set=vb.186040714921338&type=2&theater.
29 Chung and Pan. 2014. 'KMT is again world's richest party'. *Taipei Times*, 24 July, 3.
30 Interview, 5 August 2013.
31 Interview, 5 August 2013.
32 Interview, 20 December 2012.
33 Interview, 4 January 2014.
34 Chen Man-li is one of the few exceptions to this rule as she had previously been a DPP National Assembly member.
35 Interview, 17 December 2012. Chen had originally been in the DPP herself, serving as director of the party's Women's Affairs Department, and was elected as a National Assembly member in 2005. She was expelled from the DPP on being nominated by the GPT in 2007.
36 Interview, 17 December 2012.
37 Interview, 17 December 2012.
38 Interview, 4 January 2014.
39 Interview, 5 August 2013.
40 Interview, 17 December 2012.
41 Interview, 17 December 2012.
42 Interview, 17 December 2012.
43 Interview, 17 December 2012.
44 Interview 4 January 2014.
45 Interview 4 January 2014.
46 Interview, 4 January 2014.
47 Interview, 4 January 2014.
48 www.greenparty.org.tw/news/20140623/157.
49 Focus group, 17 December 2012.
50 Focus group, 17 December 2012.
51 Focus group, 17 December 2012.
52 Supporter Interview 5, 21 July 2013.
53 Focus group, 20 December 2012.
54 These are Karen Yu, Chen Man-li and Wang Jung-chang (王榮璋).
55 Focus group, 17 December 2012.
56 Interview, 17 December 2012.
57 Interview, 20 December 2012.

58 www.greenparty.org.tw/news/20150128/240.
59 Focus group, 17 December 2012.
60 Focus Group, 17 December 2012.

Bibliography

Adams, James, Michael Clark, Lawrence Ezrow and Garrett Glasgow. 2006. 'Are niche parties fundamentally different from mainstream parties? The causes and the electoral consequences of Western European parties' policy shifts, 1976–1998'. *American Journal of Political Science*, 50(3), 513–29.

Arrigo, Linda and Gaia Puleston. 2006. 'The Environmental movement in Taiwan after 2000: Advances and dilemmas'. In Dafydd Fell, Henning Klöter and Chang Bi-yu (eds), *What has Changed? Taiwan Before and After the Change in Ruling Parties*. Wiesbaden: Harrassowitz, pp. 165–85.

Budge, Ian and Hans-Dieter Klingemann. 2001. 'Finally! Comparative over-time mapping of party policy movement'. In Ian Budge, Hans-Dieter Klingemann, Andrea Volkens, Judith Bara and Eric Tanenbaum (eds), *Mapping Policy Preferences*. Oxford: Oxford University Press, pp. 19–50.

Cabestan, Jean-Pierre. 2008. 'A new constitutional balance and the prospect for constitutional change in Taiwan'. In Steven Goldstein and Julian Chang (eds), *Presidential Politics in Taiwan: The Administration of Chen Shui-bian*. Norwalk, CT: Eastgate, 29–47.

Carter, Neil. 2007. *The Politics of the Environment*. Cambridge: Cambridge University Press.

Copper, John. 1993. 'The Role of Minor Political Parties in Taiwan'. *World Affairs*, 155(3) (Winter), 95–110.

Doyle, Timothy. 2005. *Environmental Movements in Majority and Minority Worlds*. London: Rutgers University Press.

Duverger, Maurice. 1954. *Political Parties, Their Organization and Activity in the Modern State*. London: Methuen.

Election Study Center. *N.C.C.U., important political attitude trend distribution, National Chengchi University Party Preferences Trend Distribution in Taiwan (1992/06~2014/12)*. Available online at http://esc.nccu.edu.tw/course/news.php?Sn=165.

Fell, Dafydd. 2005a. *Party Politics in Taiwan*. London: Routledge.

Fell, Dafydd. 2005b. 'Success and failure of new parties in Taiwanese elections'. *China: An International Journal*, 3(2), 212–39.

Fell, Dafydd. 2006. 'The rise and decline of the new party: Ideology, resources and the political opportunity structure'. *East Asia*, 23(1), 47–67.

Fell, Dafydd. 2014. 'Measuring and explaining the electoral fortunes of small parties in Taiwan's party politics'. *Issues and Studies*, 50(1), 153–88.

Fell, Dafydd. 2016. 'Small parties in Taiwan's 2016 national elections: A limited breakthrough?' *American Journal of Chinese Studies* (forthcoming).

Fell, Dafydd and Peng, Yen-wen. 2016. 'The electoral fortunes of Taiwan's Green Party: 1996–2012'. *Japanese Journal of Political Science*, 17(1), 63–83.

Harmel, Robert and Kenneth Janda. 1994. 'An integrated theory of party goals and party change'. *Journal of Theoretical Politics*, 6(3), 259–87.

Ho, Ming-sho. 2003. 'The politics of anti-nuclear protest in Taiwan: A case of party-dependent movement (1980–2000)'. *Modern Asian Studies*, 37(3), 683–708.

Ho Ming-sho. 2006. *Green Democracy* [綠色民主]. Taipei: Socio [群學].

Hood, Steven. 1996. *The Kuomintang and the Democratization of Taiwan*, Boulder, CO: Westview.

Hsieh, John Fuh-sheng. 2002. 'Change and continuity in Taiwan's electoral politics'. In John Hsieh and David Newman (eds), *How Asia Votes*. New York, NY: Chatham House, 32–49.

Inglehart, Robert. 1997. *Modernization and Postmodernization*. Princeton, NJ: Princeton University Press.

Liao, Da-chi and Chen, Po-yu [廖達琪 and 陳柏宇]. 2013. 'Internet: A tool for mobilizing the politically marginalised' ['網路: 政治邊陲者的動員工具']. In Liao Da-chi, Hung Yung-tai, Lin Jih-wen, Lin Fu-jen, Liu Cheng-shan, Chen Po-yu, Wang Hong-en, Li Cheng-hsun and Chen Li-hsuan (eds), *Internet Democracy* [網路民主]. Taipei: Wunan, pp. 101–28.

Lucardie, Paul. 2000. 'Prophets, purifiers and prolocutors: Towards a theory of the emergence of new parties'. *Party Politics*, 6(2), 175–85.

McCarthy, John D. and Mayer N. Zald. 2001. 'The enduring vitality of the resource mobilization theory of social movements'. In Jonathan H. Turner (ed.), *Handbook of Sociological Theory*, 533–65.

Meguid, Bonnie. 2008. *Party competition between Unequals: Strategies and Electoral Fortunes in Western Europe*. Cambridge: Cambridge University Press.

Müller-Rommel, Ferdinand. 1998. 'The new challengers: Explaining the success of green and right-wing populist parties in western Europe'. In Annie Laurent and Bruno Villalba (eds), *Les Petit Partis*. Paris: L'Harmattan, pp. 119–41.

Petrocik, John. 1996. 'Issue ownership in presidential elections: With a 1980 case study'. *American Journal of Political Science*, 40(3), 825–50.

Pan, Han-sheng. 2006. 'Where the air is thin and polluted, create the oxygen to produce a rainbow' ['空氣稀薄更加污濁, 製造氧氣催生彩虹']. Available online at http://2012.greenparty.org.tw/index.php/election/election-database/2006election/488-20061214.

Rigger, Shelley. 1999. *Politics in Taiwan: Voting for Democracy*. London: Routledge.

Rigger, Shelley. 2001. *From Opposition to Power: Taiwan's Democratic Progressive Party*. Boulder, CO: Lynne Rienner.

Rüdig, Wolfgang. 2012. 'The perennial success of the German Greens'. *Environmental Politics*, 21(1), 108–30.

Stockton, Hans. 2010. 'How rules matter: Electoral reform in Taiwan'. *Social Science Quarterly*, 91(1), 21–41.

Spoon, Jae Jae. 2011. *Political Survival of Small Parties in Europe*. Ann Arbor, MI: University of Michigan Press.

TVBS Poll Center. 2001, 16 January. 'Survey on the judicial ruling on fourth nuclear power station'.

TVBS Poll Center. 2010, 13 April. 'Survey on death sentence and satisfaction with public security'. Available online at http://home.tvbs.com.tw/static/FILE_DB/PCH/201004/doshouldo-20100413191826.pdf.

TVBS Poll Center. 2011, 7 June. 'Party image survey (legislative party list support rate)' ['政黨形象 (不分區立委支持度)']. Available online at http://home.tvbs.com.tw/static/FILE_DB/PCH/201106/di95o2n2v2.pdf.

TVBS Poll Center. 2013, 14 November. 'Survey on the diverse family bill'. Available online at http://home.tvbs.com.tw/static/FILE_DB/PCH/201404/20140401151506973.pdf.

TVBS Poll Center. 2014, 24 April. 'Survey on the fourth nuclear power station'. ['核四公投議題民調']. Available online at http://home.tvbs.com.tw/static/FILE_DB/PCH/201404/20140426181527706.pdf.

11 Rising from the ashes?

The trade union movement under Ma Ying-jeou's regime

Chiu Yu-bin

1 Introduction

Taiwanese society has witnessed the sharp growth of income inequality in the new millennium. A research paper co-authored by Chu Ching-yi (朱敬一), a former minister in Ma Ying-jeou's government, has pointed out that although the Gini co-efficient of 0.34 is not very impressive compared with Hong Kong and Singapore, the income of the top wage earners has risen significantly since the late 1990s. In 1998, the income of the richest 5 per cent of people was 32.74 times that of the poorest 5 per cent of people. The figure has tripled in 13 years to 96.6 times in 2011 (Chu and Kang 2015). This figure would be too embarrassing if it exceeds 100, so the government announced that it would stop publicizing the figures to the public.[1] Chu and his colleagues warned in another paper that during the economic crises in 2002 and 2008 only the richest 10 per cent of people could recover from the fluctuation and keep growing richer, while the income of the remaining 90 per cent dwindled after the turmoil (Chu *et al.* 2015). In terms of working conditions, three notable phenomena are the stagnation of wages, the prevalence of irregular employment and long working hours. The average wages in manufacturing and service industries have stagnated since 1998. Irregular employment such as part-time jobs, outsourcing and contract jobs and labour dispatch has swelled since 2000. The number of part-timers and dispatch workers grew from around 650,000 (6 per cent of total employment) in 2008, when the national labour statistics started to document the figures, to 776,000 (9 per cent). Regarding working hours, Taiwan's annual working hours are around 2,124, which is the fourth highest in the world, following Singapore, Hong Kong and South Korea, where the wage levels are all higher than Taiwan. Long working hours, which have been particularly prevalent in electronic manufacturing, security service, hospitals, transportation services and retail, have become a national issue after several overworking-related deaths have happened since 2011. Regarding the prospect of personal future, a survey has indicated that most people feel the trend of downward mobility of social class and express an anxiety about the deterioration of income inequality (Lin 2015). All these phenomena might be considered important social background that contributed to the emergence of the Sunflower Movement in 2014.

However, there was no substantial fightback in the new millennium from the trade union movement, which was once militant during the democratic transition at the turn of the 1990s. The conservative unions, which have close ties to the Kuomintang (the Nationalist Party, hereafter KMT), did not play an active role and largely remained docile. On the other side, those independent unions that thrived in the 1990s have failed to launch substantial campaigns to defend workers against attack from the state and capital. Two main national union federations, the old, pro-KMT Chinese Federation of Labor (CFL) and the once-active Taiwan Confederation of Trade Unions (TCTU), both lost the momentum to lead the national labour resistance. This chapter aims to review the trajectory of the trade union movement after President Ma came to power in 2008 in order to understand the characteristics of the labour resistance in a deteriorating environment. To do this, however, one cannot ignore the legacy left by the industrial relations in the pre-democratic period and the trajectory of autonomous labour movement emerging from the democratic transition after the late 1980s. In next paragraphs, therefore, I will start by briefly reviewing how the autonomous trade union movement grew up during the democratization and, following this, in the third part I will illustrate the institutional design of trade unions left by the authoritarian rule that conditioned the development of the new union movement. In the fourth part, I will examine the performance of national union federations, which have often played a significant role in labour resistance in the newly democratic countries. The ups and downs of the new national federation, the Taiwan Confederation of Trade Unions, in the first decade of the new millennium will be reviewed. The fifth part mainly reviews the recent resurgence of labour militancy, followed by the sixth part on the development of union organizing after the amendment of the Trade Union Law. The seventh part examines the relations between labour unions and politics, in particular the political practice of certain autonomous unions triggered by the drastic political change since the 2014 local election. In the conclusion, the challenges of the union movement will be discussed.

2 Brief history of the autonomous trade union movement

With sparse strikes and disputes, industrial relations had been peaceful during the authoritarian period. Although we might not overlook the importance of workers' non-obvious ways of resistance before the democratic transition (Ho 2014), it was in the second half of 1980s that labour started to organize autonomously and take actions openly. The two waves of strikes in 1988 and 1989, shortly after the lifting of martial law in 1987, announced that the period of labour quiescence had come to an end. Industrial action appeared in transportation, petrochemicals, manufacturing, textiles and garments, food processing and service industries. In this period, not only did the progressive labour NGOs emerge, but also the unions were formed in the unorganized workplaces. The number of unions organized by company or factory had grown from 1,160 to 1,354 between 1988 and 1989. Most of the unions formed in this period called themselves autonomous unions, in order to separate themselves from the old-style, conservative unions. Furthermore, those autonomous unions started to form union federations (generally called Federation of Industrial Unions, hereafter FIU) after 1994 at city/county level. Three factors can explain this move. First, between 1989 and 1993 the state and capital launched collaborated oppression on those autonomous unions, which led to around 300 to 400 unionists being illegally sacked and dozens of them being prosecuted (Wu and Liao 1991). It exposed the vulnerability of these autonomous unions – an average membership of 519 in 1991 – and, therefore, revealed the necessity of solidarity among autonomous unions (Chiu 2011a). Second, in the first half of the 1990s the protests brought by factory shutdown, reallocation, and redundancy soared and exhausted the autonomous unionists and the labour NGO organizers. An active union federation at city or county level could more efficiently help those suffering workers, mostly unorganized, and might ease the burden of those experienced unions and labour NGOs. Third, several labour NGOs poured significant energy into several main industrial counties and cities into building local FIUs. As a result, with help from NGOs, eight local FIUs were established between 1994 and 2000 and became the backbone of the national labour movement.

In the mid-1990s, another group of unions joined the FIUs, becoming an important part of the autonomous union movement: the state-owned enterprise (SOE) unions. According to the Trade Union Law, in the whole of the public sector only the SOE employees were allowed to unionize, while the teachers and public servants had been deprived of the right of unionization. SOE unions, which had been under the tight authoritarian control of the KMT since the 1950s, have experienced threats of privatization since the late 1980s. Grass-root SOE workers in petroleum, telecoms, water, railways, wine and tobacco successfully removed the pro-KMT and pro-management leadership and gained union autonomy in the mid-1990s. These SOE unions, along with the FIUs, launched a project to form a new national union federation in late 1997. After two and a half years of preparation, in May 2000 the Taiwan Confederation of Trade Unions (TCTU) was established by eight nationwide enterprise unions (seven of them SOE unions) and eight local FIUs, consisting of around 300,000 members. The then newly elected president, Chen Shui-bian, announced immediately that his government would recognize the TCTU. The formation of the TCTU formally terminated the old, conservative Chinese Federation of Labour's monopoly over labour representation.

However, the continuous decline of union presence in the workplace since 1990 did not stop after the formation of the TCTU (see Figure 11.1). The crisis is clear: the autonomous union movement is losing its strength in the traditional manufacturing sector and failing to represent workers in emerging industries such as electronic and service industries, which in particular are not receptive to union activity. The autonomous union movement might be familiar with how to fight against the government and the individual capitalists, but it lacks momentum and knowledge about how to organize the unorganized. Declining membership is not an uncommon problem for unions around the world, but Taiwan's problem is largely thanks to the legacy of union regulation left by the authoritarian state.

3 The institutional legacy of authoritarian period

To understand Taiwan's union movement, one must not overlook the rigid union structure and regulations left by the KMT authoritarian rule, which not only dominated post-war union development but also conditioned the organizing capacity of the nascent autonomous union movement. It is notable that not all regulations in the authoritarian period were negative and some first-generation unionists were able to cleverly adopt some regulations as resistance strategies (Chiu 2010, chapter 2). However, in terms of organizing development, we can see many negative legacies. For example, the Trade Union Law clearly banned teachers and public servants from unionization. One of the consequences was the underdevelopment of white-collar unionism and this left a social image that unions are something only for blue-collar workers. The most decisive part regarding the union organizing was the union constituency, i.e. the boundary of unionization. Before the amendment in 2011, the Trade Union Law (enacted in the 1940s when the KMT still ruled China) only recognized two types of unions: (1) industrial unions and (2) occupational unions. No other types of union, for example industry-based unions or miscellaneous unions, would be recognized by the government. The first type of union, 'industrial union', refers only to the organizing territory within a company or factory where the number of employees is more than 30. In order to avoid confusion created by the official term 'industrial union', I mainly describe this kind of union as a company- or factory-based union (廠場工會, CFBU hereafter), which more clearly defines the character of unions of this kind and is a term that has been used extensively in the labour movement.

The second type, 'occupational union', refers to unions organized by the workers in the same occupation in the same city or county. Theoretically, occupational unions were designed in the West to be craft unions; however, they have never operated in that way. According to the Ordinance of Labour Insurance, the occupational unions were developed as insurance agents for (1) self-employed workers, (2) employees working in small businesses where there are fewer than 10 employees, and (3) small business owners, while enterprises with more than 10 employees are the agents. In other words, the reason for these occupational workers to join the occupational unions is to be covered by national labour insurance including medical care, industrial accident compensation and pensions. In fact, large amounts of insurance fees (normally collected once every six months in advance) and commissions from the government are great incentives for organizing occupational unions so that most of them are actually controlled by the employers rather than grass-roots employees. As a result, unions of this kind during the authoritarian period were generally corrupt, part of the authoritarian establishment and extremely passive in the labour struggles of the 1980s. Thanks to the institutional design of the national labour insurance and the prevalence of small enterprises, occupational unions not surprisingly have outnumbered the CFBU in union number and membership (see Figure 11.1).

The rigid union structure brings difficulties in union organizing at the company or factory level. The Trade Union Law raises another barrier against union organizing (particularly in CFBU): the minimum to form a union of 30 initiating members. It is not difficult to get 30 workers from different workplaces in an occupation or industry. However, for employees in a company or factory, getting 30 dissatisfied workers is not an easy task if there is no existing labour dispute. In many cases, the active workers who were interested in union-building found it difficult to find enough colleagues to meet the threshold. It is also easy for management to bust a union-building process by intimidating the initiating members. The high threshold of forming a new union has limited the possibility of organizing the unorganized.[2] Finally, if a CFBU cannot be built up successfully, all efforts will be in vein. Those workers favouring a union cannot join any other CFBUs. In the cases of redundancy or factory closure in a unionized workplace, those redundant workers lost the union membership. Given the fact that industry-wide unions are outlawed, those two groups of workers remained unorganized. In short, the size of a CFBU is not decided by the efforts of union leaders but by the size of the company. This explains the steady decrease of CFBUs in number and membership.

One can see the institutional design of the KMT's union regime divides labour into three segments: (1) employees in small workplaces (fewer than 10 employees) and the self-employed: this section constitutes 53.3 per cent of the

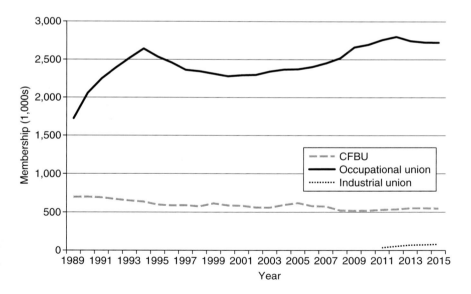

Figure 11.1 Union membership in Taiwan, 1989–2015.

Source: *Yearly Statistics Bulletin*, Ministry of Labor, Executive Yuan.

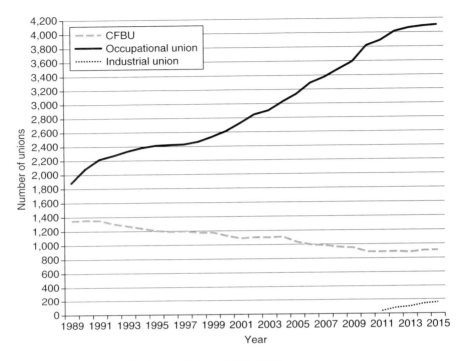

Figure 11.2 Number of unions in Taiwan, 1989–2015.
Source: *Yearly Statistics Bulletin*, Ministry of Labor, Executive Yuan.

working population and traditionally belongs to the organizing territory of occupational unions; (2) employees in larger enterprises (more than 30): this section constitutes 28.4 per cent of working population and is regarded as the main area of autonomous union movement; and (3) the remaining 18.3 per cent are the employees in medium-sized companies (10–30 employees), whose union rights have in fact been deprived. The bedrock of the autonomous union movement was in segment (2), or, more precisely, the workplaces hiring more than 100 employees (which only accounted for 15 per cent of the whole working population). Some scholars have pointed out that the rigid union regulations have prevented the CFBU unionists from having ambitious organizing strategies and launching aggressive organizing (Ho 2006, 2008; Chiu 2011b). As a result, the 2.7 million or so occupational union members have been 'locked' into the current union structure and left no chance to be organized by the autonomous union movement. All resistance prior to the Trade Union Law 2011 amendment, which legalized the industry-based union, exclusively came from CFBUs. However, the size of CFBUs is small and it is difficult for them to resist the attack from the government and management during the strikes. In the first half of the 1990s, right before the democratization, those unions suffered serious attack from the state and the capitalists. Many unions collapsed. The remaining ones gradually distanced themselves from militant unionism. Strikes or confrontational industrial actions gradually disappeared from the union agenda. To survive in the company became the priority of every CFBU. Putting it simply, we can find a more pragmatic mindset within the union leaders since the mid-1990s, compared with their counterparts in the second half of the 1980s.

4 Weak national federations, active local federations

If we deduct the members of occupational unions, which in fact function as agencies of the Labour Insurance Bureau, from the total union membership, the figure of union density (CFBU members/employed + self-employed) was around 6.23 per cent in 2000.[3] It was in these circumstances that unions started to form a new union federation at the local level – as they needed a united front to help each other. Therefore, the first Federation of Industrial Unions (FIU, 產業總工會) was established in Taipei County in 1994 and then some seven other FIUs appeared in other cities/counties over the next six years. These FIUs became the solidarity centre of individual CFBUs, dealing with labour disputes, conducting labour education programmes, mobilizing the protests and negotiating with local government. As a result, the FIUs became the backbone of labour resistance from the mid-1990s. However, the resources of FIU were limited, because its member unions could only contribute 4–6 per cent of their income to the federation. Two reasons prevented the member unions from paying more to the FIUs: first, the rival CFL's local federations, largely composed of occupational unions, only collected 1–2 per cent of income from their member unions. Second, due to their small size, CFBUs could not afford to pay too much to the federation. One consequence was that FIUs could only hire one to three full-time officers to deal with daily affairs. So the strength of a FIU still relied on the voluntary contribution of veteran unionists from some large and experienced affiliates.

In countries experiencing democratic transition, an effective national union federation can help individual union struggles, network the activists, coordinate the information and knowledge of the struggles and fight against the undemocratic regime from the standpoint of the working class (Seidman 1994; Koo 2001; Hirschsohn 2002). Furthermore, many studies reiterate the importance of national union federations when discussing the union revitalization (Heery *et al.* 2000; Heery and Simms 2008, Foerster 2003; Fairbrother and Yates 2003; Milkman and Voss 2004; Simms *et al.* 2013). In the era of neo-liberal globalization, irregular employment, labour flexibility and the degradation of working conditions are common challenges for labour. Thus, a national federation is crucial in terms of union organizing and revitalization: e.g. to fight against neo-liberal policies and union-busting, to develop mapping of organizing on a national scale, to provide resources and training and to coordinate the organizing activities between different unions. In this regard, those autonomous unions, which never received any help from the conservative and pro-KMT CFL, were understandably eager to form a new national union centre from the late 1980s.

The attempt finally succeeded in 2000, when the Taiwan Confederation of Trade Unions was established by FIUs and some large SOE unions.

However, the pragmatism of CFBU still dominates the new TCTU. Most of its member unions expect federations, local or national, to solve their own problems rather than national labour issues. Not many union leaders see TCTU as an organization to launch national campaigns and demonstrations against neo-liberal policies, or as a headquarters to organize the unorganized. Instead, TCTU is expected to meet the pragmatic needs of each member union. This pragmatism was further consolidated after the TCTU re-election in 2003. Before the election, several SOE or privatized SOE unions were invited to join the TCTU, which disrupted the fragile balance between the public and private sector, and thereafter SOE unions gradually dominated the executive board. The DPP government (the Council of Labor Affairs) intervened in the election by encouraging some pro-DPP unions, mostly SOE or ex-SOE unions joining the TCTU, to support the DPP-favoured candidate. As a result, the DPP-favoured candidate defeated his rival, who was supported by most independent unions, by a narrow margin.[4] It led the TCTU to become a national centre that was more interested in the SOE-related issues other than general labour issues and gradually embraced strategies such as negotiations and lobbying instead of street protests. The move of the new leadership angered several active local FIUs whose members were mainly in the private sector. The TCTU has since 2004 gradually played a role in serving its large member unions, mostly SOE or ex-SOE unions, which were mainly interested in negotiating with the government on their specific issues. Between 2002 and 2006, the DPP government launched several neo-liberal policies such as introducing flexible working hours, labour dispatch, and the reform of the national pension scheme. The TCTU has been heavily criticized for its poor performance in resisting these attacks on labour. An FIU leader described the TCTU as 'an organisation for press conferences and statements'.[5]

On the eve of Ma Ying-jeou's inauguration in 2008, the TCTU had been dominated by large SOE unions, who paid little attention to the general degradation of the labour environment. As a result, several active local FIUs whose members were mainly in the private sector and were deeply affected by the neo-liberal policies decided to withdraw from the TCTU in 2005 and form another loose alliance, the Solidarity of Labour, which had roughly 100,000 members. Since then, the Labour Day Demonstrations have mainly been initiated by the Solidarity and, though the TCTU joins the demonstration from time to time, it is no longer in a leading position. The main goals of these demonstrations include: to abolish the labour dispatch and labour flexibilization, to raise the minimum wage, to reduce the long working hours and to reform the pension system. To a certain extent, the Solidarity and its affiliates have replaced the TCTU in resisting the degradation of working conditions. However, the Solidarity is a loose coalition instead of a concrete union federation – it does not even have a secretariat. It acts more like a labour advocacy group that does not effectively take on the role of organizing, bargaining and legislative campaigning.

5 The resurgence of labour militancy

It is notable that President Ma did not stop the neo-liberal labour policies initiated by the Chen Shui-bian regime, such as flexible working hours, labour dispatch and a passive attitude towards raising the minimum wage. In fact, Ma's administration launched more attacks on labour. His labour minister filed a lawsuit in 2012 against the old redundant workers who in the mid-1990s lost their jobs because their employers maliciously moved their factories to other countries without paying any compensation. At that time, there was no institutional design of unemployment allowance. The fierce protests of those desperate redundant workers forced the government to finally set up a special fund to compensate workers' loss and the government could claim the debt from their employers. Everyone knew it was an extremely difficult task because most employers had run away and relocated their assets overseas. However, the sudden move of the labour minister in 2012 to sue workers and ask them to pay back the money angered those veteran protesters as well as the new generation of labour activists, student activists and young lawyers. The two-year-long campaign ended with the government losing the lawsuit. At the same time, another strike related to the malicious factory shutdown also attracted public attention. This was the strike of the Hua-long Textile (華隆紡織) workers in Miao-li County. The Hua-long strike, which lasted 100 days and had much support from other FIUs and students, successfully forced the company's chairperson, who was a former politician, to pay the redundancy. The two campaigns reminded the public about the recklessness of the capitalists who relocated their investment overseas and the weakness of state regulations. Furthermore, President Ma initiated a policy called 'Salmon Coming Home' (鮭魚返鄉), aiming to attract overseas Taiwanese capitalists (mainly in China) to move their investment back to Taiwan by loosening labour regulations in the special industrial zones, providing financial support and tax exemption and increasing the usage of foreign workers. While many critics of the 'Salmon Coming Home' policy focused on its inefficiency in industrial upgrading, labour unions focused on how those capitalists abandoned Taiwanese workers 20 or so years ago. A union officer in Kaohsiung commented in this way:

> If we keep silent on these events, we cannot face those redundant workers throughout the 1990s. It was the sacrifice of those workers that taught us the recklessness of capitalists and forced the government to set up the unemployment allowance scheme. How can the government lure those bastards back to Taiwan with taxpayers' money? It is humiliating us![6]

Another campaign also is important in recent developments. In 2013, the government contracted out the electronic toll system of highways to a big corporation, Far-Eastern Electronic Toll Collection Co. (遠通電收) Again, this was a project initiated by the DPP government. The original collectors, many of whom had worked for 10 or more years, were all sacked. The government said that they were contract workers, so there was no need to consider their job security. The only measure of labour protection the government did was to ask Far-Eastern to find a job in the company for those collectors. It was not surprising that Far-Eastern did nothing. With the help of Taoyuan County FIU, 400 or so collectors organized themselves and started to appeal for seniority compensation, labour insurance reimbursement and diversified job placement. They adopted more radical measures in the campaign, including, in October 2014, a rally on the motorway, where several activists tied themselves on the high bar above the motorway. Then, in May 2015, the collectors occupied the office of the Bureau of Personnel Administration or the Executive Yuan for 12 hours. The campaign is still going on. One of its issues is to question the necessity of the 'contract job', which harms the job security and denies the value of seniority. In particular, the union movement accused the government of being the main user of contract and labour dispatch jobs, which had created the job insecurity.

Some union actions since 2015 are more encouraging. Pilots and flight attendants working for China Airlines (中華航空), the national flag carrier, held several protests in 2015 against the shrinking of annual bonuses, long working hours and work pressure. The pilot union held a strike ballot in May 2015. China Airlines conceded in the subsequent negotiation before the strike begun. Also in May, the union of Shin-chi (昕琦科技) Co., a contact lens manufacturer, held a strike against new regulations on employees' rotation and commuting. In June, workers in Hwa-jei Washing Co. (華潔洗滌), which is the subsidiary of China Airlines in charge of the cleaning and washing task of its flights, launched a strike to ask for wage increases, more paid holidays and a reduction in the number of migrant workers. Both strikes ended with union victory: the management in the two companies conceded to workers in less than 24 hours. Notably, Hwa-jei's strike is the first offensive strike, i.e. asking for enhanced working conditions, whereas other strikes in two decades were exclusively defensive, relating to the goals to fight against massive redundancy, to stop the possible shutdown of the company or to fight against the malicious merger. The success of Hwa-jei encouraged the China Airline flight attendants. One month after Ma stepped down as president in May 2016, the China Airline flight attendants held an unprecedented strike that brought the airline to a standstill and the management conceded within one day.

The trade union movement in Taiwan still faces huge challenges despite its recent victories. The trend of neo-liberal practice at the shop floor and national levels does not stop and the threat from the free trade ideology is still deeply rooted in the mindset of politicians, in both the KMT and the DPP camps. However, the most important challenge might come from the union movement itself. Whether the union movement can reverse the trend of low union density and transform the conservative occupational unionism into a progressive force will be the key to boost union strength in the future.

The trade union movement in Ma's Taiwan 209

6 New organizing efforts after the 2011 Trade Union Law amendment

As the result of legislative reform initiated by the autonomous union movement since the mid-1990s, the amendment of the Trade Union Law in 2011 has brought some breakthrough in terms of union organizing. The rigid regulation on union formation from the Trade Union Law has been changed: the 'industrial union' (i.e. the CFBU) has been renamed as the 'enterprise union' and a new type of union, the 'industrial union', was legalized, while the 'occupational union' remains intact (see Figure 11.3). The fact that the amendment allows workers to organize by industry provides Taiwan's union movement with an opportunity to overcome the narrow-minded, pragmatic CFBU unionism. Under the old union structure, it is obvious that the labour movement based on the company- or factory-based unionism (with the minimum requirement of 30 initiating members) can only reach a limited proportion of employees. The practice of the old Trade Union Law divided workers into three segments: (1) those working in the small businesses (fewer than 10 employees) and the self-employed, mostly joining the occupational unions in order to get the national labour insurance; (2) those working in the enterprises hiring more than 30 people, which means they are entitled to organize a CFBU; and (3) those working in enterprises employing between 10 and 30 people, a group of workers who have no need to join occupational unions (because the company has to insure them) and are deprived of the right to organize a CFBU, which needs 30 founding members. Figure 11.4 shows the proportion of three groups and public servants who have been prohibited from unionization. Given the facts that most occupational unions were conservative and that CFBUs rarely existed in companies hiring fewer than 100 employees, only 15.8 per cent of working people were the potential target of Taiwan's autonomous labour movement. This is why the amendment in 2011 is meaningful.

The legalization of industrial unions in 2011 allowed workers for the first time to organize across the workplaces. Since 2012, several industrial unions have been set up in the industries which were under-organized, for example teachers in preschool institutions (kindergarten and nursery), school teachers, security workers, social workers, workers in the hi-tech industry, employees in universities and so on. Most industrial unions are still small, but these efforts

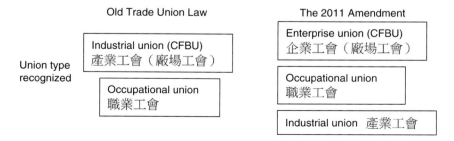

Figure 11.3 The amendment of Trade Union Law in 2011.

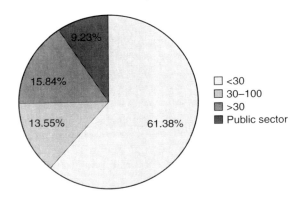

Figure 11.4 Employees by size of workplace, 2014.

Source: *Annual Report of Human Resource Statistics*, The Directorate General of Budget, Accounting and Statistics, Executive Yuan.

might shed light on the future of organizing activities in Taiwan's union movement.

First, one can see the sharp growth of unionization in the education industry. In 2012, a bunch of new industrial unions were transformed from 'teachers' associations' (教師會), mostly organized by teachers in primary schools, junior high schools and senior high schools (years 1 to 12). Those teachers' associations were the only legal organizations of teachers before 2011 but they did not have any rights of collective bargaining and industrial actions. The amendment of the Trade Union Law allowed teachers to be unionized by industry (but not by schools and institutes), so the Teachers' Association at the county/city level immediately transformed into the Teachers' Union in order to resume their union rights with the prohibition on teachers' strikes. Most local Teachers' Unions have affiliated to the National Federation of Teachers' Unions, an umbrella federation with 100,000 members. For preschool teachers, after 2011some active kindergarten teachers from southern Taiwan started to organize themselves into an industry-wide union, whose membership so far has grown from dozens to 800 or so. The final part of organizing in the education sector was the formation of the Taiwan Higher Education Union (THEU). THEU organizes employees in higher education institutions, including full-time and part-time teaching staff, administrative staff, research and teaching assistants and other employees. Its membership to date is roughly 1,300, having grown from 180 when the union was established in February 2012. THEU fiercely fought against the neo-liberal and managerialism-oriented higher education policies of Ma's government. After a series of protests in 2013, the Ministry of Education changed its review system on national universities to a more decentralized system that was more welcomed by the employees. The THEU also successfully blocked a bill initiated by the MoE that intended to separate the salary scheme of private schools from the public school scheme in 2015.

In a Confucian society such as Taiwan, teaching has been seen as an honourable occupation and hence teachers have been asked to be self-sacrificial. It took the union movement 20 years to fight for the right of unionization for teachers, a longer journey than South Korea, where the teachers were entitled to unionize in 1999. Despite the fact that there are significant opinions against educational unions (mainly from the Ministry of Education and the parents' associations), the appearance of unionization in every kind of educational institutions has 'corrected' the myth in the society – that the union is a matter only for 'blue-collar workers' – and to a certain extent encouraged more workers in the service industry (the unionization of civil servants is still outlawed).

Second, these new industrial unions have developed some organizing methods that have not been seen in the traditional union movement. Although many of the methods might have been common in the other counties, for instance pamphlet distribution, house visiting, email bombing, SMS services or social media campaigns, it is the starting point of Taiwan's union movement to accumulate its own experiences of organizing across companies/workplaces. For example, the THEU has employed a two-tier email system, one for current members and the other for potential members, who have been collected deliberately from the recommendations of current members and the list of social and political petitions over the past 10 years. The mailing system is useful in organizing when combined with special issues (e.g. the campaign against national university review and protests against irregular employment in universities).

Third, based on the experiences, some established union federations have noticed the shortage of organizing skill and knowledge and launched some preparatory work for organizing in the future. Several local federations and the industrial federations have highlighted the importance of new organizing strategies in union training programmes and regular meetings. A full-time officer of Kaohsiung City FIU told me his plan: 'We have to gradually let the delegates from different affiliates to understand the crisis so that I can get more support when I raise the plan of a new industrial union for security workers next year.'[7] Another example is the Taiwan Federation of Financial Unions (TFFU), which is organized by individual bank unions, recently formed a new financial industrial union in order to attract employees working in a non-unionized bank. The leadership understands that current knowledge would not be enough for an industrial union, so the executive committee of the TFFU has approved a series of training programmes for all full-time officers of its affiliates, including visiting the Hong Kong Confederation of Trade Unions to learn how to organize the unorganized. It is noteworthy that the most changes happened in local CIUs and industrial federations, while the national federation, the TCTU, which is dominated by large SOE unions, has shown little interest in developing the role of organizing the unorganized.

Finally, the failure of the TCTU, in particular its marginalization in the national politics of Ma's regime, has stimulated a new discussion within the autonomous union movement about the importance of an effective national union centre. The TCTU was established upon, not against, the legacy of KMT authoritarian rule, a pragmatic and narrow-minded unionism grown from the formation of the CFBU, whereas the old, conservative Chinese Federation of Labor remained dominant among the occupational unions and SOE unions. Apparently the new challenge lying ahead is not the conservatism of the old unions but the rigid union structure that obviously cannot resist the fierce attack of neo-liberalism across occupations and industries. The general secretary of the Kaohsiung Federation of Labor Unions, a local federation formed by CFBUs and some progressive occupational unions, denounced the old division of occupational unions/CFBUs:

> Putting aside the history of the corrupted and conservative occupational unionism, the occupational unions nowadays are the only unions in Taiwan that have accumulated precious experiences on how to recruit members across workplaces. If we want to organise the unorganised, in particular in the service industry, their experiences are unique and important. I think we need a new national federation that can gather different experiences and develop new organising strategies that can bring all suffered workers together.[8]

In Taiwan, one can see the gap between the current low union density and the hope for a stronger union movement among society.[9] How to fill the gap is surely the most urgent task for the autonomous union movement. As shown in the previous discussion, the change will not happen if the union movement cannot review and transcend the legacy of union structure left by the authoritarian rule. It is obvious that the once-militant company- or factory-based unionism of the late 1980s will not be able to meet the challenge of changing economic structure and industrial relations. To develop new organizing methods will require combining the experiences of blue-collar industrial unionism and the mindset of occupational unionism to organize across workplaces, as the story of organizing growth in Los Angeles service industry shows (Milkman and Voss 2004).

To gain new organizing momentum, the trade union movement needs to develop an underlying rationale of organizing, coordinated planning, comprehensive strategies, training programmes, and so on. As illustrated in part four of this chapter, the experiences of union renewal in the West have shown that many of these tasks often rely on a proactive national union federation. Can the Solidarity of Labour be transformed into a new confederation to replace the TCTU, equipped with stronger organizing ambitions and more comprehensive organizing strategies? So far the discussion has been brought up among Solidarity's affiliates since 2014, but no conclusion has yet been reached. In the second term of Ma Ying-jeou's presidency, we witnessed the resurgence of labour militancy and some new organizing efforts brought about by the amendment of the Trade Union Law. However, the limited resources and the loose structure of the Solidarity of Labour made it difficult to take the responsibility of coordinating the national resistance and envisaging more effective national organizing strategies to enhance the low union density. So far the momentum of new organizing mainly comes from the local FIUs. For example, most workshops and training courses since 2014 on organizing irregular workers, dispatch workers and youth labour have been held by local FIUs or the TFFU, not by the Solidarity of Labour. The Solidarity did not play any role in new organizing campaigns mentioned above, while several nascent industrial unions have received certain help from FIUs.

7 Unions in politics

It is notable that pro-KMT unions did not play a significant role during Ma's period in government. The CFL and its affiliates were sidelined and no pro-KMT union leader was recruited into cabinet or the KMT central committee after Ma came to power in 2008. Interestingly, a similar situation happened to the DPP. In the 2012 general election (both presidential and legislative), the DPP's chairperson and presidential candidate, Tsai Ing-wen, who used 'social equality and justice' as her campaign slogan, declined to nominate any leaders from the autonomous unions into the DPP's legislator PR candidacy list. Even after its defeat, the DPP still showed a lukewarm attitude towards the labour protests mentioned in previous paragraphs. A veteran unionist described his disappointment with the DPP:

> When the DPP was small, they said they were too small to help labour; when it won the president in 2000, they said they were minority in the Legislative Yuan so they cannot do anything; now they rule many local governments, they said 'please wait until we win the President and Legislative Yuan in 2016.' Does this party really care about working people?[10]

It explains why many autonomous unions that used to be pro-DPP lost their interest in supporting it. In Ma's terms, the unions kept fighting against anti-labour policies not only at the national level but also at the local level, including cities/counties where the DPP was in power. For example, for those active union federations in Kaohsiung where the DPP ruled with a comfortable majority, the local government was not friendly at all. Active union federations in Kaohsiung had to fight against the municipal authority's outsourcing and labour dispatch policies. It seriously disappointed the autonomous unions, most of which had been holding big hopes for better treatment from a grown-up DPP since the democratic transition in the 1990s.

The political atmosphere has changed drastically since late 2014 when the KMT was trapped in a fierce power struggle. Once the high popularity of President Ma Ying-jeou's first term had disappeared, his government showed no willingness to accept criticism for dealing with controversial social issues such as labour disputes, land expropriation and brutal eviction, corruption in high-rank officials and injustice in judicial practice. The situation was getting worse in the spring of 2014, when the Sunflower Movement erupted. The sentiment did not stop at criticizing Ma and his team but all of his party. A slogan has since gone viral: 'If the KMT doesn't fall, Taiwan is no way to be good'. (國民黨不倒, 台灣不會好). Eight months after the Sunflower Movement, the DPP won a landslide in the local election. And, in Ma's stronghold, Taipei City, the KMT candidate was defeated by an independent politician. An interesting development was that new mayors of Taipei City and Taoyuan City recruited two active unionists each into the cabinet as the Chief of Labour Bureau. Both of the unionists-turned-officials have exercised the power from which the union movement had indirectly benefitted. The Chief of the Taipei Labour Bureau, Lai Shiang-ling (賴香伶) who was a former organizer of immigrant workers, exercises the power to inspect working hours in the media industry, which is notorious for its long working hours and working pressure. The move stimulated several media employees to form their own unions. Lai's counterpart in Taoyuan City, who was the general secretary of the Taiwan Railway Workers' Union, also used the power of workplace inspection on the companies involving labour disputes in Taoyuan, including those of flight attendants and pilots and Hua-Jei's workers.

Since President Ma's second term, some small parties that have been concerned about the growing social discontent over social inequality and wage stagnation started to draft pro-labour platforms and establish certain connections with progressive unions. The 18-year-old Green Party Taiwan (GPT), which for the first time won two local council seats in 2014, has tried to develop connections with autonomous unions in Kaohsiung and Taipei. A few unionists took up positions in GPT's secretariat and central committee. In January 2015 a bunch of founding members of the Taiwan Higher Education Union joined the newly formed Social Democratic Party (SDP). In July, GPT and SDP decided to form a coalition for the 2016 general election. Eleven candidates ran for district seats and six for the PR seats (which needed to pass the threshold of 5 per cent vote). The coalition decided to nominate the general secretary of the Chung-hwa Telecom Workers' Union, Chang Li-fen (張麗芬), and put her as the first candidate in the PR list. The nomination was soon welcomed by many autonomous union leaders and several large unions and federations started to mobilize their members and to collect political funds for the campaign. Another small new party, the New Power Party (NPP), which was formed by several high-profile non-student leaders of the Sunflower Movement, also nominated a lawyer, who had voluntarily fought several labour disputes, to stand in the Hsin-chu constituency. The NPP, which, nevertheless, holds a closer position to the DPP's Tsai Ing-wen, also put pro-labour policies in its electoral platform. Although, in the end, the GPT–SDP coalition failed to win any seats (it received a 2.5 per cent share of the vote, around 300,000 votes) and the pro-labour NPP candidate did not get elected, the campaigns successfully brought up the enthusiasm of political participation among autonomous unions. After the election, the Solidarity of Labour and several FIUs held special conferences to review the GPT–SDP Alliance campaign and discuss the future of labour politics. The labour issues brought up in the election, such as working hours, labour dispatch, low wages and income inequality, somehow forced the two main parties to respond during the election and will become the crucial materials of labour movement in the post-Ma Ying-jeou era. Despite the fact that the unions are still debating their strategies for political participation, (e.g. to keep allied with the GPT–SDP alliance or to form an independent Labour Party), one can anticipate the further politicization of the union movement in the future.

8 Conclusion

Looking back, the degradation of working conditions and labour protection in the eight years of Ma Ying-jeou's presidency was highly related to the weakness of the trade union movement, which was not only trapped in the institutional legacy left by the long-term authoritarian rule but also was weakened by the DPP administration between 2000 and 2008. Facing the fact that Ma's economic and financial policies strongly favoured the capitalist class, in particular the large corporations and the business groups who invested in China, the weakened TCTU failed to take on the leading role of national labour resistance. As a result, in the first term of Ma's presidency only a few local federations in Taoyuan City, Taipei City, Tainan City and Kaohsiung City and their loose national network, the Solidarity of Labour, fought against neo-liberal labour policies. It was not until 2012 that we saw increasing labour militancy under the efforts of these union federations, including several labour disputes and strikes that gradually attracted public attention. Some successful strikes in 2015 and 2016 might be quite encouraging. However, it is too soon to reach the conclusion that the union movement has found its momentum to stand up against the neo-liberal DPP government after 2016. The challenge lying ahead of Taiwan's trade union movement is the low union coverage. While most occupational unions function as national labour insurance agencies and remain conservative, the members of CFBUs and industrial unions only accounted for 6.22 per cent of employees in 2014.[11] To radicalize the occupational unions and to organize the unorganized are the keys to improve the strength of trade union movement in Taiwan. One positive development that occurred under Ma's administration was the amendment of the Trade Union Law, which loosened the rigid regulation of union formation. Under the old regulation, the CFBU and occupational unions actually divided workers instead of uniting them; unions were confined to a specific factory, company or occupation. The amendment in 2011 brought the basic freedom of unionization to Taiwanese working people, who can finally organize across different workplaces and occupations. The next challenge will be to what extent the current union movement can grasp the new institutional opportunity to enlarge union coverage. Obviously it needs the additional backup such as resources and coordination from union federations or large national unions. In Taiwan's case, it is the local federations that are taking up the role. It is noteworthy that the pro-KMT CFL and its local affiliates were sidelined in Ma's administration. Those autonomous local federations have therefore occupied a more prominent role in national labour campaigns. In other words, there is no competition from the conservative union federations. It might send a message to workers in trouble about which side they can approach and who can really help them. That is why we can see more workers in dispute coming to FIUs for assistance and later being unionized by the FIUs.

As happened in 2000, the party rotation in 2016 provides another political opportunity for the trade union movement. The last opportunity did not bring much positive impact on the development of trade unions – and even caused the split of the TCTU. Will the developments seen in the second term of Ma Ying-jeou's presidency, i.e. the build-up of union militancy, the practice of politicization and the deregulation of union formation, help the trade union movement to meet the challenges brought by the new political opportunity? The answer lies in the capability of FIUs to enlarge the union membership at the local and industrial levels and to build a more substantial and comprehensive national network.

Notes

1 'Ministry of Finance: The Figure of Income Gap Will Not Open the Public' (貧富差距恐破百倍 財部不公布了). *Liberty Times* (自由時報), 29 April 2014.
2 The minimum number of workers to form a union in Hong Kong is seven and in Japan it is 20. There is no regulation on minimum initiating members in South Korea. Namely, two workers can theoretically form a union.
3 Calculated from the *2000 Report on the Manpower Utilization Survey*, The Directorate General of Budget, Accounting and Statistics, and the *Yearly Statistics Bulletin*, Ministry of Labor.
4 Regarding the government intervention, see 'The government-backed candidate to launch a campaign in the TCTU election' (全國產總改選 官派大反攻). *China Times* (中國時報), 15 May 2003; 'Lu Tien-lin won the TCTU president with a three vote margin' (全產總理事長改選 盧天麟三票險勝). *China Times* (中國時報), 20 June 2003.
5 Interview with an executive office of the Kaohsiung City Federation of Industrial Unions (高雄市產業總工會), 12 December 2014.
6 Interview with an executive office of the Tainan Federation of Industrial Unions (台南市產業總工會), 30 October 2014.
7 Interview with the general secretary of Kaohsiung City Federation of Industrial Unions (高雄市產業總工會), 15 Dece 2014.
8 Interview with the general secretary of Kaohsiung Federation of Labor Unions (大高雄總工會), 10 January 2015.
9 For the public anticipation of stronger trade unions, see Chang and Chang (2010).
10 Interview with an executive office of the Taoyuan City Federation of Industrial Unions (桃園市產業總工會), 6 January 2015.
11 Calculated from the *2014 Report on the Manpower Utilization Survey*, Directorate General of Budget, Accounting and Statistics, and the *Yearly Statistics Bulletin*, Ministry of Labor.

Bibliography

Chang, Chin-fen and Heng-hao Chang. 2010. 'Who cares for unions? Public attitudes toward union power in Taiwan, 1990–2005'. *China Perspectives*, 2010/3, 64–78.
Chiu, Yu-bin. 2010. *Haunted by the past, organising the future: Independent labor movements in Hong Kong and Taiwan*. PhD thesis, University of Essex.

Chiu, Yu-bin. 2011a. 'Old constraints and future possibilities in the development of Taiwan's independent labor movement'. *Capitalism, Nature and Socialism*, 22(1), 58–75.
Chiu, Yu-bin. 2011b. 'A Comparison on the Independent Union Movements in Hong Kong and Taiwan' ['工會作為階級行動者？ 對台灣與香港獨立工會運動的歷史考察']. *Hong Kong Journal of Social Science* [香港社會科學學報], 41 (Autumn/Winter).
Chu, Cyrus Ching-yi, Teyu Chow and Sheng-cheng Hu. 2015. 'Top income shares in Taiwan 1977–2013'. *World Top Incomes Database Working Paper* (2015/2).
Chu, Cyrus Ching-yi and Ting-yueh Kang. 2015. 'Social inequalities during economic transformation' ['經濟轉型中的「社會不公平」']. *Taiwan Economic Forecast and Policies* [臺灣經濟預測與政策], 45(2), 1–22.
Fairbrother, Peter and Charlotte A. B. Yates (eds). 2003. *Trade Unions in Renewal: A Comparative Study*. London and New York, NY: Continuum.
Foerster, Amy. 2003. 'Labor's youth brigade: What can the organizing institute and its graduates tell us about the future of organized labor?' *Labor Study Journal*, 28(3), 1–31.
Heery, Edmund, Melanie Simms, Rick Delbridge, John Salmon and Dave Simpson. 2000. 'The TUC's organising academy: An assessment'. *Industrial Relations Journal*, 31(5), 400–415.
Heery, Edmund and Melanie Simms. 2008. 'Constraints on union organising in the United Kingdom'. *Industrial Relations Journal*, 39(1), 24–42.
Hirschsohn, P. 2002. 'From grassroots democracy to national mobilization: COSATU as a model of social movement unionism'. In J. Kelly (ed.), *Industrial Relations: Critical Perspective on Business and Management*. London: Routledge.
Ho, Ming-sho. 2006. 'Challenging state corporatism: The politics of Taiwan's labor federation movement'. *China Journal*, 56, 107–27.
Ho, Ming-sho. 2008. 'A labor movement without class identity: Taiwan's autonomous unions and the limits of the brotherhood' ['沒有階級認同的勞工運動：台灣的自主工會與兄弟義氣的極限']. *Taiwan: A Radical Quarterly in Social Studies* [台灣社會研究季刊], 72, 49–91.
Ho, Ming-sho. 2014. *Working Class Formation in Taiwan: Fractured Solidarity in State-owned Enterprises, 1945–2012*. London: Palgrave Macmillan.
Lin, Thung-hong. 2015. 'Causes and consequences of increasing class inequality in Taiwan' ['臺灣階級不平等擴大的原因與後果']. *Taiwan Economic Forecast and Policies* [臺灣經濟預測與政策], 45(2), 45–68.
Koo, Hagen. 2001. *Korean Workers: the Culture and Politics of Class Formation*. Ithaca, NY, and London: Cornell University Press.
Milkman, Ruth and Kim Voss. 2004. (eds) *Rebuilding Labor: Organizing and Organizers in the New Union Movement*. Ithaca, NY: Cornell University Press.
Seidman, Gay. 1994. *Manufacturing Militance: Workers' Movements in Brazil and South Africa, 1970–1985*. Berkeley, CA: University of California Press.
Simms, M., J. Holgate and E. Heery. 2013. *Union Voices: Tactics and Tensions in UK Organizing*. Ithaca, NY: Cornell University Press.
Wu, Nai-Teh and Jin-kwei Liao. 1991. *The Counterattack from the Empire: Dismissal of Union Officials, the Labour-Management Act and the Class Conflict* [帝國大反擊：解雇工運幹部、勞資關係法和階級衝突]. Paper presented at the Conference on Labor Market and Industrial Relations, Institution of Social Sciences, Academia Sinica, Taiwan, June 1991.
Liberty Times (自由時報).

China Times (中國時報).
Annual Report of Human Resource Statistics, The Directorate General of Budget, Accounting and Statistics, Executive Yuan.
Report on the Manpower Utilization Survey, The Directorate General of Budget, Accounting and Statistics, Executive Yuan.
Yearly Statistics Bulletin, Ministry of Labor, Executive Yuan.

12 A team player pursuing its own dreams

Rights-claim campaign of Chinese migrant spouses in the migrant movement before and after 2008

Lara Momesso and Isabelle Cheng

Introduction

Since the early 2000s, citizenship legislation regulating marriage migration from China and South East Asia to Taiwan has become one of the most debated public policies in Taiwan (Friedman 2012, 2010; Liao 2009; Yang and Lee 2009; Kaneko 2009: 23; Tsai and Hsiao 2006: 5). From the Democratic Progressive Party (DPP) government of 2000–08 to that of the Kuomintang (KMT) after 2008, each ruling party left its mark on the shaping of the legislation that safeguards the eligibility of migrant spouses for citizenship rights (Cheng and Fell 2014: 17–21). While the legislation was evolving, the migrant movement was at the forefront, campaigning for reforming the restrictive and discriminatory legislation. The rights-claim movement of migrant spouses is spearheaded by the Alliance for Human Rights Legislation of Immigrants and Migrants (AHRLIM) (移民／住人權修法聯盟). Having the TransAsia Sisters Association, Taiwan (TASAT) (南洋台灣姊妹會), as its original and core member, AHRLIM is an umbrella alliance forged in 2003 and composed of a large number of social organizations advocating for the improvement of human rights of women, labour, migrant spouses and migrant workers (Hsia 2006a: 97, 2006b: 34–5, 2008: 188, 2009b). One founding member is the Marriage Association of Two Sides of China (MATSC) (中華兩岸婚姻協調促進會),[1] a self-help organization independently established by Chinese migrants and their Taiwanese spouses in 1998, which later received governmental recognition for their capacity of advocating for the well-being and rights of marriage migrants from the People's Republic of China (PRC) in Taiwan.

It has been well documented that the migrant movement under the leadership of AHRLIM achieved its goal of improving the legal treatment for South East Asian spouses during the second DPP presidency. Indeed, the Immigration Act was amended in November 2007 largely in accordance with the demands raised by the movement. The requirement of financial sufficiency for citizenship eligibility was dropped, the right to work was granted and the right to reside after the cessation of marriage was partially permitted (Hsia 2006a: 107, 2009b: 371;

AHRLIM 2013; Liao 2009: 398). After the KMT returned to power in 2008, AHRLIM continued to lobby on behalf of South East Asian spouses for the amendment of the Nationality Act and to mobilize the support for equalizing legal treatments for Chinese and foreign spouses.

Against the backdrop of the well-studied AHRLIM leadership during the DPP era, however, what has not been sufficiently examined is the strategic division of labour within the alliance, which may hold the key to deciphering contrasting interests within the migrant movement. From the outset of the alliance, it appears opaque as to how individual organizational members, such as MATSC, contributed to the overall formation of the campaign strategy, the mobilization of social support and their lobbying for legislative reform. As a result, the internal dynamics, which made the migrant movement in Taiwan different from other movements examined in this volume, remains unknown. Given MATSC's representation of the huge constituency of marriage migrants from the PRC, a close look at its position and contributions within the alliance will offer a key to understanding the internal dynamics of the migrant movement in Taiwan. In this light, this chapter aims at examining the campaign of AHRLIM after 2008 during the KMT administration, with a focus on the overlapped as well as divergent interests between MATSC and AHRLIM. This chapter will compare the changed political environment before and after 2008 and the strategies employed by the migrant movement as a response to the new political opportunities after 2008. Specifically, this chapter aims to answer the following questions: (1) how did the change of ruling party in 2008 contribute to the emergence of new political opportunities available to the migrant movement? (2) How did MATSC and AHRLIM negotiate with the changed political environment emerging after 2008? (3) What achievements have been attained by AHRLIM as a whole and MATSC in particular? Underlining MATSC's somewhat peculiar role and its strategies within the alliance, this chapter argues that the migrant movement in Taiwan should be understood not as a unified entity but as a conglomeration of sometimes conflicting interests.

Examining the migrant movement: political opportunity theory

To grasp the complex negotiation between the state and the migrant movement, this chapter builds on the analytical concept of political opportunity. Political opportunity theory argues that social movements in general, and their values, strategies, alliances and actions in particular, are not only a consequence of a lack of representation in social and political contexts but also related to the operation and development of the political system where they emerge (Tarrow 1988: 428). Thus, social movements may shape, or be shaped, by the opportunities and constraints of the socio-political context in which they form and exist. Moreover, they may engage with politics by asking for inclusion of new issues and concerns in the political debate (Scott 1991: 24) and, in some cases, they may enter the political and institutional arena and directly negotiate with the state apparatus (Foweraker 1995: 62).

Along this line, political opportunity theory sees social movements as a rational action undertaken by groups of citizens in opposition to institutional actors whose actions have an impact on the interest of citizens. The focus lies on the dynamic negotiation between the two sides (Carty 2011: 10–11). To further enhance the dynamism of this negotiation, McAdam and colleagues (1996) introduce two concepts of *mobilizing structures* and *framing processes* (McAdam *et al.* 1996: 2). Mobilizing structures refer to the strategies conceived by social groups allowing drawing resources from various avenues so as to advance social campaigns. These resources include knowledge, funding, organizational structure, media attention and political elites' support (Carty 2011: 9–10). Framing processes refer to the shared cognitive worldview in which social movements and state institutions mediate their different interpretations of existing ideology, norms and values. Within this process, not only do social movements identify new problems and develop their moral appeals; they also envisage their unique solutions, so that the link between *why* the movement is campaigned and *how* it evolves is synergic (Carty 2011: 12–14).

Built on political opportunity theory and the concepts of mobilizing structure and framing process, this chapter will shed light on the following two issues: (1) how the migrant movement in Taiwan shifted its strategy as a consequence of changed political opportunities after 2008; and (2) how interests of different migrant groups coexist within the movement as a consequence of the availability of new political opportunities.

A dichotomized view of the migrant movement: the known and the unknown

Current literature on the migrant movement in Taiwan is problematically dominated by a dichotomy of inside-out and outside-in perspectives. The former is written by involved activists reporting how the alliance waged its campaign as an aligned movement negotiating with state structures (Liao 2009; Hsia 2006a, 2008, 2009a, 2010, 2013). The latter prioritizes the strategies developed by single group members to negotiate with state structures (Tseng *et al.* 2013; King 2011).

As activists who founded AHRLIM, Hsia (2006a, 2008, 2009a, 2010, 2013) and Liao (2009) take an *inside-out* perspective, chronicling the progress of the alliance and analysing its strategy. Prioritizing the perspective of migrant spouses from South East Asia as the main interest group and active members within the alliance, Hsia assesses their activism, particularly at the early stage, as being short of critical assets, such as networks, legal knowledge and language proficiency (Hsia 2010: 104). This evaluation seems to suggest that they cannot *independently* and *autonomously* found formal organizations. Nevertheless, arguing along the lines of the empowerment of the oppressed (Hsia 2006a), contentious collective politics (Hsia 2008), transversal politics (Hsia 2008), multiple citizenship (Hsia 2009a) and multiculturalism (Hsia 2013), Hsia asserts that, being empowered by their participation in the movement, migrant spouses have become 'historical subjects' capable of changing social relations. Despite the significance of this scholarship for the understanding of the migrant movement in Taiwan, these insiders' accounts are nevertheless given from the stance of the 'privileged local activists' (Hsia 2010: 104) who anchored, orchestrated and choreographed the proceedings of the alliance.

It should also be pointed out that these studies draw heavily from the experiences of South East Asian spouses. Yet these experiences are not entirely identical with those of other migrant groups, such as marriage migrants from the PRC and labour migrants. In other words, this *inside-out* scholarship overlooks the fundamental heterogeneity of interests and identities within the movement. Thus, these studies do not fully inform how other crucial group members, such as MATSC, operated inside and outside the movement. The stressed sisterhood among migrants and the celebrated comradeship among group members induced by consensus-seeking gloss over divergent or even conflicting interests among member organizations. These deficiencies flatten the complex heterogeneity, constituted by gender and ethnicity, within the alliance and, as a result, dismiss the critical diversity of interests that derive from the heterogeneity within the movement.

Parallel to this scholarship, there is a separate strand of studies on the campaign mobilized by marriage migrants from the PRC in cooperation with their Taiwanese partners. In this light, Chao's *inside-out* accounts provide valuable biographical insights into individual migrants' motivations of participation in the campaign and their interpretations of the impact of the nationalistic 'Love Taiwan' discourse on their personal life (Chao 2006). Yet, viewed from the theory of political opportunity, Chao's anthropological observations do not illuminate how the collective actions of migrant spouses from the PRC and their Taiwanese partners are possible in the first place. They also do not attend to how PRC marriage migrants' campaign fitted into the broad migrant movement spearheaded by AHRLIM.

Taking an *outside-in* perspective, and treating PRC migrant spouses' campaign as contentious politics, Tseng and colleagues (2013) analyse the political environment where MATSC campaigns were waged. By scrutinizing the legislation, they demonstrate that the legislation inaugurated by the KMT and DPP was a reflection of the fluctuating Taiwan–China relations. Under this overarching political setting, they elaborate other parameters which also affected the advance of the campaign, including anti-China nationalistic sentiment, the gender bias of women's groups towards marriage migration and the legal restrictions on the political rights of PRC migrant spouses. Although acknowledging that PRC marriage migrants and their foreign counterparts encountered a socio-political environment that is not entirely identical, the authors do not delve into how the two groups diverged in terms of their interests, agenda setting and strategies. Thus, they give an impression that the PRC marriage migrants' right-claim campaign was an independent and isolated incident. They also overlook the essential role played by Taiwanese spouses in the campaign and the complex power relation between husband and wife, which also shapes the overall outcomes of the movement.

A juxtaposition of these two strands of literature shows that their strength is also their weakness. The *inside-out* accounts focus on AHRLIM and value the universal sisterhood among migrant spouses but fall short of revealing the internal heterogeneity of interests within the alliance. The *outside-in* perspective focuses on PRC marriage migrants' campaign and sheds light on opportunities and constraints arising from the socio-political environment, but it is insensitive to the support rendered by civil society as epitomized by the success of AHRLIM. Moreover, none of these studies examine transnational factors that are beyond the national level and, as a result, fail to challenge the inclination, common to the literature on social movements in Taiwan, that treats domestic politics as the dominant contributing factor for the evolution of migrant movement in Taiwan.

Seeing the migrant movement as an alliance of divergent interests and intrinsically transnational, this chapter aims at addressing the disjointedness embedded in the literature reviewed above. This chapter regards the migrant movement in Taiwan as a flexible alignment in which component groups act at times as in a united front and at other times pursue their own agenda when the environment is ripe for changes favourable to a specific group. In this vein, AHRLIM is not only a collective actor that makes claims on behalf of all organizational members and the mass of migrants, but it is also a heterogeneous entity composed of different identities and interests derived from nationality, ethnicity and gender. While this chapter explores how the migrant movement led by AHRLIM took advantage of the new political opportunities rendered by the change of ruling party in 2008, it will also highlight how MATSC sprang into action in the new socio-political environment and pushed through their own agenda.

To enable the *outside-in* and *inside-out* perspectives, this chapter utilizes two sets of primary source materials. First, the *Official Gazette of the Legislative Yuan* was employed as an archival resource to understand the political dynamics between the movement and their collaboration with legislators. Recording the interaction between government officials and legislators at the deliberation meetings discussing migration legislation, the *Gazette* also renders insights to the attitudes and mentality of political actors that reflect the overall social discourses surrounding migrant spouses. Second, in-depth interviews with MATSC board members and observations of its closed-door activities and public events between November 2010 and October 2011 were utilized so as to understand the operation of the organization. Finally, this chapter also benefits from more recent interviews with an academic activist and a number of KMT politicians conducted in May and July 2013.

The following section will examine the socio-political environment that shaped the actions of AHRLIM, as well as those of MATSC. Under the shared but different forms of discrimination, AHRLIM and MATSC developed different strategies of collective negotiation within the socio-political environment. Before the formation of AHRLIM, South East Asian spouses were mainly represented by TASAT, whereas PRC spouses were largely represented by MATSC. The different process and mobilization strategies of TASAT and MATSC are crucial to understand the divergent interests housed within AHRLIM.

MATSC: a hard-earned recognition

The years under the DPP presidency corresponded to a rising rate of marriage migration, in particular migration from the PRC (MoI 2013). Migrant spouses from South East Asia and China found themselves in a discriminatory and exclusionary social-political environment, yet they were imposed on by different patterns of discrimination (Chen and Yu 2005; Tsai 2011). Despite the celebratory publicity of embracing multicultural values, the DPP government inaugurated the requirement of Chinese language proficiency for citizenship eligibility for South East Asian spouses, who were regarded as inferior ethnic others and incapable mothers (Cheng I. 2013; Cheng and Fell 2014). Their questioned motherhood, symbolized by their inability to use the Chinese language, was seen as deteriorating the *quality* of the host nation and, as such, was considered to be a threat (NSC 2006: 61; Hsia 2007a). In contrast, PRC marriage migrants are particularly politicized. They were seen as an '*enemy within*', owing to the concern of their indoctrination of communist values, which are alien to the way of life of Taiwan (Cheng 2014). As their political loyalty was questioned, they, as a political force, were feared for their potential to compromise Taiwan's de facto independence vis-à-vis China (Lu 2008: 171; Yang and Lee 2009: 75).

In this hostile socio-political environment, both communities were confronted by restrictive legislation adopted by the DPP government intending to slow down the approval of their citizenship applications. For all migrant spouses, an entry clearance interview was introduced in 2003 in order to deter human trafficking under the disguise of marriage. However, South East Asian spouses and PRC spouses are regulated by different laws for their citizenship eligibility. The former are under the Immigration Act and Nationality Act, whereas the latter are under the Act Governing Relations between Peoples of the Taiwan and the Mainland Area (henceforth the Cross-Strait Act) (Cheng and Fell 2014: 17–21). In the past, South East Asian spouses faced a high financial requirement for citizenship eligibility and they lost the right to reside after the cessation of their marriage. As for migrants from the PRC, they were entirely dependent on their Taiwanese spouses' sponsorship for their residency. There was a limitation on their right to own property, they could not work until after six-year residency and their incomes were heavily taxed. The defining difference of the legal treatment between the two categories is the required length of residency for citizenship eligibility. For foreign spouses, it was no less than four years, in addition to the renunciation of their original nationality. For PRC spouses, it was no less than eight years, after the DPP government failed to prolong it to 11 years in 2002–03 (Tseng *et al.* 2013). Furthermore, they were denied the right to assemble and to found or join social organizations (Tseng *et al.* 2013; Chao 2006).

Before 2008, the restrictions on South East Asian spouses were the top priority on the reform agenda of migrant movement (Hsia 2009b: 371; Liao 2009: 398).

The different treatments as outlined above highlight the fact that PRC and South East Asian spouses were situated in a similar *as well as* different sociopolitical environment. As a wife-mother, both were seen as inferior ethnic others and a threat to the host nation. On the other hand, the hostility towards the migrants from the PRC and from South East Asian countries was differently constituted. PRC migrants were politicized by the antagonism across the Taiwan Strait and the anxiety of protecting Taiwan's challenged sovereignty, whereas the South East Asians were pathologized as having the potential for the deterioration of Taiwan's prosperity. The shared experiences of encountering hostility paved a common ground for their collaboration within AHRLIM. Yet, the different substance of the hostility foretold their distinctive interests and strategies.

From the mid-1990s, various migrant spouse organizations started to emerge in civil society. Facing the DPP's conservative attitude towards social movements (Ho 2005: 411–13), these dispersed organizations formed AHRLIM, an inclusive organization flexible enough to house various organizations focusing on migrants' well-being. It was during the first DPP presidency that confrontation at a national level between the government and the alliance kicked off. Founded by Taiwanese activists in the name of the migrant community for pursuing the reform of immigration legislation, AHRLIM proved to have a stronger impact than individual organizations and amplified the empathy of a still relatively fragmented civil society for the well-being of labour and marriage migrants in Taiwan. Thus, it is argued that the founding of AHRLIM symbolized the burgeoning of the migrant movement in Taiwan (Hsia 2008: 194).

Yet, long before AHRLIM was conceived, MATSC had already established its presence in the civil society of Taiwan, since December 1998 when social movements had gradually become a 'permanent, routine and legitimate feature' in the newly democratized society of Taiwan (Chang 2004; Ho 2010: 10). Unlike their South East Asian counterparts, who faced a language barrier and, as a result, who relied on local activists' anchoring in the rights-claim movement, MATSC's campaign was relatively autonomous and independent of guidance from influential academics. However, a peculiarity of MATSC is that the organization was nominally founded by Taiwanese spouses and families because, as explained above, of the legal deprivation of the right of PRC marriage migrants to form or join social organizations.

The cooperation between husbands and wives in creating and developing their campaign is a defining characteristic distinguishing MATSC from other organizations within AHRLIM. This spousal cooperation contributed to its distinctive strategies and values, which were different from those of TASAT, an advocacy organization for South East Asian spouses. First of all, the spousal cooperation of MATSC highlighted its endogenous agency as the organization was not set up by Taiwanese activists. Both Chinese and Taiwanese spouses held the ownership of their social campaign and directly participated in the negotiation with the state. PRC spouses particularly regarded themselves as insiders of the host society, given the perceived cultural proximity between Taiwan and China. In contrast, TASAT was founded by Taiwanese activists in the name of South East Asian migrants, whose foreign cultural inheritance singled them out as *the other* in the Taiwanese society. AHRLIM, having its roots in TASAT, holds similar principles. Thus, the empowerment of migrant spouses was assisted by the advocacy of Taiwanese activists. Second, the spousal cooperation within MATSC meant that the blame on patriarchy as the root cause of the issues of marriage migration was spared by MATSC's campaign publicity. After all, the spousal working partnership was critical to the operation of its social campaign. In contrast, TASAT's stance was informed by a feminist critique on patriarchy. The critique argues that the difficulties encountered by migrant spouses in their daily life is rooted in marriage itself, the unequal power relations between wife and husband within the family and the consequential legislation that reinforces the unequal power relations. Thus, some academic activists called for 'liberat[ing] immigrant women from marriages' (Cheng S.-y. 2013: 17), an appeal that never featured in MATSC's campaign publicity. Instead of blaming marriage, MATSC pointed their criticism at the state, whose discriminatory legislation has impacts on both husbands and wives. As the President of MATSC, a Taiwanese husband, explained, 'If your wife is discriminated, you are also discriminated' (interview, 28 July 2011, Taipei). Third, the spousal cooperation also fed into MATSC's issue-framing strategy, which characterized their petition as one for maintaining an undisrupted family life for husbands and wives and parents and children, rather than for migrant spouses only (Tseng *et al.* 2013: 209). With this essential difference explained, the next section will analyse AHRLIM's strategies prior to 2008, which prioritized the interests of South East Asian marriage migrants over those of PRC migrants.

Before 2008: pale in the background

After the DPP assumed power in 2000, human rights became a key element of the party's construction of Taiwan's self-identity. This construction was epitomized by the slogan of 'Nationhood of Human Rights' and the establishment of the National Human Rights Commission. This self-identity was given a boost after Taiwan ratified the International Covenant on Civil and Political Rights and the International Covenant on Social, Economic and Cultural Rights and voluntarily made them applicable in the domestic laws.

Thus, when the DPP was in power, human right discourses proved a useful resource for framing the issue of migrant rights and mobilizing political support from legislators. As a matter of fact, before the discourse of human rights earned wide political currency in the 2000s, framing the rights of migrant spouses as universal human rights was already commonly employed as a campaign strategy. Not only was it those foreign spouses who petitioned legislators who evoked this concept (LY 1998a: 303), but KMT and DPP legislators also appealed to human rights when sponsoring initiatives changing legislation. They sometimes cited relevant international law-making so as to enhance the credibility of their appeal (LY 1998b: 828, 843; LY 1999: 414). As shown in the deliberation of the draft bill of the Immigration Act in 1998 and 1999, the passing of the law itself was taken by legislators as a signifier of how the Taiwanese state treated foreign nationals and how it would implement constitutionally protected human rights. The promulgation and implementation were further considered in relation to whether Taiwan could be seen as being civilized, progressive, democratic and under the rule of law (LY 1998a: 297; LY 1998b: 828; LY 1999: 229). These records illuminate that, in addition to being a human rights issue, the legal treatment for immigrants was also conceptualized as that of reinforcing self-identity and the grooming of self-image, a reoccurring theme that the movement utilized in their campaign in the last decade (LY 2005: 121–4).

Thus, similarly to the strategies undertaken by other social movements in the second half of the 1990s (Ho 2010), in 2005 AHRLIM lobbied for support within the Legislative Yuan and obtained bipartisan endorsement of 60 legislators for their bill amending the Immigration Act. AHRLIM's amendment bill was guided by the synergy between activism and professionalism. That is, inside the alliance, legal experts' professionalism was directed by first-hand knowledge of real cases and identification of potential problems provided by grass-roots organizations (Liao 2009: 401–3). Externally, staging public protests, organizing public consultation meetings and hosting press conferences were the most effective means to raise public awareness and showcasing the agency of the movement (Hsia 2006b: 22–3). Its campaign included the mobilization of large-scale protests resisting the financial requirement for PRC migrants' citizenship eligibility in March 2004, denouncing the vice education minister's comment on the alleged high fertility of immigrant spouses in July 2004, criticizing the Naturalisation Test in July 2005 and opposing the high threshold for foreign spouses' financial sufficiency in September 2007 (Hsia 2006b: 31–2, 2009b: 371).

The DPP's authorship of the human rights discourse seemed hypocritical given that the party was taken accountable for promulgating and implementing hostile legislation towards migrant spouses. Thus, appealing to self-identity and highlighting the gap between rhetoric and reality became AHRLIM's effective strategy to lobby the support of DPP and TSU legislators (Hsia 2013: 142–6). A largely unnoticed external input that strengthened the opportunity to build on the human rights discourse was the pressure from the US government. In 2003, Taiwan was accused by the US government of turning a blind eye to marriage migration being abused by smugglers for sex and labour exploitation. Taiwan's claim to champion human rights protection was at stake, and the state, as well as the people of Taiwan, was taken to be accountable for the violation of human rights of migrant spouses. The sense of urgency of addressing the US criticism was shared by the executive and legislative branches across the board. Thus, the external US pressure opened a new window of opportunity for the movement to win bipartisan support for amending the legislation (Cheng and Momesso, forthcoming).

Similar to the overlooked US pressure, there is no attention paid to the contribution of transnational and regional networks to the enhancement of the advocacy of the movement. The Asian Pacific Mission for Migrants (APMM) and the

Action Network for Marriage Migrants' Rights and Empowerment (AMM♀RE) (of which TASAT is a member) offered the indigenous movement opportunities of exchange, discussion and connection across borders. APMM is now included as one of AHRLIM's group members, together with the Migrant International-Taiwan Chapter. The flow of information from APMM and AMM♀RE with regard to national policies, migrants' living conditions and related actions provided significant insights to practitioners and activists in Taiwan, who built on these examples and developed their own agenda and strategies (Cheng and Momesso, forthcoming).

Since 2003, AHRLIM has attempted to bridge the gap between PRC spouses and South East Asian spouses by emphasizing the shared interests and suggesting how the two groups could benefit from each other's support. According to an academic activist who was deeply involved in the movement, the fact that PRC spouses do not have a language barrier and had experiences in organizing collective actions could prove useful for South East Asian spouses who were inexperienced in this regard. However, considering the complexity of citizenship legislation and avoiding to be overstretched by fighting on two fronts, AHRLIM prioritized the reform of the Immigration Act and Nationality Act and set aside the reform of the Cross-Strait Act as a later task (interviews, 9 June 2011 and 15 July 2013, Taipei). AHRLIM's success in reforming the two laws constituted a precedent with which to push for the reform of the Cross-Strait Act (Hsia 2009b: 379). In other words, although MATSC was one of the founding members of AHRLIM since 2003, only in the last years of the DPP government could MATSC reap the benefit of its membership of this alliance. This lower priority suggests that during the DPP era, in spite of AHRLIM's activism, MATSC did not feature significantly in AHRLIM's campaign. The prioritization and the division of labour were not advantageous for MATSC to further its pursuits.

On top of the internal disadvantage, the external socio-political environment was not beneficial for MATSC either. Although the human rights discourses seemed useful for framing the issue for South East Asian spouses, when it was applied to the Chinese, its universality failed to cross the rigidity of identity politics. Instead, hyped nationalistic sentiments during the DPP's first presidency proved obstructive for MATSC. As mentioned above, with the collaboration of the TSU legislators, the DPP government attempted to prolong the qualifying residency for citizenship eligibility of PRC spouses to 11 years. This motion was tabled in overwhelming nationalistic sentiments which liberally accused PRC spouses of being disloyal to Taiwan (Tseng *et al.* 2013: 215). Thus, while under the DPP most social movements gained access to participate in the decision-making process of the state and obtained official recognition as the legitimate representatives of their constituencies (Ho 2010: 408–11), the channels to gain face-to-face negotiation with the government were denied to MATSC. This was largely because the DPP government saw their actions as interference with the domestic politics of Taiwan and a transgression of the permitted purpose of their entry to Taiwan (Tseng *et al.* 2013: 214). Related to the volatile nationalistic sentiments were Taiwan–China relations, which also confined the advancement of the collective actions of PRC spouses. As pointed out by a KMT legislator, the support of the blue camp for PRC spouses was externally checked by Taiwan–China relations. When the relationship went sour, none of the pan-blue parties could afford to sanction an all-out campaign for helping PRC migrants (interview, 10 July 2013, Taipei).

Thus, while AHRLIM was making its demands heard by the state and society, MATSC found itself entrapped in a hostile environment during the DPP era. The political opportunity created by the human rights discourse was unavailable to them. Moreover, their communication with the general public was impaired by the fanfare of the nationalistic discourse. Their non-confrontational actions, such as petitioning at government officials (often used during the KMT era) and seeking legislators' support, had not yielded any fruit. A MATSC board member recalled that, at that point, the organization had realized that they had no other options but resorting to more assertive and confrontational actions so as to pile pressure on the DPP government (interview, 8 October 2011, Taipei). In other words, MATSC found itself contemplating a more effective mobilizing structure whereby their issue-framing strategy could be utilized. Assisted by the Taiwan New Immigrants Labour Rights Organization (臺灣新移民勞動權益促進會) in terms of knowledge and resources, in November 2002 MATSC organized a large-scale protest in front of the Legislative Yuan against the proposed prolongation of the required residency for citizenship eligibility and asked for the recognition of PRC university degrees. The fact that the protest was joined by migrant mothers and their children drove home the message that marriage migration was a matter of family well-being rather than the one of bogus marriages for illegal employment or prostitution, as postulated by the DPP government. The escalated confrontation between MATSC and the DPP government reached a peak in 2003, when PRC spouses who joined demonstrations were threatened with expulsion (Tseng *et al.* 2013: 214). In September, nearly 3,000 PRC migrants and their supporters marched through Taipei and protested against the DPP's initiative of extending the required residency from eight to 11 years. As it turned out, this initiative was blocked in the Legislative Yuan in 2003. In the DPP's later years, before it was succeeded by the KMT in 2008, other improvements were put in place, such as granting the right to work, recognizing PRC university degrees and granting the right to reside in Taiwan in cases of the death of Taiwanese spouses. As a consequence of these successful actions, MATSC, as an advocacy organization, became more visible and assertive and it won the trust, among organizations advocating the well-being of PRC spouses, as their major representative (Tseng *et al.* 2013: 215).

After 2008: winning recognition

The KMT presidency after 2008 was marked as a dim period for social movements to the extent that whether social movements were able to continue was questioned (Ho 2010: 16). Nevertheless, for the migrant movement, and in particular for MATSC, the opposite was true. As a matter of fact, MATSC saw new opportunities opening up after the KMT returned to power. The new political environment was underlined by the KMT's growing interest in safeguarding the votes of PRC spouses, as mentioned by a KMT legislator who was involved in the migrant movement (interview, 15 July 2013, Taipei). According to the above-cited academic activist, the ultimate source of such support came from the president himself, who, during the election campaign, made the equalization of legal treatment between PRC and South East Asian spouses a personal commitment. It was not only a presidential promise, but also in the interests of some KMT legislators. For instance, the above-cited KMT legislator explained that supporting Chinese spouses for legal reform in the Legislative Yuan was in tandem with winning their votes in the constituency. Given that his constituency was home to a large number of PRC spouses and their mainlander veteran husbands, he had to prevent candidates of the People First Party (PFP) and the New Party (NP) from eroding his support base among mainlander (*waishengren*) voters. This was because the other two parties had a free hand to advocate even more favourable treatment for marriage migrants from the PRC when the KMT was inclined for a slower change to the legislation. This competition was fiercer under the single non-transferable vote in the multi-member district system (SNTV-MMD), as small parties with an extreme policy stood a good chance of winning seats (see Göbel 2012 for a discussion of the impact of the change in voting system). Yet, once the SNTV-MMD system was replaced by a majority system, the threat from small parties was abated (interview, 10 July 2013).

In such favourable environment, face-to-face negotiation between MATSC and the government was made possible. Members of MATSC noticed that their interactions with government officials improved significantly and more intensive interactions in turn led to a stronger support of government officials. As there was a more constructive attitude towards each other, public confrontation was spared and replaced by closed-door meetings either at the governmental premises or in MATSC office. For instance, in 2011, ahead of the general election of 2012, MATSC organized a couple of rallies calling on the two main parties to respond to the appeals of PRC spouses. The DPP did not respond to their call. In contrast, as a member of the MATSC board revealed, the KMT government received the protesters in a closed-door meeting with the vice chairman of the Mainland Affairs Council (MAC), where a promise of equalizing the qualifying length of residency for citizenship eligibility was made (interview, 8 October 2011, Taipei). Also, later on, exchanges of views on the phone and mutual visits between MATSC and the state apparatus (including personnel of the MAC and the National Immigration Agency) became normal practice. At long last, MATSC, along with the Chinese Association for Relief and Ensuing Service (CARES) (中華救助總會), an organization providing services to PRC spouses, became one of the major communication channels between the state and PRC spouses. In this new political atmosphere, MATSC committed itself to coming to the aid of PRC spouses. It regarded AHRLIM's expertise in law-making and its previous success in pushing reform as a 'yardstick' to reform the Cross-Strait Act. The above-mentioned activist explained that their collaboration on the draft bill of amending the Cross-Strait Act drew from the legal expertise of AHRLIM and the grass-roots feedback of MATSC, which was gained from its rich experiences of a 10-year campaign (interview, 9 June 2011, Taipei). The collaboration notwithstanding, joint actions between the two remained limited after 2009. One MATSC board member attributed the lack of deeper and continuing cooperation to their divergent interests derived from the dual legal track system (interview, 2 March 2011, Taipei). AHRLIM continued to appeal to the human rights discourses and mobilize legislators' support for its campaign on reforming the Nationality Act. In April 2013, AHRLIM presented its draft bill to the Legislative Yuan and its goals were the legal acceptance of dual nationality, granting migrant spouses the right to serve public office with immediate effect after acquiring citizenship, and applying the regulations for foreign spouses' naturalization to foreign widows or divorcees (AHRLIM 2013; Cheng S.-Y. 2013).

As a result of AHRLIM and MATSC's campaigns, the long-awaited reform of the Cross-Strait Act was finally achieved in August 2009. The marriage brokering industry was outlawed. For both PRC and foreign spouses, the financial requirement was dropped. For PRC spouses, the right to reside after the cessation of marriage was granted, but for foreign spouses this was premised on their gaining the custody of their children. As for PRC spouses, they were permitted to work as soon as they entered Taiwan, a right that had already been granted to their South East Asian counterparts by the previous DPP government. The most fought for reform – equalizing the qualifying period of residency for PRC and foreign spouses – was not realized, however. It was not until November 2012 that the appeal for equalization was finally accepted by the KMT government, who included this amendment in the draft bill to be passed by the Legislative Yuan (Cheng and Fell 2014: 91). Yet, as of January 2016, marriage migrants from the PRC are still required to reach six years of residency before they become eligible for citizenship (Tseng et al. 2013). Thus, the president's commitment notwithstanding, inside the government an agreement on the equalization was hard to reach.

Conclusion

This chapter showed that the migrant movement in Taiwan has not been the result of a linear process, nor can it be interpreted solely as a united and concerted effort for all migrants. Centred on the differentiated rights of PRC and South East Asian spouses derived from the dual legal track, this chapter compared the development of AHRLIM, as an umbrella alliance, and MATSC, as a component organization within the alliance, so as to highlight the internal heterogeneity of the migrant movement in Taiwan as well as its distinctive opportunities and constraints derived from the change in the ruling party.

The parallel existence of, and loose working relationship between AHRLIM and MATSC manifested in different histories, development paths and outcomes of the members within the movement. Self-regarded as insiders within the Taiwanese society, PRC spouses, with the indispensable help of their Taiwanese partners, were able to exercise their agency against the unfavourable structures embodied by the nationalistic politics and the national security discourse. In contrast, being *the other* in the Taiwanese society, the empowerment of South East Asian spouses was assisted by the guardianship of local activists. By exploring this difference, this chapter drew a dynamic picture closer to the reality rather than adding on the empathy and universal sisterhood celebrated by established literature. Our findings underlined that heterogeneity within the movement is the strength as well as the weakness of the campaign.

Bringing together both *outside-in* and *inside-out* perspectives, this chapter identified two fundamental parameters of the evolution of migrant movement. An *outside-in* perspective was beneficial to trace how the migrant movement continuously reconfigured its agenda according to the changed political opportunities and the divergent interests of its member organizations. In this regard, this chapter highlighted previously unnoticed external influences during the DPP era from the US, as well as transnational and regional networks. As a whole, these factors contributed to framing the movement into the human rights discourse, enhancing support from the legislative and executive branches and mobilizing transnational and regional resources. After 2008, the KMT government held a more accommodative attitude towards spouses from the PRC and subsequently developed a closer working relationship with MATSC. Consequently, the broader alliance adjusted to these changed political opportunities.

An *inside-out* perspective was essential to look at the internal divide as a consequence to the unequal legal status between PRC spouses and their South East Asian counterparts. The mutual constitution of the two parameters was evident in how AHRLIM and MATSC set their agendas in accordance with the availability of political opportunities before and after 2008. Thus, a dynamics of change and continuity was depicted in the sense that the migrant movement constantly adjusted its strategy while its internal divide remained. The utility of an inside-out perspective is also found in illuminating the divide within the movement. Although AHRLIM attempted to bridge the differences between various migrant groups, its prioritization nevertheless reinforced this division. Under the DPP administration, being denied by the chance of tapping into the resources derived from the human rights discourses, MATSC was set aside as a second priority within AHRLIM. As a result, it was left with no options but undertaking more confrontational presentation of their views to the government and the general public. After 2008, while AHRLIM worked closely to reform the Cross-Strait Act, MATSC continued its campaign on a relatively independent basis even when the KMT was in power.

To conclude, our analysis showed that political opportunities did make a difference to how the migrant movement adjusted its strategies so as to advance its causes. Yet, along with political opportunity, mobilizing structure and the framing process, the impact of the internal heterogeneity cannot be overlooked so as to fully understand the development of the rights-claim movement of migrant spouses.

Note

1 In addition to TASAT and MATSC, the other group founding members were the Awakening Foundation (婦女新知), the Association for the Development and Care of Foreign Spouses (外籍配偶成長 關懷協會), the Taiwan International Family Association (台灣國際家庭互助協會), the Taiwan Migrants' Forum (台灣外勞行動), the New Immigrants Labour Rights Association (新移民勞動權益促進會), the Female Labour Rights Association (女性勞動者權益促進會), the Labour Rights Association (勞動人權協會), the Taiwan Association for Human Rights (台灣人權促進會), the Rerum Novarum Center (新事勞工服務中 心) and a few other organizations (Hsia 2009b: 369; Hsia 2007b).

References

AHRLIM. 2013. *When Will a Foreign Land Become a Homeland? Press Release on 18th March*. Available online at http://tahr.org.tw/node/1209 (accessed 14 May 2014).
Chang, Hsuan-chun [張瑄純]. 2004. *Practices of Using the Internet by Cross-Strait Couples for Striving for Citizenship – A Case Study on 'Cross-Strait Park' and 'Cross-Strait Family Forum'* [兩岸婚姻者爭取大陸配偶公民權的網路實踐一以「兩岸公園」，「兩岸家庭」論壇為例]. Master's thesis, National Chung-Cheng University (in Chinese).
Chao, A. 2006. 'Politics of sentiment and alternative social justice: how mainland spouses have engaged in social movements in Taiwan' ['情感政治與另類正義: 在台大陸配偶的社會運動經驗']. *SOCIETAS: A Journal for Philosophical Studies on Public Affairs* [政治與哲學評論], 16 (March), 87–152 (in Chinese).
Carty, V. 2011. *Wired and Mobilizing: Social Movements, New Technology, and Electoral Politics*. New York, NY: Routledge.
Chen, C.-y. J. and T.-l. Yu. 2005. 'Public attitudes towards Taiwan's immigration policies' ['台灣民眾對外來配偶移民政策的態度']. *Taiwanese Sociology* [台灣社會學], 10, 95–48 (in Chinese).
Cheng, I. 2013. 'Making foreign women the mother of our nation: the exclusion and assimilation of immigrant women in Taiwan'. *Asian Ethnicity*, 14(2), 157–79.
Cheng, I. 2014. 'Bridging across or sandwiched between? Political re-socialisation of Chinese immigrant women in Taiwan'. *Asian Ethnicity*, 17(3), 414–34. doi: 10.1080/14631369.2014.973003.
Cheng, I. and D. Fell. 2014. The change of ruling parties and Taiwan's claim to multiculturalism before and after 2008'. *Journal of Current Chinese Affairs*, 43(3), 71–103.
Cheng, I. and L. Momesso. Forthcoming. 'Look, the world is watching us! An examination of the change of immigration policy during the Ma administration by the Spiral Model Theory'. *Journal of Current Chinese Affairs*, forthcoming.
Cheng, S.-Y. 2013. 'Women who must stay: citizenship, residence and marriage status of immigrant women in Taiwan'. *Migrant Monitor*, 2013(2). Available online at www.apmigrants.org (accessed 20 May 2014).
Foweraker, J. 1995. *Theorizing Social Movements*. London: Pluto Press.
Friedman, S. 2010. 'Marital immigration and graduated citizenship: post-naturalization restrictions on mainland Chinese spouses in Taiwan'. *Pacific Affairs*, 83(1), 73–93.
Friedman, S. 2012. 'Adjudicating the intersection of marital immigration, domestic violence, and spousal murder: China-Taiwan marriages and competing legal domains'. *Indiana Journal of Global Legal Studies*, 19(1), 221–55.
Göbel, Christian. 2012. 'The impact of electoral system reform on Taiwan's local factions', *Journal of Current Chinese Affairs*, 43(3), 69–92.

Ho, M.-s. 2005, 'Taiwan's state and social movements under the DPP government, 2000–2004'. *Journal of East Asian Studies*, 5, 401–25.

Ho, M.-s. 2010. 'Understanding the trajectory of social movements in Taiwan (1980–2010)'. *Journal of Current Chinese Affairs*, 39(3), 3–22.

Hsia, H.-s. 2006a. 'Empowering "foreign brides" and community through praxis-oriented research'. *Societies Without Borders*, 1, 93–111.

Hsia, H.-c. 2006b. 'The making of immigrants movement: politics of differences, subjectivation and societal movement'. *Taiwan: A Radical Quarterly in Social Studies*, 61, 1–71, March 2006.

Hsia, H.-c. 2007a. 'Imaged and imagined threat to the nation: the media construction of the "foreign brides phenomenon" as social problem in Taiwan'. *Inter-Asia Cultural Studies*, 8(1), 55–85.

Hsia, H.-c. 2007b. *The Brief History of TransAsia Sisters Association, Taiwan*. Available online at http://tasat.org.tw/enPage/290 (accessed 11 November 2014).

Hsia, H.-c. 2008. 'The development of immigrant movement in Taiwan: the case of Alliance of Human Rights Legislation for Immigrants and Migrants'. *Development and Society*, 37(2), 187–218.

Hsia, H.-c. 2009a. 'Foreign brides, multiple citizenship and the immigrant movement in Taiwan'. *Asian and Pacific Migration Journal*, 18(1), 17–46.

Hsia, H.-c. 2009b. 'Intellectual intervention and the making of im/migrant movement I' ['知識介入與移民／工運動的推進（一）']. T*aiwan: A Radical Quarterly in Social Studies* [台灣社會研究刊], 74 (September), 367–82 (in Chinese).

Hsia, H.-c. 2010. 'The subjectivation of marriage migrants in Taiwan: the insider's perspectives'. In A. Choudry and D. Kapoor (eds), *Learning from the Ground up: Global Perspectives on Social Movements and Knowledge Production*. London: Palgrave Macmillan, pp. 101–18.

Hsia, H.-c. 2013. 'The tug of war of multiculturalism: contestation between governing and empowering immigrants in Taiwan'. In A. E. Collins, L. Francis and B. S. A. Yeoh (eds), *Migration and Diversity in Asian Contexts*. Singapore: Institute of Southeast Asian Studies, pp. 130–59.

Kaneko, K. 2009. 'Foreign migrants in Taiwan and Japan: a comparative analysis'. *Asia Journal of Global Studies*, 3(1), 22–36.

King, W. 2011. 'Taiwanese nationalism and cross-strait marriage – Governing and incorporating mainland spouses'. In S. Gunter and J. Damm (eds), *Taiwanese identity in the 21st century. Domestic, regional and global perspectives*. London: Routledge, pp. 176–96.

Ministry of Interior (MoI). 2013. *Statistical data of foreign spouses and mainland (Hong Kong and Macao included) spouses in each county and city according to the status* [各縣市外籍配偶人數與大陸 (含港澳) 配偶人數按證件分]. Available online at www.moi.gov.tw/stat/index.aspx (accessed 20 January 2015).

LY (The Legislative Yuan). 1998a, 16 December. 立法院第三屆第六會期內政及邊政, 外交及僑 政, 交通, 司法四委員會併案審查「入出國及移民法草案」第二次聯席會議紀 錄, 249–305.

LY (The Legislative Yuan). 1998b, 21 December. 立法院第三屆第六會期內政及邊政, 外交及 僑政, 交通, 司法四委員會併案審查「入出國及移民法草案」第三次聯席會議 紀錄, 807–70.

LY (The Legislative Yuan). 1999, 20 April. 立法院公報第八十八卷第十九期院會紀錄, 97–230.

LY (The Legislative Yuan). 2005a, 16 November. 立法院公報第九十五卷第三期委員會會議紀 錄, 119–72.

Liao, B. Y.-H. 2009. 'Intellectual intervention and the making of im/migrant movement II' [知識介入與移民／工運動的推進,二]. *Taiwan: A Radical Quarterly in Social Studies* (台灣社會研究刊), 74 (in Chinese), 383–405 (in Chinese).
Lu, M. 2008. *Gender, Marriage and Migration. Contemporary Marriages Between Mainland China and Taiwan*. PhD thesis, Leiden University.
McAdam, D., J. D. McCarthy, and M. N. Zald (eds). 1996. *Comparative Perspectives on Social Movements: Political Opportunities, Mobilizing Structures, and Cultural Framings*. New York, NY: Cambridge University Press.
NSC (National Security Council). 2006. *National Security Report* [國家安全報告]. Taipei: NSC (in Chinese).
Scott, A. 1991. *Ideology and Social Movements*. London: Allen and Unwin.
Tarrow, S. 1988. 'National politics and collective action: recent theory and research in Western Europe and the United States'. *Annual Review of Sociology*, 14, 421–40.
Tsai, M.-C. 2011. '"Foreign brides" meets ethnic politics in Taiwan'. *International Migration Review*, 45(3) (Summer), 243–68.
Tsai, Y.-H. and H. H. M. Hsiao. 2006. 'The non-governmental organizations (NGOs) for foreign workers and foreign spouses in Taiwan: a portrayal'. *Asia Pacific Forum*, 33 (September), 1–31.
Tseng, Y.-C., I. Cheng and D. Fell. 2013. 'The politics of the mainland spouses' rights' movement in Taiwan'. In D. Fell, K.-f. Chiu and P. Lin (eds), *Migration to and from Taiwan*. London: Routledge, pp. 205–26.
Yang, W.-Y and Lee, P.-R. 2009. 'The citizenship dilemma of mainlander spouses in Taiwan: the conspiracy of nationalism and patriarchy' ['大陸配偶的公民權 困境一國族與父權的共謀']. *Taiwan Democracy Quarterly* [臺灣民主季 刊], 6(3), 47–86 (in Chinese).

13 All our relations

Indigenous rights movements in contemporary Taiwan

Scott Simon

For many observers of Taiwan, the election of Ma Ying-jeou as president of the Republic of China in 2008 seemed like a watershed moment in the island's history and even to some like a step backwards. A generation of Taiwan studies scholars had come to maturity since the inaugural conference of the North American Taiwanese Studies Association in 1994. Over two and a half decades, Taiwan was transformed in intellectual discourse from a laboratory of Chinese culture to an ontological subject in its own right that merited a worldwide network of conferences, book series, journals and the creation of Taiwan studies programmes. In Taiwan, intellectual and literary currents of *bentuhua*, with increased valorization of a local Taiwanese identity as opposed to a state-sponsored Chinese identity (Makeham and Hsiau 2005), followed by dynamic social movements of feminism, labour, environmental, anti-nuclear and, not least, indigenous movements, made it appear as if the Taiwanese were becoming masters of their own destiny. Intellectual discourse focused on democracy, especially since the end of martial law led to a flowering of social movements (Blundell 2012; Fell 2012: 178).

The rise of the Democratic Progressive Party (DPP), with the election of Chen Shui-bian in 2000 and his re-election in 2004, seemed to confirm teleological notions of a Taiwanese *Volksgeist* emerging from the tragic imposition of what Hill Gates once described as a 'rump' state dependent on the United States for its very survival (Gates 1979: 393). Murray and Hong (1994), who caused much brouhaha in anthropology when they argued that social scientists had ignored the real Taiwan while looking for China on the island, seemed vindicated, but for less than a decade. The 2008 presidential election and 2012 re-election of Ma Ying-jeou were initially interpreted as the triumphant return of the Chinese Nationalist Party, whose Sino-nationalist essence is easily obscured in English by habitual use of the acronym KMT but is never ignored in Taiwan. This political change in a democratic system made it appear as if a sizeable portion of Taiwan's population were at ease after all with being somewhat Chinese, especially as the new government made it clear from the beginning that they sought rapprochement with the People's Republic of China and that the new president embraced symbols of pan-Chinese identity in public speeches and rituals.

Chinese-ness was back in vogue, or was it? Were 'Asian values' coming back to Taiwan? Was the supposed 'chaos' of social movements about to take a back seat again to 'Confucian' notions of social harmony? One productive way to understand change and continuity is through an analysis of Taiwan's social movements before and after 2008. Were they ever really bound so intimately with the emergence of a Taiwanese *Volk* on the world stage of democratic yearnings? Is the rise or fall of social movements dependent on the vagaries of electoral politics? Or do they have a momentum entirely of their own? The social movement for indigenous rights is especially relevant to this discussion. The vibrancy of all social movements is a sign of the strength of democracy; but the indigenous movement appears especially indicative of Taiwan's national identity because it draws attention to a non-Chinese specificity of Taiwan. Taiwanese nationalists have long gazed nostalgically at the island's Austronesian minorities, often imagining them as their own Polynesian ancestors rather than as political agents with their own priorities (Munsterhjelm 2014). There is a risk, however, in any analysis that frames indigenous people as 'non-Chinese' rather than on their terms.

In this chapter, I examine political change in Taiwan since 2008 through the prism of the indigenous rights movements that claim to speak for the half a million people of Austronesian descent and identity on the island.[1] To a degree even stronger than the already quite diverse marriage migrant movement (Momesso and Cheng, this volume), the indigenous social movement is plural. A vast range of disparate events, from protests in Tokyo against the inclusion of indigenous Formosan warriors in Japan's nationalistic Yasukuni shrine (Simon 2006a) to alliances between indigenous activists and pro-independence groups to include indigenous rights in a new constitution (Simon 2006b), are promoted by political actors in the name of indigenous social movements. Worldwide, indigenous social movements, of which the *yuanzu minzu* (原住民族, 'original dwelling peoples') of Taiwan are one local inflection, are unique among social movements because they claim a temporal and relational identity based on 'prior-ity' (Pratt 2007: 398) before the arrival of new groups and state forms on a given territory. Indigenous people are aware that their ancestors were 'here' before the arrival of the state and that they, to some extent, continue to live in a colonial existential situation. Unlike all other social movements, which merely demand better policy and law, they base their political goals on the legal principle of self-determination (Niezen 2010: 113), with the goal of eventually determining independently most of the policies that affect them.

In a reflection on changes in Taiwan's indigenous movements since 2008, I reflect upon four recent unfoldings. I prefer to refer to them as unfoldings, rather than as developments, in order to avoid any impression of linear development or teleological assumptions. The four most visible unfoldings are an increasing emphasis on livelihood issues, the rise of non-church actors, the use of new social media and a radical rethinking of party politics. Since all of these have roots that predate 2008 by decades, it is necessary to begin by placing them in their historical context. This makes it clear that indigenous people have been autonomous political actors, negotiating their relationship with the state, for much longer than the other social movements. In fact, the ontological basis of indigeneity on Taiwan has its roots in Japanese colonial policy.

A brief history of Taiwan's indigenous–state relations

From a historical perspective, the political experience of the Formosan indigenous peoples is very different from that of Taiwan's Han Chinese groups (despite the important differences between mainlanders and so-called 'Native Taiwanese') for the very basic reason that the mountain groups had never been governed by a state in pre-modern times, whereas settlers who came from China inherited a habitus of dealing effectively with state bureaucracies, tax collectors etc. The Qing dynasty, in over two centuries of colonization prior to the Japanese annexation of the island in 1895, subdued the *pingpuzu*, or 'plains aborigines', largely assimilating those groups into Chinese polity and cosmology over the nineteenth century (Brown 2004; Shepherd 1993; Zheng 1995). They classified the native groups as 'raw' (*sheng*, 生) or 'cooked' (*shou*, 熟) 'savages' (*fan*, 番), depending on whether or not their groups had collectively submitted to the political rule of the Chinese state. Military-enforced boundaries between the territories of the two groups were intended to protect plains peoples from head-hunting expeditions, but also protected mountain peoples from the encroachment of Hokkien and Hakka farmers onto their territory. During the Qing dynasty, as plains communities lost wars to incomers from China, refugees fled to the mountains and eastern coastal communities, making everyone aware of the danger posed by Hokkien and Hakka settlers.

In the Formosan Highlands, loose bands of acephelous societies remained autonomous until they were subjugated by the Japanese military, with the final decisive battle happening as late as 1914, when the Truku of Hualien surrendered after three months of resistance. They were subsequently integrated into the state as new institutions and organizations were created around property rights, political representation, identity and social welfare in ways that separated them from the other ethnic groups and reinforced local identities (Fujii 1997). These 'raw' groups, incorporated into a state for the first time in their history by Japan, were those that eventually adopted identities as indigenous by the end of the twentieth century. From their perspective, the state is a relatively new imposition. In fact, today's elderly people still remember what their parents told them about the social changes ushered in by foreign states.

Policy innovations for the newly subdued Austronesian peoples in Japanese Formosa amounted basically to a 'bureaucratization of indigeneity' (Simon 2012: 229) that continued to unfold after Taiwan was transferred from Japan to the Republic of China. Local people often accepted new institutions as state protection against encroachment on their lands by Hokkien and Hakka people. In terms of politics, the Japanese had required groups, even those with relatively 'nomadic' inclinations, to settle in permanent villages and create tribal councils with chiefs who would manage relationships with the Japanese police authorities. This system was modernized by the ROC with the establishment of 30 mountain townships in 1945, followed by local electoral innovations created under the slogan of 'local autonomy' (*difang zizhi*, 地方自治). This institutional innovation contributed to the formation of a local indigenous elite centred around township offices, indigenous politicians and their supporters, all very dependent upon KMT patron–client networks (Simon 2012: 123). In both the Japanese and ROC eras, indigenous collaboration with powerful outsiders protected indigenous communities from the encroachment of Hokkien and Hakka settlers. Social expectations towards chiefs were transferred to township politicians, creating some continuity in norms of local leadership. The Atayalic groups (including the Truku and Sediq) refer to the expectations that ordinary people have of these leaders in terms of the sacred ancestral law of Gaya or Gaga (Simon 2012: 230–2).

A reserve land system, based on Japanese precedents that were in turn inspired by American Indian policies (Simon 2012: 95–6), made it difficult to sell land to outsiders, even as individual landowners could return their land rights to the township office that could lease to corporate interests. The reserve system, like its precedents in North America, did not include the vast traditional territories that became classified as state property. Nonetheless, the reserve land system gave indigenous villages a land base and provided individuals with the option of staying in or, in many cases, returning to the countryside after years or decades of work elsewhere. This land base, in spite of the social upheaval that happened with indigenous people selling land to other indigenous people – an emergent elite who enriched themselves from land deals as much as from politics – kept indigenous societies more intact than they would have been if people had simply been able to sell land to outsiders when moving to the cities to work.

The post-martial law indigenous rights movements arose within, partly against but always intricately entwined with these resulting village networks in the 1980s, giving impetus to further political change in the 1990s. Even as the first social rights movements were based in Taipei and initiated by educated urban aborigines, activists always referred to their origins in the countryside and drew inspiration from those roots. The leaders of the new movements, as well as many relatively apolitical people in the villages, were fully aware of the political autonomy their groups had before colonialism, the limited autonomy their fathers enjoyed during the Japanese period (often as chiefs or members of tribal councils), and the promised autonomy of the ROC. Their communities were kept relatively intact, in locations mostly designated by the Japanese, owing to the land reserve system, which gave them a material base for their livelihoods (Simon 2015). The subsequent demands, strategies and limitations of the indigenous social movement are all rooted in this history.

The indigenous social movement before 2008

Anthropologist Fiorella Allio (1998a) dates the modern indigenous social movement back to the establishment of the magazine *Gaoshanqing* in 1983, followed in 1984 by the establishment of the Alliance of Taiwan Aborigines (ATA). It emerged within the larger *dangwai* opposition movement and was nourished by networks of the Presbyterian Church of Taiwan (PCT). Protestant influences on the movement, which included a pro-indigenous theology taught at Yushan Theological Seminary and the involvement of Canadian missionaries in the Urban–Rural Movement (URM) training school for social activists, were so influential that Michael Stainton summed it up in the title of his MA thesis as 'counterhegemonic Presbyterian aboriginality' (Stainton 1995). Ku Kun-hui observed a discursive shift in the movement in the mid-1980s from an initial concern for social welfare and individual rights to a focus on collective rights (Ku 2005: 100).

One of the first demands of the nascent movement was name rectification (*zhengming*, 正名), which in the first case meant the collective name to be used for all indigenous tribes of Taiwan. This was of course a colonial effect, as a collective name served only higher-level taxonomic classification of colonized peoples, most of whom continued to refer to themselves by local linguistic variants of words meaning 'human being'. This generic category had in colonial times changed from the 'raw' versus 'cooked' classification of the Qing dynasty and early Japanese period to the Japanese *takasagozoku* 高砂族 ('high sands' peoples, from an archaic word for Formosa), a word with positive connotations of bravery that had supposedly been designated by the Emperor himself in 1935 (Yamaguchi 1999: 32). After the ROC took over Taiwan, the government terminology had become *shanbao* (山胞, 'mountain compatriots'), with somewhat confusing inflections as 'mountain mountain compatriots' 山地山胞 and 'plains mountain compatriots' 平地山胞, the major differences being that the former groups had reserve land, whereas the latter groups did not. The idea was to include indigenous people with Chinese citizens as equals in the ROC form of republicanism. Thus the aim was to integrate them into a larger Chinese polity rather than to explicitly recognize them as small nations on their own terms.

The leaders of the emergent indigenous movement, influenced by global indigenism (Niezen 2003) and inspired by URM training taught by Mohawk activist Donna Loft, deemed all of these terms pejorative and demanded that they be called instead indigenous people (*yuanzhumin*, 原住民) (Allio 1998a: 56). They successfully lobbied the National Assembly to incorporate this new terminology in the 10 additional articles to the ROC constitution in 1994. Remarkably, they were able to get the wording subsequently altered in constitutional revisions in 1997 to *yuanzhuminzu* (原住民族). The addition of one Chinese character at the end of the word, like adding the letter -s at the end of the word 'people', effectively guaranteed the political status and participation of indigenous peoples as collectivities (Simon 2012: 182). The indigenous movement also lobbied successful for the creation of a cabinet-level Council of Indigenous Peoples in 1996, a move which basically moved government administration of indigenous affairs from the provincial to the national level.

This is not just a question of terminology or bureaucratic reorganization, because identity is crucial to formulating and claiming rights. As Niezen noted, 'Membership in a legally defined community with the potential to call upon public sympathies in defense of rights has become the single most important form of belonging' (Niezen 2010: 14). It is important to keep in mind that the names of indigenous groups and the legal definitions of community boundaries and membership were already established in the 1930s. This means that Taiwan's indigenous identity has a longer institutional history than the organizing identity of any other social movement in the country. The end of martial law enhanced the potential to call upon public sympathies, thus enabling indigenous people to launch a new social movement that could interact with other political actors.

In the 1990s, the 'Return our lands' movement demanded the return of traditional territories and reserve land that had been, through various methods, transferred to state or private non-indigenous use for such purposes as national parks and mines. As the United Nations began creating various venues for indigenous peoples to express their concerns, Taiwanese indigenous activists began attending international meetings in Geneva and New York. The main theme of the movement became political autonomy, based on the concept that indigenous peoples, as a result of their ongoing presence on a given territory before colonization, possessed inherent sovereignty. In 1999, this concept was the cornerstone of the *New Partnership Between the Indigenous Peoples and the Taiwanese Government*, signed by DPP presidential candidate Chen Shui-bian during a campaign stop on Orchid Island (Simon 2012: 183). No matter what Chen may have thought of the document, indigenous activists interpreted it as an important state-to-state treaty.

This momentum culminated in the 2005 Basic Law on Indigenous Peoples, which promised to meet most of the demands of the indigenous social movement, including political autonomy. As the Council of Indigenous Peoples expanded in size, many indigenous social activists joined the ranks of the public service. Some activists even became concerned that the movement would lose its radical edge as its leaders took government positions. In addition, indigenous legislators – guaranteed a quota of seats in the Legislative Yuan since the beginning of direct elections for legislators – became important spokespeople for indigenous rights. Although most of them tended to represent the KMT and allied pan-blue forces (Simon 2010), the Executive Yuan and the Legislative Yuan (still dominated by the KMT throughout the entire Chen administration) actually seemed to compete to demonstrate which party best represented indigenous interests.

The apparent success of the indigenous movement to quickly achieve so many of its stated goals led some observers to speculate that the state instrumentalized 'indigeneity' to claim an identity distinct from China. Tsinghua University anthropologist Ku Kun-hui (2005) showed how indigenous activists exploited political opportunities to assert their rights at a moment when Taiwan was actively seeking a non-Chinese identity. She concluded with an analysis of how the state manipulated indigenous themes to legitimate a new national identity, most prominently by the use of indigenous performers at the 2000 inauguration ceremony of President Chen Shui-bian. Michael Rudolph took the instrumentalization hypothesis by suggesting that 'all these efforts of course had not only the aim to demarcate Taiwan culturally, but also politically from China'

(Rudolph 2006: 46ff., 12). Such analysis explains well why the DPP claimed to support indigenous rights, but they overlook the long institutional history of indigeneity with roots in the colonial period. Most importantly, the identities of the island's earliest inhabitants as essentially non-Chinese and the institutional framework of differential property rights and tribal political organizations that kept those identities alive and politically salient have roots in policies that go back to Qing and, more importantly, to Japanese rule. The main demands of the indigenous rights movement are thus different from other social movements in two important ways. First, they are based on identities rooted in an ongoing colonial situation that predates even the arrival of the ROC on Taiwan, not to mention wider political conflicts about 'Taiwan' versus 'China'. Second, they are based thus on claims to sovereignty rooted in that very colonial situation. What happened between 2008 and 2016 was thus less shaped by the fact that the KMT took the reins of the government than by political dynamics in a longer period of time. We can now examine the four unfoldings that happened during Ma's presidency.

Four unfoldings since 2008

Events since 2008 reveal the need to moderate claims that indigeneity is a state effect of the last two decades, or that attention to indigeneity was *only* a way to demarcate Taiwan from China. Those arguments overemphasize the roles of Presidents Lee Teng-hui and Chen Shui-bian in creating the conditions for an indigenous social movement. In fact, the institutions of indigeneity are much older than those two politicians, as tribal councils and reserve lands were created in the Japanese era and the forms of the current system gained shape mostly under the leadership of Chiang Kai-shek. The grass-roots social movement, of course, gained steam after the end of martial law along with other social movements and Taiwan-centric intellectual currents (Blundell 2012).

The international circulation and appropriation of legal norms, institutions and strategies that may be called 'vernacularization' (Levitt and Merry 2009: 443) has a long history that was merely accelerated with participation of Taiwan in transnational indigenous movements. There were changes after 2008, but the most important changes did not necessarily begin in 2008; and they were rarely caused by the election of Ma Ying-jeou. Instead, they reveal that the indigenous social movement follows an internal dynamic that is only weakly, if at all, dependent on the political context in Taipei. The return of the KMT to the presidency certainly changed the wider context, but the indigenous movement seemed to unfold largely according to its own internal dynamics.

The first unfolding: a shift from name rectification to livelihood issues

The first generation of the modern indigenous rights movement was necessarily focused on name rectification, getting recognition as *yuanzhuminzu* rather than as *shandi tongbao*. Arguably, the previously used name of 'mountain compatriots' already entitled Taiwan's mountain groups to certain political and economic rights. The ROC signed ILO107 (the International Labour Organization Indigenous and Tribal Populations Convention) as early as 1962, created mechanisms at the provincial level for governance of mountain communities and, through the land reserve system, continued in altered form the Japanese system of recognizing a specific form of property rights for mountain groups. Even with limited privatization of land, the law prohibited mountain compatriots from selling land to non-indigenous people. In some cases, indigenous land owners still made arrangements to cede land usage to non-indigenous investors in informal land 'sales', while still retaining legal land title. In other cases, township officials pressured land owners to relinquish their rights so that township offices can then lease the required land to outside investors. This all happened under the slogan of 'local autonomy' (*difang zizhi*, 地方自治). Like ILO107 (Niezen 2003: 38), moreover, the intention of these measures was to 'modernize' the targeted communities and eventually assimilate their members into mainstream society. This has led to a situation in which township offices are the main arenas for indigenous politics.

At the international level, indigenous peoples worldwide began demanding recognition of their collective rights, including rights to land and to recognition of their inherent sovereignty, and the right to remain distinct from the wider society. These changes led to the replacement of ILO107 with ILO169 to protect these rights. This shift in discourse from indigenous people to indigenous peoples, which became a cornerstone of indigenous activities at the United Nations and in customary international law, was vernacularized in Taiwan as constitutional recognition of *yuanzhuminzu* with political rights. This fundamental change, further elaborated in the 2005 Basic Law on Indigenous Peoples, which promised the creation of autonomous zones, offered the possibility that each officially recognized 'tribe' could become a legal person in its own right with some kind of recognition of tribal inherent sovereignty (Simon and Awi 2013).

Attention to name rectification subsequently led to legal recognition of specific local groups, as local elites saw potential benefits for themselves and for their communities in terms of representation at the Indigenous Peoples Council, perhaps eventual formation of autonomous tribal self-governing bodies, and state funding for such projects as language curricula and cultural activities. Successful demands for state recognition led the number of state-recognized groups to expand from nine for the entire period from 1945 to 2000 to 14 by the end of the Chen Shui-bian presidency. In August 2014, the Kanakanavu and the Hla'alua were recognized by the state as independent from the Tsou – demonstrating that the DPP has no monopoly on this form of identity politics.

Cynical observers, especially indigenous activists, have been quick to note that the timing of these changes to tribal classification tended to be strategically planned to influence the results of local and legislative elections. Once groups are established, in what can become highly contested political struggles (see Chi and Chin 2012; Hara 2003, 2004; Huang 2013; Simon 2007, 2012: 177–206), the emergent leaders have to convince local people to change their household registration papers to the new tribal identity and support the changes.

From a village level, the rather abstract and political nature of identity changes made their necessity difficult for local people to understand. Local people often perceive the creation of new organizations, or institutional change related to new ethnic groups and proposed forms of self-governance, to be merely attempts by indigenous leaders to create new, presumably well-paid, positions for themselves. On the subject of creating indigenous autonomous regions, Rudolph thus quoted one person describing such proposals as 'only a means to get aborigines locked up in a cage so that people could look at them like monkeys in the zoo' (Rudolph 2004: 250). The problem was that most legal and institutional issues, as pressing as they seemed to activists and township political leaders, remained remote from the livelihood issues of rural workers and farmers. This social division, between those at the forefront in the political representation of difference and those who remain apolitical, is characteristic of collective rights movements everywhere (Niezen 2010: 103). In the communities where I have worked and where name rectification was a major issue, fewer people were interested in whether they were called Atayal, Truku or Sediq than in the price they could earn for selling peanuts or in how to take legal action against labour contractors who failed to pay wages.

Once tribes have been legally recognized, however, they can more effectively organize around local livelihood issues such as control of forests and shores, the danger posed by nuclear waste and the right to hunt. The list of indigenous social movement issues raised during the Ma administration is long. Non-livelihood issues that seemed less pressing to ordinary villagers included protests against the conversion of mountain townships into city districts as Taiwan revised its municipal structure to convert several counties into municipalities. Legal debates about indigenous autonomy – whether township offices or newly created tribal governments are more appropriate as institutions for implementing political autonomy – attracted the attention of indigenous activists and intellectuals but gained little traction among ordinary people (Simon and Awi 2013). During the Sunflower Movement, several indigenous rights groups took public action in support of the movement against ECFA and the Service Trade Agreement and indigenous students claimed their own public space at the demonstrations. In the villages, however, people tended to show disapproval of these actions, saying that the students had broken laws and were manipulated by larger political forces.

To ordinary villagers, debates about name rectification and autonomy seemed less pressing than livelihood issues such as post-typhoon reconstruction after Typhoon Morakot, protests against tourist development projects such as the Meiliwan resort, the Hongye Hot Springs and Sun Moon Lake; hydroelectric development at the Gaotai Dam; or road construction that involved the displacement of graves in Katipul. There have also been protests against deforestation on Bunun and Truku land and against proposals to store nuclear waste near the Paiwan village of Nantian. This latter issue, like that of storing nuclear waste on Orchid Island (Hu 2011), creates links between indigenous groups and the broader anti-nuclear movement (see Grano, this volume), even as these indigenous and non-indigenous actors may have different perspectives (Fan 2006). Perhaps the most widely supported livelihood demands are those for expanded hunting rights (Simon 2009, 2013). On this front, activism eventually led to a reform in firearms legislation to permit indigenous men to possess home-made rifles and to hunt, after application via township offices to county officials, for cultural reasons, even as trapping and any form of hunting in national parks remain illegal. These local movements, similar to those described by Cole (this volume) in non-indigenous rural communities, may very well prove to be the training grounds for new forms of activism at a broader national scale. This is related to an important second unfolding, the rise of non-church actors in the social movements.

The second unfolding: the rise of non-church actors

As noted by nearly all observers, the Presbyterian Church has played a central role in the creation of the indigenous rights movement. The first indigenous rights organization, the Alliance for Taiwanese Aborigines, was essentially a Presbyterian political alliance relying on Christian concepts of social justice and Marxian liberation theology. Beginning in the 1980s, and relying largely on international alliances that included Dr Ed File and his Mohawk wife Donna Loft from Canada, the church trained a generation of indigenous social activists in training camps known as the Urban–Rural Mission, or URM for short (Simon 2004). During this training, promising social activists learn to focus on group identity, define visions for social change, identify the causes of social pain in their communities as well as obstacles to change, and then create strategies for action. During the training, instructors proudly give examples of their direct action, as when they toppled a statue of Wu Feng, a mythical Qing-dynasty official who supposedly sacrificed his own life to convince the Tsou people to stop head-hunting, from its pedestal in Chiayi, noting that the statue has subsequently been replaced with a commemorative statue to the 2:28 Incident (Amae 2012). Graduates of URM have launched social movements including a drive to reclaim land from the Asia Cement quarry and factory in Hualien, but also the various name rectification movements. Owing to this history, an estimated 90 per cent of indigenous activists in Taiwan are Presbyterian (Amae 2012: 139).

The main weakness of this form of political organization is that it has been so closely associated with the Presbyterian churches that it has alienated members of other churches, including the Roman Catholics and the True Jesus Church. The training camps have also been held outside the local communities, meaning that they are available only to individuals who have the time and the resources to attend, creating the impression that the subsequent political demands are strategies of local elites to gain power. Even the organizers of the movement against Asia Cement, for example, were greeted with local scepticism and rumours that it was an attempt to gain a seat on the township council or, rather mysteriously, to extort financial gain from Asia Cement, as if companies paid people who organize public protests against them.

Although the Presbyterian Church was an important incubator of social movements, it is noteworthy that activism has moved beyond church networks. Although these groups are largely organized by well-educated urban-based activists, they have managed to create secular groups that also transcend ethnic or tribal identification. These new groups include the Indigenous Youth Front (原住民族青年陣線), the Taiwan Indigenous People Society (台灣原社), which is more overtly tied to demands for Taiwanese independence from the ROC, the Association of Taiwan Indigenous People Development (台灣原住民學院促進會), the Indigenous People Action Coalition of Taiwan (台灣原住民部落行動聯盟), the Association for Taiwan's Indigenous Peoples' Policy (台灣原住民族政策協會) and the Hunter Smoke Action League (狼煙行動聯盟). There is also the NGO Millet Foundation (小米穗原住民文化基金會), with strong involvement of anthropologists, which funds research and advocacy. Most of these associations are urban-based, with meetings and public events held mostly in Taipei. Members are educated indigenous people, with some support from sympathetic non-indigenous academics. There are also indigenous student associations at many universities. Although participants in these groups are often also involved in the PCT, and although PCT ministers and other leaders are active in the events they organize, these new movements are less tightly associated with the church and reach a wider public.

An interesting example is the Hunter Smoke Action League, which is rural-based and active in communities along the East Coast. Village-based members of these groups meet regularly and organize local meetings. They have in some cases used Open Space Technology (Owen 2008), which basically means occupying public space to attract participants, holding meetings in ad hoc circles in which anyone can express their concerns and then planning protest demonstrations or other strategies to address the concerns raised. The Hunter Smoke Action League has been more successful than URM at reaching out to villagers, not least because they have also been able to offer legal aid to people involved in land disputes with non-indigenous people. Participants in this movement note, however, that most people are too busy with farming and other forms of employment to pay attention to indigenous rights issues or get involved in social movement activities. Prominent in Hunter Smoke Action League activities, as well as in the environmental and anti-nuclear movements, are indigenous singers Panai Kusui (Puyuma) and Nabu Husungan Istanda (Bunun). Through their music, as well as through the Hunter Smoke Action League, they promote a post-colonial understanding of indigenous issues in Taiwan.

The emergence of a social movement external to the church means that it is less infused with Protestant theology, a format which may have pleased Presbyterians but which was equally likely to alienate members of other churches or traditionalists. A new tendency, exemplified by the Hunter Smoke Action League, is a move away from officially registered NGOs with elected boards, an organizational form which easily becomes a tool for elite competition and which can alienate grassroots people. Instead, the Hunter Smoke Action League is a loosely interconnected network of people concerned primarily with local livelihood issues, such as opposition to particular development projects or to encroachments of the Forestry Division and other government bodies on indigenous sovereignty. Every year, the Hunter Smoke Action League draws attention to their existence by lighting bonfires in villages nationwide on the emotionally salient date of 28 February, when many Taiwanese commemorate those who lost their lives in 1947, when the newly arrived ROC government violently oppressed local calls for self-rule. On a day when many Taiwanese reflect on their difficult relation with governments arriving from China, the indigenous activists affirm that they are the true masters of the land.

For the rest of the year, the Hunter Smoke Action League provides a platform for communication between local activists across Taiwan. They thus permit activists involved in a diversity of local projects to share concerns and strategies, as well as information about upcoming protests so that they can travel to other communities and mutually provide support for common struggles, especially around the aforementioned livelihood issues. Their platforms involve, above all, the creative use of new social media.

The third unfolding: the use of social media

Alternative media, or what Lee Chin-chuan called 'guerrilla media' (2003), have played an important part in Taiwan's social movements from the beginning in the forms of privately published and mimeographed magazines and newspapers and underground radio stations. The indigenous people have also felt marginalized in mainstream media, which led to Article 12 of the Basic Law, calling for the establishment of indigenous media. In 2005, Taiwan began broadcasting the first indigenous television network in Asia, with the 24-hour Taiwan Indigenous Television Network (TITV) providing news and educational programming. Established under the auspices of the CIP, there was a requirement that 70 per cent of staff be indigenous. The CIP also distributed satellite receivers to households in mountainous areas and took steps to make televisions affordable to poor families (Alia 2012: 144).

Although indigenous social activists initially hoped that new broadcast media would give them a platform to spread a political platform on indigenous rights and many of them took up employment at TITV, this state-funded medium has remained sensitive to political considerations and threats to continued funding. TITV has thus taken a relatively conservative approach, focusing on cultural and language content, which, nonetheless, does reinforce the ethnic identities of the officially recognized groups. They also have news programmes dedicated to indigenous issues, providing nationwide coverage of events, including protest actions, and other information that in the past was rarely known outside the immediate context. Most disappointing to indigenous activists has been programming on tourism in indigenous areas, emissions that are clearly created for non-indigenous viewers and do not consider the potential negative impact of tourism on indigenous communities. In September 2014, long-time Amis activist and film-maker Mayaw Biho resigned as chief director of TITV, in protest of state interference in the station's editorial operations (Loa 2014).

These traditional media outlets were soon surpassed by the Internet and growing social media, especially those such as Facebook and Twitter that are available on the ubiquitous mobile telephones. Indigenous youth have been active in blogging, with the result that they can both reinforce their own identities by using their indigenous names and make their concerns better known to non-indigenous readers. The Atayal of Smangus, involved in a legal case with the Forestry Bureau from 2005 to 2010 over the right to use fallen wood on their traditional territory, used the Smangus Community Blog in Chinese and English to attract national and international support to their cause (Reid 2011: 443).

By coincidence, the Taiwanese translation of 'blog', based on a phonetic rendering of the English word as bu-luo-ge (部落格), literally means 'tribal grid' and uses the word *buluo* used to describe indigenous communities (Zheng 2011). Many indigenous blogs are published on Coolloud.org.tw, a web-based medium for social activists established in 1997. Although this web site was originally most closely tied to the labour movement, it has become an important site for the publication of news and blogs by groups marginalized in the mainstream media. A bilingual site known as the International Platform for Taiwan Indigenous Peoples provides blogs and news for and about Taiwan's indigenous peoples and international indigenous peoples in English and Mandarin.[2]

Most of the aforementioned groups have their own websites. Most notably, however, nearly everyone in Taiwan owns a smartphone. This has become the platform for the widespread use of Facebook, YouTube and (to a lesser extent) Twitter to spread social movement ideas and information about protests or other political actions. A Google search in Chinese for Hunter Smoke Action League turns up contributions to Facebook, YouTube, Google Groups, Pixnet, Coolloud and Civilmedia.tw (which archives video footage for Taiwanese social movements). A search for the Indigenous Youth Front reveals they are active on Facebook, YouTube, Twitter and Coolloud, but have also established an autonomous bilingual web presence as 'Mata Taiwan'.[3] *Mata*, which means 'eye' in many Austronesian languages and some (but not all) Formosan languages, indicates that the web site is intended to be an eye on Austronesian Taiwan. This group, which like Hunter Smoke Action League is active in many livelihood issues, has also taken a strong public stance against the Cross-Strait Service Trade Agreement. Indigenous students from this group participated in the Sunflower Movement and also launched their own protests against that agreement in spring 2014. The Indigenous Youth Front uses Twitter and Facebook to publicize lectures and book discussion groups on indigenous rights, most of which are meetings of university students in Taipei. Mata Taiwan, in sites marked by striking photography, uses Facebook, Twitter, Pinterest, Instagram and even the Chinese blogging site Sina-Weibo in simplified Chinese characters. The postings on this latter site, compared to those on the Chinese sites, are conservative and apolitical, probably indicating some degree of censorship or self-censorship.

Those who are interested in indigenous rights are thus better informed than ever about events happening across Taiwan. Images and information about land disputes in other communities are easily available, as well as notification of protests and other events. These new social media serve multiple purposes as they can simultaneously connect local activists and reach out to the rest of the world with postings in English and simplified Chinese. An inundation of information, however, makes it unclear how people actually use the social media. Although most bloggers and creators of online content hope to reach out to a global audience, it is possible that they mainly reach people who are already interested in indigenous issues. As Niezen observed about these movements for social justice, 'outreach to publics is almost always in some way like sending a message in a bottle, oriented toward a future audience of unknown provenance and uncertain sympathies' (Niezen 2010: 26). Even at the local level, in the indigenous villages, one cannot assume that people without previous involvement in the indigenous social movements will use these media or be influenced by them in the way hoped by tech-savvy social activists. As Hsiao (this volume) noted on the Wild Strawberry Movement, social media tends to reproduce existing interpersonal networks rather than create new ones. Yet, this does not stop political actors from trying to use social media this way. The most recent group visible through its online presence on Facebook is a new political party, the Taiwan First Peoples Party.

The fourth unfolding: a new political party

Since the 1950s, indigenous people have been able to elect in democratic elections their own local representatives as township magistrate, township council members, and village heads; and only indigenous people are permitted to be magistrates in the 30 mountain townships. Yet, since direct legislative elections in the 1990s, most political energy has been devoted to a quota of indigenous legislators, half of whom are from designated mountain groups and half from designated plains groups. In 2005, when constitutional revisions reduced the total number of legislators from 225 to 113, the quota for indigenous legislators was reduced from eight to six. This suggests that indigenous groups have adequate legislative representation. Although they constitute 2.2 per cent of Taiwan's population, they have 5.3 per cent of the seats in the legislature. Yet, indigenous activists have long been frustrated with the fact that indigenous people vote overwhelmingly for the KMT and that indigenous legislators – often, but not always – tend to follow the party line rather than represent indigenous interests. Since politicians must campaign island-wide and gain votes from all tribes, moreover, small tribes have little chance to see their members elected (Allio 1998b: 47).

This electoral system has contributed to a dialogic relationship between indigenous groups and the state, through which national parties and state actors negotiate deals with powerful local individuals, groups and factions, but can have the effect of delegitimizing indigenist strategies if they become perceived as merely electoral strategies (Simon 2010). Although all candidates promise to defend indigenous rights, there is a strong tendency for the KMT and other 'pan-blue' or 'pro-unification' independent legislators to win elections. The DPP has so far only succeeded in getting elected one plains legislator, and some legislators on island-wide non-indigenous electoral lists (Simon 2010: 731). Indigenous legislators have sometimes been able to make important changes in state–indigenous relations, most notably by creating the Council of Indigenous Peoples in 1996 and by passing the Basic Law on Indigenous Peoples in 2005. They are most successful in negotiating deals with other politicians when the major parties are near parity in the Legislative Yuan and indigenous legislators can sway the balance of power in either direction (Iwan 2005).

Indigenous activists have long been dissatisfied with this situation. After President Chen Shui-bian promised that state–indigenous relations would be considered to be 'quasi-state-to-state' relations, indigenous leaders and activists met at the Council of Indigenous Peoples in the summer of 2004 to draft indigenous clauses for an eventual Constitution of the Republic of Taiwan (Working Group on Constitutional Indigenous Policy 2005). During these discussions, they examined the precedent of the Canadian Assembly of First Nations (AFN). This body, which emerged from and replaced the National Indian Brotherhood in 1985, is envisioned by indigenous people as a place for diplomatic and political relations between sovereign First Nations and, collectively through representation of chiefs from across the country, as the organization for nation-to-nation relations with Canada. This precedent has since inspired indigenous activists in Taiwan, who proudly refer to their own groups as First Nations and who aspire to a similar organizational framework. In 2004, they hoped that a new constitution for their country would include such provisions as an indigenous vice president and an indigenous assembly in parliament to institutionalize state-to-state relations. This dialogue between indigenous activists and supporters of Taiwan independence proved short-lived as their dreams crashed on the shores of political reality and long before the end of Chen's tenure. In 2005, none of this was even debated in the last round of constitutional revisions by the National Assembly, which dissolved itself in those revisions, and by 2006 President Chen was already too embattled by 'Red Shirt' protests against corruption (Shih 2007) to even entertain, let alone propose, any radical changes in indigenous policy.

After Ma Ying-jeou's election in 2008, indigenous activists decided to take independent action, with Thao Nation activist Shi Qinglong taking a leading role. Inspired by the AFN, they debated at meetings across Taiwan whether they should seek to establish an assembly or a new political party. Some even proposed a bit of a compromise by creating the 'Assembly of First Nations Party'. On 12 December 2012, veteran activists from all over Taiwan met in Taipei to formally establish the Taiwan First Nations Party. Stressing indigenous issues that other parties neglect, this constitutes what Fell (this volume), following Lucardie, calls a 'prophetic party'. At the opening ceremony, Shi was elected Chair of the First Nations Party nearly unanimously. In his investiture speech, he explained that 'First Nations' means that the indigenous people were originally in Taiwan and that outsiders should not simply declare it to have been *terra nullius*. The first goal is to obtain autonomy and other rights to order to gain equality and justice, so it is important that indigenous peoples and the state can build a new relationship on equal footing. He set the goal of getting some people elected in the 2014 local elections, and hopefully for one legislator in both mountain and plains quotas in the 2014 legislative elections.[4] In 2014, Shi presented his own candidacy as county representative in Nantou and won the election.

Shi's Thao Nation, located near Sun Moon Lake, has since the Japanese period been classified by the state to be a part of the Tsou tribe. The Japanese converted the natural lake into a reservoir for hydroelectric power and relocated the group. After the ROC came to Taiwan, the government encouraged Han Taiwanese to move into the area and promoted it as a tourist destination. On 21 September 1999, the area experienced a major earthquake, which destroyed most of their homes and left most of them unemployed. In the subsequent reconstruction, they demanded to rebuild their former community, including architecture, according to Thao cultural norms. This strengthened their ethnic identity. In 2001, the Thao were the first new indigenous group to gain recognition by the Chen Shui-bian administration as Taiwan's tenth indigenous tribe (Yayoi 2011). They remain Taiwan's smallest tribe, with a population in May 2014 of 747. Shi Qinglong became their first representative to the Council of Indigenous Peoples, where he learned about the Canadian Assembly of First Nations and began adapting to the Taiwanese situation ideas about indigenous rights that were concurrently gaining importance in customary international law. The name rectification movements of the Chen Shui-bian period thus created new institutions that incubated new political entrepreneurs and new networks. Even with a change in president, these institutions and political actors have gained a momentum of their own and may still take state–indigenous relations in Taiwan into unexpected directions. It is, however, still too early to predict how successful the Taiwan First Nations Party will be, as they still have very little electoral experience.

Conclusion

In conclusion, I would like to draw a few comparisons with other social movements in Taiwan. Most importantly, the indigenous social movement is fundamentally different from all others because its starting point is the legal principle of self-determination (Niezen 2010: 113). Built around communities that existed on the territory before the arrival of foreign states, the indigenous rights movement demands recognition, in meaningful ways, of a nation-to-nation relationship. In Taiwan, this was the spirit that attracted indigenous leaders to accept the formation of chiefdoms and tribal councils during the Japanese period, followed by 'autonomy' (自治) and township electoral politics after the arrival of the Republic of China on their territories. This is the same spirit that also animates indigenous protest movements and new political actors, including leaders of the First Nations Party. From an indigenous perspective, the goal of various political actions was the same, even before the post-martial law reframing of indigenous social movements allowed them to gain even greater traction.

What does all of this mean? In my book *Sadyaq Balae! L'autochtonie formosane dans tous ses états* I demonstrated that all of the political and social measures taken for and by the formerly acephelous societies of Taiwan, from township elections to name rectification, contributed to a bureaucratization of indigeneity. The charismatic leadership of these formerly egalitarian societies has been routinized into forms of state leadership, albeit not without resistance from 'ordinary people', whose perspectives, like those of the international indigenous movement, are still infused with ideals of equality between men, of autonomy between local groups and of spiritual notions of law. Their main preoccupations have never been to distinguish Taiwan from China, but rather to preserve their own autonomy. Historically, this has sometimes meant accepting alliances with foreign state bureaucracies, whether Japanese or Chinese, in order to limit Hokkien and Hakka access to their territories. Considering the historical tension between these ethnic groups, it is not surprising that indigenous people are reluctant to vote for what they perceive to be a Hokkien-dominated DPP (Simon 2010). They are often distrustful of other social movements, especially the environmental movements, which they perceive as dominated by Taiwanese Buddhists and thus intrinsically opposed to hunting.

We can better understand the indigenous social movements, and their resilience in the face of political change, if we think of them as composed of individual actors who continue to pursue their own livelihoods and strategies among changing circumstances. We can thus better perceive continuity in terms of the indigenous legislators, township authorities and public servants who have maintained and even entrenched their positions in Taiwan as the KMT returned to the presidency and the Executive Yuan. We can also see the importance of livelihood issues as thousands of people outside of these privileged positions seek to maintain their own lifestyles based on farming, productive labour, fishing and hunting. Taiwan's indigenous social movements seem to best gain traction when they can relate to the livelihood issues as these lifestyles are threatened by coastal development, nuclear waste storage, the criminalization of hunting etc.

But to see the social movements as *only* elite competition misses most of the picture. After all, these supposed elites, whether they are legislators, township council representatives, Presbyterian pastors, musicians or underemployed youth with university degrees, are also members of their communities, sons and daughters, brothers and sisters of 'ordinary people'. And these elites are not the only people involved in the social movements, which indeed rely for their success on the time and resources of thousands of students, workers, small entrepreneurs, farmers and unemployed individuals. These social movement supporters are quite capable of casting cynicism upon the social movements, even when speaking to outside observers, but surely their intellects are just as keen when they decide to join a demonstration or vote for a candidate as when they denounce the political activities of their pastor or an elected politician. The actions and strategies of social movement entrepreneurs and their sometimes-fickle supporters are those of neither isolated 'rational actors' nor beings overdetermined by culture, but of human beings embedded in social networks, motivated not just by power and money but also by emotion and faith.

All other social movements in Taiwan, whether they be labour, environment, feminist or LGBT, face the challenge of reaching out to millions of unrelated individuals, mostly in the urban areas from Taipei to Kaohsiung. The indigenous movement has the also quite-daunting challenge of reaching out to small communities anxious to protect their own autonomy. All four of the unfoldings described here can be viewed in this light. The shift to livelihood issues is a way of reframing indigenous rights in terms of local issues mostly conflicts with forestry officials, national parks and externally imposed development projects. The local protests attract activists from other communities and indigenous legislators but are still composed primarily of people from the directly affected community, most of whom are related to one another through what anthropologists would call agnatic and affinal kinship, through patrilineal lines and marriage networks. The rise of non-church actors is an attempt to reach across denominational lines, but largely as individual activists reach out to relatives who are members of other churches. The new social media promise to produce new networks but are in fact more likely to reproduce existing networks. Even the First Nations Party will propose candidates first in local elections and will succeed only if, like the KMT, if it can successfully mobilize kin-based and village-based networks.

The long history of indigeneity on Taiwan, its ontological grounding in nation-to-nation relations in spite of a century of bureaucratization and its embeddedness in tightly knit kin-based communities mean that the indigenous social movement is unlike any other. The indigenous movement is not at all about the emergence of a Taiwanese *Volk*; in fact, indigenous people often stress that they alone are the true Taiwanese as they deny Hokkien and Hakka the status of non-Chinese alterity. Their social movements, although they emerged at the end of martial law and at the same time as many other social movements that drew energy from dissatisfaction with the KMT, have their own internal dynamics. Eager to remain autonomous from electoral politics dominated by others, they sometimes position themselves as allies of the pan-green forces but have also been allies of the pan-blues. This was very evident when we consider that some of the same indigenous activists showed up at both the Red Shirt rallies in 2006 and at the Sunflower protests in 2014. In fact, indigenous activists often stress that debates about independence and unification are debates between Han Chinese. Ever since the Qing dynasty, but more explicitly during the Japanese period, they are more interested in indigenous–state relations, no matter who controls the state on the other side. From an internal perspective, the indigenous movement is not about Chinese versus Taiwanese identity. It is not about electoral politics and even less about Great Power politics in international relations that go beyond Taiwan. Indigenous activists are concerned internally with relations as they reach out to kin and allies in their own villages. They are concerned externally as they seek to create international relations with other political formations in Taiwan and even with allies abroad. But, true to their ancestral law, it is all about maintaining moral relations that respect the autonomy of the kin-based community.

Addendum: indigenous politics in 2016

Although the presidential and legislative elections saw DPP victories in most of Taiwan, the indigenous communities continued to support the KMT. The KMT gained a majority of the presidential vote in areas with large numbers of indigenous voters, most notably Hualien and Taitung Counties, but also in the mountain townships of Ren'ai and Xinyi in Nantou County. In the legislative elections, pan-blue incumbents Kung Wen-chi, Chien Tung-ming and May Chin were re-elected in the mountain districts, whereas DPP candidate Chen Ying took one of the plains seats. The First Nations Party failed to gain a seat and their proposed Bunun candidate for a mountain seat, Salizan Binkinuan, switched ballots at the last moment to the Christian Faith and Hope League Party (where he also lost). With such large numbers of indigenous voters expressing continued support for the KMT, which many describe as an alliance between indigenous people and mainlanders, the old dynamics continue. Moving forward, the indigenous social movements will have to collaborate with the DPP in order to promote their legislative goals, but their support among rural indigenous people will continue to be limited if they are perceived as being too close to Hokkien and Hakka 'pro-independence' political forces. The indigenous peoples may appear to be an effective symbol of Taiwan's independent identity but their own political behaviour suggests that they prefer an alliance with Chinese-oriented leaders. In this context, it remains difficult for indigenous social movements to align themselves too closely with other progressive social movements without losing credibility among the populations they are supposed to represent.

Notes

1 The reflections in this chapter are intended to update observations initially made in a research project from 2004 to 2007 that included 18 months of field research in three Truku communities on development and resistance, and are based on observations and participation in social movement actions in annual visits from 2008 to 2013. This research was first presented in oral presentations at the Freeman Spogli Institute for International Studies, Stanford University, and in a lecture at SOAS. The author is thankful to Dafydd Fell, Larry Diamond, Kharis Templeman and participants who commented on the paper at those two events. Any mistakes or omissions are those of the author alone.
2 http://iptip.wordpress.com.
3 www.pure-taiwan.info/about-us.
4 I was present at the meeting, as I was in Taiwan doing research on another topic and was invited to attend. This summary of the meeting was reported in the Taiwanese media, as in this report on ETToday: 台灣第一民族黨成立　進入國會爭取原住民權益. Available online at www.ettoday.net/news/20121212/138865.htm (accessed 6 September 2014).

References

Alia, Valerie. 2012. *The New Media Nation: Indigenous Peoples and Global Communication*. New York, NY: Berghahn.

Allio, Fiorella. 1998a. 'La construction d'un espace politique austronésien'. *Perspectives Chinoises*, 47 (May/June), 54–62.
Allio, Fiorella. 1998b. 'Les Austronésiens dans la course électorale'. *Perspectives Chinoises*, 50, 46–8.
Amae, Yoshihisa. 2012. 'The role of the Presbyterian Church in Taiwan's transitional justice'. In A. Schick-Chen and A. Lipinsky (eds), *Justice Restored? Between Rehabilitation and Reconciliation in China and Taiwan*. Frankfurt: Peter Lang, pp. 127–52.
Blundell, David (ed.). 2012. *Taiwan Since Martial Law: Society, Culture, Politics, Economy*. Berkeley, CA: University of California Press and Taipei: National Taiwan University Press.
Brown, Melissa. 2004. *Is Taiwan Chinese? The Impact of Culture, Power, and Migration on Changing Identities*. Stanford, CA: Stanford University Press.
Chi, Chun-Chieh and Hsang-Te Chin. 2012. 'Knowledge, power, and tribal mapping: a critical analysis of the "Return of the Truku People"'. *GeoJournal*, 77(6), 733–40.
Fan, Mei-Fang. 2006. 'Environmental justice and nuclear waste conflicts in Taiwan'. *Environmental Politics*, 15(3), 417–34.
Fell, Dafydd. 2012. *Government and Politics in Taiwan*. London: Routledge.
Fujii, Shizue [藤井志津枝]. 1997. *Lifan: Riben Zhili Taiwan de Jice: Meiyou Paohuo de Zhanzheng* 理蕃: 日本治理台灣的計策 沒有砲火的戰爭(一) [*Savage Administration: Plans for the Japanese Administration of Taiwan, a War without Ammunition (1)*]. Taipei: Wenyingtang [臺北市: 文英堂出版社].
Gates, Hill. 1979. 'Dependency and the part-time proletariat in Taiwan'. *Modern China*, 5(3), 381–408.
Hara, Eiko [原 英子]. 2003. 'Taiyaru Sedekku Taroko o meguru kizoku to meishô ni kan suru undo no tenkai (1) – Taroko ni okeru dôkô o chûshin ni' ['タイヤル セデック タロコ を めぐる 帰属と 名称に関する 運動の展開（１）——タロコにおける動向を中心に']. *Taiwan Genjūmin Kenkyū* [台湾原住民研究], 7, 209–27.
Hara, Eiko [原 英子]. 2004. 'Taiyaru Sedekku Taroko o meguru kizoku to meishô ni kan suru undo no tenkai (2) – Nantou ken Sedekku no dôkô o chûshin ni' ['タイヤル セデック タロコ をめぐる 帰属と 名称に関する 運動の展開（２）：南投県セデックの動向を中心に']. *Taiwan Genjūmin Kenkyū* [台湾原住民研究], 8, 94–104.
Hu, Jackson. 2011. 'Retrieving ancestral power from landscape: Cultural struggle within Yami ecological memory on Orchid Island'. In D. Blundell (ed.), *Taiwan Since Martial Law: Society, Culture, Politics, Economy*. Berkeley, CA: University of California Press and Taipei: National Taiwan University Press, pp. 173–200.
Huang, Shiun-wey. 2013. 'Cultural construction and a new ethnic group movement: The case of the Sakizaya in eastern Taiwan'. *International Journal of Asian Studies*, 10(1), 47–71.
Iwan Nawi [黃鈴華]. 2005. *Taiwan Yuanzhu Minzu Yundong de Guohui Luxian* 台灣原住民族運動的國會路線 [*La voie parlementaire du mouvement autochtone taïwanais*]. Taipei: Guojia Zhanwang Wenjiao Jijinhui [臺北市:國家展望文教基金會].
Ku, Kun-hui. 2005. 'Rights to recognition: Minority/indigenous politics in the emerging Taiwanese nationalism'. *Social Analysis*, 49(3), 99–121.
Lee, Chin-Chuan. 2003. *Liberalization without full democracy: guerrilla media and political movements in Taiwan*. Paper presented at the International Communication Association, San Diego, CA, 27 May. Available online at www.allacademic.com/meta/p112248_index.html (accessed 6 September 2014).
Levitt, Peggy and Sally Merry. 2009. 'Vernacularization on the ground: Local uses of global women's rights in Peru, China, India and the United States'. *Global Networks*, 9(4), 441–61.

Loa, Iok-sin. 2014. 'Indigenous TV chief director resigns over conflict on media independence'. *Taipei Times*, 27 September. Available online at www.taipeitimes.com/News/front/archives/2014/09/27/2003600670 (accessed 22 October 2014).

Makeham, John and A-Chin Hsiau (eds). 2005. *Cultural, Ethnic, and Political Nationalism in Contemporary Taiwan*. New York, NY: Palgrave Macmillan.

Munsterhjelm, Mark. 2014. *Living Dead in the Pacific: Contested Sovereignty and Racism in Genetic Research on Taiwan Aborigines*. Vancouver: University of British Columbia Press.

Murray, Stephen O. and Keelung Hong. 1994. *Taiwanese Culture, Taiwanese Society: A Critical Review of Social Science Research Done on Taiwan*. New York, NY: University Press of America.

Niezen, Ronald. 2003. *The Origins of Indigenism: Human Rights and the Politics of Identity*. Berkeley, CA: University of California Press.

Niezen, Ronald. 2010. *Public Justice and the Anthropology of Law*. Cambridge: Cambridge University Press.

Owen, Harrison. 2008. *Open Space Technology*, 3rd Edition. San Francisco, CA: Berrett-Koehler.

Pratt, Mary Louise. 2007. 'Afterword: Indigeneity today'. In M. de la Cadena and O. Starn (eds), *Indigenous Experience Today*. Oxford: Berg, pp. 397–404.

Reid, David. 2011. 'Nation versus tradition: Indigenous rights and Smangus'. In D. Blundell (ed.), *Taiwan Since Martial Law: Society, Culture, Politics, Economy*. Berkeley, CA: University of California Press and Taipei: National Taiwan University Press, pp. 433–62.

Rudolph, Michael. 2004. 'The pan-ethnic movement of Taiwanese Aborigines and the role of elites in the process of ethnicity formation'. In F. Christiansen and U. Hedetoft (eds), *The Politics of Multiple Belonging: Ethnicity and Nationalism in Europe and East Asia*. Aldershot: Ashgate, pp. 239–54.

Rudolph, Michael. 2006. 'Nativism, ethnic revival, and the reappearance of indigenous religions in the ROC: The use of the Internet in the construction of Taiwanese identities'. In Ahn, Krüger and Radde (eds), *Online-Religions and Rituals-Online*. Heidelberg: Online – Heidelberg Journal of Religions on the Internet No. 1/2, 2006. (www.ub.uni-heidelberg.de/archiv/6956, 17 June 2008).

Shepherd, John. 1993. *Statecraft and Political Economy on the Taiwan Frontier, 1600–1800*. Stanford, CA: Stanford University Press.

Shih, Fang-long. 2007. 'The "Red Tide" anti-corruption protest: What does it mean for democracy in Taiwan?' *Taiwan in Comparative Perspective*, 1, 87–98.

Simon, Scott. 2004. 'Grassroots education, identity and empowerment: the urban-rural mission in indigenous Taiwan'. In R. W. Heber (ed.), *Issues in Aboriginal/Minority Education: Canada, China, Taiwan*. Regina: Indigenous Studies Research Centre, First Nations University of Canada, pp. 122–41.

Simon, Scott. 2006a. 'Formosa's first nations and the Japanese: from colonial rule to post colonial resistance'. *Japan Focus*. Available online at www.japanfocus.org/products/details/1565.

Simon, Scott. 2006b. 'Taiwan's indigenized constitution: What place for Aboriginal Formosa'. *Taiwan International Studies Quarterly*, 2(1), 251–70.

Simon, Scott. 2007. 'Paths to autonomy: Aboriginality and the nation in Taiwan'. In Carsten Storm and Mark Harrison (eds), *The Margins of Becoming. Identity and Culture in Taiwan*. Wiesbaden: Harrassowitz, pp. 221–40.

Simon, Scott. 2009. 'Indigenous peoples and hunting rights'. In Errol P. Mendes and

Sakunthala Srighanthan (eds), *Confronting Discrimination and Inequality in China: Chinese and Canadian Perspectives*. Ottawa: University of Ottawa Press, pp. 405–21.

Simon, Scott. 2010. 'Negotiating power: Elections and the constitution of indigenous Taiwan'. *American Ethnologist*, XXXVII(4), 726–40.

Simon, Scott. 2012. *Sadyaq Balae! L'autochtonie formosane dans tous ses états*. Québec: Presses de l'université de Laval.

Simon, Scott. 2013. 'Of boars and men: Indigenous knowledge and co-management in Taiwan'. *Human Organization*, 72(3), 220–29.

Simon, Scott. 2015. 'Making natives: Japan and the creation of indigenous Formosa'. In Andrew Morris (ed.), *Japanese Taiwan: Colonial Rule and its Legacy*. London: Bloomsbury, pp. 75–92.

Simon, Scott and Awi Mona. 2013. 'L'autonomie autochtone a Taiwan. Un cadre légal en construction'. In I. Bellier (ed.), *Peuples autochtones dans la mondialisation: les avancées du droit*. Paris: L'Harmattan, pp. 147–64.

Stainton, Michael. 1995. *Return our Land: Counterhegemonic Presbyterian Aboriginality in Taiwan*, Master's thesis, York University, Toronto.

Working Group on Constitutional Indigenous Policy [憲法原住民族政策制憲推動小組]. 2005. *Minutes of the Meetings on the Indigenous Special Clause in the Constitution* [原住民族憲法專章會議實錄]. Taipei: Indigenous Peoples Council.

Yamaguchi, Masaji [山口政治]. 1999. *Higashi Taiwan kaihatsushi: Karenkoo to Taroko* [東台湾開発史: 花蓮港とタロコ]. Tokyo: 中日産経資訊.

Yayoi, Mitsuda. 2011. 'First case of new recognition system: The survival strategies of the Thao'. In D. Blundell (ed.), *Taiwan Since Martial Law: Society, Culture, Politics, Economy*. Berkeley, CA: University of California Press and Taipei: National Taiwan University Press, pp. 145–72.

Zheng, Chantal. 1995. *Les Austronésiens de Taïwan: à travers les sources chinoises*. Paris: Harmattan.

Zheng, Portnoy. 2011. 'Taiwan: Social media makes indigenous voices loud and clear'. *Global Voices*. Available online at http://globalvoicesonline.org/2011/03/09/taiwan-social-media-makes-indigenous-voices-loud-and-clear (accessed 20 September 2014).

14 Uneasy alliance

State feminism and the conservative government in Taiwan[1]

Huang Chang-Ling

1 State feminism and conservative government

In January 2014, the Ministry of Education in Taiwan announced the list of newly appointed members of the Commission on Gender Equality Education. The announcement immediately angered the feminist movement because two of the members had been involved in the campaigns against legalizing same-sex marriages in prior months. The Commission on Gender Equality Education (教育部性別平等教育委員會) has been a main engine in promoting gender equality since its establishment in 1997.[2] Though among the newly appointed commissioners there were also seasoned feminist activists, the appointment of the two controversial commissioners signalled that, under the conservative government, the alliance between the state and feminist movement, known as state feminism, had become really fragile or nearly broken.

State feminism has attracted the attention of feminist scholars since the 1980s, when it emerged in many countries. Mazur and McBride (2007) delineated the development of the term in three stages. At first it was a loose term to describe a range of state activities related to gender and women's issues. Later, influenced by the United Nations' agenda of women's decades and gender mainstreaming, the term was associated with women's policy agencies. The third stage illustrated intellectual endeavours by gender and women's studies scholars and they gave the term an operationalized concept – state feminism is about the interactions between women's policy agencies and feminist movements.

The impact of state feminism has been documented into two kinds: (1) policy and legal success in some policy realms; and (2) demobilization and deradicalization of the feminist movement. It has been shown that state feminism was successful in issues that have long been on the feminist movement agenda. Major policy changes or enactment of laws regarding abortion, prostitution and equal representation of men and women are usually achieved under state feminism. For policy issues that are not generally recognized as gender- and women-related, however, state feminism had clear limitations (Haussman and Sauer 2007: 5).[3] State feminism is also criticized for demobilizing and deradicalizing the feminist. Once engaged in the bureaucratic routines of state functions, portions of movement resources were directed to deal with the usually tedious bureaucratic requirement and less to advocate on gender equality (Haussman and Sauer 2007: 5).

While the strength and limitations of state feminism were shared in many countries' experiences, the literatures also tend to suggest that state feminism enjoys more success under progressive governments than conservative governments. Except for Bashevkin (1998, 1996, 1994), few studies focused specifically on the relation between conservative governments and feminist movements. Bashevkin's studies (1994) showed that under conservative governments women's interests could vary with different opportunity structures, and they were not always disadvantaged. However, Bashevkin (1996) also showed that, even if the feminist movement could still make advances under conservative government, their common ground with the conservative government was much narrower. What happened to state feminism under conservative government if it began under the progressive government in a newly democratizing country? Could state feminism survive the government change or did it disappear when the conservative party returned to power? On the other hand, in what circumstances would the conservative government be willing to continue what was achieved during the rule of the progressive government? This chapter aims to explore these questions by looking at the experience of Taiwan, a young Asian democracy that has experienced state feminism under both progressive and conservative governments since 2000.

Taiwan experienced decades of authoritarian rule before democratization began in 1987. The democratic forces eventually captured power in 2000 and feminists were brought into the government to take advantage of the opportunity to make and implement women-friendly policies. In 2008, however, the conservative Nationalist Party (Kuomintang, KMT) returned to power and the challenges to state feminism began. Based on data collected through documents, field research and personal involvement and observation of Taiwan's feminist movement, I will show in this chapter that the alliance between government agency and the feminist movement was weakened but survived after the conservative party returned to power. While state feminism withstood the attacks from the conservative social forces, a significant crack did emerge after the Ministry of Education appointed members of conservative social organizations to be the commissioners of gender equality education. The chapter concludes by arguing that, however uneasy the alliance between the state and feminist activists, the alliance is still important for the development of gender equality.

2 State feminism under the progressive government[4]

The creation of women's policy agencies or gender policy machineries in many countries was treated as the starting point of state feminism. In the 1970s, women's movements in the Western democracies regarded the state as patriarchal and unfriendly, so feminist activists usually worked outside the state. At that time, movement actors focused on advocating gender equality in societies (Banaszak *et al.* 2003: 30). In the 1980s, the movement strategies began to shift and activists not only wanted to engage the state more but also had more international mobilization (Rai 2003: 20; Meyer and Prügl 1999). Many countries created women's policy agencies in response to the women's movement's demands and the directives of international organizations such as the United Nations.

Being excluded from the United Nations (UN), Taiwan was not engaged in the UN agenda of gender equality until the early 2000s. The establishment of women's policy machinery in Taiwan had more to do with the development of the domestic feminist movement than with the advancement of the UN agenda. The first women's policy machinery was established in the capital city Taipei in 1995, after the Democratic Progressive Party (DPP) won the mayoral election and established the Taipei City Commission on the Promotion of Women's Rights (CPWR) (臺北市婦女權益促進委員會).[5] This gender commission consisted of bureaucratic members and civic members. Bureaucratic members were heads of some of the departments of the city government. Civic members were representatives of women's organizations or gender scholars. The chairperson of the gender commission was the mayor himself. Besides the CPWR, the Commission on Gender Equality Education and Commission on Women's Health (台北市教育局兩性教育暨性教育委員會) were also established under the Department of Education and Department of Health in the Taipei City government, following similar compositions of the gender commission and headed respectively by the heads of each department.

Though the Taipei City government under the DPP began to work with feminist activists through these various commissions, women's policy machinery at the national level did not emerge until 1997, after a tragedy. The DPP's director of the Department of Women's Affairs was killed at the end of 1996. The killing was believed to be a random crime at night and not politically motivated.[6] However, women's organizations protested against the state's inability to create a safe environment and demanded that the national government, still under the rule of the conservative KMT, be more responsive towards women's needs. The national government eventually established similar commissions to those in the Taipei City government. The cabinet CPWR was established and the Commission on Gender Equality Education was also established under the Ministry of Education. The cabinet CPWR met three times a year, and at first the commission was chaired by the Minister of the Interior, at that time a woman, and later the chairperson was replaced by the vice premier. Though civic commissioners would advise the government on various women's policies, gender mainstreaming was not yet a part of the policy vocabulary. Though the commission did publish works related to gender equality, its impact on government policies was not obvious under the KMT government.

In 2000, the DPP won the presidential election and the alliance between the government and feminist movement began to emerge and influence national policies. After the DPP came to power, many feminist activists were appointed as the cabinet gender commissioners, and their involvement in the policy process led to institutional transformations and implementation of gender mainstreaming.

Before these feminist activists became gender commissioners, the commission held meetings three times a year and the policy suggestions made in those meetings were not necessarily adopted or followed by line ministries. Among these commissioners, some were also seasoned feminist activists. However, at that time the major function of the commission was consultative and there was no established mechanism to follow up on the suggestions made by the commissioners.

When the DPP was first in power, the term of the KMT-appointed gender commissioners had not yet expired. Some feminist activists who were close to the DPP government made two demands. The first demand was that the commission be expanded so that more feminist activists could be commissioners. The second was that the premier, not the vice premier, should be the chairperson of the commission. The government accepted both. When more feminist activists were appointed as cabinet gender commissioners (commissioners for the cabinet CPWR), the feminist movement network was brought into the government. These feminists did not regard themselves as mere policy consultants; they thought of themselves as partners with the government in making gender policies. The cabinet gender commission was then divided into five different sections, with focuses on women's safety, health, employment and welfare, education and culture, and international participation. Besides the regular commission meetings held once every four months, civic commissioners now had section meetings on those five major policy realms and special meetings on specific policies. In other words, civic commissioners of the cabinet gender commission not only met the premier and other ministers once every four months; they were constantly holding meetings with various ministers or senior bureaucrats to discuss all kinds of policies.[7]

Around 2002 and 2003, gender mainstreaming as a movement agenda was finally incorporated by the cabinet gender commission and the alliance between the government and feminist movement was further intensified because now the civic commissioners helped to review line ministries' gender mainstreaming plans. Though many civic commissioners held full-time jobs in addition to the commission works, they were actively involved and very dedicated because of their activist backgrounds and mentality. The gender commission model was expanded into local governments in almost every city and county after 2002, and by 2008, before the conservative party returned to power, a commission-like working team was also established in every ministry.[8] The expansion of the gender commission was a significant change because it created even more institutional space that feminist activists and gender scholars could take advantage of. In order to assure the connection between the ministry-level working teams and the cabinet gender commission, members of the cabinet gender commission passed a resolution and demanded that all the ministry-level working teams should have at least one member of the cabinet gender commission on their teams. Such institutional design made Taiwan's gender policy machinery a commission-driven one, since by 2008 there were gender commissions in every ministry and in almost every local government.

Along with the development of commission governance, under the progressive government there were also enactments of important gender laws. The Gender Equality Employment Law (性別工作平等法)[9] and the Gender Equity Education Law (性別平等教育法) were passed in 2002 and 2004, respectively. The Gender Equality Employment Law had been on the feminist movement's agenda for more than a decade and was finally passed by the parliament in 2002. The Gender Equity Education Law, on the other hand, was a significant success of the alliance between the government and the feminist movement.[10] Civic members of the Commission on Gender Equality Education in the Ministry of Education began to draft the law in 2001 and when the bill was submitted to the parliament in 2004 activists and bureaucrats were on the same side to lobby for the law. The law stipulated that a gender-friendly environment was essential for students' rights to education, so it required every school, from elementary schools to colleges and universities, to establish a committee on gender equality to promote gender equality education and prevent sexual assault and harassment on campuses. The law also clearly demanded that teachers and administrators respect students' sexual orientations. In the following years the law opened the door for gay and lesbian organizations to go into many schools to educate students on gay and lesbian rights.

In addition to the legal success, the alliance between the government and feminist movement also helped to increase women's political participation. Due to the early adoption and later reforms of gender quotas, Taiwan already enjoyed one of the highest levels of female representation in elected offices in Asia. The current percentage of female representatives in parliament is 38 per cent, much higher than Japan's 9.5 per cent and South Korea's 17 per cent. In 2004, the cabinet gender commission demanded that a 30 per cent gender-neutral quota be applied to every cabinet- and ministry-level government commission, not just gender commissions. This would allow each sex to occupy at least 30 per cent of the seats on a commission. The demand became one of the resolutions of the cabinet gender commission in 2005.[11] By the end of 2007, among the 500-plus government commissions that were supposed to comply with the resolution, more than 90 per cent of them did.[12]

Despite the success through commission governance, there were also obvious limitations. The best example of the limitations was the cabinet gender commission's inability to prevent the government from including a waiting period in the draft of the Reproduction and Health Bill (生育保健法). Around the mid-2000s, the Department of Health wanted to replace the outdated Eugenics and Health Law (優生保健法), enacted in 1984, with a new Reproduction and Health Law. The religious organizations and feminist organizations fought against each other through the drafts of the bill regarding women's reproductive freedom. The religious organizations demanded the government to implement a waiting period of seven days for any woman who wanted to have an abortion and the feminist organizations wanted none of that.[13] Eventually, in the bill submitted by the cabinet to the parliament in 2006, the waiting period was reduced to three days and several cabinet gender commissioners resigned in protest.[14] Unable to win the battle within the cabinet, feminist activists turned to the parliament to block the bill. Because of the controversy about the waiting period, parliamentary members were reluctant to deliberate on the bill and it has yet to be placed on the legislative agenda.

Generally speaking, state feminism in Taiwan had its share of successes and limitations under the progressive government between 2000 and 2008. One thing indisputable, however, is that the alliance between the government and feminist movement was unprecedented. Before the feminist movement had a chance to reflect on its gains and losses under the progressive government, the conservative party returned to power and the new challenges began.

3 The weakened alliance under the conservative government

In 2008, the conservative party, KMT, returned to power in Taiwan. The government did not completely exclude feminist activists from the cabinet gender commission, but among the newly appointed cabinet gender commissioners were people who did not have much feminist background or who were members of conservative women's organizations. The alliance between the government and the feminist movement, however, was at first only weakened, not broken.

Because the term of the cabinet gender commissioners was not synchronized with the election cycle, when the conservative government returned to power in 2008 the premier could assemble the new cabinet but he could not reappoint the civic gender commissioners until their term expired, which was one year away. In other words, institutionally, the premier and his cabinet had to work with the feminist activists who were left in the cabinet from the previous government. In 2009, when it was time to appoint new cabinet gender commissioners, the government excluded those close to the opposition party but not all of the progressive feminist activists. There were notable changes, of course. For example, the National Women's League of the Republic of China (中華民國婦女聯合會), usually known by its shortened name 婦聯會), known for its close relation with the conservative party, now had its deputy secretary appointed as a civic member of the cabinet gender commission. The Awakening Foundation (婦女新知), a feminist organization known for its long-term advocacy on gender equality policies and laws, no longer had its president appointed as a cabinet gender commissioner, breaking a long-term tradition observed since the birth of the gender commission. There were also civic organization members or scholars who became commissioners but had no particular background in women's affairs. The government, however, kept some of the commissioners who worked with the progressive government before and that was enough to maintain a weak alliance with the feminist movement. Table 14.1 shows the composition of the cabinet gender commissioners since the conservative government returned. As shown in the table, between 2007 and 2009, when the conservative government had to work with the civic commissioners left from the previous progressive government, the number of commissioners who had connections to the feminist movement or opposition party

Table 14.1 Cabinet Commission on the Promotion of Women's Rights (CPWR) member composition

Term year	Total # of cabinet CPWR members	Number of civic members	Number of members who have movement or progressive party connections
2007–09	30	17	12
2009–11	31	18	8
2011–13	31	18	6
2013–15	35	18	7

Source: Compiled by the author with data from the Department of Gender Equality of Executive Yuan, Republic of China.

was relatively high. After 2009, that number went down but remained stable throughout the rule of the conservative government.

The conservative government's willingness to work with some of the feminist activists in the cabinet gender commission was partially related to the fact that Taiwan's gender policy machinery did not have a full-time bureaucratic unit until 2012. Before all the government gender commissions emerged from the mid-1990s, bureaucratic units such as the departments of women's affairs in the national or local governments treated women's affairs mainly as an issue of welfare delivery, not an issue of gender equality. The situation changed when the various gender commissions were established but the government's commitment to promote gender equality still fell short of establishing a high-level bureaucratic unit to be in charge of planning and making gender policies. Starting from 2003, the feminist movement demanded the government to establish a high-level bureaucratic unit for women's policies. Within the feminist movement, there were vehement debates about the proper institutional design. Some argued for a new ministry, like the Korean Ministry of Gender Equality. The advantage of this ministry-model was transparency and an independent budget. Others argued for a bureaucratic unit within the cabinet. The advantage of this department-in-cabinet-model was its bureaucratic power over line ministries. The debate lasted for a few years. Eventually in 2009 the government decided to adopt the department-in-cabinet model and that decision also allowed preservation of the cabinet gender commission. According to the new design, the cabinet gender commission would be renamed the Gender Equality Committee (GEC) of the Executive Yuan (行政院性別平等會；行政院性別平等處) and remained the decision-making body for women's and gender equality policies. The newly created Department of Gender Equality functioned as the secretariat to execute policies and decisions made by the GEC.

The government's decision to opt for the bureaucratic model instead of the ministerial model was related to its intention to downsize the government, since the bureaucratic model would only have created a bureaucratic unit within the cabinet and the unit would not have an independent budget. However, the government's decision also had an institutional impact that kept partisan politics distant from the gender policy machinery. Unlike the position of a minister, the head of the Department of Gender Equality within the cabinet would not be a political appointee. Instead, that position needed to be filled by a civil servant. The head of the Department of Gender Equality therefore was basically a senior civil servant executing policies approved by the cabinet Gender Equality Committee, which in turn consisted of civic members that might or might not be politically close to the ruling party.

Such institutional design could also partially explain why some feminist activists were appointed as civic members of the cabinet gender commission. Though the commissioners were appointed by the premier, it was the civil servants that prepared the list of potential commissioners for the premier to select. Thus, as long as the activists were willing to work with bureaucrats in promoting gender equality, they had a chance to get invited back to serve in the commission, even if they, as individual voters, might not be supporters of the conservative party.

The irony was that if the conservative government really cared about gender policies and had its own gender-related agenda, then the department-in-cabinet model could be as political as the ministerial model, because, after all, the premier himself was both the chairperson of the Gender Equality Committee and the boss for the head of the Department of Gender Equality. He held the power to appoint the committee members as well as the head of the department. However, if the premier did want to politicize the gender policy machinery, then he needed to first make sure that the head of the Department of Gender Equality, supposedly a senior civil servant, was a good executioner of his gender-related political agenda. And then he needed to make sure that he appointed the right kind of Gender Equality Committee members that would not oppose his agenda during the committee meetings. All these works probably meant he had to pay more attention to gender policies then he was willing to. And this has been why the department-in-cabinet model seemed to have been less affected by partisan politics.

Another institutional reason that the alliance between the government and feminist movement somehow remained was because of the gender equality working teams in the line ministries. When all the ministries, under the demand of the cabinet gender commission, had to establish a gender equality working team that included civic members, the ministries needed to find scholars or activists who had gender knowledge and understood the work of the ministries. When there were all these positions to fill, it was no surprise that at least some feminist activists would be invited to be the civic members of the gender equality working teams at the ministry level. In other words, the weak alliance between the conservative government and the feminist movement was not exactly a result of the intent of the government but a result of institutional demand.

Between 2008 and 2012, under the conservative government, because of the feminist activists in the cabinet gender commissions and in the line ministries' working teams, there were still advancements made by the feminist movement. Besides the creation of the Department of Gender Equality within the cabinet, the government passed the Enforcement Act of the Convention on the Elimination of All Forms of Discrimination Against Women (CEDAW) (消除對婦女一切形式歧視公約施行法) and a new Gender Equality Policy Framework (性別平等政策綱領) in 2011. Both had many feminist activists involved. Though Taiwan is not a UN member, the Taiwanese parliament ratified CEDAW in 2007 and the government, with the help of feminist activists, prepared the first national report in 2009. Unable to send delegates to the UN for the report to be reviewed, the Taiwanese government invited some CEDAW committee members to Taiwan to help review the national report and the NGO's shadow reports. However, up until 2009, there was no consistent enforcement of the convention and no systematic review of laws and regulations to see if any of them violated CEDAW. Under the demand of the feminist movement and with the support of the cabinet gender commission, the government submitted the bill of the Enforcement Act of CEDAW to the parliament and got it passed. The Gender Equality Policy Framework was initiated by civic members of the cabinet gender commission in view of the fact that the old framework, written and passed in 2005 under the progressive government, needed to be updated. The commission invited other gender scholars to participate in drafting the framework, and, before the framework was formally approved by the cabinet, it was presented to all ministries and to women's organizations, conservative or progressive, in every city and county. The framework was a comprehensive document and served as a 'to do list' for the newly created Department of Gender Equality.

When the Department of Gender Equality was finally established in the cabinet in 2012, the major tasks taken up by the department were three pillars: promoting gender mainstreaming, enforcing CEDAW and implementing the Gender Equality Policy Framework. All three tasks began under the rule of the progressive government, and all three tasks had feminist activists involved and working with the state, regardless of whether the government was progressive or conservative. The policy continuity was there but the alliance between the government and the feminist movement was different. Under the progressive government, when a large number of activists were appointed as commissioners, the feminist movement network was brought into the government. Under the conservative government, however, some of the feminist activists stayed on as commissioners but the feminist movement network was no longer in the government. The difference was mainly about the communications and interactions among civic commissioners before they attended the commission or working team meetings. Under the progressive government, such kinds of communication usually allowed the activists to have more strategic thinking in their interactions with the bureaucrats. For example, they would try to solve their differences beforehand and avoid raising different opinions when facing bureaucrats, so that the bureaucrats could not use differences of opinion among civic commissioners as an excuse for not taking actions. This 'united front' was easier to form among the commissioners under the progressive government since most of them shared feminist values. However, under the conservative government, such a united front became harder to form because the composition of the commission changed. When pre-meeting communications did not exist or became rare, the agenda that could be pushed by the civic gender commissioners was affected. Though there was no significant regression of state feminism before 2013, the pace of the progression was slowed down. One example of the slowdown was gay and lesbian rights. In the Gender Equality Policy Framework, after rounds of discussions the government still refused to make a clear commitment to enact the Civil Union Law or to legalize same-sex marriages. The wording in the section regarding same-sex marriages turned out to be very vague, stating only that the government would make efforts to create social understanding and consensus on this issue. The issue of same-sex marriages, however, became the focal point of the gender equality struggles in 2013.

4 State feminism challenged

In 2012, the conservative party KMT won re-election again in Taiwan and, not long after that, the already weakened alliance between the state and feminist activists was challenged by the conservative social forces which rallied against gender equality education and same-sex marriages.

The conservative forces' challenge against gender equality education first emerged in the spring of 2011, and the target was gay and lesbian education. After the Gender Equity Education Act was passed in 2004, the Commission on Gender Equality Education in the Ministry of Education soon decided to emphasize three tasks in schools: relationship education, sexual education and gay and lesbian education. A new curriculum guideline for grades 1 to 9 was scheduled to be in effect in August 2011,[15] and the Commission on Gender Equality Education had made sure that gay and lesbian education would be included as part of the gender equality education in the guideline. The commission also invited scholars to write a teachers' resource manual in which there were candid discussions on human sexuality, including homosexuality and transgender identities.

In the spring of 2011, a petition initiated by the Taiwan True Love Alliance (臺灣真愛聯盟), connected to Christian churches, demanded that the Ministry of Education stop teaching students about gays and lesbians and called for the suspension of the new curriculum guideline. The petition misunderstood the teachers' resource manual as a new textbook for elementary and junior high school students and questioned the appropriateness of the content. Though feminist as well as gay and lesbian organizations countered with news conferences and releases to clarify the misunderstanding and defended the teachers' resource manual, the True Love Alliance successfully lobbied the parliament to stop the Ministry of Education from implementing the new curriculum guideline. The parliament also demanded the Ministry of Education to hold public hearings on this issue. Feminist and gay and lesbian organizations had by then also formed the Friendly Taiwan Alliance (友善臺灣聯盟). In the following months, the two alliances fought against each other in all of the public hearings held by the Ministry of Education. Meanwhile, the civic commissioners of the Commission on Gender Equality Education were working hard within the ministry to fight for the inclusion of gay and lesbian education in the curriculum guideline. Eventually, in the spring of 2012, the Ministry of Education presented a report to the parliament and the curriculum guideline remained intact. The only revision made was on a competence indicator for junior high school students. In the original guideline, one of the students' competence indicators would encourage students to understand their own sexual orientations, and that indicator was changed to teach students to respect other people's sexual orientations. The change, therefore, was not a compromise on the curriculum guideline, only a compromise on the competence indicators for students. The curriculum guideline that included gay and lesbian education withstood the attack from the True Love Alliance partially, if not mainly, because of the work of the Commission on Gender Equality Education.[16]

Though gender equality education did not experience huge setbacks under the attack from the True Love Alliance, the conservative forces' attempts to reorient the direction of gender equality education continued and their mobilization for opposing same-sex marriages exerted enough pressure for the conservative government to eventually compromise the integrity of the Commission on Gender Equality Education. Since the mid-1980s, there had been sporadic efforts in Taiwan to demand the legalizing of same-sex marriages. The momentum picked up in 2009, when the Taiwan Alliance to Promote Civil Partnership Rights (TAPCPR) 臺灣伴侶權益推動聯盟, usually known for its shortened name, 伴侶盟, was established. The alliance aimed at revising the Civil Law to recognize civil partnership and legalize same-sex marriages. In October 2013, the TAPCPR announced that, with the help of a female DPP parliamentary member, the organization was ready to submit the bill they had drafted. The announcement immediately led to the formation of the Alliance for Protecting Families (臺灣守護家庭行動聯盟, usually known for its shortened name, 護家盟), which opposed same-sex marriages. The TAPCPR's bill consisted of three parts: recognizing civil partnership, legalizing same-sex marriages and allowing 'multi-member families' – a family form that could be but not necessarily is polyamorous. The DPP politician only submitted the part on same-sex marriage to the parliament for deliberation, but the Alliance for Protecting Families focused their attacks on the part of 'multi-member families'. The same-sex marriage bill quickly passed the first reading in the parliament, and the Alliance for Protecting Families, along with other non-religious conservative forces, mobilized a huge rally to prevent the bill from entering the second reading. Between October and December 2013, the fight between the pro and con camps of same-sex marriages was very much like the replay of the fight over the curriculum guideline a year and half before. The only difference was that the fight was even more vehement and had many more people involved. Surveys conducted a year before showed that more than 50 per cent of Taiwanese supported same-sex marriage, and younger generations overwhelmingly so. Therefore, besides the rallies each held on the streets, social media were also battlegrounds.

The conservative forces' mobilization successfully blocked the bill from entering the second reading of the parliament after the Alliance for Protecting

Families lobbied and exerted pressure on both the KMT and the DPP parliamentary members. It turned out that the party whips of both parties had sided with the Alliance for Protecting Families and the only parliamentary members who continued their support for same-sex marriages were a few female DPP politicians.[17] In early 2014, accompanied by the KMT parliamentary members, the Alliance for Protecting Families met with the premier and demanded that the Commission on Gender Equality Education be 'diversified' to include representatives from religious organizations and parental organizations, both close to the conservative camp. Soon after, the Ministry of Education announced the list of commissioners for the 2014–16 Commission on Gender Equality. Though there were credible activists and scholars on the list, the appointment of people who had openly opposed same-sex marriages shocked and angered feminist and gay rights organizations. Despite protests from these organizations, the Ministry of Education continued to cite 'respecting diversity' as a reason for such appointments. Though there has yet been no obvious regression of the work of the Commission on Gender Equality Education, preliminary evidence shows that the function of the commission has been affected by the two members close to the Alliance for Protecting Families.[18]

5 Uneasy alliance

Between 2008 and 2014, state feminism survived under Taiwan's conservative government. The government continued the work initiated during the rule of the progressive government by creating the Department of Gender Equality within the cabinet, releasing a new policy framework for gender equality and enacting a law to enforce CEDAW. The gender commissions in the cabinet or line ministries also demonstrated their strength when their agendas were attacked by the conservative forces. However, state feminism under the conservative government also showed significant cracks in one of the most important gender commissions – the Commission on Gender Equality Education. It remains to be seen, however, whether in the future there will be other cracks and whether the cracks will eventually break the alliance between feminist activists and the state.

Taiwanese feminists began to engage the state in an active way from the mid-1990s and the engagement was never easy. In many ways, it was a mutual learning experience – feminists learned the workings of the state and the state learned about feminist values. The engagement undoubtedly brought challenges to the feminist movement. Besides the usual issues raised in the literature of state feminism, such as dual constituencies, the redirection of movement resources to accommodate the bureaucratic process of the state or the deradicalization of the movement, the development of state feminism also made it more challenging for the feminist movement to connect with the youth. Engaging the state requires knowledge of the state, and that knowledge could be tedious, boring and sometimes even difficult for young people to get a hold of because it is usually about understanding how the bureaucratic process works.[19]

The continuity of state feminism was also a double-edged sword. On the one hand, it showed that state feminism in Taiwan was not affected very much by partisan politics because it allowed the feminist movement to keep its influence in the policy making process to some extent. On the other hand, however, it also meant that the feminist movement's agenda was not able to drive any political party's major agenda. This was particularly clear on the issue of same-sex marriages. When both the KMT and DDP were under pressure from the lobby of the conservative forces, neither party showed a commitment to legalize same-sex marriages.

Generally speaking, Taiwan's experience has shown that state feminism under the conservative government might slow down the pace of gender equality development, but it has not reversed the course of actions taken under the progressive government – at least, not yet. This means that, once feminist activists find a way to engage the state, as long as they keep engaging, the state would become more gender-friendly. The alliance might be uneasy between the feminists and the state, especially under the conservative government, but it is important and even necessary for the development of gender equality.

Notes

1 This chapter was originally published in the *Journal of Gender Studies* (Japan), Volume 18, 7–20 (2015). Reproduced with permission from the *Journal of Gender Studies*, Ochanomizu University, Japan. For the original version, see www.igs.ocha.ac.jp/igs/IGS_publication/journal/18/18e.pdf. I would like to thank the helpful comments from the two anonymous reviewers. The research for this chapter is supported by Taiwan's Ministry of Science and Technology: NSC101–2420-H-002–017-MY3.
2 When it was established in 1997, it was called 教育部兩性平等教育委員會, and in 2001 the name was changed to the current one.
3 The studies that Haussman and Sauer (2007) mentioned include Stetson (2001), Outshoorn (2004) and Lovenduski *et al.* (2005).
4 I am sure there will be disagreement from scholars or social activists in Taiwan when I use the term 'progressive government' to describe the government under President Chen Shui-bian of the Democratic Progressive Party. However, since progressiveness can be a relative concept in terms of the political spectrum, I stick to that term in this chapter for analytical purposes.
5 Later, under Ma's Taipei City government, the name was changed to 臺北市女性權益促進委員會.
6 The case was not solved and the killer is still at large.
7 The bureaucrats, of course, did not like these changes and had their share of doubts and reservations on gender mainstreaming. See Peng (2008).
8 For a description of this process, see Huang (2008).
9 It was called 兩性平等工作法 when it was enacted in 2002 and then in 2007 the name of the law was changed to its current name.
10 For a comparison of the state–society relationship in the enactment process of the Domestic Violence Prevention Act, enacted under the conservative government in 1998, and that of these two gender laws, see Yang (2006).
11 See the Twenty-Second Meeting Minutes for the Executive Yuan Commission on the Promotion of Women's Rights: www.gec.ey.gov.tw/Upload/RelFile/1508/719858/2dd73a76–5610–4485–81ba-ef68f0f1a68.pdf. Executive Yuan is the name of Taiwan's cabinet.
12 This percentage is calculated from the meeting documents for the Twenty-Seventh Meeting of the Executive Yuan Commission on the Promotion of Women's Rights. The meeting documents were data and documents prepared by bureaucrats for the

commission's meetings. Unlike the meeting minutes, these documents have not been released online.
13 Technically speaking, Taiwanese women had reproductive freedom in the old Eugenics Law because one of the conditions under which legal abortion was allowed was very vaguely worded.
14 I was among those who resigned.
15 In Taiwan, all the textbooks used by the schools, from elementary to high schools, have to follow the curriculum guideline designed by the Ministry of Education.
16 Unable to change the curriculum guideline, the True Love Alliance came up with a new tactic. In 2013, the alliance changed its name to the Taiwan Gender Education Development Association. The name, in both Chinese and English, was extremely close to the Taiwan Gender Equality Education Association, an organization established 10 years earlier and well known for its efforts in advocating for gender equality education. Once the True Love Alliance changed its name, the organization began to advocate a conservative version of gender education, of which one of the main ideas was that gays and lesbians were corrigible.
17 Though the bill on legalizing same-sex marriage got blocked, Taiwan was still regarded as the beacon for gay and lesbian rights in Asia (Jacobs 2014).
18 I was told that civic commissioners spent a lot of time fighting and arguing within the commission, mainly because there is always difference of opinions between the two conservative members and the rest of the commission.
19 For example, it takes some experience for civic commissioners to understand how to push the right button when they demand bureaucrats to take actions. Bureaucrats usually would not take initiatives to accomplish the tasks that civic commissioners demand unless the tasks are specifically assigned to them. To make sure the tasks are correctly assigned, civic commissioners need to have some knowledge about the functions of different units within the cabinet or the ministry.

References

Allsopp, Jennifer. 2012. 'State feminism: Co-opting women's voices'. Available online at www.opendemocracy.net/author/jennifer-allsopp-0.

Banaszak, Lee Ann, Karen Beckwith and Dieter Rucht. 2003. *Women's Movements Facing the Reconfigured State*. Cambridge: Cambridge University Press.

Bashevkin, Sylvia. 1994. 'Confronting neo-conservatism: Anglo-American women's movements under Thatcher, Regan and Mulroney'. *International Political Science Review*, 15, 275–96.

Bashevkin, Sylvia. 1996. 'Losing common ground: Feminists, conservatives and public policy in Canada during the Mulroney years'. *Canadian Journal of Political Science*, 29, 211–42.

Bashevkin, Sylvia. 1998. *Women on the Defensive: Living through Conservative Times*. Chicago, IL: University of Chicago Press.

Hankivsky, Olena. 2008. 'Gender mainstreaming in Canada and Australia: A comparative analysis'. *Policy and Society*, 27, 69–81.

Haussman, Melissa and Birgit Sauer. 2007. *Gendering the State in the Age of Globalization: Women's Movements and State Feminism in Postindustrial Democracies*. Lanham, MD: Rowman & Littlefield.

Huang, Chang-ling. 2008. *Engaging the State: Civil Society and the Institutional Transformation of Democracy*. Paper presented to the Conference on Democratic Consolidation in Taiwan, Stanford Center on Democracy, Development, and the Rule of Law, 30–31 May.

Jacobs, Andrew. 2014. 'For Asia's gays, Taiwan stands out as beacon'. *New York Times*, 29 October.

Lovenduski, Joni, Petra Meier, Diane Sainsbury, Marila Guadagnini and Claudie Baudino. 2005. *State Feminism and Political Representation*. Cambridge: Cambridge University Press.

Mazur, Amy G. and Dorothy E. McBride. 2007. 'State Feminism since the 1980s: From loose notion to operationalized concept'. *Politics & Gender*, 4, 501–13.

Meyer, Mary and Elisabeth Prügl. 1999. *Gender Politics in Global Governance*. Lanham, MD: Rowman and Littlefield.

Outshoorn, Joyce. 2004. *The Politics of Prostitution: Women's Movements, Democratic States, and the Globalization of Sex Commerce*. Cambridge: Cambridge University Press.

Peng, Yen-wen. 2008. 'When bureaucrats meet feminists: Exploring the progress and challenges of gender mainstreaming in Taiwan'. *Soochow Journal of Political Science*, 26, 1–59.

Rai, Shirin. 2003. *Mainstreaming Gender, Democratizing the State? Institutional Mechanisms for the Advancement of Women*. Manchester: Manchester University Press.

Siim, Birte and Hege Skjeie. 2008. 'Tracks, intersections and dead ends: Multicultural challenges to state feminism in Denmark and Norway'. *Ethnicities*, 8, 322–44.

Stetson, Dorothy McBride. 2001. *Abortion Politics, Women's Movements and the Democratic State: A Comparative Study of State Feminism*. Oxford: Oxford University Press.

Yang, Wan-ying. 2006. 'A comparative analysis of the process of gendered law-making in Taiwan'. *Taiwanese Journal of Political Science*, 29, 49–82.

Index

Page numbers in *italics* denote tables, those in **bold** denote figures.

02 Activist Society 77, 121
1984 (Orwell) 77
2:28 Incident 245
228 Massacre 18
818 Land Justice (and Government Demolishment) Movements 137, 138, 139
901 Anti-Monopoly Alliance 137
901 demonstration 78–81, 82
929 Citizen Action Alliance 137

Act Governing Relations between Peoples of the Taiwan and the Mainland Area 224
Action Network for Marriage Migrants' Rights and Empowerment (AMM♀RE) 227–8
adultery, decriminalisation of 185
AEC 164
AF (Awakening Foundation) 138, 144, 147, 149, *149*, 185, 233n1, 263
AFN (Assembly of First Nations), Canada 250, 251
agency 15–16
AHRLIM (Alliance for Human Rights Legislation of Immigrants and Migrants) 219–20, 221, 222, 223, 225, 226, 227, 228, 229, 230–1, 232
Ai Weiwei 83
Alliance for Protecting Families 268–9
Alliance for Taiwanese Aboriginals 245
Alliance of Anti-Forced Eviction 94
Alliance of Taiwan Aborigines (ATA) 239–40
Allio, Fiorella 239
AMM♀RE (Action Network for Marriage Migrants' Rights and Empowerment) 227–8

animal rights 184–5
anti-casino movements 4, 5, 55–6, 66–7; development pattern 8; impact assessment 11, 13, 16; Mazu 4, 8, 11, 13, 16, 55–6, 61–7; Penghu 4, 8, 11, 13, 16, 55–61, 66, 67
anti-corruption movement *see* Red Shirt anti-corruption movement
anti-globalization movements 27, 142–4
Anti-Kuokuang Petrochemical Industry Movement 20
Anti-Media Monopoly Movement 4, 50, 54, 67, 71, 93, 116, 125, 136, 137, 140; development pattern 9, 15; impact assessment 10, 12, 13, 16; roots of 5, 6, 72, 73–6; *see also* media monopolies
Anti-Nuclear Abolition Platform 172n9
anti-nuclear movement 2, 4, 26, 54, 67, 138, 139, 154–5, 170–1; development pattern 8, 15–16, 72–3, 76–85; early political alliances 157–8; and the GPT (Green Party of Taiwan) 178, 183; impact assessment 10, 11, 12–13, 73, 85–8; nuclear referendum issue 160, 165–6, 168, 183; organizational structure 158–9; political situation 2014 onwards 167–70; public opinion 15, 154, 163–5, 183; roots of 6–7, 155–7; significant trends since 2008 159–65; and the Sunflower Movement 147, 165, 166–7, 170–1
APMM (Asian Pacific Mission for Migrants) 227–8
Appendectomy Project 130
Apple Daily 74, 79, 82, 88
Arab Spring Movement 34
ARATS (Association for Relations Across the Taiwan Strait) 20, 120

Arrigo, Linda 168
Asia Cement 245
Asian Pacific Mission for Migrants (APMM) 227–8
Assembly and Parade Act 5, 13, 20, 22, 25, 39, 76–7, 173n9
Assembly of First Nations (AFN), Canada 250, 251
Association for Relations Across the Taiwan Strait (ARATS) 20, 120
Association for Taiwan's Indigenous People's Policy 246
Association for the Development and Care of Foreign Spouses 233n1
Association of Taiwan Indigenous People Development 246
Association of Taiwan Journalists 78
ATA (Alliance of Taiwan Aborigines) 239–40
Atayalic groups 239
Atomic Energy Council 164
autonomous trade unions 200–2, 205–6, 212, 213, 214, 215
Awakening Foundation (AF) 138, 144, 147, 149, *149*, 185, 233n1, 263

banks, Chinese 146–7
Bashevkin, Sylvia 259
Basic Law on Indigenous Peoples, 2005 241, 243, 247, 250
Batto, Patricia 75
BBS (Bulletin Board System) 35; Wild Strawberry movement Internet usage case study 37, 38–50, **40**, **41**
Beckershoff, André 4, 9, 11, 113–33
'Black Box' 117, 120, 126
Black Island Nation Youth Alliance 4, 15, 23–4, 25, 26, 27, 29, 115, 117, 128, 130, 137
BOT (build-operate-transfer) projects 58
Bourdieu, Pierre 113–14, 119–20
Buddhism 252
Bulletin Board System *see* BBS (Bulletin Board System)

Cable Radio and Television Act 85
Café Philo 130, 131
California, US 55
Canada, AFN (Assembly of First Nations) 250, 251
Caohwei, Master 60
CARES (Chinese Association for Relief and Ensuing Service) 230
Carmines, Edwards 10

Carter, Neil 9, 178
casino industry 54–5; *see also* anti-casino movements
Castells, Manuel 38
'causal-process observation' 37, 49
CCP (Chinese Communist Party) 115, 117, 146
CCW 147, 149, *149*
CEDAW (Convention on the Elimination of All Forms of Discrimination Against Women) 266, 269
CEPA (Closer Economic Partnership Agreement) 142
CET (Citizen of the Earth) 136, 137, 138, 139, 147, 148, 149, *149*, 173n9, 190, 194
CFBUs (company- or factory-based unions) 202, 203, **203**, **204**, 204–6, 209, *209*, 212, 215
CFL (Chinese Federation of Labor) 200, 201, 205, 212, 213, 215
CGU (Chang Gung University) 82–3
Chang Ching-chung 113, 117, 118
Chang family, Dapu 102, 103, 104, 106, 139
Chang Fu-shun 82–3, 89n2
Chang Gung University (CGU) 82–3
Chang Li-fen 214
Chang, Flora 75
Chao, A. 222
Chen Chi-chung 147
Chen Dung-Sheng 164
Chen Man-li 188–9
Chen Shui-bian 19, 57, 75, 97, 158, 201, 207, 236, 241, 242, 243, 250, 251
Chen Wei-ting 23, 26, 28, 76, 83, 106, 117, 121, 130, 167
Chen Ying 254
Chen Yu-ching 6
Chen Yunlin 5, 8, 19–20, 39, 120, 140
Chen, Ketty W. 4, 5, 7, 8, 10, 92–112
Chen, Sean 82, 85
Cheng Nylon 107
Cheng, Isabelle 7, 8, 219–35
Chernobyl nuclear accident 155
Chi-Ting Self-Help Group 106
Chiang kai-shek 242
Chiang Wei-hua 6, 9
Chiang Wei-ling 83
Chiang Wei-shui 18
Chien Tung-ming 254
China (People's Republic of China) 1; gender rights 146; marriage migration from 6, 7, 219, 220, 222, 223, 224–5, 227, 228, 229, 230, 231; relationship

Index 275

with Taiwan 2, 3, 6, 10–11, 20, 75, 93, 107, 115; student movements, 1989 36; *see also* China factor
China Airlines 208
China factor 5, 6, 15, 16, 22–3; anti-globalization path 142–4, 149, *149*; cross-strait-centred involvement path 139–41, *141*, 149, *149*; CSO changing epistemology and perception of 147–8; pro-democracy/human rights path 144–7, 149, *149*; and the Sunflower Movement 116–17, 134–6, 139–50; and the Want Want/CNS deal 75
China Network Systems *see* CNS (China Network Systems)
China Television (CTV) 74, 76
China Times 42, 74, 75, 76, 78, 79, 81, 83, 164
Chinatrust Charity Foundation 82
Chinese Association for Relief and Ensuing Service (CARES) 230
Chinese Civil War, 1949 18, 95, 97
Chinese Communist Party (CCP) 115, 117, 146
Chinese Federation of Labor (CFL) 200, 201, 205, 212, 213, 215
Chinese Nationalist Party 236; *see also* KMT (Kuomintang)
Chiu Hei-yuan 86–7
Chiu Hua-mei 185, 188, 189, 190, 191
Chiu Yu-Bin 5, 7, 8, 199–218
Chomsky, Noam 23, 83
Chou Kuei-tien 156
Christian Faith and Hope League Party 254
Chu Bing-kun 102
Chu Ching-yi 199
Chu Feng-min 101
Chu, Eric 168
Chuang, Y.-C. 19
Chung Tien Television (CtiTV) 74, 76, 78, 79, 84
Chung-hwa Telecom Workers' Union 214
Chungli Incident, 1977 108n2
Citizen 1985 Action Alliance 4, 24–6, 28, 136, 145, 147, 149, *149*
Citizen of the Earth (CET) 136, 137, 138, 139, 147, 148, 149, *149*, 173n9, 190, 194
Citizen's Union 192
Civil Disobedience (Chen Yu-ching) 6
civil society in Taiwan 2, 19–20, 30, 115–17, 130–1, 145–6, 150, 171; Mazu 62–4; *see also* social movements in Taiwan

civil society organisations *see* CSOs (civil society organizations)
Civil Union Law 267
Clark, John D. 36, 38
Closer Economic Partnership Agreement (CEPA) 142
CNS (China Network Systems) 13, 74, 75, 76, 88; *see also* Anti-Media Monopoly Movement; Want Want China Times Media Group
Cole, J. Michael 4, 6, 8, 12, 15, 18–33, 150
Commission on Gender Equality Education 12, 258, 260, 262, 267–8, 269
Commission on the Promotion of Women's Rights (CPWR) 260, 261, 263, *264*
Commission on Women's Health 260
company- or factory-based unions (CFBUs) 202, 203, **203**, **204**, 204–6, 209, **209**, 212, 215
constitutional revisions 11
Convention on the Elimination of All Forms of Discrimination Against Women (CEDAW) 266, 269
Coolloud.org.tw 248
Council of Indigenous Peoples 240, 241, 250, 251
Covenant and Conventions Watch 94
CPWR (Commission on the Promotion of Women's Rights) 260, 261, 263, *264*
Cross-Strait Act 228, 230–1
Cross-Strait Service Trade Agreement *see* CSSTA (Cross-Strait Service Trade Agreement)
CSAW (Cross-Strait Agreement Watch) 140, 141, *141*, 142, 145, 146–7, 148, 149, *149*
CSOs (civil society organizations) 134–6, 148–50, *149*, *150*, *151*; anti-globalization path 142–4, 149, *149*; cross-strait-centred involvement path 139–41, *141*, 149, *149*; mobilization networks 136–8; movement tactics 138–9; pro-democracy/human rights path 144–7, 149, *149*; *see also* NGOs (non-governmental organizations)
CSSTA (Cross-Strait Service Trade Agreement) 1, 4, 11, 13, 23–4, 30, 87, 92, 113, 114, 117, 129, 134, 144, 145, 146, 148, 166, 187, 194, 244, 248; *see also* DFACSSTA (Democratic Front against the Cross-Strait Service Trade Agreement); Sunflower Movement

CtiTV (Chung Tien Television) 74, 76, 78, 79, 84
CTV (China Television) 74, 76
culture workers, Mazu 65

dangwai ('outside the party') movement 18, 22, 74, 240
Dapu Borough, Miaoli County, land justice movements 1, 4, 7, 10, 12, 22, 94, 96, 97, 100, 101–7, 108, 118, 137, 139
Dapu Self-Help Organization 101
death penalty 3, 16, 42, 185–6
Democracy Tautin 130
Democratic Front against the Cross-Strait Service Trade Agreement *see* DFACSSTA (Democratic Front against the Cross-Strait Service Trade Agreement)
'democratic groups without leaders' 46–8
Democratic Progressive Party *see* DPP (Democratic Progressive Party)
democratization 170–1
demolitions, forced *see* land justice movements
Deng Pi-yun 38
Department of Cultural Affairs, Taipei 98
Department of Gender Equality 264, 265, 266
DFACSSTA (Democratic Front against the Cross-Strait Service Trade Agreement) 6, 8, 117–18, 130, 135, 138, 140, 143, 147, 148, 149; membership list *150*; *see also* Sunflower Movement
Diani, Mario 36
Domestic Violence Prevention Act, 1998 270n10
DPP (Democratic Progressive Party) 1, 11, 30; failures of 7, 21, 22, 145, 178, 213; foundation of 18, 74–5; and indigenous rights 12, 241–2, 249–50; and land justice 95; and the migrant spouse rights movement 219, 222, 224–9, 230, 231, 232; nuclear power policy 155, 157–8, 159, 160, 163, 164, 165, 166, 169, 170, 171, 183; post-2016 administration 13; and social movements 2–3, 11, 12, 14, 21, 29, 43; and state feminism 259–63, 270; and the trade union movement 206, 208, 213, 214

Earl, Jennifer 36
Ebsworth, Rowena 4, 5, 6, 9, 71–91
ECFA (Economic Cooperation Framework Agreement) 10–11, 20, 23, 115, 117, 140, 141, 244
ecologies 42, 45, 46; Internet as 37; *see also* virtual ecologies
Economic Democracy Union 130
education, unionization of 210–11
EIA (Environmental Impact Assessment) 158, 183
electoral campaigns, cost of 187–8
electoral system 177, 178, 182, 190–1, 230, 249–50
Enforcement Act of the Convention on the Elimination of All Forms of Discrimination Against Women (CEDAW) 266, 269
English language 32n17
enterprise unions 209, **209**
Environmental Impact Assessment (EIA) 158, 183
Environmental Impact Assessment Committee 11
environmental movements 1, 4–5, 58–60; and the GPT (Green Party of Taiwan) 178, 182–5, 194, 195; roots of 6–7
ethnicity, of protesters 100, 107
ETToday 42
Eugenics and Health Law 262
evictions, forced *see* land justice movements
Executive Yuan 15, 23, 28, 30, 39, 82, 122, 123

Facebook 27, 34, 35, 49–50, 77, 78–9, 80, 82, 83, 86, 125, 193, 248
Fair Trade Commission (FTC) 23, 86
Faith and Hope Alliance 186
Fan Yun 38
Far-Eastern Electronic Toll Collection Co. 207–8
Farglory Construction Group 184
Farmers' Movement, 1988 107
Federations of Industrial Unions (FIUs) 201, 205–6, 211, 213, 215, 216
Fell, Dafydd 1–17, 19, 177–98
Female Labour Rights Association 233n1
File, Ed 245
Fire Ex 1, 32n20, 105
FIUs (Federations of Industrial Unions) 201, 205–6, 211, 213, 215, 216
Formosa Incident, 1979 108n2
Formosa Plastic Group 164
Formoshock 130
Fourth Nuclear Power Station 3, 7, 8, 10, 11, 12–13, 16, 139, 143, 154, 155, 160, 161, 162, 163, 166, 167–71, 183

framing processes 221
Free Taiwan Front 129
free-rider problem 35, 36
Freeman 38
Friedman, Milton 72, 73
Friendly Taiwan Alliance 267
FTC (Fair Trade Commission) 23, 86
Fukushima Dai-ichi nuclear disaster, 2011 7, 26, 139, 154, 156, 160, 163, 164, 165, 170, 171, 183
fundraising 188
'Fury' rally 21, 24, 85

gambling industry 54–5; *see also* anti-casino movements
Gaoshanqing magazine 239
Gates, Hill 236
GCAA (Green Citizens Action Alliance) 136, 137, 138, 139, 142, 143, 144, 145, 147, 148, 149, *149*, 158–9, **159**, 160–1, 173n9, 183, 184
GEC (Gender Equality Committee) 264, 265
gender equality 185–6
Gender Equality Employment Law, 2002 262
Gender Equality Policy Framework 266, 267
Gender Equity Education Law, 2004 262, 267
Gerbaudo, Paolo 38
Gini co-efficient 199
Golden Brick *see* Huaguang Community, Taipei
Golden Melody music awards ceremony, 2015 1
Gongliao, How are you? 13, 183
Gould, Roger V. 36
GPT (Green Party Taiwan) 5, 11, 158, 167, 169, 171; development pattern 15; and the DPP 12, 191; electoral performance since 2008 177–8, *179*, *180*, 181–2, 194–5; impact assessment 8, 14, 16; and the labour movement 214–15; organizational structure 189–90; political opportunity structure 182, 187–94, 195; political project 182–7, 194; political resources 182, 187–90, 194–5; roots of 7
Grand Assembly, Wild Strawberry Movement 46, 48
Grano, Simona 4, 7, 8, 11, 12–13, 15–16, 154–76

Green Citizens Action Alliance (GCAA) 136, 137, 138, 139, 142, 143, 144, 145, 147, 148, 149, *149*, 158–9, **159**, 160–1, 173n9, 183, 184
Green Party Taiwan *see* GPT (Green Party Taiwan)
Green Party, Germany 178, 184
Gu Zhong-hua 38
guerrilla tactics 21, 104–5; and the anti-CSSTA movement 23

hair and beauty salon industry 144, 147
Hakka people 238, 239, 252, 253, 254
Harmel, Robert 190
Harrison, Mark 75
high school curricula, revision of 6, 29, 34, 35, 108n5
High Speed Rail (HSR) area 104
Hla'alua people 243
Ho Hai Yan Rock Festival 161
Ho Ming-sho 4, 6, 8, 16, 54–70, 156, 160, 166, 182
Hokkien people 238, 239, 252, 253, 254
Homemakers Union 189
homosexuality *see* LGBT rights
Hong Keelung 236
Hong Kong 142; Umbrella Movement 32n13
Hong Kong Federation of Trade Unions 211
Hou, Jeff 94, 106
Hsai, H.-c. 221–2
Hsiao Chia-chi 106
Hsiao Yeh 163
Hsiao Yuan 4, 9, 14, 34–53, 193, 249
Hsieh, Frank 19
HSR (High Speed Rail) area 104
Hsu Shih-jung 95, 96, 109n9
Hsu Szu-chien 4, 6, 7, 8, 12, 15, 134–53, 194
Hsu Wen-yen 192
Hsu Yung-ming 169
Hsu, Victoria 186
Hua-long Textile 207
Huaguang Community, Taipei 4, 22, 94, 96, 105, 107, 108
Huang Chang-Ling 5, 7, 8, 15, 258–72
Huang Kuo-chang 32n23, 76, 78, 79, 87, 129–30
human rights 144–7; and marriage migration 226–7
Hung Chung-chiu 24, 26, 32n23, 34
Hung Hsiu-chu 168
Hung Tzu-yung 32n23

Hunter Smoke Action League 246–7, 248
Hwa-jei Washing Co. 208

ILO107 (International Labour Organization Indigenous and Tribal Populations Convention) 243
ILO169 243
Immigration Act 219, 224, 226–7, 228
income inequality 199
Independent Taiwan Study Group 138
Indigenous People Action Coalition of Taiwan 246
Indigenous Peoples Council 243
indigenous rights movement 5, 237–8; development pattern 8; and the DPP 12, 241–2, 249–50; historical context 238–9; impact assessment 12, 16; Internet and social media use 237, 247–9, 253; livelihood issues 237, 243–5, 252–3; name rectification *(zhengming)* 240–1, 242–3, 244, 245, 251; new political party 237, 250–1, 253, 254; non-church actors, rise of 237, 245–7, 253; post-2008 era 243–54; pre-2008 era 239–42; roots of 7
Indigenous Youth Front 246, 248
industrial unions 202, **203, 204**, 209, **209**, 211, 215; *see also* CFBUs (company- or factory-based unions)
InfraVest Corp 31n4
Innolux Corporation 101
International Covenant on Civil and Political Rights 95, 226
International Covenant on Economic, Social and Cultural Rights 95, 226
International Herald Tribune 84
International Platform for Taiwan Indigenous Peoples 248
Internet and social movements 4, 14–15, 27, 34–5, 193–4; and the anti-CSSTA movement 23; and indigenous rights movement 237, 247–9, 253; and mobilization structures of social movements 35–7, 44–6, 49; and organizational structures of social movements 37–8, 46–8, 49; Wild Strawberry case study 37, 38–50, *40*, **41**
irregular employment 199
Island's Sunrise (Fire Ex) 1, 32n20, 105

Janda, Kenneth 190
Jang Show-ling 75
Japanese colonial era in Taiwan 7, 18, 238–9, 240, 242, 253

Jhunan Science Park 101
Jiang Peng-chien 107
Jiang Yi-huah 99, 103, 104, 120, 122, 127, 128, 168
Jiebeiyu 59–60
Joint Congress (Sunflower Movement) 123–4

Kanakanavu people 243
Kao Cheng-yan 158, 183
Kaohsiung City FIU 211
Kaohsiung Federation of Labor Unions 212
Kaohsiung Incident, 1979 18, 74–5
Keane, John 74
Ker Chien-ming 127
Ketagalan Boulevard 24, 25, 28, 92, 104, 105, 138, 141
Kimport, Katrina 36
KMT (Kuomintang) 14, 30; authoritarian governing style 7, 15; death penalty 185; government, 2008–2016 1, 3, 6–7, 54, 58, 66; and indigenous rights 242, 254; land appropriation policies 93–108; and media monopolies 85; and the migrant spouse rights movement 219, 220, 222, 226, 228–9, 229–31, 232; nuclear power policy 154–5, 156, 157, 158, 159, 163, 164, 165–6, 167–8, 171, 183; opposition period 2000–2008 19; and social movements 11–12; and state feminism 258, 259, 261, 263–70; and the trade union movement 200, 201, 203–4, 207, 208, 210, 212, 213–14; wealth of 187–8; *see also* Ma Ying-jeou
Ko I-chen 163, 184
Kongliao 155, 158–9, 160, 164
Koo, Jeffrey Jr. 82
Ku Kun-hui 240, 241
Kung Wen-chi 254
Kuokuang Petrochemical Plant 16, 54, 67; *see also* Anti-Kuokuang Petrochemical Industry Movement
Kuomintang *see* KMT (Kuomintang)

Labour Day Demonstrations 206
Labour Insurance Bureau 205
Labour Party 14, 169
Labour Rights Association 233n1
labour unions *see* trade union movement
Lai Chung-chiang 117
Lai Shiang-ling 214
Lai, Jimmy 79, 81–2
Laid-Off Workers Alliance 105

land justice movements 3, 54, 93–4, 183; Dapu Borough, Miaoli County 1, 4, 7, 10, 22, 94, 96, 97, 100, 101–7, 108, 118, 137, 139; Huaguang Community, Taipei 4, 22, 94, 96, 105, 107, 108; and KMT land appropriation policies 93–108; roots of 7
Lanyu Island 183, 184
leadership: charismatic 23, 26; and democratic organizational structures 38; Wild Strawberry Movement 46–8
League for Mazu's Future and Hope (Mazu weilai xiwang lianmeng) 66
Lee Chin-chuan 247
Lee Ching-hua 165
Lee Ming-Tsung 39, 40, 43
Lee Teng-hui 3, 142–3, 242
Legislative Yuan 19, 85, 87; occupation by Sunflower Movement 1, 2, 26, 27–9, 92, 93, 100, 106, 114–15, 118–29, 130–1, 134
LGBT rights 11, 15, 146, 185–6, 194, 267–9; *see also* same-sex marriage
Li Ken-cheng 190, 194
Li Yi-chieh 192
Liang Yi-chih 186, 187
Liao, B. Y.-H. 221
Liberty Square 39, 76–7, 120, 121, 163
Liberty Times 75, 79, 164, 168
Lin Chao-xin 76, 79
Lin Cheng-hsiu 187
Lin Fei-fan 23, 24, 26, 28, 77, 100, 117, 120, 121, 130
Lin I-hsiung 11, 166, 171, 183
Lin Pin-kuan 58, 59
Lin Sheng-hsiang 1
Lin Shu-wen 104
Lin Ya-chi 98
Lin, Edgar 172n3
Ling Tzung-kuei 83
Liu Cheng-hung 97, 101, 103–4, 106
local identity, and anti-casino movements 59–61, 67
Loft, Donna 240, 245
Longshan Temple 107
Losheng Sanatorium 19, 22, 25
Lost Wonderers of the Golden Block 93
Low, Setha 94
Lu, Annette 74–5
Lucardie, Paul 177, 178, 182, 194
Lungmen nuclear power plant *see* Fourth Nuclear Power Station

Ma Ying-jeou 4, 10, 12, 13, 16–17, 19–20, 58, 75, 115; approval ratings 31n4; first term 4, 8, 10, 20–1, 213, 218; second term 6, 7, 8, 13, 20–1, 30, 92, 93–4, 95, 97–108, 144–5, 162, 171, 212, 214, 216, 219; and the Sunflower Movement 120, 122, 127, 128; *see also* KMT (Kuomintang)
MAC (Mainland Affairs Council) 230
Macau 6, 54
marriage migration *see* migrant spouse rights movement
Mason, Paul 83–4
Mata Taiwan 248
MATSC (Marriage Association of Two Sides of China) 219, 220, 222, 223–6, 229, 230, 231, 232
May Chin 254
Mayaw Biho 247
Mazu anti-casino movement 4, 8, 11, 13, 16, 55–6, 61–7
Mazur, Amy G. 258
McAdam, D. 221
McBride, Dorothy 258
media costs, electoral campaigns 187–8
media environment 193
media monopolies: legislative discussions since 2013 85–7; *see also* Anti-Media Monopoly Movement; Want Want China Times Media Group
Mele, Christopher 36
Migrant International – Taiwan Chapter 228
migrant spouse rights movement 5, 6, 7, 219–21, 223–6, 231–2, 237; development pattern 8, 9; DPP era, 2000–2008 226–9; impact assessment 12, 13; *inside-out* perspective 221–2, 224, 232; *outside-in* perspective 222–3, 232; post-2008 era 229–31; roots of 6, 7
Millet Foundation 246
Ministry of Education 29, 82, 210; *see also* Commission on Gender Equality Education
Ministry of Justice: and the Huaguang Community 97–101
Ministry of the Interior *see* MOI (Ministry of the Interior)
Miramar resort, Taitung County 7, 183
MMD (multiple member district) electoral system 182, 190–1, 230
MND (Ministry of National Defense) 24
Mob, The (Chiang Wei-hua) 9
mobilizing structures 221
MOI (Ministry of the Interior) 96; occupation of 24, 94, 102, 105–7, 118, 137, 139

280 Index

Momesso, Lara 5, 7, 8, 219–35
Moore, Sheehan 92
movement momentum 8
multiple member district (MMD) electoral system 182, 190–1, 230
Murray, Stephen O. 236

Nabu Husungan Istanda 246
NALWSF (National Alliance of the Laid-Off Workers from the Shut-down Factories) 136, 137–8, 139, 143
name rectification *(zhengming)* 240–1, 242–3, 244, 245, 251
National Alliance for Workers of Closed Factories (NAWCF) 25
National Cheng Kung University (NCKU) 77, 121
National Chengchi University (NCCU) 77, 95
National Communications Commission (NCC) 23, 74, 75–6, 84, 85, 86
National Federation of Teachers' Unions 210
National Human Rights Commission 226
National Immigration Agency 230
National Nuclear Abolition Action Platform 172n4
National Police Agency (NPA) 32n14
National Security Bureau (NSB) 25
National Taiwan University (NTU) 76–7
National Tsing-hua University (NTHU) 76, 83, 121
National Women's League of the Republic of China 263
Nationality Act 220, 224, 228, 231
Naturalisation Test 227
NAWCF (National Alliance for Workers of Closed Factories) 25
NCC (National Communications Commission) 23, 74, 75–6, 84, 85, 86
NCCU (National Chengchi University) 77, 95
NCKU (National Cheng Kung University) 77, 121
neoliberal policies 115–16
network analysis 36–7
New Immigrants Labour Rights Association 233n1
New Partnership Between the Indigenous Peoples and the Taiwanese Government 241
New Party (NP) 177, 181, 182, 188, 230
New Power Party (NPP) 14, 32n23, 87, 129–30, 181, 184, 192, 193, 195, 214

'new social movements' theory 37, 83–4
Next Media 13, 23, 79, 81–2, 85, 86, 88
NGOs (non-governmental organizations): and the Sunflower Movement 115, 118, 121, 122, 124, 127, 130; *see also* CSOs (civil society organizations)
Niezen, Ronald 240–1, 249
Nip, Joyce Y. M. 36, 37
No Nuke Action campaign 161, **162**
No Nuke Street Band 160, 161
North American Taiwanese Studies Association 236
NP (New Party) 177, 181, 182, 188, 230
NPA (National Police Agency) 32n14
NPP (New Power Party) 14, 32n23, 87, 129–30, 181, 184, 192, 193, 195, 214
NSB (National Security Bureau) 25
NTHU (National Tsing-hua University) 76, 83, 121
NTU (National Taiwan University) 76–7
nuclear waste 156, 164, 183, 244–5; *see also* anti-nuclear movement
Nuclear-Free Homeland Committee 11, 160

occupational unions 202–3, **203**, **204**, 209, **209**, 212, 215
Occupy Wall Street Movement 34
Official Gazette of the Legislative Yuan 223
Offshore Islands Development Act 54, 55, 56, 58
Olson, Mancur 35
Open Space Technology 246
Orchid Island 156, 241, 244
Ordinance of Labour Insurance 202
Orwell, George 77

Pan Han-sheng 181, 184, 189, 191, 192, 193
Panai Kusui 1, 246
party system 191–2
PCT (Presbyterian Church of Taiwan) 240, 245–6
Peckham, Michael 38
Peng Yen-wen 4–5, 7, 8, 11, 14, 177–98
Penghu anti-casino movement 4, 8, 11, 13, 16, 55–61, 66, 67
Penghu Anti-Gambling League (Penghu fandu lianmeng) 57, 58, 59, 61, 68m13
People's Democratic Front 192
People's Republic of China *see* China (People's Republic of China)
PFP (People First Party) 80, 188, 230

police and social movements 4, 5, 7, 20, 39, 95–6; Citizen 1985 rallies 25
political opportunity theory 220–1, 222
Polleta, Francesca 38
Presbyterian Church of Taiwan (PCT) 240, 245–6
press freedom 72, 73–4, 75
'prophetic parties' 177
public opinion 15; anti-nuclear movement 15, 154, 163–5, 183; LGBT issues 186; social movements in Taiwan 15
'purifier parties' 177

Qing dynasty 238, 240, 242, 253

Radical magazine 121
Radio and Television Act 85
Rawnsley, Ming Yeh T. 167
Red Shirt anti-corruption movement 3, 19, 138, 250, 253
redundancy 207; *see also* NALWSF (National Alliance of the Laid-Off Workers from the Shut-down Factories); NAWCF (National Alliance for Workers of Closed Factories)
Reproduction and Health Bill 262–3
Rerum Novarum Center 233n1
reserve land system 239, 241
resilience, of social movements 24, 30
resource mobilization theory 35, 37, 182
'Return our lands' movement 241
Right Thing, The (Chiang Wei-hua) 6, 9
Roman Catholic Church 245
Rüdig, Wolfgang 184
Rudolph, Michael 241, 244
Russia 55

Safeguard East Coast Alliance 106
Safeguard Miaoli Youth Alliance 93, 105
Salizan Binkinuan 254
Sallaz, J. 55
'Salmon Coming' Home 207
same-sex marriage 11, 13, 15, 186, 258, 267–9; *see also* LGBT rights
San-Ying Aboriginal Community 106
Sandel, Michael 84
Satellite Broadcasting Act 85
scientology 38
SDP (Social Democratic Party), Taiwan 14, 130, 177, 181, 192, 214
Sediq people 239
self-determination, principle of 237, 251
Self-Help Group Against Eviction for Railroad Relocation in Tainan 106

shanbao 240
shandi tongbao 243
Shaoxing Community 106
Shi Qinglong 250–1
Shih Hsin University 96
Shih Ming-teh 31n2
Shin-chi Co. 208
Shyr, Howard 85, 86
Simon, Mark 86
Simon, Scott 5, 7, 8–9, 12, 16, 236–57
Sina-Weibo 248
Sinan Mavivo 183
Singapore 54
size, and social movements 8, 21–9
SMD (single member district) electoral system 177, 178, 182, 190–1
Smith, Neil 94
SNTV-MMD (single non-transferable vote in the multiple member district) electoral system 230
Social Democratic Party (SDP), Taiwan 14, 130, 177, 181, 192, 214
Social Democratic Party, Germany 178
social media 14–15, 27; Anti-Media Monopoly Movement 72, 77, 78–9; anti-nuclear movement 161; indigenous rights movement 237, 247–9, 253; Sunflower Movement 125–6
social movements in Taiwan 1, 2–3, 16–17, 194, 237, 251–3; 'coolness' of 28–9; agency of 15–16; connections between 8, 12–13, 21–3; CSO movement tactics 138–9; development patterns 3, 8–9; explanations for development patterns 3, 14–16; external impacts of 10–14; impact assessment 3, 9–10; mobilization structures 35–7, 44–6, 49, 136–8; organizational structures 37–8, 46–8, 49; political opportunity theory 220–1, 222; politicization of members 9–10; public opinion 15; resilience of 24, 30; root causes of 3, 5–7; *see also* civil society in Taiwan
social networks 36, 114, 121
SOE (state-owned enterprise) unions 201, 206, 212
Solidarity of Labour 206, 212–13, 215
South Africa 55
South East Asia, marriage migration from 7, 219, 220, 221–2, 223, 224–6, 227–8, 230, 231, 232
South Korea 54
Stainton, Michael 240

282 *Index*

state feminism 5, 7, 8, 11–12; and conservative government 258–9; under progressive government 259–63
state-owned enterprise (SOE) unions 201, 206, 212
Stein, Laura 36
Stimpson, James 10
strikes 200, 207–8, 215
Su Beng 28
Su Herng 7
Sunflower Movement 4, 26, 30, 34, 35, 50, 54, 67, 107, 113–14, 187, 244; and the anti-nuclear movement 147, 160, 166–7, 170–1; and CSOs (civil society organizations) 134–6, 142, 148–50, *149, 150, 151*; development pattern 8, 9, 15; impact assessment 10, 11, 12, 13, 14, 16, 129–31, 150, 194, 195; media strategy 124–6; occupation of Legislative Yuan, 2014 1, 2, 26, 27–9, 92, 93, 100, 106, 114–15, 118–29, 130–1, 134; organizational structures 119–20, 123–4; roots of 2, 7, 115–18, 199
Sungshan Tobacco factory 184
synchronization 113–14, 119–20, 130–1

TAAYRF (Taiwan Alliance for Advancement of Youth Rights and Welfare) 10, 142, 147, 149, *149*
TAHR (Taiwan Association for Human Rights) 137, 138, 143, 146–7, 149, *149*, 233n1
Taipei Main Railway Station 138
Taipei Prison 97–8; *see also* Huaguang Community, Taipei
'Taipei Roppongi' 98
Taipower (Taiwan Power Company) 155, 156, 164, 165
Taiwan: democracy 2, 16, 47, 92–3, 117, 126, 144–7; Japanese colonial era 7, 18, 238–9, 240, 242, 253; relationship with People's Republic of China 2, 3, 6, 10–11, 20, 75, 93, 107, 115
Taiwan Alliance for Advancement of Youth Rights and Welfare (TAAYRF) 10, 142, 147, 149, *149*
Taiwan Alliance for Victims of Urban Renewal 94
Taiwan Alliance to Promote Civil Partnership Rights 186
Taiwan Alliance to Promote Civil Partnership Rights (TAPCPR) 268
Taiwan Anti-Gambling League 57, 60, 63, 64, 67

Taiwan Association for Human Rights (TAHR) 137, 138, 143, 146–7, 149, *149*, 233n1
Taiwan Association of University Professors (TAUP) 140, 141, 145, 147, 148, 149, *149*
Taiwan Confederation of Trade Unions (TCTU) 200, 201, 206, 211–12, 215, 216
Taiwan Cultural Society 18
Taiwan Democracy Watch (TDW) 137, 138, 140–1, 143, 145, 146, 147, 148, 149, *149*, 169
Taiwan Environmental Protection Union (TEPU) 155–6, 158, 161–2
Taiwan Federation of Financial Unions (TFFU) 211
Taiwan First Nations Party 250–1, 253, 254
Taiwan First Peoples Party 249
Taiwan Higher Education Union (THEU) 210, 211, 214
Taiwan Independence Alliance 187
Taiwan Indigenous People Society 246
Taiwan Indigenous Television Network (TITV) 247
Taiwan International Family Association 233n1
Taiwan Labor Front (TLF) 137, 138, 142, 145, 147, 148, 149, *149*
Taiwan March 130
Taiwan Migrants' Forum 233n1
Taiwan New Immigrants Labour Rights Organization 229
Taiwan Railway Workers' Union 214
Taiwan Referendum Alliance 32n16
Taiwan Rural Front (TRF) 23, 94, 105, 106, 137, 138, 139, 142–3, 147, 149, *149*
Taiwan Solidarity Union (TSU) 80, 177, 188, 192, 227, 228
takasagozoku 240
TAPCPR (Taiwan Alliance to Promote Civil Partnership Rights) 268
TASAT (TransAsia Sisters Association, Taiwan) 219, 223–4, 225–6, 228
TAUP (Taiwan Association of University Professors) 140, 141, 145, 147, 148, 149, *149*
TCTU (Taiwan Confederation of Trade Unions) 200, 201, 206, 211–12, 215, 216
TDW (Taiwan Democracy Watch) 137, 138, 140–1, 143, 145, 146, 147, 148, 149, *149*, 169

TEPU (Taiwan Environmental Protection Union) 155–6, 158, 161–2
TFFU (Taiwan Federation of Financial Unions) 211
Thao Nation 250, 251
Themudo, Nuno S. 36, 38
THEU (Taiwan Higher Education Union) 210, 211, 214
Times Weekly 76, 79
TITV (Taiwan Indigenous Television Network) 247
TLF (Taiwan Labor Front) 137, 138, 142, 145, 147, 148, 149, *149*
Tokyo, Japan 98
tourism 58, 60, 62; and indigenous rights 244; *see also* anti-casino movements
Tourist Casino Management Act 68n1
Trade Union Law 88n1, 200, 201, 202, 203; 2011 amendment 204, *209*, 209–10, 212, 215
trade union movement 5, 82, 88n1, 200, 215–16; authoritarian period, institutional legacy of 202–5, **203**, **204**; brief history 200–2; development pattern 8; FIUs (Federations of Industrial Unions) 201, 205–6, 211, 213, 215, 216; impact assessment 14; impact of Trade Union Law amendment, 2011 **209**, 209–13, **210**; labour militancy, resurgence of 207–8; in politics 213–15; roots of 7
TransAsia Sisters Association, Taiwan (TASAT) 219, 223–4, 225–6, 228
Transportation and Communications Committee 85, 87
Tree Party 14, 169, 189, 192
tree protection campaigns 183–4
TRF (Taiwan Rural Front) 23, 94, 105, 106, 137, 138, 139, 142–3, 147, 149, *149*
True Jesus Church 245
True Love Alliance 267, 268
Truku people 239
Trust Act 86
trust, and online services 36, 37
Tsai Chi-hao 191–2, 193–4
Tsai Eng-meng 4, 23, 74, 75, 76, 77, 82, 84, 86, 87, 88
Tsai I-lun 4, 6, 8, 16, 54–70, 166
Tsai Ing-wen 1, 129, 130, 131, 168, 169, 171, 213, 214
Tsai, Alex 130
Tsai, Frida Pei-hui 96, 106, 109n9
Tsao Ya-ping 64

Tsay Ting-kuei 32n16
Tseng, Y.-C. 222
Tsou people 243, 245, 251
TSU (Taiwan Solidarity Union) 80, 177, 188, 192, 227, 228
Tsui Shu-hsin 159, 166, 173n9, 183
Tu Wen-ling 169
Twitter 34, 248
Typhoon Morakot 244

Umbrella Movement, Hong Kong 32n13
United Daily News 75, 83
United Nations: and gender issues 258, 260, 266; and indigenous rights 241, 243
URM (Urban-Rural Mission) 240, 245
US, social movements 36, 38, 49

Victims of Urban Renewal and Eviction 105–6
virtual ecologies 35, 37; BBS as 40–2, **41**, 49; as mobilization structures 45–6, 49
voting age 191

wage stagnation 199
Wang Chung-ming 167
Wang Dan 28
Wang Jia case 31n5
Wang Jin-Pyng 127–8, 146
Wang, Xavier 185
Want Want China Times Media Group 4, 6, 13, 23, 71, 72, 74, 75–86, 87, 88, 193; *see also* Anti-Media Monopoly Movement
Weidner Resort Development Inc. 62, 64, 66
Wen, Calvin 184
White Terror 18
Wild at Heart Legal Defence Lawyers Association 183
Wild Lily Movement, 1990 10, 12, 18, 19, 28, 49
Wild Strawberry Movement 4, 20, 24, 34, *39*, 54, 76–7, 89n2, 93, 117, 119, 120, 140; development pattern 9, 14, 15; Internet usage case study 35, 37, 38–50, *40*, **41**; roots of 5–6, 7
Winkler, Robin 170
women's movement: Taiwan (*see* state feminism); US 38
Work Congress (Sunflower Movement) 123–4
working conditions 199

working hours, excessive 199
World Nuclear Association 155
Wu Den-yih 22, 101, 103
Wu Feng 245
Wu Jieh-min 147, 151n1
Wu Ken-cheng 86
Wu-er Kaixi 28
Wu, Charo 79

Xi Jinping 6, 20–1, 129

Yang Chang-ling 188, 189, 190
Yang Shui-sheng 65, 66
Yanliao Anti-Nuclear Self-Help Association 156
Youth Alliance Against Media Monsters 22–3, 26, 77, 78–9, 80, 81, 82, 83–4, 85, 86, 87–8
Youth Alliance for Miaoli 23–4, 25
YouTube 248
Yu Chin 107
Yu Chung-tien 104
Yu, Karen 188–9, 193
Yuanli Self-Help Group against Wind Turbines 106
Yuanli Self-Help Organization 25
yuanzhuminzu 237, 240, 242

Zhao Ding-xin 36, 45
zhengming (name rectification) 240–1, 242–3, 244, 245, 251
Zhongxiao East Road 82
Zhongshan South Road 28, 106
Zhongxiao West Road 26, 139, 167
zili jiuji ('self-relief') activism 19, 22
Zone Expropriation Act, 1969 96–7